THE EXPENSE OF VISION

Laurence B. Holland
THE EXPENSE OF VISION
ESSAYS ON THE CRAFT OF HENRY JAMES

THE JOHNS HOPKINS UNIVERSITY PRESS
Baltimore and London

To
Eugene Holland
Louise Bedwell Holland
and the memory of
F. O. Matthiessen

The Johns Hopkins University Press, Baltimore, Maryland 21218
The Johns Hopkins Press Ltd., London

Originally published by Princeton University Press, 1964
Johns Hopkins Paperbacks Edition, 1982

Library of Congress Catalog Card Number 81-48195
ISBN 0-8018-2755-8

CONTENTS

FOREWORD

ANYONE who read *The Expense of Vision* when it first appeared in 1964 will have been prepared for much that has appeared since that time on the theory of the novel and on the works of Henry James. Nearly two decades later it remains one of the most inward and enlightening commentaries, setting an invigoratingly high standard for any future studies of the fiction and of James's own critical writings. I know of nothing that more intelligently inquires into the problematic relationship of his most important novels to the larger questions of form—fictional, cultural, and social—addressed in the Prefaces. Not surprisingly, one of the very best single essays on James written in the next decade—in *A Future for Astyanax* by Leo Bersani, a critic thoroughly conversant with European critical thinking—expresses and everywhere reveals a special gratitude to Laurence Holland's distinctly American book.

Its American accent is nowhere more pronounced, however, than in its being theoretical only by inference and out of obligation to the deepest impulses of the Jamesian *oeuvre*. Holland works always with remarkable suppleness of mind inside the performative drama of James's writing, he brilliantly traces the connection between the lives enacted in the fiction—an Isabel Archer in *Portrait of a Lady* or a Strether in *The Ambassadors* —and the central terminologies of James's criticisms, and he is reluctant to disengage himself from this intricate task for the sake of theoretical pronouncements. And yet he convincingly demonstrates that the novel—the genre that with James went through one of its most decisive transformations—is in itself a kind of critical text, an inquiry into the movements of power, the nature of temporality, the virtues of fabrication, the pains of transgression, and the repression of desire by the exigencies of form. Particularly in his discussions of *The Golden Bowl,* he examines more effectively than has anyone before or since why for James the act of novelistic composition brought into play authorial passions equivalent to those that his characters are themselves trying to understand and to manage. *In* his fiction, no less than in his essays, reviews, and travel writing—as we can now see from Holland's appended study of *The American Scene*

—James was always the critic at work, the greatest critic America has yet to produce, and Holland is really the first to prove this in a detailed and persuasive manner.

The connections thereby established between James's novels and his inferable concerns for literature as a social and political form bear directly on the persistent charge that he was somehow insufficiently historical or that he was out of touch with American realities. That such allegations are still being made is only another indication that literary criticism never sufficiently takes advantage of its best findings in order to move forward to questions still unanswered. Holland's book is thus as fresh and necessary now as it initially was, and its publication and availability in paperback provide an occasion to celebrate one of those rare critical works that is wholly worthy of its great subject.

RICHARD POIRIER

PREFACE

IN *The American Scene* James made some brief remarks about social rituals at the Metropolitan Opera which illuminate his own ambitions and define the approach which the following essays take in exploring his writing. Ladies attending the opera who don a tiara for the occasion, James remarked, are assuming a peculiarly American burden. That institution is virtually the only one in America which affords a pretext for the costumed drama they want to enact, yet the occasion does not call for head-gear quite so resplendent. In Europe or in "worlds otherwise arranged," ceremonious custom assigns and sanctions the roles to be played: "the occasion itself, with its character fully turned on, produces the tiara." In New York, by contrast, the crown itself must endow the occasion with the importance it otherwise lacks, the symbol must lend to the event its eventfulness: the "symbol has, by an arduous extension of its virtue, to produce the occasion."

It is precisely that ambition which is served by James's art, though his interests extended beyond the particular occasion and symbol he mentioned, beyond even so stylized and modern an art as grand opera or so heavily financed an edifice as that which houses it. His was not a merely literary symbolism in the narrow sense, as the late F. O. Matthiessen helped us to see in *Henry James: The Major Phase* (New York, 1944); James's was not an art which began with a literary symbolic form and then built poems or novels around them. Yet his works *are* symbolic constructs of a more ambitious order whose motive lies deeper than the strictly literary aims which implement it. This is the ambition which James shared with writers as different from him as Whitman and Joyce: the determination to forge or shape a changing world, to create a society, to take his place in a community-in-the-making by joining in the process of making it.

James's fiction as well as his criticism reveals a deep concern with the very nature of authority, particularly with the sanctioned power of important institutions in the culture and society he knew. More particularly, he was fascinated with the authority he himself exercised as an author of fiction, selecting subjects, contriving plots, ordering his materials, using and reshaping the institution of the novel, and, as Professor Edel has helped us to see, marketing his fiction in a world which needed prompting to buy or read it. James performed that constructive task and exercised his power in a world he helped to make, and his career is best understood in the light of his own recognition of what such a responsibility entails for the author who shoulders it.

The communities that were taking shape on either side of the Atlantic were not local habitations in which he could automatically inherit a tranquil place, and his expatriation has dramatized the dislocations which characterize the culture in which his art matured, his tenuous ties to the capitals of power in which he lived or visited. Yet tenuous ties remain ties; expatriation, and the alienation which is both its cause and consequence, are social phenomena, not social voids or escapes from social relations. Natives and foreigners become aliens only by virtue of residence *in* a society whose structure renders them alien. And James's expatriation, like Benjamin West's before him or T. S. Eliot's and Hemingway's afterward, did not create the vacuum for his imagination that Van Wyck Brooks abhorred in *The Pilgrimage of Henry James* (New York, 1925). If it deprived James of certain securities known to people who had settled into the routines and habits of either American society or its European counterparts, it did not rule out involvements of a more hazardous kind with the middle-class world of change and crisis, with the culture of capitalism, which followed the American, French, and industrial revolutions. Though misunderstanding of James's expatriation and his concern for form in the narrowly technical sense have obscured the nature and extent of these involvements, his fiction itself, and his mature criticism, virtually lay them bare by drawing attention to the full and varied implications of his form.

It was the achieved form of one of his novels (*The Wings of the Dove*), not its meaning, that James was discussing in its preface when he insisted on the close scrutiny which he demanded of readers, and the behavior of his form in the finished work must take precedence over prior models in literature or patterns of meaning which lie outside his fiction, even when and if those precedent patterns were among his materials. For the actual behavior of his form alone determines his fiction's relevance, marks the axes of its relations with actualities beyond it: the symbol alone defines finally the occasion it consummates. The textures and movement of James's prose, the rhythm of his structure, do not produce the fixity of reference and narrow range of emblematic patterns which Professor Quentin Anderson's allegorical reading in *The American Henry James* (New Brunswick, 1957) requires; his insistence on the relevance of a Swedenborgian frame of reference derived from James's father's theology remains unconvincing. The novelist was not so much using or following given and settled conventions of value, structures of thought, or novelistic practices, as he was establishing conventions of his own. To speak more precisely, he was, in his major works, converting earlier habits of thought, mere formulations of feeling, and literary practice into *new* or at least newly constituted conventions to which he gave the full sanction of the achieved form which he created from his materials.

Both James's criticism and his fiction suggest the relevance of tangible institutions and virtually demand that we give attention, as he clearly did, both to the complexities and to the elemental if sometimes obvious features of the institutions of marriage, the family, and publishing, money-making and the social and economic symbolism of money, forms of diversion or entertainment, the institution of manners in America, and governing standards of taste in the arts in the nineteenth century. Whether or not James approved of them, whether his relation to them was direct or tangential, the fascination of these institutions exerted a continuous pressure on the diction, structure, and import of his writings, and convenient though it might be to separate these matters out as background, they prove to be intimately related not only to James's materials but to his plots, his imagery and diction, his very forms. The best way to consider the background and the foreground of the fiction itself is in the light of their intimate connection in the finished art.

Art or aesthetic reality was not for James an order of value to be ranked in relation to others but a process of creation to be engaged in, with a product—the union of form and vision which in the late Prefaces he came to call a *marriage*—to be fashioned and enjoyed. And the process of making his novels is what joined him to the world he knew and rendered in his art and kept him from sorting his characters into categories of good and evil with serenely Olympian assurance and detachment. Neither his criticism nor his fiction makes paramount the rigor of moral judgment which Professor Dorothea Krook's *The Ordeal of Consciousness in Henry James* (Cambridge, 1962) overemphasizes and which Professor Richard Poirier, in *The Comic Sense of Henry James* (New York, 1960), makes the basis of James's comic strategies in the early fiction. We critics have tended to make James guilty of the " 'flagrant' morality" which his father taught him to disdain. The moral implications of James's fiction are to be found not only and not principally in the judgments he passes on his characters but in the fully creative function of James's form, whether comic or otherwise. His form often creates the follies it mocks, and on occasion he celebrates them rather than simply evaluating or correcting them. Like gods and other parents, authors not only confront moral problems but create them, and James constantly confessed this fact in his fiction. One of his chief contributions to the lyric dimension of English fiction is his distinctive fusion of moral and technical concerns, which has the effect of founding his moral vision on the act and form of intimate confession.

His relation with his reader, his rhetoric, is telling in this connection. The formal means he uses to arouse interest, to woo the reader, to make the reader believe or entertain the fiction and be entertained by it, create moral issues for both author and reader which James was keenly aware of. He neither ignored the reader out of concern for the objective integrity of his novel nor was content simply to tell and show the reader things. His aims were more in keeping with the activist conception of art that is characteristic of American Thoreaus and Melvilles: he wanted not only to *show* things to the reader but to *act upon* him. The result in James's fiction is an intimacy of address to the reader which has all the contingencies and moral resonance of intimacy. By splicing the conventions of the novel of manners and the Gothic novel, he virtually created the *intimate* novel in English, though this is not to say that intimacy takes the form of exposed nakedness in the lives of the characters he depicts. It is both notorious and true that James's characters —probably even their innermost psyches—remain costumed.

Moreover his concern for his own privacy and for that of others impelled him to convert an habitual reticence into the controlled tact of his narrative mode. James's intimacy is the intimacy of a novelistic form, placed in the near presence of the reader with a strange combination of caution and candor.

Correspondingly James's form—his imagery, his plot—involves him intimately with his characters and creates moral issues in its own right, whatever the presumed motives of his villains and heroines whose actions are shaped in part by the form. Only by considering simultaneously James's treatment of his reader and his treatment of his characters can we properly take the measure of his fiction, and this task is possible only if we make the further effort to follow the very process by which his novels come to be what they are. They do not simply unfold from given premises or simply present the certain findings of earlier experiments of the imagination which are then recorded and demonstrated in the novel; they make the original experiments themselves, undergo the task, and share at least in creating the results or hypothecating them in a world of perilous promise facing an uncertain future. Whatever tiaras James used, their function was determined, they were even transformed, by the process of his using them. The light his fiction sheds is not that of a mirror; it is the light of magic and implemented, not reflected, power. If his fiction has, as some think, a merely tangential relation to actualities beyond it—or if, as seems more likely, this is the fate of any art—James's form defines the tangents which relate life to his art by giving a central position to the institutions and activities which we must focus on: the courtships and marriages, the exploitation and the deceptions which are practiced on some of his characters, the endowments of money and the acquisition of possessions which move his plots, the sacrifices exacted in the very process of transformation.

James had the "grasping imagination" which he once said was necessary to meet the challenge presented to the artist by American civilization, and the result is his distinctly modern art, founded on a strange commerce with his characters and readers, and on the combination of commitment and devotion which the following essays attempt to analyze.

While working on James I have had the help of countless

friends, students and colleagues who have every reason to expect my gratitude whether or not they are pleased with the result. Among them is Mrs. Helen Wright, who typed the manuscript with a degree of care and editorial assistance which are deservedly well known. Others are Joseph W. Fitchett, Jr., Arthur R. Gold, the late Dr. James E. Moss, Paul Levine, and Professors Lawrance R. Thompson, Howard C. Horsford, Richard M. Green, and Alfred Schwarz. Professor C. L. Barber read a crucial part of the manuscript and made suggestions which I wish again to thank him for.

I want particularly to thank John William Ward for his attention to the manuscript and his interest over a long period in the issues concerning James and American culture which it treats. And there are others from whom I have learned whose contributions do not show in the footnotes. The writings of Professor Kenneth Burke and the essays of Professor Harry Levin on the institution of the novel have made contributions too extensive to itemize. Professor Perry Miller first taught a generation of us that literary history could be dramatic for the very reason that the historical past itself was an urgent drama, and Professor Richard Blackmur has shown how poetry can be quickened into life even by unlikely materials.

Among my teachers is my wife, Faith Mackey Holland. She joins me in inscribing the dedication. She has every conceivable right to do so.

ACKNOWLEDGMENTS

THE author gratefully acknowledges indebtedness to: the University Research Fund of Princeton University for funds to type the manuscript; the Johns Hopkins Press and the editors of *ELH: A Journal of English Literary History* for permission to use material from the author's essay on *"The Wings of the Dove"* in that journal; and to Richard Wilbur and the editors of Harcourt, Brace & World for permission to quote from "An Event" in *Things of This World*.

". . . you must live upon the country you traverse."
Henry James, *The Tragic Muse*

The artist and his work are not to be separated. The most wilfully foolish man cannot stand aloof from his folly, but the deed and the doer together make ever one sober fact.
Henry Thoreau, *A Week on the Concord and Merrimack Rivers*

CHAPTER ONE

James's *Portrait*

So I seemed to have arrived at this: doubtless I have methods, but they begot themselves, in which case I am their proprietor, not their father.

Mark Twain, in *The Art of Authorship*

. . . Keep thy Shop, and thy Shop will keep thee.

Ben Franklin, *Poor Richard Improved*

[I]

THE *PORTRAIT*'S PREFACE

THE WORD "ado," even when expanded to the more impressive phrase "ado about something," is a strangely frivolous term for what James named on other occasions the "Action" of a novel, or for what, over a stretch of nine pages in the preface to *The Portrait of a Lady,* he refused to call by the name he thought "nefarious," its " 'plot.' " Indeed frivolity may be (on my part) too mild a word when we recall that the *Portrait*'s ado entails, among other things, the arrangement of a large endowment of money, a fraudulent deception, and a disastrous marriage for its heroine. Yet frivolity is often enough the acknowledged index of anxious concern rather than the mask or denial of it, and one need not assume that James was hiding something (from himself or his readers) nor imagine that he was evading an important issue when he wrote carefully of "organizing an ado about Isabel Archer." The preface sets that remark in the virtual center of a highly metaphorical context; the essay is important not primarily as an explicit argument nor even as a statement of intentions but as a sensitive exploration, employing the instrument of metaphor, which moves beneath the more explicit discourse of the preface, refining and at times running counter to it. Its full relevance to the *Portrait,* and its brilliance as an essay in its own right, come to light only when read with full attention to its metaphorical details and to the intimate drama which moves implicitly within the more explicit argument. It becomes a conscience-stricken inquiry into the deepest implications of James's craft, undertaken at a time when, in preparing the revisions for the New York Edition of his fiction, James had engaged his mature creative powers in a direct confrontation of his imaginative work. What the preface can help us to see, if we follow the admittedly "long way round" it takes to get to its turning point, is that this process, a form of self-recognition for the artist, is central to the novel itself.[1]

[1] *The Art of the Novel: Critical Prefaces,* ed. Richard P. Blackmur (New York, 1946), pp. 48, 15, 42, 53, 48, 47.

3

Indeed, the process of self-recognition is more penetrating in the *Portrait* than in the critical essays, or even those stories which deal with professional artists as particular cases, where we might be more tempted to look for it. And the *Portrait* speaks with the firm authority of a masterpiece and accordingly affords a commanding perspective on those occasions in James's career when he penetrated most deeply into his resources, his material and talent. It enables us to reexamine the connections among James's moral, social, and aesthetic themes in the light of his concern for form and to redefine James's relation to the society which has had to be interested, whether eagerly or reluctantly, in making and remaking things, in measuring the cost of human institutions and aspirations.

Of the many images of the artist which James employed, one of his favorites and most famous is that of the architect, but James's treatment of it in the preface to the *Portrait* accords it a curiously dubious status: the image does reveal some of James's deepest apprehensions about the act of imaginative vision but remains silent on the issue of "action" or the "nefarious" plot which most troubled him. The writer as architect, in his more public and active role, builds his structure, piling "brick upon brick" until, "scrupulously fitted together and packed in," they form the "large building" of the *Portrait*. The famous passage about the "house of fiction" develops the architectural image more amply, assigning to the artist a more private position inside a completed building and the ostensibly more restful occupation of a "watcher" whose sole activity is to observe: the "consciousness of the artist" stands behind the "dead wall" of a building enclosing him, equipped "with a pair of eyes, or at least with a field-glass," and scrutinizes life through the window of his particular literary form.[2]

These architectural metaphors are relevant to the *Portrait*—if for no other reason than that they place the author *inside* his finished dwelling and call into question his edifice by alluding to its "dead wall"—yet the image of architecture does not dominate the preface because it does not satisfactorily come to grips with the assertion which James made the basis for the explicit argument of the preface. This is the assertion that the "figure"

[2] *Ibid.*, pp. 55, 48, 46.

4

of Isabel (whatever its origin in James's acquaintanceship or reading) came first and alone without involvement in setting or action, an "unattached character" who was "not engaged in the tangle, to which we look for much of the impress that constitutes an identity." She was a "single character" given alone, as Turgenief had claimed his own were given, without the "situations" and "complications" which launch novels into "movement" and which identify a hero's world or "fate." The problem for the writer was, later, to "imagine, to invent and select and piece together . . ." the figure's world and "destiny." [3]

James had described this strategy before, as being Turgenief's, in his essay of 1884 on the Russian. It was based on the priority of character over "plot" and consisted in deriving the action "from the qualities of the actors" rather than from a "preconceived" plan. Its antithesis, as James then formulated it, was the novel with the *imposed* form of a *story* or "dance—a series of steps . . . determined from without and forming a figure," a strategy whose very weakness was the basis of its appeal: that of reminding readers "enough, without reminding them too much, of life." The "architecture" was *associated* loosely with plotted action as the great asset that both Scott and Balzac, unlike Turgenief, could add to their "precious material." In the late preface to the *Portrait,* however, the metaphor of architecture is *opposed,* in James's analysis, to the *action* of the novel or story. Moreover, it fails to govern the argument which James makes explicit.[4]

The architectural images do not, for one thing, precisely locate or place Isabel. (Was she part of the structure, or did she stand, "in perfect isolation," as a center around which the "spacious house" was constructed, or was she the "plot of ground" on which the edifice was built?) Neither could architecture account for the "ado" about Isabel and the need to excite the reader's interest by the acts of characters who surround her: when thinking of the novel's action and characters in relation to "the reader's amusement," James swiftly abandoned buildings and summoned up "Roman candles and Catherine-wheels." [5]

[3] *Ibid.,* pp. 44, 47, 42, 43, 47, 43, 48.
[4] *Partial Portraits* (London, 1888), pp. 314-316.
[5] *The Art of the Novel,* pp. 48, 52-53.

5

The language of fireworks, however, was but a momentary seizure. James immediately set aside the question of the reader's excitement and confined himself to the questions of action and character without reference to the reader; and in writing that he simply awoke one day "in possession" of the characters who were "the concrete terms of my 'plot' " [6] he had returned to the terms of discourse, basically metaphorical in function, which actually carry the burden of the essay's searching inquiry. The terms prove in James's handling to be adequate to the resources of inspiration and method which literature shares with other arts while being more distinctly literary than architecture and fireworks; and some carry psychological implications while being tangibly institutional. Without suppressing or obscuring their multiplicity of reference, the preface underscores certain particular metaphorical connotations: they are either literary ("actors," "characters," "figure," "fable") or commercial ("pedlar," "contract," " 'tip' "). In the case of "possession," "*disponible*," " agents," and "business," they prove to be both.

In attempting to trace the "growth in one's imagination" of the germ of his novel (to reconstruct "the history of the business," as James put it alternatively), James left the reader standing before a dead wall which was, in part at least, of James's own construction. He did not name the prototype in actual life of any of his characters. In the case of the Touchetts, their friend Madame Merle, her lover Gilbert Osmond and their daughter Pansy—those who helped to awaken the novel's heroine and to arrange her marriage—James declared that his memory was "a blank as to how and whence they came," that he simply "waked up one morning in possession of them." On the other hand, the "grasp of a single character" that inspired the novel was an act whose origin James recalled but chose not to retrace. The figure of Isabel was simply "an acquisition," tormenting in its fascination of long standing, by now rendered "familiar" but not at all "blurred" in its "charm" for having been in James's "complete possession" for "a long time." [7]

For all the characters, then, what the preface does is not to identify their actual prototypes but, by returning repeatedly to

[6] *Ibid.*, p. 53.
[7] *Ibid.*, pp. 42, 53, 47.

the question of their origin, to define James's relation to them as materials, chosen or given, for his novel. The preface becomes simultaneously technical and intimately personal, as concerned with the relation of Henry James to his "setting" as with Isabel's to hers, and troubled by the phenomenon which is the essay's subject: namely the process by which resources, thematic and formal, and the pressures of actual life, from within and without, become the developing design of art. It is to this problem that the preface returns again and again in its tacking movement, every shift of which is significant, from the notations of publishing data and the recollections of Venice, which open the essay, to the last paragraphs with their acknowledged admiration for two of the novel's scenes and their apology for having overdone one character in an effort to be entertaining. The more deeply the essay probes this problem, the more troubled it is, and the more it depends on one of James's most congenial vocabularies, the language of commerce.

The imagery of trade was of some use in assessing the merits of the finished novel, for while James could admire its spaciousness as architecture, he could also praise its "economy" and compare the excitement of Isabel's meditation scene to certain staples of adventure fiction, the capture of a "caravan or the identification of a pirate." But the imagery of commerce is used chiefly to provide a setting for the artist himself, placing him in relation to his society and in relation to the "ado" about Isabel. This is the task which the opening paragraphs assume by dwelling, with little ostensible pretext, on the enticements of Venice, where James had passed a mere "several weeks," as he remembered it, of the more than a year and a half he had spent writing the *Portrait*. In the attractions of the Venetian scene he had sought inspiration for the right phrase and "next happy twist of my subject," but he had had to acknowledge that the scenes of Italy were "too rich in their own right" to perform that service; it was "as if he were asking an army of glorious veterans to help him arrest a pedlar who has given him the wrong change." Better, on reconsideration, to work in more "neutral" surroundings to which "we writers may lend something of the light of our vision." But Venice is too proud for the "charity," as James called it, of a loan. She prefers to initiate transactions: to give outright munificent gifts, for instance. But to "profit" by them the writer must either be idly "off duty" or bound to Venice's exclusive service. The novel at hand had nothing to do with Venice's service (its settings lie elsewhere), but there were, nevertheless, rewards; the transactions simply proved to be more complicated. To turn to Venice is "wasted effort," but nonetheless "strangely fertilizing"; "cheated and squandered" the effort always is, whether by "high-handed insolent frauds" or by "insidious sneaking ones." The issue depends on *"how"* the attention has been beguiled, but the preface does not stipulate a preferred way; suffice it that even on the most astute "designing artist's part," try as he does to "guard him against their deceits," there is "always witless enough good faith" and "anxious enough desire" to render him the dupe of such deceptions.[8]

The process of writing is placed by this reminiscence in a context where the author may be shortchanged by his work but will not ask help from a world engrossed in larger preoccupations; where a loan, even if a "charity," is humiliating; where the free gifts of life are the rewards only of idle indulgence or of a constricted service; where the writer's precautions against fraud are merged ambivalently with a desire to be cheated; and where gains for art may possibly accrue through being wasted and defrauded.

It is against that setting of profit, swindling, and wastage that James proceeded in precisely the next sentence to deny that his novel originated in "the conceit of a 'plot,' nefarious name," though eight pages later, by using the term, he conceded that the *Portrait* does have one. But now he declared that the *given* was not an action that "launches a novel immediately into movement" but the isolated figure of Isabel. James's scruples clearly go beyond disapproval of melodramatic contrivances or the flimsy intrigues of poorly made well-made plays and call into question the very function of *plot.* Moreover, they render the discussion of the relation of character to action more urgent than was the case in the earlier essay on Turgenief because they call into question the ground of James's responsibility for his *own* novel. Impelled by this concern, the preface proceeds

8 *Ibid.,* pp. 57, 40-41.

through the paragraphs that discuss the relation between morals and art. It avoids settling for either of two complex alternatives but is haunted and quickened by both. First: that authorship consists in the initiation of an action; that an author's responsibility stems from the creation of that action; and that to organize the *Portrait's* particular plot around Isabel Archer is in itself reprehensible. The second alternative: that authorship consists not in beginning anything but in the careful arrangement of given materials; and that to "place" and draw out the given subject of a portrait leaves the author detached and morally unaccountable for its consequences. The preface analyzes and refines the question as it approaches the point later where it can speak of the "ado about Isabel," its anxiety acknowledged and mastered because it has already discovered, in the figure of a shopkeeper, the image which gives both the terms "ado" and "plot" their precise connotations.

The essay proceeds from Venice to establish the central figure's given isolation and, with Turgenief's help, to insist that the imagination selects not simply any situations and complications for its heroes but those most "favorable to the sense of the creatures themselves, the complications they would be most likely to produce and feel," that indeed the artist simply watches as the characters "come together" and, themselves, engage in actions and difficulties. But the essay does not linger long on this point; it returns to the question of origins, declaring, still with the aid of Turgenief, that the characters simply accumulate, though to be sure the writer is "always picking them over, selecting among them"; they are so to speak "prescribed and imposed" on the artist by the life he encounters, and it is irrelevant therefore to quarrel with his subject.[9]

Particularly the "dull dispute over the 'immoral' subject and the moral," which darkened, James said, the critical climate of his early career, seemed now "inane" from within the perspective he proceeded to establish. Significantly, the preface does not mention formulations of moral truth or wholesome principles for the guidance of conduct—the moralistic frame within which the question is argued conventionally. There too, no doubt, lay the dullness and the inanity. More significant by far

9 *Ibid.*, p. 43.

9

is this section's silence on the matter which the preface elsewhere makes most urgent, namely the question of the author's transactions, the question of what, if anything beyond merely picking over his store of subjects, the writer actually does. The famous paragraphs on the "moral sense of a work of art" and "the house of fiction," which together defend the writer's "boundless freedom" to take up any subject and to project "any vision," neglect anything a writer might be said to *do* and speak of him instead as a passive medium.[10]

He is neither the sower of his story's seed nor its cultivator; he is its "soil"; the "quality and capacity" of that soil to nourish the "vision" growing there accounts for any moral quality the work may acquire. The "artist's humanity" is admittedly crucial in giving his given subject the mark of "intelligence" or "experience" which makes the work "genuine" and, moreover, gives the work its "moral sense," the "last touch of the worth of the work." Yet what that "humanity" or "sensibility" is, is a medium, whether "a rich and magnificent medium" or "a comparatively poor and ungenerous one." The moral value of the finished work, as James had stressed in his earlier studies of Baudelaire and Hawthorne, is not formulated beforehand and placed there by the writer but is an increment deriving from the richness, or poverty, of the writer's inspiration and temperament, which are part of his medium. The passage concludes by removing the discussion from the conventional language of morals and the question of the artist's intent to the terms of price and the function of form: the novel's value as a form is its "high price," its power to "preserve [its] form with closeness" while sustaining a pressure which threatens to shatter it, remaining "true to its character" only insofar as it "strains, or tends to burst, with a latent extravagance, its mould." The form and the pressure, rather than wisdom or point, are the measure of the novel's price. When the preface returns to the question of the author himself, rendering the writer as a "watcher" behind the dead walls of the house of fiction, it probes beneath the writer's actions, even the crucial act of seeing, to the sheer state of consciousness which conditions what he

10 *Ibid.*, p. 45.

sees, and finally to his sheer being ("what the artist is") which accounts for the range and nature of what he is conscious of.[11]

So complex was the process James recognized, and so circuitous, consequently, was the "long way round" the preface takes in getting to its turning point, the final account of the "grasp," the "acquisition" of Isabel Archer. To complete the "history of the business," ascertaining what "had extraordinarily happened" to the imagination and precisely how it could "take over" the character of Isabel would in any case be "so subtle, if not so monstrous, a thing" as to be impossible. But the essay quickens as it probes further than before, and refines the question so precisely as to challenge what began as its basic assertion. The disposable figure, it now seems, was to begin with launched in movement; it was "in motion . . . , in transit"; it was certainly "bent upon its fate—some fate or other." How did the figure become so "vivid" if it were not involved in some "tangle" of conditions "to which we look for much of the impress that constitutes an identity," and if it remained in its isolation still "to be placed," since we usually account for vividness of characters "just by the business of placing them"? [12]

The preface discovers its answer suddenly in an analogy (a "superfine" one, James felt) for the translation of life into art that recognizes the multiple expectations and contingencies which inhere in a creative process, and which, for those in the modern world, inhere in the profession of letters. It brings into focus, along with the world of affairs in Venice, the writer "picking over" his stock of subjects and *taking over* the figure of Isabel, and it presents an artist who is at once the receiving medium of his material and the manipulator of it. The image is presented in the course of acknowledging that the given character is vivid because it has already *"been* placed—placed in the imagination that detains it, preserves, protects, enjoys it, conscious of its presence in the dusky, crowded, heterogeneous back-shop of the mind very much as a wary dealer in precious

[11] *French Poets and Novelists* (Leipzig, 1883), pp. 64-65; *Hawthorne,* in *The Shock of Recognition,* ed. Edmund Wilson (Garden City, N.Y., 1947), p. 471; *The Art of the Novel,* pp. 45-47.
[12] *Ibid.,* p. 47.

odds and ends, competent to make an 'advance' on rare objects confided to him, is conscious of the rare little 'piece' left in deposit by the reduced, mysterious lady of title or the speculative amateur, and which is already there to disclose its merit afresh as soon as a key shall have clicked in a cupboard-door." The disposable figure of Isabel, accordingly, was a " 'value' " that James had, as he said, "all curiously at my disposal" in the gift shop and pawnshop of the creative mind.[13]

The passage recalls an enterprise tangibly actual in the history of institutions and quite significant for James's conception of his office: the shop which combined a retail trade with the business of pawn, the owner serving as broker for secondhand *objets d'art* and advancing money in anticipation of their sale, and acquiring items on deposit as security for small loans at high interest rates, acquiring ownership and free to sell the objects if not redeemed in a stipulated time. Its transactions—including the charity of its loans—are commercially rather than industrially productive and are sought, whether out of indigence or desperation, by individuals without routine access to the institutions of large-scale enterprise who have some pressing private need for money but no negotiable security other than their belongings. To such a shop—a curiosity shop in function, a pawnshop by prior association in James's imagination—come the Prince and Charlotte Stant in *The Golden Bowl* to look over the poetry of its contents, objects of "old gold, old silver, old bronze, of old chased and jewelled artistry," its "small florid ancientries, ornaments, pendants, lockets, brooches, buckles, pretexts for dim brilliants, bloodless rubies, pearls either too large or too opaque for value . . . cups, trays, taper-stands, suggestive of pawn-tickets, archaic and brown, that would themselves, if preserved, have been prized curiosities." (I, 107.)*

In such a shop, the artist is at once a doer, a medium, and an environment or setting for what is done. He is indeed implicated in his art, though not alone by choices and preferences

13 *Ibid.*, pp. 47-48.
* References enclosed in parentheses in the text are to James's fiction and, unless otherwise identified, to the New York Edition: *The Novels and Tales of Henry James*, 26 vols. (N.Y., 1907-1917). *The Golden Bowl* is contained in volumes XXIII and XXIV, and *The Portrait of a Lady* is contained in volumes III and IV, of that edition. All other footnotes appear at the bottom of the page.

among his characters but by assent to the functions inhering in his craft and office, his relation revealed not chiefly in the gestures of passing judgment and sentence upon characters or principles but in those of shared recognition, felt acknowledgment, or confession. The imagination, James goes on to say, is a "wary dealer," in a position to enjoy the acquisitions it protects as well as to profit from the charitable transactions with the customers, including the hard-pressed lady of title or the adventuresome amateur, who placed them there. There remains the problem, however, of how to dispose of the object detained in transit, and James's wariness included the "pious desire," as he called it, "but to place my treasure right. I quite remind myself of the dealer resigned not to 'realize,' resigned to keeping the precious object locked up indefinitely, rather than commit it, at no matter what price, to vulgar hands. For there are dealers in these forms and figures and treasures capable of that refinement." [14]

The image of the broker is profoundly apt because it defines a suspension of multiple contingencies. It is the figure for a process rather than for the origin, simply, or the mere denouement of one. The role presented for the artist embraces the arrangements he makes and any actions he initiates, but even more important is another feature of the image: namely, that instead of emphasizing mastery of intentions, on the writer's part, or known certainties of achievement, it defines a suspension of contingent possibilities. The possibilities defined include four: that the "pious desire" might prove ineffectual and the figure be acquired and defiled to the profit of the dealer; or that the treasure in transit might remain locked up for the occasional enjoyment of the broker alone; or that the figure might be sold into the hands of a worthy purchaser; or that a reduced lady of title, a daring amateur, might herself complete the transaction by returning to take up the form. The *Portrait* itself, as will be seen, manages to redeem all these possibilities, but the preface at hand proceeds to rephrase its statement of the writer's task: to "imagine" and "piece together" the surroundings of the figure already "bent upon its fate" and already deposited in the imagination which apprehends it, to figure out

[14] *The Art of the Novel*, pp. 47-48.

what could be the "destiny" of one among "millions of presumptuous girls" who "daily affront their destiny," this was "what one was in for—for positively organizing an ado about Isabel Archer." [15]

The task was all the more difficult because James had welcomed the challenge of an experiment—centering the interest in the unprepossessing girl's consciousness itself rather than buttressing the "'mere' young thing," as Shakespeare and George Eliot had done, with an entourage of equally important characters or an appropriate Romeo or Anthony. Yet, however interesting the heroine became, any shortcomings in the unbuttressed young thing would have to be compensated by the excitement of the action in order to provide fireworks for the reader's amusement. Quite suddenly, in answer to James's question "Well, what will [Isabel] do?" the agents of the fable "as if by an impulse of their own" came into view. They were the "concrete terms of [his] 'plot,' " and James's terms for his relation to them were "possession," "trust," and "contract." His actors assured him that they would show him what Isabel would do if he simply would "trust them"; James did, "with an urgent appeal to them to make it at least as interesting as they could. . . . They were like the group of attendants and entertainers who come down by train when people in the country give a party; they represented the contract for carrying the party on. That was an excellent relation with them. . . ." [16]

James proceeded to define an equally businesslike relation with his audience: it was that of the canny servant and scrupulous employee. Dishonorable though it was, as James said, even to think of "benefits," the artist had one benefit to which he could justifiably think himself "entitled": that of "the simpler, the very simplest, forms of attention," the "'living wage'" which the reader might be expected to pay. The more *discriminating* attention, the "finer tribute," the writer might *"enjoy"* when it came, but he could expect it only as a "'tip,'" by "taking it as a gratuity 'thrown in,' a mere miraculous windfall, the fruit of a tree he may not pretend to have shaken," a "golden apple . . . straight from the wind-stirred tree." The writer

15 *Ibid.*
16 *Ibid.*, pp. 49, 53.

THE PORTRAIT'S PREFACE

will never cease, "in wanton moods, to dream of some Paradise (for art) where the direct appeal to the intelligence might be legalized," but these dreams remain sheer "extravagances." [17]

In speaking of himself as expecting payment but resigned to receiving only minimum wages from his audience of employers, or as expecting to be wasted and cheated by the process which fertilizes the imagination, or as resigned to foregoing profit so as to preserve a figure in his shop from desecration, or as making himself responsible, within his chosen office, for arrangements of matters which he did not initially control or possess, James acknowledged forms of experience which are shared by a number of characters in the novel but which are realized chiefly in the destiny of Isabel. But the preface also reveals other recognitions which are more unusual with brokers: that to protect, preserve, and arrange a figure in the imagination's shop was to "grasp" and possess it, for enjoyment if not for profit; that to receive "in deposit" and "take over straight from life" a figure that was placed there was to be involved in the act of placing it there in the first place; that to contract with entertainers for the "ado about Isabel" was to be in league with them and accordingly to be implicated in the action which James, though he disliked to, brought himself to name the "plot." The preface's uneasy candor in drawing attention to the novel's plot suggests the extent of James's involvement in his fiction: the watcher at the window inside the House of Fiction was also a colleague in the plot. It suggests indeed that James's fiction displays not the remote manipulations which André Gide found to be his deficiency but the very "multiplicity of his intimate connivances" which Gide demanded of the great artist. Yet, as James wrote of Turgenief, "What he thought of the relation of art to life his stories, after all, show better than anything else." In *The Portrait of a Lady*, the plot proves to reveal the form not only of its author's mediation but of the novel's social and aesthetic implications as well.[18]

Moreover, the plot, more clearly than other components in

[17] Ibid., p. 54.

[18] Gide, "Henry James," in The Question of Henry James: A Collection of Critical Essays, ed. F. W. Dupee (New York, 1945), p. 253. James, Partial Portraits, p. 303.

the novel, reveals the *Portrait*'s place in American cultural history. Far from being incidental to these historical considerations, a mere archaic artifice in a field of *realistic* techniques, moral themes, and social comment, the plot is central. And it is central also in defining the *Portrait*'s chief distinction as a literary form: its success in transforming its materials at once into movement and into visual, strictly representational, form. The novel imposes the burden of considering James's role in writing it, its place in American literature, its themes, and its representational strategy in their shared connection with the movement of the plot.

[II]

THE PLOT

IF JAMES's remarks in the preface can serve as a warning against ignoring the importance of the plot, they should warn too against reducing it to cliché oppositions of characters, abstract antitheses, or capsule summaries (Girl gets Money; American Girl marries Middle-aged Expatriate) at the cost of obscuring its very function as a form of action: its function as a relational form among events, which embraces not only motives and occasions but the full complexity of those events.

As the form of the novel's action, the plot relates to each other the main events on which the action turns; the plot encompasses each event in its integrity (including motives of the characters but other pressures as well) while giving them together a shape and significance beyond the mere impingements of cause and effect, or linear sequences of desire and attainment, effort and failure, which would otherwise be their only connections. One of its central functions is to define the action, form being in relation to works of art what James once said it was in relation to the emotions: "the most definite thing about them." What the plot does is to connect monetary transactions with both marital and parental concerns and with aesthetic concerns as well, and to reveal a profound displacement which is of particular importance in American cultural history: a movement in which the possibilities for experience of one generation are shifted to seek their fulfillment in the prospects of a younger. In defining or shaping the limits of the action, the plot operates by inclusions but as well by exclusions, presenting each of the events which it encloses as a substitute for other possibilities which it brings to light only to postpone or exclude.[19]

The first of these events in the novel's history is the occasion when the expatriate Mrs. Daniel Touchett, still married to her banker husband but "virtually separated from him," stops in Albany when in America on business to adopt or *take* up her niece for a trip abroad. Isabel, when her aunt unexpectedly ap-

[19] "Daudet," *Partial Portraits*, p. 207.

17

peared, was awaiting a call not from a surrogate parent but from her suitor, Caspar Goodwood. (I, 23-27, 33.)

The second event is the occasion when the aging banker is persuaded by his son, Ralph Touchett, to divide the son's inheritance in half so as to augment a bequest to Isabel of £5,000 to over £60,000. The father had planned to give it all to Ralph in anticipation of his marrige to Isabel; Ralph wanted, in securing this advantage for Isabel, to meet " 'the requirements of my imagination,' " having ruled out for himself a full " 'natural life,' " including the possibility of marriage to Isabel, because he was dying of tuberculosis. (I, 265, 259.)

The third occasion occurs when the widow Madame Merle undertakes to arrange the marriage of young Isabel to Madame Merle's former lover, a forty-year-old widower, Gilbert Osmond. She hoped to " 'amuse' " and renew her former lover's interest in life, but one of her chief motives was to provide a suitable stepmother, a sizable dowry, and eventually an advantageous marriage for Pansy Osmond, her illegitimate daughter whom she has never been able to acknowledge. Her project is a substitute for prospects that have proved to be impossible, including the assumption of " 'visible property' " in her own child, marriage with Osmond, or the marriage with a truly " 'great man' " that earlier had been her ambition. The prospect of Pansy's marriage, and the viability of Isabel's, are the pressing issues at the novel's end. (I, 343; II, 366, 368-370.)

A fourth occasion occurs when Gilbert Osmond's sister, the Countess Gemini, discloses to Isabel the facts of Madame Merle's and Osmond's affair, Pansy's parentage, and the arrangement for Isabel's marriage. Still married to her Italian husband, but childless since the death of her own three children, she has pursued a virtually independent career in a "labyrinth of adventures." Once she had hoped that Isabel, as Osmond's wife, would triumph over him and put him in his place. Now she is moved by Isabel's deep trouble and has discovered reasons for encouraging Pansy's love for young Ned Rosier. Bored finally by her silence and by Isabel's delusion, "leaning far out" of the "window of her spirit," she tells what she knows and Isabel sits "staring at her companion's story as at a bale of fantastic wares

some strolling gypsy might have unpacked . . . at her feet."
Asked how she knows, she leaves Isabel with the declaration:
" 'Let us assume that I've invented it!' " (i, 404, 402; ii, 226,
361, 368, 372.)

The movement of the plot which shifts the ambitions and opportunities for experience from one generation to another is
familiar enough in any epoch or society—part indeed of the
very action of history—but one which the American imagination
has characteristically found to be problematical and obsessively
fascinating. The American can neither ignore the interaction of
past, present, and future nor take it tranquilly for granted.

Obviously he heightens an awareness of distinctions among
the generations when emphasizing the antagonisms among
them—as when Jefferson, attempting to institutionalize revolution, insisted that the past was dead and that a generation's extent could and should be precisely delimited to twenty years,
or when Emerson warned against enslavement to the past in
The American Scholar.[20]

But the American sharpens the distinctions among the generations even when cultivating the connections among them,
the continuities of history and the patterns of tradition. One
such American (Cotton Mather in the *Magnalia*) exhorts a
lapsed generation to look backward and forward, Janus-like, in
an expanding crisis, backward to the heroic fathers and exemplars whom he resurrects, forward to an unresolved but prefigured future of "REVOLUTION" and "REFORMATION."
Another (Whitman in *Democratic Vistas*) declares: "America,
filling the present with greatest deeds and problems, cheerfully
accepting the past, including feudalism, (as, indeed, the present
is but the legitimate birth of the past, including feudalism,)
counts, as I reckon, for her justification and success, (for who,
as yet, dare claim success?) almost entirely on the future."
More recently, a third (T. S. Eliot in "Tradition and the Individual Talent") warns against a "blind or timid adherence" to
tradition, yet insists on cultivating the "consciousness of the
past—not only of the pastness of the past but of its presence,"

[20] *The Life and Selected Writings of Thomas Jefferson,* ed. Adrienne Koch
and William Peden (New York, 1944), pp. 413, 674-676.

counting tradition highly valuable but insisting that it "cannot be inherited" and that consequently "one must obtain it by great labour." [21]

There is in American literature one image of this disturbed, this labored concern for history which is as grotesque and apt as the above quotations taken together: "the charming picture," as James called it, in Hawthorne's *The Dolliver Romance,* of a great-grandfather as old as Lear, cut off from "the entire confraternity of persons whom he once loved" and unable to follow them in death because he is held back by the clutched "baby-fingers" of his three-year-old great-granddaughter. The girl's name, Pansy, is echoed in *The Portrait.* More enchanting in its juxtaposition of past, present, and future is a description that is echoed in the *Portrait*'s opening setting in the "perfect middle of a splendid summer afternoon," the description of what Hawthorne found to be a typically English summer day with "positively no beginning and no end," where "Tomorrow is born before Yesterday is dead. They exist together in a golden twilight where the decrepit old day dimly discerns the face of the ominous infant; and you, though a mere mortal, may simultaneously touch them both, with one finger of recollection and another of prophecy." [22] (I, 1.)

James quoted this description admiringly and referred to "the charming picture of the old man and child" in the critical work on Hawthorne which he published in 1879, the year before he began work in earnest on the *Portrait.* James's immersion in the writings of Hawthorne is well known, but his *Hawthorne* proves to have a particular relevance for the *Portrait* and its plot, for Hawthorne was the one prose master of James's American predecessors to combine an obsessive interest in the past with a resolute commitment to the future. The *Portrait* itself includes echoes of Hawthorne which are rendered important by the plot, and James's published study of his master discloses not

21 Mather, *Magnalia Christi Americana, or, The Ecclesiastical History of New England* . . . , 2 vols. (Hartford, 1853), II, 653. Whitman, *The Complete Poetry and Prose of Walt Whitman,* ed. Malcolm Cowley, 2 vols. (New York, 1948), II, 208. Eliot, *Selected Essays, 1917-1932* (New York, 1932), p. 4.

22 Hawthorne, *The Works of Nathaniel Hawthorne,* Standard Library Edition, 15 vols. (Boston, 1882-1891), XI, 20. James, *Hawthorne,* in *The Shock of Recognition,* p. 546.

a strict model for his plot but the very matrix of its fabrication.[23]

One echo is admittedly faint: the notice taken of an art which Madame Merle shares with Hester Prynne: her "wonderful tasks of rich embroidery . . . an art in which her bold, free invention was as noted as the agility of her needle." Another echo is stronger, however, during the important scene when Osmond and Pansy are first introduced and Madame Merle broaches her plan for Osmond's and Isabel's marriage. Osmond remarks of Pansy: " 'She's as pure as a pearl.' " Madame Merle continues: " 'Why doesn't she come back with my flowers then. . . . She doesn't like me.' " Later, it seems to Isabel that Pansy indeed might "make a perfect little pearl of a peeress." Her endowment with money and the translation of Little Pearl into a peeress is the denouement of *The Scarlet Letter*. That novel, the less famous work by John Gibson Lockart to which James compared it, and James's remarks about both underscore the importance of the *Portrait's* plot and illuminate its significance. (I, 273, 350; II, 175.)

The Lockart novel to which James compared *The Scarlet Letter* is the *Life of Mr. Adam Blair* (1822). The burden of James's comments—he dismissed "simple resemblances and divergences of plot"—is to establish the "cold ingenious fantasy," the "passionless quality" of Hawthorne's novel about adultery in contrast to the "something warm and straight-forward" in the lesser novelist's treatment of the same subject. The paragraphs which explore the comparison, however, suggest a seminal reminiscence which owes less to the demands of the argument at hand than to the very "resemblances and divergences of plot" which a comparison of the two works brings to light. Indeed, the compulsive attraction of the comparison for James is suggested by his remark that "if one has read the two books at a short interval, it is impossible to avoid confronting them." (One slight measure of the lasting fascination for James of Lockart's book is that the names of its two principal characters, those of the wife and the widower who commit the adultery, are Charlotte and Adam, the names decades later of the adulterous wife and the widower she marries in James's *The Golden*

23 *Ibid.,* p. 561.

Bowl, and that the name of Adam Blair's young wife, who dies in the first chapter, is Isabel.) [24]

The important similarity which a comparison of the two works throws into relief is the ambivalent splicing in each of the roles of lover and parent, and the dominance finally of the institution of the family and the role of parent. (James noted that in both novels a "charming little girl" stood between the "guilty pair," and he recalled that his earliest memory of *The Scarlet Letter* [derived from a painting before he knew more than the cover of the novel] was the ineradicable image of its "two strange heroines," Hester and her daughter Pearl.) Both novels dramatize, among other things, the problematical responsibilities of parenthood, treating parenthood as a virtual mission beyond a mere physiological and perfunctory familial role, while subjecting it to the challenge of a crisis.[25]

In Lockart's work, the Reverend Adam Blair is plunged into melancholy by his wife's death, when the tutelage of his little daughter Sarah "had devolved upon him." Townspeople soon begin to single out not so much a new wife for Adam as a "step-mother" for Sarah, and one local lady with a "motherly manner" suggests that a visit from an old friend of Adam and Isabel, Mrs. Charlotte Campbell, would dispel Adam's gloom. During Charlotte's stay, neighbors are struck by her "unwearied attention to little Sarah Blair." One of the melodramatic crises of the story centers on the daughter's fate; it occurs when Adam tries to save Sarah from drowning, and both are rescued opportunely by Charlotte. After the seduction scene (in which Charlotte and liquor play the leading roles), Adam's remorse leads him to the verge of suicide, until Charlotte checks him. Each then acknowledges his betrayal of Adam's late wife: " 'Oh Isabel, my Saint, my wounded Saint, my Isabel!' " and " '. . . sainted Isabel—thee too I have injured—thee too have I robbed.' " Later (after Charlotte's death, Adam's confession to his presbytery and retirement to the life of a peasant, and finally his restoration to his congregation), Sarah turns down "many wooers" and devotes her life to caring for her father.

24 *Ibid.*, pp. 513-514.
25 *Ibid.*, pp. 513, 510.

When he dies, twenty years later, she retires, still unmarried, to the peasant cottage that had been the scene of her father's "lonely life of penitence" and spends "the evening of her days in calmness," respected by the entire parish.[26]

In *The Scarlet Letter*, too, the role of parent is one of the first motives introduced, in the incident when Chillingworth consents to perform a parental task, reluctantly because he is not the child's father, by administering medicine to Pearl in the prison, and in the incident when Hester succeeds against the magistracy (with Dimmesdale's cautious support) in keeping Pearl in her care; indeed, the motive is established the moment the tale's "two strange heroines" appear in the prison door. Also, Hester and Dimmesdale, like Charlotte and Adam, are brought to acknowledge that they have wronged the husband (though they do not call Chillingworth a saint). Hester's lonely return to New England at the end is reminiscent of Adam's "lonely life of penitence" and of Sarah's return, unmarried, to the peasant cottage in the evening of her life.

Yet it is the contrasting denouements of the two novels which is most suggestive. That of Adam Blair looks backward in tribute to Adam's memory; the parish and Scotland continue on, but no tangible future for the community is adumbrated, and Sarah and the Blairs are cut off from any future whatever ("With her, the race of the Blairs in that parish ended—but not their memory."). While Sarah has virtually become a matriarch—Adam's "only hand-maid—his only household"—without actually being either wife or parent, and while she has virtually replaced her father in the community's affection, her devoted care and subsequent retirement are the gestures of filial, not parental, responsibility. By contrast, *The Scarlet Letter* culminates in the adoption of parental responsibilities by all the principal adult characters, and this movement is projected ahead into an hypothetical future which is adumbrated in Hester's anticipation of "a brighter period" of history when "the whole relation between man and woman" will be founded "on a surer ground of mutual happiness," but which is prefigured

[26] *Some Passages in the Life of Mr. Adam Blair and the History of Matthew Wald* (Edinburgh, 1871), pp. 15, 17, 31, 57, 119, 121, 173, 166, 174.

more immediately and tangibly in the prospect of Little Pearl.[27]

Under many pressures of personal motive, institutions, and circumstances, Hester first and then Dimmesdale are brought to acknowledge their passion as lovers and their responsibilities as Pearl's parents (Pearl wanders off but near at hand while they reaffirm their love in the forest, and she will accompany them in their projected escape). In Dimmesdale's case, the two roles of lover and parent are acknowledged jointly when he calls: " 'Hester . . . come hither! Come, my little Pearl' " and makes his public confession. Significantly it is Pearl's kiss, however, not Hester's, that Dimmesdale begs at the end, and Pearl's bestowal of it seals the confession and insures her development into a mature woman.[28]

Hawthorne's "Conclusion" completes these patterns and embodies their more harmonious resolution in a prefigured future for Pearl at the cost of presenting a chapter that is too sharply detached from the body of the main novel and not fully anticipated by the movement of the story. It is nonetheless germane to its themes. Roger Chillingworth's death, along with Dimmesdale's death and Hester's self-denial at the end, underscore the novel's final emphasis on the subsequent destiny of Pearl, and moreover, their last acts authenticate and launch it. Dimmesdale's confession and his request for Pearl's embrace is matched by "the matter of business" which Hawthorne relates concerning Hester's husband. Chillingworth's last act, in a will executed at his death by the Governor and the Reverend Mr. Wilson, was virtually to adopt Pearl, administering not medicine but property by making her his heir; she becomes "the richest heiress of her day, in New England" when Chillingworth bequeaths her "a very considerable property, both here and in England." Hester's trip away with Pearl, then her separation from her to return to New England, make possible the independent adult life "in another land" which the mature Pearl is believed to enjoy. In what nation, or even on what continent, Pearl resides, the novel does not stipulate. Nor does it

[27] Lockart, *Adam Blair*, pp. 174, 166. Hawthorne, *The Complete Novels and Selected Tales of Nathaniel Hawthorne*, ed. Norman H. Pearson (New York: Modern Library, 1937), p. 240.
[28] *The Scarlet Letter*, *ibid.*, p. 233.

state whether the "armorial seals" of Pearl's letters home, with "bearings unknown to English heraldry," are more exalted in status than the "half-obliterated shield of arms" which characterized the "antique gentility" of Hester's family in Jacobean England. The bearings may be unknown to any established heraldry or class structure whatever in the hypothetical world of Pearl's fulfillment, though they contrast distinctly with the peasant background of Adam Blair. Other features of Pearl's world, however, are more clearly prefigured. They include the monetary wealth and affection which are displayed in the presents Pearl sends her mother and the "beautiful tokens" she sews for her, in the "lavish richness of golden fancy" which Hester has indulged earlier in embroidering the letter and now in sewing garments for a grandchild who can wear them more openly in that other land, and in the marriage of Pearl, whom Hawthorne believes to be "not only alive, but married, and happy, and mindful of her mother," and herself the parent of a child.[29]

If *Adam Blair* and *The Scarlet Letter* together define some of the main pressures that impel the plot of James's *Portrait*—patterns of marital and familial responsibility—Hawthorne's masterpiece more particularly guides its orientation. The relation between comfortable security and high status of an archaic aristocratic sort, which is suggested by Hawthorne's vocabulary but left fanciful and shadowy in Pearl's case, becomes problematic in James's novel. The "matter of business" and the role of money on which the "Conclusion" of *The Scarlet Letter* turns (and which is of genuine concern in the "Custom House" preface) are treated more emphatically by James. The place of "golden fancy," the role of the imagination, becomes more important, indeed central, in the *Portrait*. And *The Scarlet Letter*'s projection toward a resolution in a prefigured future becomes an even stronger thrust in the *Portrait*, which too confronts a future it would seek to form, though significantly it conceives that future as an urgent and unresolved crisis rather than as the hoped-for resolution of one. James's finished novel confirms what his remarks on *Adam Blair* and *The Scarlet Letter* suggest: a response to Hawthorne's novel so profound as to

[29] *Ibid.*, pp. 238-239, 118, 239.

25

constitute a reworking of the earlier work's materials, a commitment of James's imagination to the fundamental impulsions which are given concrete form in Hawthorne's masterpiece.[30]

The reworking entailed, however, one basic transformation of its materials: to bring the institution of marriage into the center of focus, to treat the "great undertaking of matrimony" as a vital and problematic form, and to mold the action around and within it, rather than to leave that institution remote in the background and dim in the future and to found the present action on alternatives to it. If James's imagination resurrected his cousin Minnie Temple in creating Isabel Archer, it also brought back the Isabel who existed in name only in Lockart's novel and assigned to her as wife the burdens of tutelage, rescue, and experience which she shares with Charlotte Campbell, Hester Prynne, and later Madame Merle. (II, 360-361.)

The two views of marriage that are polarized in *The Scarlet Letter* are presented also in the *Portrait*: the sheerly conventional marriage figured in the failure of Hester and Chillingworth (their marriage the emptiest of conventions, their relation now a shadowy perfunctory marriage still recognized but buried in secrecy and in the past, without foundation in behavior or desire) and the marriage posited for Pearl, marriage as a form of fruition and aspiration. But in James's work they are manifest in many and complex versions which render their extremes less patently antagonistic. Marriage as a hollow factitious form—viewed at one point in the *Portrait* as the " 'ghastly form' "—and marriage as a form of fulfillment and creative possibilities—called at one point "the magnificent form"—are more intimately and problematically related. Indeed, one of the creative functions of the plot is to constitute this close relation between the two by splicing together the immediate plan for Isabel's marriage and the more long-range provisions, still unsettled at the novel's end, for Pansy's. The splicing is strengthened by the fact that Isabel and Pansy attract common suitors. Lord Warburton, whose proposal Isabel turns down, is later an unsuccessful suitor of Pansy. And the younger Ned Rosier, who loves Pansy and whom Pansy would like to marry, had been at the age of twelve a childhood ac-

[30] E.g., *ibid.*, pp. 104, 107.

quaintance, an "angelic" infatuation, of Isabel. (II, 433, 356; I, 306; II, 218.)

James's plot accordingly enabled him to solve a technical problem that Hawthorne handled less satisfactorily (the structural relation between the bulk of the work and its conclusion, between the destiny of Hester, Dimmesdale, and Chillingworth and that of Pearl) and to mediate more successfully the shift from the older generation's opportunities to the younger's that his novel helps to make a burden and a mission for American culture. The process by which the plot orients the novel's movement, drawing the characters into the action it shapes while delineating their characters, is displayed in the amplitude of character, imagery, and incident of the *Portrait* itself.

[III]

THE MARRIAGE

THE first of the important characters to be engaged by the plot and implicated in its moral consequences are those who initiate it and display the main outline of its significance, the interconnection of marital and familial, monetary, and aesthetic concerns: the older Touchetts, Daniel and Lydia, still linked but no longer intimate in their "experiment in matrimony." They find awakened interest, and Mrs. Touchett finds convenience as a hostess, in the niece they have taken up and are supporting while diverting her from the dry sands of German philosophy to a more direct exposure to Europe and the past. It is Mrs. Touchett's telegram (she has mastered " 'the art of condensation' ") that announces in Chapter One that she has " 'Taken sister's girl' " and that Isabel is soon to arrive at Gardencourt. Touchett himself, with his earned and banked resources, long ago bought a house, which imaged all English history since Edward VI, for the simple reason that it was "a great bargain." But as a consequence of this purchase he now has it in his "careful keeping" and has acquired "a real aesthetic passion" for his Gardencourt. He stands firm against the aimless boredom, the jocular detachment, of his son and his son's friend, Lord Warburton, and has suggested that Warburton " ' "take hold" of something' "—indeed marry an interesting woman so that his " 'life will be more interesting,' " though he jokingly excludes the niece of whose impending arrival he has just heard. Later, in his bequest to Isabel, he deliberately consents to play along with his son's plan to make Isabel rich although he fears it is risky to the point of being irresponsible, even " 'immoral.' " (I, 11, 31, 13, 3, 11, 264.)

That plan, if immoral, is also creative. Ralph Touchett's plan is founded on renouncing prospects of marriage with Isabel and on translating his affection into something paternal and fraternal instead. And it is founded on actions in which *both* the renunciation and the use of his inherited wealth are fused. If he is, as one character claims, " 'Prospero enough to make

28

[Isabel] what she has become,' " he is nonetheless like the plotter Iago in wanting to " 'put money in her purse.' " He wants to put money in her purse so that he might, and she might, "meet the requirements of their imagination." With his permissive and playful imagination, he has, as he remarks, " 'amused myself with planning out a high destiny for you' " and after her disastrous marriage to Osmond he spends what time he can watching her, entertained in trying to see through the mask of tranquil satisfaction she has assumed. He presses the limits of their "tacit convention" not to discuss Osmond's conduct openly, for he is so involved in her predicament that he feels "an almost savage desire to hear her complain of her husband," longing "for his own satisfaction more than for hers" to show that he understood her situation, trying again and again "to make her betray Osmond" though "he felt cold-blooded, cruel, dishonourable almost, in doing so." He is turning about in pained fascination the figure detained in the imagination's shop. It is an anguished entertainment, founded on money and imagination, love and sacrifice, and when Isabel later disobeys her husband to rush to Ralph's deathbed, his affection for his cousin becomes adoration in his final declaration. (I, 169, 260, 261, 265; II, 69, 251-252, 417.)

Unlike Ralph, who has renounced the prospect of marriage, his friend Lord Warburton, young Ned Rosier, and Caspar Goodwood find their place as suitors in the novel's action. Warburton exerts a definite but ambivalent charm throughout the novel. He pursues an active career in Parliament and is a "nobleman of the newest pattern" for he combines the security of his wealth and station with the programs of the " 'radicals of the upperclass' " who, in Daniel Touchett's view, indulge in their theories as a luxuriously safe " 'amusement' " without profound commitment. Isabel continues to like Warburton's manliness and all "his merits—properties these partaking of the essence of great decent houses, as one might put it." When he proposes to her she feels "that a territorial, a political, a social magnate had conceived the design of drawing her into" his "system," though she recognized that in his genuine tact and decency he was "looking at her with eyes charged with the light of a passion that had sifted itself clear of the baser parts

of emotion—the heat, the violence, the unreason. . . ."
Though he insists that he simply offers her " 'the chance of
taking the common lot in a comfortable way' " she declines his
" big bribe" on the grounds that she cannot detach herself from
" 'the common lot,' "—from the " 'usual chances and dangers,
from what most people know and suffer,' "—that, as she says,
" 'I can't escape my fate.' " (I, 95, 101-102, 418, 144, 148, 162,
186-187.)

His presence becomes more disturbing in the later part of
the novel; at the age of 42 he has become Pansy's suitor, and
Madame Merle and Osmond find him the answer to their ambitions for Pansy, and Osmond demands that Isabel encourage the
match. Though Isabel finds Warburton's friendship a comfort
—"it was like having a large balance at the bank"—it becomes
problematical because there are definite grounds for the suspicion Ralph and the Countess Gemini share: that a large
part of Warburton's interest in Pansy is the desire to be near
her stepmother. There is a complicated emotional involvement beneath the oddity, as Osmond puts it to Isabel, that
" 'Pansy's admirers should all be your old friends.' " Isabel displays more interest in Warburton's robust masculinity than she
did earlier, noticing now how Pansy gives "quiet oblique
glances at his person, his hands, his feet, his clothes," how
Pansy's "eyes, as usual, wandered up and down his robust
person as if he had offered it to her for exhibition." These are
the observations of a vicarious participant. (II, 212, 151, 302,
182, 177, 213.)

Warburton and Isabel tacitly recognize this involvement on
one occasion when Isabel "met his eyes, and for a moment they
looked straight at each other," and this recognition simply
tightens her dilemma, for the plot has created a situation which
complicates the relation between her roles as wife and parent
and her relation with her former suitor: to obey her husband's
demand by encouraging Warburton's courtship of Pansy would
prove that she did not fear Warburton's presence but risk making her relation to him more intimate; to disobey her husband
out of concern for Pansy's feelings by encouraging Pansy's favorite, Ned Rosier, would safeguard her conduct from emotional
complications with Warburton but virtually acknowledge that

she fears Warburton's proximity and envies Pansy his affection. She assures Warburton he may court Pansy if he pleases, but instantly afterward promises Ned to " 'do what I can' " to favor his suit; yet even after Pansy confesses her love for the younger man, Isabel does not speak in his favor but speaks, albeit without force, of Pansy's obligation to respect her father's desire and of the importance of Warburton's title and fortune. (ii, 221-222, 254-261.)

The crisis is not resolved by Isabel but by a decision of Warburton which is in keeping with the basic design of the plot. He withdraws without making a proposal, understanding Isabel's predicament and recognizing that the younger girl is not in love with him. Later when Isabel learns that Warburton, after a courtship of three weeks, has married " 'A member of the aristocracy; Lady Flora, Lady Felicia—something of that sort,' " she reflects that Warburton "was dead for poor Pansy; by Pansy he might have lived." But instead of becoming the perfect little pearl of a peeress, Pansy will wait in hopes of marrying Ned who looks to her so like a "nobleman." (ii, 408-409, 261.)

Before Pansy's prospects and Isabel's concern turn from Warburton to the young man, Ned Rosier's place in the action seems inconsequential, for there is justice in Isabel's feeling that Ned is "really so light a weight. He was much more of the type of the useless fine gentleman than the English nobleman," and Warburton is probably not envious in remarking that Ned still " 'doesn't look much more than twelve today.' " He is an American expatriate and dilettante (" 'There's nothing for a gentleman in America' "). And he lacks not only Warburton's title but a career (" 'American diplomacy—that's not for gentlemen either' "), and instead of Warburton's radical views he has the "grim politics," reactionary and Napoleonic, which he parrots (prophetic soul) from one Mr. Luce. Yet for all the novel's frivolous attention to the decorations of his mantelpiece, his prominent position in the plot suggests his importance, for he is carefully introduced just after Madame Merle learns that Isabel has inherited a fortune, and his arrival in Rome is the first narrated incident to follow Isabel's marriage. With his "cultivated tastes" and collection of bibelots, he all but lives at the auctioneer's, yet he could not possibly have a career as shopkeeper because, as he says, " 'I can buy very well, but I can't sell.' " In the course of the novel, however, he has found temporarily a place in the world of affairs. He has been drawn into the final crisis by paying court to Pansy and rendering himself eligible by the commerical transaction which he announces to Isabel when he finds her seated in the "despoiled arena" of the Coliseum: he has sold his *objets d'art* (all but his enamels) for $50,000 cash. (II, 175, 218; I, 304, 307, 309, 308; II, 341.)

Ned's relation with Isabel spans the years from their childhood to a point which lies beyond the range of her personal desire, but the relation of Caspar Goodwood is at once more confined and more intimate. The first suitor to propose to Isabel (in Albany), he is the last to confront her in the novel, when he tries to persuade her to leave her husband. With his square jaw and the "hardness of presence, in his way of rising before her" that Isabel finds disagreeable, his manner presents a distinct combination of masculine vigor and the awkward and genuine assertiveness of the American businessman. Isabel is critical of the sameness of his apparel, the simplicity of his manner, and later his literalness, and she early compares the prospect of "conquest at her English suitor's [Warburton's] large quiet hands" to the more unsettling prospect of letting Caspar "take positive possession of her." He manages a large cotton mill in Massachusetts and is the son of its founder; his business acumen, energy, and career distinguish him from both Warburton and Rosier. So complete is his association with the realm of business that in a later scene with Isabel, when restating his love for her and trying to understand her distance from him, his very idiom makes the world of business the dividing line between himself and the intimacy of Isabel's feelings: the phrase "none of my business" becomes a virtual refrain as he concedes, time and again, that " 'It's none of my business— very true. But I love you.' " (I, 161-165; II, 293, 311, 318-319.)

Yet within the novel's perspective her feelings are related, curiously, to his business, for his business capacity includes the "sharp eye" that has already led him to one patented invention and it includes "the art," as James said, "of managing men."

Two statements which James added in revision enforce Goodwood's connection with the plot and the artistry of making it: in his "clear-burning eyes" sits "some watcher at a window," and he is expected someday to "write himself in bigger letters." [31] It is he, Isabel expects, who will see through her mask if anyone can and "make . . . out, as over a falsified balance-sheet . . . the intimate disarray of her affairs." He had "invested his all in her happiness, while the others had invested only a part." The plot renders these scattered metaphors central, rather than peripheral or incidental, to the novel's design. By the final chapter, when Caspar's strong desire is buttressed by Ralph's last request to " 'Do everything you can for her; do everything she'll let you,' " Caspar's "aimless, fruitless passion" has become profound and possessive, and the plot has made of him an image of a grasping and possessive imagination. (I, 163-164, 162, 164; II, 282, 432.)

The plot's chief instruments and artificers, however, are those who give the confluence of events its distinct shape: Madame Merle and her former lover, Gilbert Osmond. With one marriage a failure, others are seemingly out of the question for Serena Merle, and she finds it impossible to acknowledge Pansy Osmond as her daughter. She conceives the simultaneous arrangement of Isabel's marriage and the provision eventually for Pansy's, hoping to " 'amuse' " her former lover and urging him to " 'profit' " by her deep familiarity with social arrangements. She is an expatriate, so steeped now in " 'the old, old world' " as to be " 'the great round world itself.' " Madame Merle seems to be deeply conventional in a world where the conventional touches upon everything, including, as Isabel recognizes, language itself. Not only does Madame Merle practice the arts of conversation and the needle, to say nothing of music, but she paints: she "made no more of brushing in a sketch than of pulling off her gloves." Isabel's partial awakening to the facts of her betrayal include the recognition (which the preface was to echo later) that Madame Merle had been a powerful "agent" in her "destiny." (I, 343, 279, 362, 274, 272; II, 322.)

Indeed, she has done for James what the Countess Gemini finally divulges that she has done for Osmond: " 'She has worked

[31] Cf. p. 99 of the first edition, Boston, 1881.

for him, plotted for him, suffered for him; she has even more than once found money for him.' " Her plotting, once it is revealed, not only calls forth Isabel's scorn but her compassion when she recognizes that Madame Merle has, as the Countess says, " 'failed so dreadfully that she's determined her daughter shall make it up.' " Her own ambitions and desires, like Isabel's, are channeled, by the plot she does so much to instigate, into the prospects for Pansy's marriage. Her final failure is to be excluded even as a silent partner from the arrangements she had wanted so much to be " '*my* work' " by Osmond who abandons her. (ii, 372, 370, 338.)

It is Osmond who is stirred to a renewed interest in life by collaboration in his colleague's plot. An "odd mixture of the detached and involved," living by himself in a "sifted, arranged world" in Italy, "thinking about art and beauty and history," this proud " 'provincial' " is an American expatriate artist and dilettante. He longs nostalgically for the authority of a pope and suggests occasionally in his demeanor a "prince in exile," a " 'prince who has abdicated in a fit of fastidiousness and has been in a state of disgust ever since.' " He is the incarnation of taste and, as he himself puts it, " 'convention itself.' " He had once had the decency to acknowledge his own daughter Pansy and, unlike Madame Merle's husband who rejected the child utterly, to make himself responsible for her care; during his engagement to Isabel he suggests that together they will "make up some little life" for Pansy, as if they were to invent it; late in the novel, "playing theoretic tricks on the delicate organism of his daughter," and wanting to "show that if he regarded his daughter as a precious work of art it was natural he should be more careful about the finishing touches," he sends her back to the Roman convent to insure her complete subservience to his will. (i, 367, 371, 377, 427, 352, 358; ii, 21, 81-82, 348-349.)

He is imaged as a commemorative "gold coin" and is discovered late in the novel devoting his art to copying an illustration of an "antique coin," scorning money but using and seeking it. His old villa in Florence—"a blank-looking structure," broken by only "a few windows," its front façade the "mask" rather than the "face of the house"—harbors inside a large "writing-table of which the ingenious perfection bore the stamp" not of Renaissance Florence but of "London and the nineteenth century." There lives the man "with eyes at once vague and penetrating . . . , expressive of the observer as well as of the dreamer," to whose "deep art" Isabel eventually succumbs. If he discreetly seeks public approval, looking "out of his window even when he appeared to be most detached from it" so as to gain its recognition rather than to "enlighten or convert or redeem it," he is also the watcher inside their common dwelling whom Isabel recognizes in her long night of meditation—the watcher who "seemed to peep down from a small high window and mock at her." "Her mind," she comes to understand, "was to be his. . . . He would rake the soil gently and water the flowers. . . . It would be a pretty piece of property for a proprietor already far reaching." He is the figure—the watcher inside the House of Fiction—in whom Caspar recognizes much later a "demonic imagination." (I, 329; II, 352; I, 325, 327-328; II, 62, 196-198, 200, 313.)

So intimately is James implicated in the action of his novel that letters he was writing while working on the *Portrait* are echoed in the passages where Osmond's mind and feelings are stirred by the workings of the plot and he proposes marriage to Isabel. James wrote that he was "much more interested in my current work than anything else," that he was "working with great ease, relish, and success," that his work would bring $6,000 from serialization alone, that it would "rend the veil" which covered his "ferocious ambition," that it would be from the finished *Portrait,* his most ambitious early effort, "that I myself shall pretend to date." [32] It is Ralph who notices that the costumed "fine lady" which the once "free, keen" Isabel has become "represented Gilbert Osmond," who now "was in his element; at last he had material to work with." His calculated effects "were produced by no vulgar means, but the motive was as vulgar as the art was great. . . . 'He works with superior material,' Ralph said to himself; 'it's rich abundance compared with his former resources.' " It is the excitement of such opportunities that earlier had awakened Osmond. Just

[32] Quoted by Leon Edel in his "Introduction" to *The Portrait of a Lady* (Boston: Riverside Edition, 1956), pp. vi, viii.

before his proposal Osmond finds himself pleased with his newly aroused "sense of success," feeling that his earlier successes had rested "on vague laurels," and that his present success was "easy . . . only because he had made an altogether exceptional effort." While the "desire to have something or other to show for his 'parts' . . . had been the dream of his youth," now it was to materialize with Isabel's help and at her expense: "If an anonymous drawing on a museum wall had been conscious and watchful it might have known this peculiar pleasure of being at last . . . identified—as from the hand of a great master—by the so high and so unnoticed fact of style. His 'style' is what the girl had discovered with a little help; and now, beside herself enjoying it, she should publish it to the world without his having any of the trouble. She would do the thing for him and he would not have waited in vain." In this view of Osmond are joined both the finished work of art—the drawing with which Osmond is associated so intimately—and the master whose style was displayed in making it. (II, 143-144, 11-12.) [33]

The useful girl is Isabel with her combination of caution and curiosity, inexperience and alertness, and the strength of will which leads her to confront life's options " 'So as to choose.' " Her suspicion of the poisoned cup of experience and her fear of suffering are countered by her desire to join in what ordinary " 'people know and suffer.' " Her desire "to leave the past behind her" and encounter always fresh beginnings is balanced by her deepening response to the appeal of the past and tradition. Her acknowledged ignorance "about bills" or " 'anything about money' " is countered by the definiteness of her aversion " 'to being under pecuniary obligations' " and the assurance of her delusion that in going to Europe she is literally " 'travelling at her own expense.' " The "something cold and dry in her temperament" which an "unappreciated suitor"

---

[33] The passage about the anonymous drawing was added in revision. It reinforces the association in the original edition between Osmond's courtship of Isabel and the aims of art. The earlier version included the reference to his London writing desk, described him as a "watcher," and associated Osmond's marriage to Isabel with the desire to make himself felt "deeply" rather than on vast "multitudes." In 1881, Osmond had been inspired by Isabel to write a sonnet. See pp. 198, 263, 267, 375-376, of the 1881 edition.

would notice is countered by the boldness of her "ridiculously active" imagination which renders her vulnerable to delusions, being so "wide-eyed" as to suffer from "seeing too many things at once" and incurring the "penalty of having given undue encouragement to the faculty of seeing without judging." Her mind in sum is a "tangle of vague outlines at the start," but the interaction of her capacity for experience with the plot which forms that experience joins her conscience and her imagination and fills in the outlines of both Isabel's and the *Portrait*'s vision. (I, 93, 187, 41, 28, 34, 57, 71, 42, 66-68.)

In the course of experiencing the lures and pressures that shape her destiny in the novel, the action brings her maternal instincts into the foreground. Mrs. Touchett's taunting fear that Isabel may decide that her " 'mission in life's to prove that a stepmother may sacrifice herself—and that, to prove it, she must first become one' " is confirmed by Isabel's feeling toward Pansy and by her eventual actions, and it is given another dimension by Isabel's late recognition that her feeling for Osmond himself contained "a maternal strain—the happiness of a woman who felt that she was a contributor, that she came with charged hands." (I, 398; II, 192.)

Moreover, the plotted action which involves her with Osmond and Pansy dissociates both Isabel and finally Pansy from the securities and settled conventions of the strictly aristocratic tradition, embodied in Lord Warburton, and involves each instead in something more problematical and hazardous. For Pansy it is the prospect of a marriage founded on no more than sheer mutual affection and a great sufficiency of cash; Pansy herself, whom Isabel feels to be a blank page she hopes will be filled with "an edifying text," displays nothing but her fragile charm and the genuineness of her devotion; Ned Rosier has neither settled status nor job and office, his mind and tastes are not exceptional, and his only recommendation is the genuine commitment defined by his courtship and the sale of his prized treasures. (I, 401; II, 174.)

Isabel's involvement is with the actual form of her strange marriage with Osmond. Within that form Isabel's and Osmond's child is born (he dies at the age of six months) and Isabel acquires her stepdaughter. Within a few years, however, it is clear that intimacy between Isabel and Osmond has ceased, and by the end his attitude is one of contempt; as Isabel finally tells him, " 'It's malignant.' " Yet the form, as a sheer institutional form, still holds and within it takes place a striking confrontation when Isabel distinguishes between her own and her husband's conceptions of aristocracy and tradition. It is not only striking but significant because their different attitudes together reveal conflicting tendencies that are widespread in American culture but which are particularly pressing in the Genteel Tradition, and these tendencies are embodied in the marriage which the plot has figured for them. (II, 354.)

Isabel's view of aristocracy is distinguished by being ethical and experiential and envisions the reconciliation of duty with enjoyment: the "union of great knowledge with great liberty; the knowledge would give one a sense of duty and the liberty a sense of enjoyment." Osmond's is at once more formal and more active; it is "altogether a thing of forms, a conscious, calculated attitude." And while both characters respect tradition, the "old, the consecrated, the transmitted," and both speak as if dissociated from it and encountering it from some distance, Isabel's attitude is eclectic and based on her determination "to do what she chose with it." Osmond's view is at once more conservative in its deference to older social patterns, more desperate in his sense of alienation from them, and more radical in his means to attain them, as befits the prince in exile from America and would-be pope who longs for the deference paid an aristocrat but has not inherited the traditional aristocratic forms. He has a "large collection" of traditions and feels that the "great thing was to act in accordance with them" rather than to choose among them; and his proprietorship, like his manner, is founded on the realization that distinguishes him from the European who could simply find or tranquilly inherit his traditions: Osmond, the American expatriate, knows that "if one was so fortunate as not to have [tradition] one must immediately proceed to make it." (II, 198-199.)

Isabel's determination to "choose," and Osmond's to construct or "make," are sharply delineated by the mutual antagonism of the two characters, but they are joined in perilous proximity by the bond of their marriage and both are related to other social realities which are part of their American background. These are the money economy and obsessive attitudes toward money, which characterize the culture of American capitalism, and characteristic American attitudes (one utilitarian, the other guilt-ridden) toward inherited wealth.

Osmond, the son of a "rich and wild" father and a mother who combined a practical "administrative" view with a talent for poor poetry, has made in his expatriation a " 'wilfull renunciation' " which is nonetheless a social construct; it is founded on the habitual intent to utilize economic resources without creating them and is centered on his immediate family. Determined " 'not to strive nor struggle' " in the business world, yet content with the independent income derived therefrom (though he thinks it " 'little' "), he carefully harbors and manages his economic resources, buys and builds his collection and refines his tastes, buys and constructs his walled substitute for a world of forms which he might prefer to have inherited. Making his " 'life an art' " as he advised Isabel to do, he attempts to mold Pansy, with his "artistic" or "plastic view" of her capacities, in accordance with his desire for dominance. He is the genteel embodiment of "convention" in a strikingly modern version recognizable since 1789: convention become conscious and deliberate, the result less of habit and tacit agreement than of calculated control, deliberate formulation, and the determination not simply to order life as it is but to shape it more firmly and actually change it. When the opportunity to gain Isabel and her fortune presents itself, he is happy for the opportunity to put it and her to use. (I, 402, 404, 381; II, 84.)

Isabel and her fortune come to be as closely associated in her own mind as they are in Osmond's and as they are throughout the novel. In Chapter I Daniel Touchett, after reading the reference in his wife's telegram to Isabel's being " 'independent,' " asks this question: is the word " 'used in a moral or in a financial sense?' " His question proves to have point. After Isabel has accustomed herself to the fact that she is rich, she is enchanted by a "maze of visions" of what a generous, independent, responsible girl could do with such resources, and her fortune "became to her mind a part of her better self; it gave her importance, gave her even, to her own imagination, a certain ideal beauty." Her attitude has less conscious origins in her temperament and in her environment, the attitudes toward experience and money being so intimate that the novel renders the one the image of the other. When Osmond proposes, Isabel is checked by a sense of dread, her hesitancy being founded on "the force which . . . ought to have banished all dread—the sense of something within herself, deep down, that she supposed to be inspired and trustful passion." Yet that fount of passion is one which Isabel inclines to save as against the alternative she anticipates, that of spending it entirely: "It was there like a large sum stored in a bank—which there was a terror in having to begin to spend. If she touched it, it would all come out." (This analogy between a bank and Isabel's capacity for passion was added in revision.) By the time she is engaged, her consent is taking the form of an act of absolution and benefaction but also of proprietorship. (I, 13, 321-322; II, 18.)

She is gratified by Pansy's affection, for "Pansy already so represented part of the service she should render," and if she feels "humility" in surrendering to Osmond, she feels also "a kind of pride" in the knowledge that "she should be able to be of use to him" and that "she was not only taking, she was giving." When Isabel looks back on her decision later, she recognizes that she never would have married him "but for her money." Her money had been the contribution to the marriage that appealed to her "maternal strain," yet the indelicacy of having merely inherited it was also a "burden" on her conscience which she longed to transfer to someone else. "What would lighten her own conscience more effectually than to make it over to the man with the best taste in the world" when she could think of no charitable institution as interesting as he? "He would use her fortune in a way that would make her think better of it and rub off a certain grossness attaching to the good luck of an unexpected inheritance." Moreover, she had felt that the "subtlest . . . manly organism she had ever known had become her property, and the recognition of having but to put out her hands and take it had been originally a sort of act of devotion." (II, 82-83, 192-194.)

These divergent views—of proprietorship, the propriety of money, domestic economy, parental care, tradition, and aristocratic forms and values—are held juxtaposed within the bond of Isabel's and Osmond's marriage. Their variety, their tension, and their proximity are an indication that not only the separate views themselves but their interconnections are being examined, and that the form which joins them, the marriage, is being subjected to a test under the pressures shaped by the plot. Indeed, the marriage institution as displayed is not a settled institutional mold but is a form in the process of being shaped. The terms "experiment" for the Touchetts' marriage and "undertaking" for matrimony in general are decidedly apt in the context of the *Portrait*—and with them the term "form," which is used by Caspar when condemning the " 'ghastly form' " which Isabel's marriage has become and is used also when Osmond, urging Isabel not to leave, is said to speak "in the name of something sacred and precious—the observance of a magnificent form." (I, 11; II, 356, 360-361, 433.)

For the *Portrait* reveals in the institution the principal functions of a form: the capacity to sustain a fully developed relationship; but also the capacity to precede the full development of a process or experience while yet prefiguring it, and thus to shape the plans and aspirations for personal and social experience, to embody emerging possibilities as well as actual achievements; and the capacity to survive the process or experience itself, remaining a skeletal but nonetheless real image of possibilities no longer (or not yet again) actual. Within the context of the *Portrait,* the marriages of the Countess and much later of Warburton image the institution reduced to its most factitiously conventional status, while Daniel Touchett's hopes for Ralph's and Isabel's marriage, and earlier for Warburton's, and Isabel's hopes for Pansy's, view the institution as a form of aspiration and commitment, with the Touchetts' marriage (and Henrietta Stackpole's) falling in between.

Indeed, the *Portrait* gives body to ambivalent remarks James made in letters to his brother and Grace Norton, in 1878 and 1881, on the subject of marriage, confirming his intention not to marry but insisting on the importance of the institution, associating the form of marriage with commitments of the profoundest sort, and displaying a firm regard for the institution despite his own decision. He wrote that "I believe almost as much in matrimony for most other people as I believe in it little for myself," and that "one's attitude toward marriage is . . . the most characteristic part doubtless of one's general attitude toward life. . . . If I were to marry I should be guilty in my own eyes of inconsistency—I should pretend to think quite a bit better of life than I really do." These letters make the form of marriage an image of commitments to life itself, whether within or beyond the range of one's actual conduct. These are commitments which James's imagination entertained and made in his fiction, if nowhere else, and they are at issue in the *Portrait*.[34]

There the plot—like the world it represents endowing and then drawing on Isabel's banked resources of temperament and inheritance—focuses first on the prospective form of her marriage; then as that becomes a hollow shell it widens its focus to include the prospects for Pansy's. In the process, Isabel's acts of confronting and imagining experience become acts of paying and suffering and responsible commitment as she is led by her husband "into the mansion of his own habitation" and made a victim of her world (including her own temperament and illusions) and of the *Portrait* which creates and paints her. (II, 196.)

[34] Quoted by F. O. Matthiessen, *The James Family* (New York, 1947), pp. 294-295.

[IV]

THE PORTRAIT OF A LADY

THE "ado" about Isabel which is formed by the plot is in perfect keeping with a carefully measured visual strategy that is one of James's most impressive contributions to the English novel: the achievement, to use the language of painting, of *representational* form. Not only the settings, but the actions of the characters and even the limits which circumscribe the range of their experience, are rendered in visual terms. The novel's chief aim—"to represent life"—which James said it shared with history and with painting in "The Art of Fiction" (1884), is in the *Portrait* a distinctly painterly objective. And the plot, though a form of movement and (as James's preface was to confess) a form in part imposed on the action, is perfectly fused with the patterns of vision.[35]

While James does present explanatory comment (notably in Chapter IV) and uses significant allusions and settings (including meaningful names and the like), the *Portrait* is not *founded* in the strict sense on certain fictive modes to which the novel genre has frequent recourse: rhetorical strategies of assertion and moral suasion, emblematic strategies, or the referential mode of explicit reporting with critical and reflective comment *about* its subject. James's form enables him to encompass both the acts of describing his material and assessing it in an act of visual representation. The *Portrait* is not a "record" or "replica," to use Professor E. H. Gombrich's terms, but, like portraits on canvas as Gombrich has shown, is an illusionist "model" resulting from an act of projection, the projection of a form. The image of the world rendered, and a moral perspective on it, are joined in a form which presents convincing models of actuality (the actualities of scene, character, customs, ideas, feelings) because instead of *imitating* or *referring to* them it *represents* them; it reveals them in the vividness of their body and contour by virtue of the heightened vividness of

[35] *Partial Portraits*, pp. 378-379.

its own formal artifices, which are projected with all the gradations and completeness, the finish, and the pressure of effect
that James's medium can manage.[36]

In his *Hawthorne* James's remarks on Hawthorne's relation
to Puritanism indicate his own conception of a painterly *objectivity* which he thought displayed in Hawthorne's treatment of "the Puritan conscience" and which, however great its
risks, need not result in the severance of the pictorial from the
moral sense and so reduce a novel to a "succession of minute
paintings on ivory," as James had felt in 1876 to be the case
with the Goncourt brothers. Hawthorne treated the Puritan
conscience, James wrote, as a pigment: he "played with it and
used it as a pigment; he treated it, as the metaphysicians say,
objectively." [37]

Such a treatment can apply to an author's own judgments as
well. So to treat the moral dimension of his material, whatever
its origin, is to make it part of the medium itself and thus to
associate it intimately, not remotely, with other resources (of
setting, metaphor, convention, and the like) and with his manipulations of them. Consequently, in the novel as finally constituted, the presented image embraces both the *subject* and
an implicit moral perspective on it; the image of the actual
world and the novel's moral pressure are joined in the perspective of the novel's visual form. James's stance in the opening paragraph of the *Portrait* is not that of a direct observer
divorced from his medium (a watcher standing outside his
House of Fiction, or a commentator registering observations),
nor that of a narrator in the strict sense, but that of a painter,
rendering "the peculiarly English picture I have attempted to
sketch." And his visual strategy entailed extension of even so
finished a sketch into full and specifically representational form,
a process which involves expanding and building up the sketch,
filling in its outlines. (James in 1886 took Howells to task for
neglecting to "paint, to evoke the conditions and appearances,

36 *Art and Illusion: A Study in the Psychology of Pictorial Representation*
(New York, 1960), pp. 28, 90, 110.

37 *Literary Reviews and Essays by Henry James* . . . , ed. Albert Mordell (New
York, 1957), pp. 159, 162; *The Shock of Recognition*, p. 471.

to build in the subject.") In this process the plot is central, for in it the novel's movement and its perspective join. (I, 2.) [38]

In placing the characters as it draws them into the action, and in giving its events their coherence—Mrs. Touchett's visit, Daniel Touchett's bequest, Madame Merle's plan, and the Countess' display of her wares—the plot gives them a projective form which is viable in impulse and movement and is distinct and recognizable, thereby defining their limits and yielding a perspective on them. As a shaping plan it is the pattern of the *fictive* world; it mediates between the separate persons, objects, and events in that fictive world and constitutes a perspective on it.

A corresponding function is performed by the plot in mediating between the novel and the *actual* world from which it takes its materials: it molds not only the fictive world but the actual one. The plot is the projected *scheme* which molds the actual world it images and seeks to shape, the seminal form which startles and intrigues the reader for the very reason that it confronts his actual world with a definite perspective on it which is recognizably an artifice and a distortion, yet a relevant version of that world. The plot acts upon the reader, shaping his insights and expectations, and through him acts upon the familiar actual world, pressing upon it a cast more firmly shaped, orienting its movement in a pattern which it projects. It creates an image of things as they are which is also a prospective view of what they are coming to be under the double pressure of processes outside the novel (which it renders) and the novel's own exertions, the "ado" which the novel makes in shaping those processes, whether to endorse or to alter them. The plot is discernible in the *Portrait* as an artifice, yet it becomes an instrument of representational form because the projected scheme is made to emerge gradually in an ample variety of incident and character, instead of turning on sudden or extreme shifts which are the work of a very few agents; in other words, the plot so informs the action that it becomes implicit, rather than obtrusive, in the novel's vision. In orienting the

[38] *Henry James: The American Essays,* ed. Leon Edel (New York: Vintage Books, 1956), p. 155.

movement of the novel, the plot's own fulfillment in ample
and clear detail is made implicit in the process it helps to
form, namely the expansion and completion of a sketch into the
full visual portrait promised in the title. As a form of expectation it anticipates and becomes both the action of the characters and the act of portraying them. Each process becomes
the embodiment of the other as one detail after another is
simultaneously launched into movement and placed in perspective, and as the form establishes a representational scale
which measures the action along with the delineated characters,
the movement along with the imagery and the structure of the
composition.

The *Portrait* begins with a set piece it calls a "sketch" which
opens into a landscaped vista, an expansive tableau, and is
filled in with an amplitude of historical and observed detail.
Space recedes in depth, measured in plausible gradations as the
tea-time hours of "the perfect middle of a splendid summer
afternoon" become "a little eternity" and "angular," "straight"
shadows lengthen on "the smooth, dense turf." The pace is
slow, the talk and even a small terrier are "desultory"; the attitudes, though relaxed, are deliberate, ceremonious, statu-
esque; the prose presents not the illusion of full movement but
the nonetheless rounded illusion of merely latent energies, the
postures and visual configurations which suggest both immanent vitality and decay. As if within a frame, hung upon a wall
or easel, figures sit or stroll undisturbed in equilibrium; the
natural setting of the park blends with the "cushioned seats,"
the "rich-coloured rugs," the "books and papers" which furnish
it "like a room" and make the outdoors seem "the extension
of a luxurious interior." All is poised in a state of suspension
within which the novel begins to unfold arcs of widening,
deepening recognition. These arcs of vision, even at the start,
are infused with the scheme or plot—the taking up and taking
hold, the giving—which has been projected in creating them.
(I, 1-5.)

The first paragraph moves from ritual to vision, from its
notations concerning the "ceremony known as afternoon tea"
to those tracing the glances of two of the characters which define a process of vision; one "looked with a certain attention at

the elder who, unconscious of observation, rested his eyes upon the rich red front of his dwelling." Soon the elder Touchett is proposing that, as an antidote to the " 'bore of comfort,' " Lord Warburton " 'take hold of a pretty woman' " and Warburton, even before hearing of Isabel's impending arrival, agrees that he will " 'lay hands on one as soon as possible and tie her round my neck as a life preserver.' " When Isabel is introduced in the opening of the next chapter, Ralph's "eyes were bent musingly on the lawn; so that he had been an object of observation to a person who had just made her appearance in the ample doorway for some moments before he perceived her." The sudden darting movement of his terrier leads his eye to the girl who "at first sight looked pretty." Instantly Isabel's independence is apparent—to Warburton, in " 'the way she handles the dog' " and to Ralph who finds her displaying " 'a remarkable air of property' " in the terrier. When she asks " 'Couldn't we share him?' " Ralph offers the dog as an outright gift. Before introducing her to the others, he declares that he is " 'delighted to see you' " and Isabel surveys the scene "with an eye denoting clear perception." The plot moves implicitly in these details of incident and observation. (I, 2, 6, 11, 16-18.)

So basic is the visual strategy that the action's culminations, as Dorothy Van Ghent has shown, are consistently recognition scenes,[39] the most intimate being that in Chapter Forty-two. Isabel sits alone in meditation on the "impenetrably black" shadows which lurk in the "mansion" of her husband's "own habitation" behind the "pictured tapestries," and which are a "creation and consequence of her husband's very presence." His presence is the "evil eye" of a watcher in the "house of darkness, the house of dumbness, the house of suffocation" and, as the preface helps us to see, the house of fiction where the watcher's "beautiful mind indeed seemed to peep down from a small high window and mock at her." The chapter leaves her standing in mute recognition, "gazing at a remembered vision." (II, 188, 190, 196, 205.)

She recognizes, in the light now of tested experience, the

---

[39] *The English Novel: Form and Function* (New York, 1953), p. 216.

knowledge whose germ she had brought with her from America, that " 'the cup of experience' " is " 'poisoned.' " It is true, however, that her early determination not to touch the cup but " 'to look about' " her instead, " 'to see for myself,' " presents an antithesis between *seeing* and the full partaking of experience which is important to the novel. Indeed the " 'show' " to which Ralph has bought a " 'ticket' " is conceived as a spectacle which he is determined to " 'see' " though doomed to stand off from as a mere onlooker. And it is true that the performance of Madame Merle and Osmond when Isabel first meets them looks like a play which Isabel merely watches from a high-priced seat while taking no part on stage in the conversation. But this antithesis between sight and experience is later qualified, and the remark that Isabel drained "cup after cup" in sight-seeing on her tour of the Near East before her marriage is an index of the extent to which *seeing,* for Isabel and reader alike, has been transformed from a sketchy substitute for full experience to a means of attaining and sharing in it. Nonetheless, the path that Isabel takes at the end is a relatively safe substitute for the passionate possession discovered to her in Caspar's kiss and for the complications his entreaty would lead to. The formal triumph of the *Portrait* is precisely that the limitations of Isabel's and the other characters' experience, as well as the kinds of experience in which they do engage, are both mediated through the representational form. (I, 213, 210, 355; II, 38.)

The taste of experience is glimpsed in the "unusually large cup" which Daniel Touchett sips in the opening sketch, and in the cracked coffee cup which Madame Merle asks Osmond to be careful of when impugning his harsh treatment of Isabel, the cup that Madame Merle stood holding and "looked at . . . rather abstractedly" after being abandoned by her lover. And the architecture of windowed houses, churches, convent rooms, galleries, and ruins is rendered in distinct detail, its tangible solidity felt in being seen. (I, 1; II, 337-338.)

Moreover, the numerous scenes in galleries and the metaphor of painting not only serve the functions of setting, characterization, and theme but help transform the inky prose, the bare printed sequence of chapters, into visual form, as when

Ralph is scrutinized as if "he himself had been a picture" and he associates himself with a painted musician in a canvas by Lancret, or when Osmond is rendered as a painting about to be identified, or when Isabel stands "framed in the gilded doorway," become at last the "picture of a gracious lady." (I, 124; II, 105.)

The visual embodiment suggested by the metaphors of painting and the focus on the experience and vocabulary of sight is enforced even by the fiction's structure, which consists of three main segments, marked by a distinct lapse of time between each of them. For whether that structure is conceived as the skeleton of an embodied action, the tangible spatial form of a House of Fiction, or as the framed and patterned composition of a representational painting, it reveals the fleshed and plotted contours of visual form. One compositional unit encloses the first twenty-one chapters, which build up to four crucial chapters, each of which is shaped by the main impulsions and contours of the plot. One is Chapter Eighteen, where Isabel first meets Madame Merle and where, also, Ralph persuades his father to leave Isabel a fortune. The next is the chapter where Madame Merle aimlessly proposes someday to introduce Isabel to her friend Osmond; the same chapter terminates in Daniel Touchett's death, which puts into effect his benefactions. The third is Chapter Twenty, where Madame Merle learns of Isabel's inheritance and where also Ned Rosier is introduced. The last is Chapter Twenty-one, where Isabel assents to the possession of her fortune. The final compositional unit includes the last twenty chapters; it opens with the arrival of Ned Rosier in Rome to court Pansy and closes with Isabel's return to Rome at the end. Between it and the first is the central block of fourteen chapters. It terminates in Chapter Thirty-five with final preparations for Isabel's marriage, which are sealed when Pansy accepts her stepmother (" 'I shall have a beautiful sister' ") and Isabel insists that Pansy stay at her side while the Countess chats on looking at her and talking (in the revised version) "as if seated brush in hand before an easel, she were applying a series of considered touches to a composition of figures already sketched in." The central block begins in Chapter Twenty-two where lies, accessible to sight, the occasion when the destinies of the novel's two strange heroines (Isabel and Pansy) are linked by Madame Merle's proposal to Osmond that he make an ado about Isabel and seek to marry her. (II, 84, 86.)

James's success in giving his novel the sense of completion while nonetheless projecting it under pressure into an unresolved future, indeed a crisis, toward which Isabel moves at the end, is one of his triumphs and an emphatically modern one; it is in large part the result of his adherence to the rigors of formal composition deriving from the logic of his plot in its fusion with the strategy of a sketch and painting to create the *Portrait*'s full representational form. For the view which opens the novel of an aging American banker, his dying son, and their British friend strolling in a foreboding atmosphere of ennui and decay, is not completely composed until impelled to its completion and filled in in depth by subsequent episodes. They include the scene when Isabel leaves Osmond, first "lingering long enough to embrace with her eye his whole deliberately indifferent yet most expressive figure," then feeling a cold mist descend as she turns to encounter the Countess and her tale, and then leaving Rome to be present at Ralph's death. This movement culminates in Isabel's envy of Ralph's tranquillity in approaching death, in her own desire to "cease utterly," in her envy of "valuable 'pieces' " or *objets d'art* which never change "but grow in value while their owners loose inch by inch youth, happiness, beauty"—in the view finally of Isabel sitting limp in a tomb-like Gardencourt, the "victim of idleness" with "her hands, hanging down at her sides" and displaying "a singular absence of purpose." Likewise the quickening of life and interest and imagination which Mrs. Touchett's telegram and Isabel's arrival bring to the men at Gardencourt at the end of the first chapter is completed only by Isabel's reawakening at the novel's end. The novel is virtually framed by these two scenes which begin and complete the pattern of its events and stand so close in the foreground for the reader, the one encountered first in anticipation and initiation, the other encountered first in the retrospect of memory. (II, 391, 403, 429.)

But the novel is composed also by two scenes which stand deeper inside the House of Fiction, further back in the measured perspective of its space. In early spring of 1871 in Albany Isabel had been "looking for a visit" from Caspar when the sound of approaching footsteps turned into the visible figure of Mrs. Touchett "who paused there" in the doorway and "looked very hard at our heroine." In late May in 1877 after Ralph's funeral, the pattern is completed when Isabel glances into the thick twilight of Gardencourt; footsteps she had not heard become the figure of Caspar, who for the last time stands "looking at her." And then, "with a motion that looked like violence, but felt like—she knew not what," he "grasped her by the wrist" to begin their final interview. (I, 31; II, 429.)

That interview is the last occasion which is given shape by the emerging form of the novel's plot. There Caspar *takes up* Isabel, his personal desire strengthened now by Ralph's plea to " 'do everything she'll let you,' " and over her protest that " 'You had no business to talk about me,' " he makes the fervent plea in which Isabel encounters for the first time the address of utter and possessive passion. It was "the hot wind of the desert," "potent, acrid, and strange" in its taste, and in prospect like death itself: for him to "take her in his arms" would be "the next best thing to her dying." Yet the embrace seems also a sinking into "a kind of rapture" as he exclaims " 'be mine as I am yours.' " It is a descent into experience which momentarily obliterates her consciousness yet reawakens her to life through Caspar's firm "act of possession," his grasp and lightning kiss. (II, 432-436.)

In sustaining Caspar's embrace, then breaking away from him, Isabel is not choosing; that she has done before and gradually, in marrying Osmond, taking responsibility for her mistake with a mixture of pride and humiliation, implying she should return to Pansy and then making that into an obligation. She now is undergoing the active surrender or commitment in consent which authenticates the fusion of her decisions with her destiny and provides the ground and form for, or constitutes, the possibilities made real by James's *Portrait*. (II, 386, 396.)

One of these possibilities is the contingent future of meaning and urgency, of quickening crisis, which is not taken for granted but prefigured, indeed created, at the novel's end. However unlikely its prospect, Ned and Pansy's marriage has not been finally ruled out, and Pansy's future is not settled, though Pansy is so vanquished as to be ready to follow whatever Madame Merle and Osmond next improvise; Madame Merle had earlier recommended to keep Ned " 'on hand; he may be useful.' " And Isabel, though wrapped in a "grey curtain of . . . indifference" after her departure from Ralph's bedside, feels that deep within her, "deeper than any appetite for renunciation—was the sense that life would be her business for a long time to come." She expects that her life after returning to Osmond will be " 'a scene' " which will endure for the rest of her life. Somber as the prospect is, the future burgeons with the drama which Isabel helps to make. (II, 385, 115, 392-393, 398.)

The pressure exerted by the novel at the end constitutes the role of parenthood as a mission, when Isabel's maternal feeling, a factor in drawing her to Osmond and his daughter in the first place, impels her to return to protect and comfort Pansy, even if it proves to be too late to help her. The relation of Isabel and Pansy is companionable rather than authoritarian (they are close to each other in age, and they embrace "like two sisters" at their final interview), and it is exemplary in the world it has helped to make, the society which expects parents to be not only the authors and guides but the companions of their children and makes heroes out of Huck and Tom, Miles and Flora, Holden Caulfield and the host of strange children who follow after Little Pearl. (II, 386.)

The role of parenthood is sanctioned in the act of constituting also the viability of social form, the instituted form of marriage and the instituted form of art. Isabel gives consent, in full knowledge of its cost and possible horrors, to the "undertaking of matrimony"—the institution which Tocqueville had found so exceptionally strong in America that, while the unmarried girl "is less constrained than elsewhere, the wife is subjected to stricter obligations." [40] And through her action the *Portrait* makes its commitment to the "ghastly" form which even in its hollowness sustains the memory and possibility of the "mag-

[40] *Democracy in America*, tr. Henry Reeve, ed. Phillips Bradley, 2 vols. (New York, 1945), II, 201.

nificent form" and which holds forth, however perilously and conventionally, the possible reconciliation of use with benefaction, of measured control with companionable and passionate affection, of choosing with making, of knowledge and duty and enjoyment with conscious calculation and form.

Yet in making this commitment, Isabel's action and the pressure the novel exerts prefigure the transformation of the "experiment." If her return to life and to her marriage makes the bond more demanding as a form of obligation, it also makes of the woman's role something more dignified than mere formalistic, deferential, and passive assent; it founds marriage in part on the vigorous determination which Isabel has displayed in choosing a husband before and which now takes her back to play an active role in the "scene" she can anticipate. When viewed in the context provided by the other marriages in the novel, Isabel's action now, like her act in marrying Osmond originally, founds the institution in part on the ambitious purposes, deliberate choice, and active consent of the woman. In her combination of resolute independence of act with her insistence on the strictness of the bond, in her determination to play a role as parent, and in the prospect, unlikely though it is to be achieved, of Ned and Pansy's union, the *Portrait* prefigures some of the conspicuous features of marriage in modern America.

The form of marriage is validated in the act of validating also the instituted form of art, in the achieved instance of James's *Portrait*. Isabel had early impressed Warburton as " 'having mysterious purposes—vast designs,' " and as wanting only " 'to amuse' " herself and selecting therefore " 'great materials; the foibles, the afflictions of human nature, the peculiarities of nations' "; she now finally constitutes this novel's form, straining with a latent extravagance to burst its mold, but preserving the form with closeness, returning to Pansy, this reduced lady of title and daring amateur, to redeem the figure in the imagination's shop, to take up the burden of the form. This is the act which joins her finally in insight, suffering, and watchful care to the author who took her up and placed and portrayed her. This is the novel's high price indeed, which Isabel, with her banked resources of money, her stern conscience, her imagination, and her determination has the strength and is made to pay. (I, 111-112.)

The power of the closing episode derives from the multiplicity of implications imaged in their embrace and Caspar's lightning kiss. For it embodies not only Caspar's sensuous vigor, possessiveness, and business commitments which Isabel rejects or is held back from by the "something cold and dry" in her temperament and by the obligations she now feels to Pansy and her marriage; the grasp of Caspar's embrace images also the alternatives Isabel knows. These include the deprivation of death which she has witnessed and longed for, the watchful scrutiny of a grasping imagination which she has suffered, and along with these the resurgence of interest, will, and vitality which also have become her destiny once the Touchetts have taken an interest in her, found her convenient and amusing, endowed her and adored her; once Madame Merle and Osmond have used her in the form of marriage "like an applied hung up handled tool," once Pansy and Ned have turned to her, once Caspar has embraced her, and once James, in league with all of them, had taken "complete possession" of her as the subject, watched and represented, of his *Portrait*. The embrace escapes the language of vision, but it is framed and imaged by it:

"He glared at her a moment through the dusk, and the next instant she felt his arms about her and his lips on her own lips. His kiss was like white lightning, a flash that spread, and spread again, and stayed; and it was extraordinarily as if, while she took it, she felt each thing in his hard manhood that had least pleased her, each aggressive fact of his face, his figure, his presence, justified of its intense identity and made one with this act of possession. So had she heard of those wrecked and under water following a train of images before they sink. But when darkness returned she was free."

After running through the darkness toward the house, she "looked all about her; she listened a little; then she put her hand on the latch. She had not known where to turn; but she knew now. There was a very straight path." (II, 379, 436.)

That path, so plotted, and Isabel's movement along it, so determined, are the adopted burden of the *Portrait*'s form.

CHAPTER TWO

The "Little Drama of My 'Spoils'"

Authors are actors,
books are theatres.
Wallace Stevens, *Opus Posthumous*

"We are the makers of manners, Kate"
Shakespeare, *Henry V*

[I]

THE MAKERS OF MANNERS

SET against the tableau and vista, the amplitude of representational detail, which surround the "ceremony of afternoon tea" at the opening of *The Portrait of a Lady*, *The Spoils of Poynton's* opening pages present a strikingly significant contrast. Representational space is virtually nonexistent; it is evoked, insofar as it is *there* at all, by the reaction of one Mrs. Gereth to a situation that chafes her. The coherence of the opening sentences derives from her aroused feelings and from an emerging pattern of social pressures which is defined in an abstract, piecemeal fashion—"church," a "punctual meal," and "imbecilities of decoration"—rather than from the outlines and masses of a completely visualized, or fully embodied, scene. Waterbath when first named is a construct of punctual routines and destinations rather than a place; one can make an inventory of items (named persons, a bench, a grassy bank, a church, corridors, souvenirs, blue saucers), but the local habitation has no architecture, no landscape. Within this abstracted space, nothing stands poised or suspended. The fictive illusion instantly moves. (3.)*

The pace is swift, the prose virtually turns in traumas of discovery and bursts of activity, as "suddenly it seemed" to Mrs. Gereth that she could wait no longer for relief, and "Suddenly, at a turn in the walk, she came upon" Fleda Vetch seated in "deep and lonely meditation." Mrs. Gereth does not *have*, she clutches at, an idea. Two lovers, Owen Gereth and Mona Brigstock, scramble up an embankment. Of the first chapter's mere thirteen words of spoken dialogue, fifteen per cent are jammed into the exclamation " 'Horrible—Horrible!' " The narrator is less conspicuous than in *The Portrait* (where he stands beginning his sketch), but the prose style is more prominent in its own right. A pent-up energy impels the prose as sentences pause,

---

* References enclosed in parentheses in the text are to the New York Edition, *The Spoils of Poynton* being volume x of that edition. Other footnotes appear at the bottom of the page.

before their completion, not to relax but to find release in active movement: when Fleda confronts the "acres of varnish" that mark the vulgarity of the Brigstocks' Waterbath, "It was [her] conviction that the application of it, by their own hands and laboriously shoving each other, was the amusement of the Brigstocks on rainy days." On a brief walk, positions shift in a pattern of movement which prefigures the novel's action: Mona Brigstock and Owen Gereth are separated temporarily, as Owen and his mother, Mona and Fleda, walk in pairs; then Fleda and Owen are placed together; at the chapter's end, Fleda alone speeds on a train toward London. Nothing is framed or poised or portrayed; everything moves. (3-5, 7-10.)

The difference in achieved form between the manner of the completed *Portrait* and that which unfolds in the first chapter of *The Spoils* is an important one; it can tentatively and metaphorically be described as the difference between a painting and a play, or as that between a representational art and an expressionistic one. But the difference is exaggerated by the contrast between them at the cost of obscuring an effect—the predominance of their medium and *manner*—which is shared in common when painter's canvas and the playwright's stage are not simply used as points of reference for narrative prose but are adopted virtually as a novelist's materials. Treacherous though analogies among the arts can be, they must be considered in connection with James, because both his critical theory and his fiction draw heavily on them for more than illustrative and ornamental flourishes, and because they prove to be indispensable for defining the matrix in convention and the achieved form of James's art. In converting the strategies of painting and the drama, along with traditional narrative techniques, into the instruments of his craft, James established a relationship among his form, the subject and content of his fiction, and its effect—that is, created a style—which cannot be ignored even if our sole interest in James's works were to interpret their meaning. For his style became so integral to his art as to affect the very cast and orientation of its meaning as well as the vitality of its form.

This is true of *The Portrait* as well as of the three late masterpieces where its effects are most telling, but it is of particular importance to *The Spoils of Poynton*—the "little social and psychological picture" which was to have "the completeness of the drama-quality" [1] when James began to work it out in his notes, the "picture of a conflict" as he called it in the preface later, "the little drama of my 'Spoils.' " [2] For that pivotal novel (marking James's return after his failure in the theater to fiction as the major resource for his talent) reveals the first signs of James's late prose style which Professor Joseph Warren Beach noticed;[3] and it displays the strategies of both the painter and the dramatist, functioning in a counterpoint between theme and technique, which contribute to both the novel's distinct *manner* and its meaning. James's style enables us to see that while in *The Portrait* he refashioned the novel of manners by transforming traditional novelistic techniques into visual representational form, in *The Spoils* he undertook the more ambitious task that was to be accomplished fully only in the novels of the later "major phase": the conversion of the novel of manners into a fully dramatic form in a style which links James to the bolder innovations of earlier American literature and to nonrepresentational forms of recent art.

The Spoils of Poynton itself best reveals the particular sense in which James's fiction is *symbolic,* responding to a pressure toward extension of meaning and form in a mode he shares with Hawthorne and Melville. Moreover, *The Spoils* best displays the way in which James characteristically treated the prospect of historical transition. And the novel itself, finally, reveals the very basis of dramatic action as James conceived it in his later fiction. Yet the innovations in *The Spoils* are so profound, however tenuously achieved, that to appreciate the novel and the function of James's manner it is necessary first to consider the role of manners in American society and the novel of manners as a creative form, giving due weight to the viability of each before relating them to James's particular talent

1 *The Notebooks of Henry James,* ed. F. O. Matthiessen and Kenneth B. Murdock (New York, 1947), pp. 136, 198.

2 *The Art of the Novel*, pp. 123, 126.

3 Joseph Warren Beach, *The Method of Henry James* (rev. ed., Philadelphia, 1954), pp. 233-234.

and style and to currents of taste in the other arts which helped to shape his imagination and his very conception of dramatic art.

To do so entails resisting a traditional American nostalgia and setting aside certain assumptions which characterize the most provocative essays on both subjects in recent literary discussion, those by Professors Lionel Trilling and the late Richard Chase.[4] The nostalgia is for a state of affairs, a society or community, in which manners and their connection with other institutions and values are clear-cut, already settled and *given,* and for that reason serviceable for novelists. In the Old World, where the "fluid" class structure of America did not prevail, upper classes were sufficiently "stable," in Professor Trilling's view, for their cultural patterns to become "authoritative" and their manners distinct. Called into question they may be, as Professor Trilling finds to be the case since the eighteenth century, by "the tension between a middle class and an aristocracy," but while they survive they are thrown by that class tension into "observable relief," the heightened clarity which makes them available to a fortunate Jane Austen. Her values preexist in the materials and conditions of her art; she need simply reveal and illuminate them. In Professor Chase's view, a considerable variety of manners in Europe, and class conflict, bring manners there into vivid contrast.[5]

One assumption congenial to this nostalgia is that manners relate in relatively stable and prosaic ways to the other institutions and values which they reflect. The result is that manners —which are forms inhering directly in behavior, a medium of forms in which the momentum of behavior itself and pressures

[4] "Manners, Morals, and the Novel" and "Art and Fortune" in *The Liberal Imagination* (Garden City, N.Y.: Anchor Books, 1953); and Chapter 8 and also Chapters 1, 3, 6, and the second appendix in *The American Novel and Its Tradition* (Garden City, N.Y.: Anchor Books, 1957). Another perceptive study which treats manners in connection with the international theme in James is Professor Christof Wegelin's *The Image of Europe in Henry James* (Dallas, 1958). Two articles on James's attitudes toward manners without reference to the American scene or the genre of the novel are the exchange between Alwyn Berland and G. H. Bantock, "James and Forster: The Morality of Class" and "Morals and Civilization in Henry James" in *The Cambridge Journal*, VI and VII (February and December, 1953), 259-280 and 159-181.

[5] Trilling, *The Liberal Imagination*, pp. 251, 249. Chase, *The American Novel*, p. 159.

from outside behavior meet—are translated too readily into mirrors of the other realities which they presumably reflect. Manners, for Mr. Trilling, simply stand for things, moral values or ideals particularly, and comment on them: they are "the living representation of ideals and the living comment on ideas." The "hum and buzz of implication" (Trilling's excellent metaphor for what all is mediated by manners) is quickly identified with or reduced to the "intentions of men's souls" and "ideas"; the "attitudes, gestures, and conventional responses" (Chase's description of manners) cease almost instantly to be recognized as social forms and are translated into the expressed attitudes themselves, the actual responses, of the social class, the epoch, and the "school of thought or conduct" which gives them sanction.[6]

In America, according to Professors Trilling and Chase, manners are all but invisible and seldom of consequence for novelists. They are inconsequential because, as Professor Trilling explains, the tension between an aristocracy and a middle class does not exist and manners accordingly are nearly uniform, and because, in Mr. Chase's words, only rarely have there been "momentarily settled social conditions involving contrasting classes with contrasting manners"; or manners are unimportant because Americans are so unwilling to confront the realities of class, as Professor Trilling insists, and so distrustful of society and its conventions that affirmations of value (according to Professor Chase) are wholly "personal and intuitive."[7]

It is true certainly that Henry James, like Cooper and Hawthorne before him, was one of many American writers to voice the lament for the "absent things" lacking in America, including "a complexity of manners and types." His fears about America's "blankness" in the early book on Hawthorne were based on his recognition, as phrased in the later Prefaces, that "the interest of contrasted things" was what both the dramatist and "the painter of life and manners" depend on. He was cer-

[6] Trilling, *The Liberal Imagination,* pp. 250, 201, 206, 250. Chase, *The American Novel,* p. 157.

[7] Trilling, *The Liberal Imagination,* pp. 249, 207. Chase, *The American Novel,* pp. 158-159.

tain, as he wrote in 1913, that in Europe life was better prepared because so much more was *given*—much of "the work of discrimination and selection and primary clearing of the ground" was already accomplished. In a late essay on Balzac, he deplored again "the fatal fusions and uniformities . . . , the running together of all the differences of form and tone, the ruinous liquefying wash of the great industrial brush over the old conditions of contrast and colour. . . ." [8]

Yet it is a mistake to consider the question of manners wholly within this perspective or to assume that James always did, for James knew the passion which Ezra Pound found described in *The Ivory Tower,* the "peculiarly American passion for 'art,' for having a system in things . . ." and as early as 1875 James knew some of the consequences. In view of the monotonous tenor of American society, he remarked in a review of Howells, we Americans must find "contrasts," "salient points," and "chiaroscuro" in "fields where a less devoted glance would see little more than an arid blank, and, at the last, we manage to find them. All this refines and sharpens our perceptions . . . and stimulates greatly our sense of proportion and form." The recognitions we may draw from these considerations—that manners are instituted forms which are capable of mediating in complex ways a wide variety of values and the very resonance of experience itself, and that the chiaroscuro of contrast may be found in areas other than those produced by sharply defined class conflict—enable us to distinguish American manners and establish their relation to James's treatment of the novel of manners. For American manners prove to have more to do with James's form than with his subjects. [9]

It is not simply that manners may be thrown into observable relief by social tensions other than conflicts between classes, including tensions within the middle class itself, but that they have been thrown into relief by phenomena of a different sort which

8 *The Shock of Recognition,* p. 459; *The Art of the Novel,* pp. 198, 199; *The Letters of Henry James,* ed. Percy Lubbock, 2 vols. (New York, 1920), II, 298; *Notes on Novelists* (New York, 1914), p. 151. James's position on this matter is placed historically by Wegelin, *The Image of Europe in Henry James,* pp. 9-31, 152-166.

9 Pound, *Make It New* (London, 1934), p. 302. James, *Literary Reviews and Essays,* p. 214.

have been important to the modern imagination and which have been crucial in shaping the acute self-consciousness which has characterized American cultural nationalism since Mather's *Magnalia*. These include the differentiation of rural and urban populations, and ethnic and dialect groups, which Mr. Trilling mentions to discount.[10] Two others are the myth of Nature, which calls all manners into question, and comparative sociology, which even in its earliest or *amateur* forms (the *Jesuit Relations* or Melville's *Omoo* and *Typee*) compares American and European manners to those of Indians and South Sea islanders. Regional and national self-consciousness, and the modern historical consciousness (even in the form of Gibbon, and surely in the form of Robertson and Scott), are other cultural pressures which bring the question of manners into prominence. More dramatically since 1776 or 1789, there are the *élan* and programs of revolution, which relate so directly to manners as to prescribe fashions and fabrics in wearing apparel and to alter forms of address.

The importance of all these matters in American culture can help us to recognize that in social experience, as in some laboratories, the reality observed is being changed under the high-powered illumination of the instruments which scrutinize it— that the scrutiny of actuality is part of a process which alters it —and that American society has manners which stand in observable relief for the very reason that they are, and are thought to be, unfinished; they are still consciously being cultivated and shaped; they are not "settled" but still in the process of formation. This is the manifest assumption of nineteenth-century comment on American manners and is more important than what the commentators say *about* the actual manners they scrutinize. The facility with which Cooper, in *The American Democrat* (1838), shifts from statements about existing manners to fears or hopeful prophecies for their future is evidence to the point. So is his tone, when writing of an America where "classes run into each other more easily and the lines of separation are less easily drawn": his is the frantic air of one who is not so much recording as *making* distinctions. Much as he hopes that "Facts are not to be changed by words"—that "life is a

10 Trilling, *The Liberal Imagination*, p. 250.

series of facts" and that "Idle declamation" cannot change "inequalities of condition, of manners, of mental cultivation" nor "language and deportment alter the relations of a society" —his every page reveals that these facts are being challenged and their proportions altered, if not basically changed, not only by those deficient in manners and by "pretenders" to good breeding whose "affectations" are a caricature of refinement, but by Cooper himself. He combats the retrogression in American manners with a written prescription for their improvement and presents a model for the "principles" and "deportment" of a "democratic gentleman." American Liza Doolittles may be foolish to think that "language and deportment can alter the relations of a society," but the Professor Higgins of Cooperstown, with all the scrupulous distinctions and cultivation of propriety that he can muster, undertakes to alter those relations by contrasting debased linguistic usages and social manners to earlier patterns which he prefers, and by creating the model of the new Democratic Gentleman who combines the heroism of simplicity, candor, and independence with the heroism of cultivated refinement.[11]

Comparably, James's comments, even when dwelling emphatically in *The American Scene* (1907) on the "absence of forms," the "apparent void" of an America virtually without manners, adumbrate a process by which manners are created rather than a fixed "blankness" or a static contrast between class patterns of behavior. Suburban villas, confronting the void with nothing but their expensiveness, revealed no manners which were "projected inwardly" to protect privacy but revealed instead to James (as to Veblen) the "candid look" of their pecuniary cost, projected "outward" to create the "air of unmitigated publicity." The result was a social drama, in preparation if not in progress: "the great adventure of a society reaching out into the apparent void" and, subject to whatever pressures lurk beneath the "void," striving "to gouge an interest *out* of the vacancy, gouge it with tools of price, even as

[11] "On Station," "An Aristocrat and a Democrat," "On Language," "On Deportment," and "On American Deportment" in *The American Democrat*, ed. Robert E. Spiller (New York: Vintage Books, 1956), pp. 81, 152, 80, 153-154, 95.

copper and gold and diamonds are extracted . . . from earth-sections of small superficial expression." It was a "general effort" at which James, the "story-seeker," was "quite intimately present." [12]

James emphasized the "complete abolition of *forms*" in a society where houses declare " 'We are only installments, symbols, stop-gaps' " having " 'nothing to do with continuity, responsibility, transmission,' " but James did so as part of the process of studying the emergence of new forms, "the possible evolution of manners, the latent drama to come," extending in his expectations "the idea of the possible drama" and finding (in the example of New England) an America where the stage was set for "the production and the imposition of forms." What he found typified in New England summer colonies was scarcely new in 1907; it was a formerly successful rural land prepared, like a willing woman, to join with an "urban class," begging it to " 'live upon me and thrive upon me' " and even more to " 'live *with* me, somehow, and let us make out together what we may do for each other—something that is not merely estimable in more or less greasy greenbacks.' " The forms emerging from such a union seemed to have in part a pecuniary base, however, being founded on the prevailing standard of high wages for employees. Another standard governing the creation of forms was the "propriety" founded on the native residents' refusal to be condescendingly patronized and the consequently firm manner of assertively fastidious democrats who demand to be admitted at the front door and who ask for the "woman" of the house when bringing a message from the " 'washerlady.' " Though the "form of Democracy" was "monstrous" (a "huge democratic broom . . . brandished in the empty sky"), what intrigued James profoundly, nevertheless, was not simply a fixed contrast between the "summer people" and the local residents but their interaction and the ensuing drama. It promised the "aesthetic enrichment of the summer people" and a comparable enrichment for the local community which grew to like the "forms" introduced by the urban visitors; it promised, in sum, the "evolution of manners," the

[12] *The American Scene,* ed. W. H. Auden (New York, 1946), pp. 9-13, 22-23.

"latent drama," the "production and the imposition of forms." [13]

Whether uniform or not, manners in America are in the making, with the important result that they are conspicuous since they are insistently aiming for, even straining for (as in Cooper's case), a degree of embodiment or completion which is partially but not yet finally achieved. The form, bulging and showing a bit, stretches beyond any achieved equilibrium toward a fuller definition and embodiment which it anticipates and incubates. This conspicuous aiming or anticipating and incubating not only lie behind the manners, in behavior and its motives, but are featured in the manners themselves. And these qualities define the particular sense in which American manners are not significant in a fixed sense but exploratively symbolic. Ben Franklin in homespun, Walt Whitman in the open shirt, Mark Twain with all the displayed impedimenta of his innocence abroad, T. S. Eliot with an umbrella wrapped tighter than the native Londoner's—all are like the movie sheriffs and cowboys in that they choose their costume carefully, and it is not the particular costume but the self-conscious insistence with which it is worn that is distinctly archetypal.

Fitzgerald caught the self-consciousness perfectly in his remark about his character Joseph Bloeckman: "His expression combined that of a Middle Western farmer appraising his wheat crop and that of an actor wondering whether he is observed—the public manner of all good Americans." [14] The manners are not the mere representation of fixed values which Americans express, nor simple comment on them. Neither are they founded on a settled, referential sign language pointing to formulated categories of status and class, nor are they the full embodiment that may be observed in the habitual behavior of characteristic European societies. The manners are a symbolic form which the American adopts and molds in estimating or aiming for both the self and the society which he seeks to make.

Tocqueville noticed but misread the evidence when he remarked that in America manners "form a light and loosely

13 *Ibid.*, pp. 11, 20-26, 54-55.
14 Fitzgerald, *The Beautiful and Damned* (New York, 1922), p. 94.

woven veil through which the real feelings and private opinions of each individual are easily ascertainable" and attributed the transparency of manners to a suspicion of all forms as such. Tocqueville's comment suggests that the manners are visibly separate from, detached from, the feelings they express.[15] Yet the form is often dense, rather than transparent, and seldom loosely worn, even when it seems so; its flexibility is taut and controlled, and its detachment from the behavior and feelings (which Tocqueville perceived so keenly) results not only from a suspicion of form itself (which is deeply embedded in the modern mind and in American culture) but paradoxically from the American's determination nonetheless to make one, actually to construct a manner, an effort which detaches the manner, so shapes it as to heighten it or abstract it, and thus throw it into observable relief. It is in this heightened prominence, this insistent, anxious *aiming* which inheres in forms of behavior, that the histories of American manners and American literature join, compelling us, with James in mind, to consider the novel of manners with attention not to its special subject but to its conventional form.

That the genre tends toward stylization is suggested by some of the predecessors which on the surface it most resembles: the literature of courtship, Shakespeare's idyllic comedies, Restoration comedy, and the literature of sensibility. The qualities which it shares with these can scarcely be circumscribed by the prosaic descriptive "realism" which Professor Chase finds to be the defining characteristic of the *novel* as distinguished from the *romance,* even when one recognizes the carefully controlled focus with which the novel of manners "concentrates so calculatedly" on the actual manners it would "report." Mr. Trilling likewise insists that the novel is a "genre with a very close and really a very simple relation to actuality," that great novels "deal explicitly" with ideas, that the novel's action is the "notation and documentation" of the will's actions. He complains of Dreiser that he "could not report the social fact with the kind of accuracy it needs." Suspicious of novels displaying "an affinity with poetry," Mr. Trilling looks forward to the revival of "a natural prose," a "straight-forward

15 Tocqueville, *Democracy in America*, II, 219, 25, 35.

prose." While the terms *render* and *report* or *notation* and *documentation* may be acceptable for the relation between prose fiction and the reality it describes with more or less closeness and completeness, they are so general as also to encompass expert journalism while failing to do justice to the complexities of *Robinson Crusoe*, to say nothing of other novels which precede and follow the career of Jane Austen.[16]

Likewise to *advance* or *invoke* moral standards, whether personal or social in sanction, may be central to the purpose of the novel of manners, but it does not exhaust the complex relations between an author's attitude and either the world he depicts or the readers' world he seeks to mold. The variety of conventions within English fiction and the novel of manners eludes the characteristic *realism* which a theory of referential description and comment would stamp upon them. The conception of the novel as an observational report rather than as a creative activity obscures some resources of the novel of manners specifically, which were particularly suited to James's most extended ambitions.

What defines a novelistic genre is not so much its subject and the invoked moral standards of its authors but its stance: the formal posture and generic orientation of its imaginative action. In the case of the novel of manners, its stance is that of analytic scrutiny. And what needs emphasis is not the minuteness or rigor of the scrutiny but the probing, piercing nature of its discernment which is obscured if one assumes that analysis, like a descriptive report or act of observation, is a mode of simple detachment or disengagement which removes the author to some safe distance from his subject. Rather it is a mode of controlled penetration, the imagination moving first toward, then within, a deepening reality which engages it.

In the case of Jane Austen (which Professor Chase rightly calls the "purest" case) her deliberate form and measured vocabulary indicate control and concern rather than separation or indifference, intimate perception and imaginative involvement in those events which her fiction renders, rather than remoteness and safe immunity. She penetrates into her mate-

16 Chase, *The American Novel*, pp. 246, 157. Trilling, *The Liberal Imagination*, pp. 263, 249-250, 207, 251, 255, 259.

rials instead of simply sorting them into categories of status, type, and motive. The types are there (notably in such characters as Wyckham and Lady Catharine) but instead of being simply described and judged, they are placed in actions (dances, parties, and the like) which are rendered vividly because the characters are probed from a point of view near and even within the actions presented. The exercise of pride and prejudice, and their moderation, are actions Austen's imagination engages in rather than patterns of behavior which she merely observes in the persons and institutions she describes.[17]

In her novels of manners, the strictly analytic mind finds its first developed convention in English fiction, and so does the perspective which in Austen is in complete fusion with the analytical power, the perspective of irony. For her irony is a governing perspective, rather than a mere rhetorical device, and while it is far from indicating moral indifference or detachment, as Professor Trilling has rightly insisted, neither does it indicate a disguised and simple moral choice as is sometimes assumed to be the case. It indicates the imagination's engagement, intimate but controlled, with the complexities of its materials. Irony sustains discrepancies among modes of perception which are actually suffered or felt in their multiplicity because they are the result of opening up and probing a reality which the imagination thereby penetrates. Diverse responses and angles of vision, functioning reciprocally, are held together, in suspension and under pressure; the observer and the realities observed (whether they might tend otherwise to fly apart or to dissolve indistinguishably in solution) are held suspended in an operation which mutually engages them. The novel of manners, as its resources are revealed in the achievement of Jane Austen, can penetrate experience and thereby found fiction on the sufferance and impress of the performed and witnessed act. The novel can become not a demonstration of experience already tested but the searching experiment itself, an experience and trial of the not yet, and not otherwise, known.[18]

Whatever the limitations of Austen's fiction (James admired but inclined to discount her merits and to stress the limits of

17 Chase, *The American Novel,* p. 157.
18 "Mansfield Park," *The Opposing Self* (New York, 1955), p. 206.

her range) she reveals within the genre of the English novel
of manners a convention which is central to James's art. The
analytic mode, however, was one whose assets and risks James
measured in the works of other writers whose fiction bore
more directly on his own. One was Hawthorne, whose *Scarlet
Letter* not only displays the mode in its own unrelenting scrutiny but images it in the actions of Chillingworth. In his *Hawthorne*, James expressed the concern (which he shared with
Hawthorne himself) that the analytic mind was dangerous,
noting that in *The Blithedale Romance* Coverdale's "analytic
nature" had much "in common with that of his creator," being
"half a poet, half a critic, and all a spectator," and James
noted that some of Hawthorne's companions at Brook Farm
thought him "an intellectual vampire" in "analyzing their characters, and dissecting the amiable ardor . . . which he was
too cold-blooded to share." In *The Scarlet Letter*, the actions
of Chillingworth present both the horrifying dangers and the
great asset of analysis when conceived as a mode of the imagination. The possible ruin and excruciating torture of Dimmesdale, the "violation of the sanctity of the human heart," are
clearly the cost of Chillingworth's "constant analysis of the human heart" even if the torture were to prove purgative for
Dimmesdale in the end. Yet the great asset of the analytic
mode is that it becomes intimate and dramatic.[19]

In this connection the transformations of Chillingworth's
plans for revenge are instructive. Intending first to reveal the
truth and to weigh it in the role of "severe" but unbiased
judge, as if investigating a "geometrical problem," Chillingworth was subsequently seized by a deeper purpose, a revenge
that would be "intimate" and would terminate in Dimmesdale's open confession to the one man who would deny him forgiveness. When Dimmesdale's refusal to confess balked that
purpose, Chillingworth's aim for intimate revenge was translated into an action equally satisfying for him, an intimacy
which is also a drama and a drama in which Chillingworth becomes both an actor and an author: "He became . . . not a

---

19 James, *The Lesson of Balzac* in *The Question of Our Speech, The Lesson
of Balzac: Two Lectures* (Boston, 1905), p. 60; *The Shock of Recognition*, pp. 528,
493. Hawthorne, *The Complete Novels and Selected Tales*, pp. 200, 184.

spectator only, but a chief actor, in the poor minister's world. He could play upon him as he chose." If he would subject him to "a throb of agony" or a "sudden fear," the agony and the terror were immediately forthcoming in the magic of Chillingworth's "art." The "prying" and "probing" of his effort "to bring his mind into . . . affinity" with his patient's become the obsessive determination to probe "to the bottom" Dimmesdale's case, "were it only for the art's sake." [20]

Analytic scrutiny took one form, a conspicuously intimate and dramatic one, in Chillingworth's art and in Hawthorne's art, but other versions of an essentially analytic mode appeared in fiction which is in many ways the opposite of Hawthorne's, the novel of manners, strictly considered, in France. The fusion of a modern analytic mode with the novel of manners in France was one of the things that struck James in remarking that the English, whom Taine had credited with inventing the genre, had been supplanted by the French; where Dickens and Thackeray had been the match for George Sand and Balzac earlier, now Daudet was supreme, and in discussing Daudet and Maupassant he revealed his conception of analysis as a form of penetration. As displayed in the generic *realism* emerging in French fiction, the analytic mode was "the analytic consideration of appearances." It included the close attention to actualities or "appearances," to tangible objects or "things," and the strategy of "notation" and "enumeration"; it provided explicit "complicated explanations" and techniques of "illustration," as found in Daudet and Balzac. Yet if these are the *techniques* of analysis—explicit enumerative notation recording the actualities of appearance and the "associations awakened by things" —they are not the generic behavior or *action* of analysis; that action is to probe, to probe into the "most unlighted corners of our being," to follow along "the most devious paths of experience," to break actuality down into its components or, as James wrote, to "divide" the world of appearance "into its parts." Maupassant, too, James insisted, used the analytic mode (despite Maupassant's denial of it), though in a different version which eschewed the techniques of explicit explanation. His "particular analysis" was the search for sexual motiva-

[20] *The Complete Novels and Selected Tales*, pp. 166-167, 157, 165.

tion, and its action James described as "peeping behind the curtain" so as to discern the characters' motivations.[21]

It was because the novel of manners afforded a mode of analytic penetration that it was so appropriate an instrument for James, even when obsessed by Gothic terrors or gripped by the "imagination of a disaster" which he shared with his heroine in *The Spoils of Poynton*—indeed whenever he gave more than perfunctory exercise to the *"grasping* imagination" which he so clearly possessed, and which is figured in the plot and commerce of *The Portrait of a Lady* and its later preface. The analytic imagination he particularly had in mind was one he named, in the preface to *The Princess Casamassima*, the "penetrating imagination," which, along with "the sense of life," prepared or "armed" him to cope with the "mysteries abysmal" of subversion which operated beneath the "smug surface" of London. The phrase "penetrating imagination" was one which James could apply to diverse writers: to Hawthorne's "delicate and penetrating imagination" for instance, and to Flaubert, whose "extraordinary penetration" James praised in 1878 and again in 1902, admiring "the fertilization of subject by form, penetration of the sense, ever, by the expression—the latter reacting creatively on the former." The full implications of the phrase, however, for James's conception of the imagination and for his dramaturgy and style, are revealed by the remarks it echoes: Ruskin's description, in *Modern Painters,* of the "penetrating, possession-taking faculty" which he termed the "highest intellectual power of man," the "penetrative imagination." [22] (262.)

Ruskin's description of the imagination's "seizing" of reality, taking possession of it, is more frantic than his first example (Dante) might suggest, but it nonetheless illuminates James's early and famous remark that American civilization would "yield its secrets" only to a "really *grasping* imagination" and that while Howells lacked this power, "Of course I don't."

21 *Partial Portraits*, pp. 195, 206, 258.

22 *Henry James: Letters to A. C. Benson and Auguste Monod . . .* , ed. Edward E. Benson (London, 1930), p. 35; *The Art of the Novel*, p. 78; *The Shock of Recognition*, p. 448; *French Poets and Novelists*, p. 206; *Notes on Novelists*, p. 103. Ruskin, *The Complete Works of John Ruskin* (New York: Society of English and French Literature, n.d.), III, 165.

Ruskin declared that the imagination in its "mode of apprehension" thrusts beyond all "outward images," indeed "ploughs
them all aside, and plunges into the very central fiery heart
. . . and drinks the very vital sap of that it deals with. . . ."
He goes on: "Every character that is so much as touched by
men like Aeschylus, Homer, Dante, or Shakespeare is by them
held by the heart; and every circumstance or sentence of their
being, speaking, or seeming is seized by process from within;
. . . it is the open sesame of a huge, obscure, endless cave,
with an inexhaustible treasure of pure gold scattered in it: the
wandering about and gathering of the pieces may be left to any
of us . . . ; but the first opening of that invisible door in the
rock is the work of the imagination only." [23]
    Its exercise varied in intensity and vigor and consequent
effect, but it is by precisely such an imaginative act, and the
vicarious engagement with experience which it entailed, that
James created his best fiction; and it is the accord of that
"grasping," "possession-taking," or "penetrating" imagination
with the generic convention of the novel of manners that
rendered that form, its latent as well as its demonstrated capacities, serviceable to James's ambitions. Yet his grasp of the
novel of manners entailed the transformation of the form in a
way that returns us to the question of American manners, to
James's preoccupation with his role as painter and dramatist,
and to his characteristic style. For in exploiting the novel of
manners James seized it as a form rather than as a subject, and
it is to his manipulation of the form, the style displayed in his
usage of it, that both American manners and the American
literary tradition relate. What American writers share with
their compatriots is their anxious awareness of form as problematic (which is not to imply necessarily their approval of it
or a developed capacity for appreciating it); and what American manners have in common with the characteristic forms of
American literature (including the ostensibly allegorical or
openly symbolic modes of Poe, Hawthorne, Melville, and Whitman) is the insistent prominence, the somewhat detached and
heightened display, the bold "relief" of their form.
    This is not to say that the achieved forms of American mas-

23 James, *Letters*, I, 30-31. Ruskin, *Works*, III, 164-165.

terpieces are identical, nor that their styles are utterly the same, but that they share one important feature: the self-conscious, anxious determination to create a manner is conspicuously articulated in the style itself, under pressures which Franklin's *Autobiography* is the first American classic to define. There (in the letter from his friend Benjamin Vaughan which Franklin shrewdly included as if Franklin still needed prompting) the assertion is made that "the manners and situation" of the new America, far from being inconsequential, are interesting and instructive and that particularly Franklin's "pacific, acquiescing manners," if widely publicized, would show that greatness can reside in the ordinary or "domestic" man. Vaughan urged Franklin to continue his autobiography and the projected treatise on "The Art of Virtue" so as to justify the new society, to prove that genuinely virtuous principles were the cause of the "immense revolution of the present period." In the light of the mission which Vaughan's letter endorsed, Franklin's carefully pruned, scrupulously managed prose style appears as one appropriate instrument of the deliberately managed life, including the carefully cultivated manners, which the *Autobiography* projects.[24]

When, in the "Continuation" finished in 1784, Franklin completed his famous list of virtues and his regimen for rehearsing them, he acknowledged imperfections in his performance but attributed to his "little artifice" the success and happiness he enjoyed. What his "little artifice" entailed was the translation of a plan into rehearsals in conduct and the translation of those rehearsals into habitual performance, culminating in a "change in my manner" of speech and expression. The change in manner, his notorious triumph, was to create a style which would support the illusion or "appearance" of one virtue, humility, which he could not actually attain: to enact, that is, in manner and in the conduct of language the virtue he aimed for. For the language of "dogmatical expression" or "fix'd opinion" he substituted the phrases *"I apprehend,* or *I imagine* a thing to be so or so; or it *so appears to me at present."* Though this adopted "mode" was "first put on with some violence to natural inclina-

24 Benjamin Franklin, *Autobiography . . . and Selections from His Other Writings* (New York: Modern Library, 1932), pp. 81, 83, 85.

tion" it became "easy" and "habitual," and it explained, Franklin thought, along with his "character of integrity," why he exercised such influence and "generally carried [his] points." In
Franklin's life, a manner became a deliberately improvised and
rehearsed artifice, a carefully aimed performance. And in his
Autobiography that performance was extended to create the
gestures adequate to the pressure and intention behind it, including the desire to display and acknowledge the cultivation
of manner which was at once the matrix and the aim of his
style.[25]

Comparable pressures and ambitions have left their mark in
the distinctive features of other American classics. Whitman
heightened the artifices of authorship by drawing attention to
his poem's very stance ("I celebrate myself, and sing myself"—
"I lean and loafe at my ease"). That bravura, along with Ish-
mael's at the opening of *Moby-Dick,* is archetypal; it is the articulation of the pressure to make radical experiments with
form. Huckleberry Finn's self-conscious interest in his own bib-
liography (he refers readers to *Tom Sawyer*) and his troubled
interest in style, like his author's two prefatory notices to the
reader about the book's narrative method and colloquial idiom,
bring into unusual prominence the form of Twain's masterpiece; they draw attention to, rather than obscure, the artifices
of the prose, which in the narrative itself are made vivid by
the supple interplay of idioms and the highlighting of stylistic
and theatrical parody. A comparable prominence of form is
displayed in the conspicuous theatricality and the posturing
convolutions of the prose of Melville's *The Confidence-Man,*
and in the variety of formal conventions in *Moby-Dick,* where
essays, theatrical scenes, dances, sermons, parodies, flights of
rhetoric and lyric invocations are rendered distinct, each set off
in its discrete identity (at times labeled), whether by arranged
contrast or fortuitous juxtaposition.

And the manner in which Melville's fiction probes beneath
and beyond the given significance of its symbols is one which it
shares with Hawthorne's usage of his openly allegorical materials in *The Scarlet Letter.* In Hawthorne's work the traditional referential devices and the generic emblematic strategy

[25] *Ibid.,* pp. 103-104.

of allegorical signification are employed but transformed in the process of using them: they are rendered more conspicuous as sheer artifice by being made at once more abstract and elemental. The title names neither Adultery nor Able or Angel but evokes their common abstract initial. (Imagine Bunyan's Christian as "C" or Dante's Treason as "T," or Spenser's Una and her friend as "U" and the "Red Cross K.") *The Scarlet Letter*'s meaning is virtually spelled, not signified, as if the fiction's conventional language were being sacrificed to an alphabet distilled from it, its full rhetorical resources being distended into firm though delicate strands of sheer feeling and movement, its emblems being recast in a process of creation; and instead of veiling a stipulated meaning it insistently hypothesizes one, in elaborations which match the ceaseless embroidering of Hester's needle. It does not spell out a previously formulated meaning but symbolizes one it seeks, measuring and estimating the vision burgeoning within it.

It is the conventional style which these works together suggest that James's fiction displays, however different from each other are the personal styles of the authors and however complex the fully achieved styles of particular works. The style as characterized by its *stance* or *attack* is a version of *expressionism,* if that term is conceived as a generic mode of the imagination, embracing different personal and period styles, whose distinguishing feature is *pressure* and which is founded on the "desire to exceed the inherent qualities of the medium," the aim which Herbert Read has discerned in the predominant expressionism of American painting since John Marin.[26] The style is generically expressionistic in that immediate access to the work is not directly through a represented subject (though one is usually recognizable), nor through an aesthetic or emotional response which is prior to its subject (though such a response is strongly projected), but through the contortions of a conspicuously wrought form, one which relates both to a represented subject and to an appropriate reaction, and mediates them. Its contortions are sometimes a *distortion* of norms of actuality or value; but sometimes they are the norms them-

[26] Herbert Read, "Some Observations on Art in America," *The Philosophy of Modern Art* (New York: Meridian Books, 1955), pp. 283, 284.

selves, the seminal or typical experience, under intense pressure. In any case, the contortions are the forms taken by processes and experience in a state of crisis, in the throes of transformation.[27]

James's predilections in painting for the nineteenth century and earlier periods (notably the Renaissance), his early distaste for the Impressionists, and his virtual silence on the Postimpressionists are well known; only gradually, under the impact of Whistler and Sargent, did he come to appreciate the Impressionists, and Roger Fry testified to James's "disturbed hesitations" in 1912 before Matisse, Picasso, and Rouault. Yet this reaction should not obscure the fact that James's art is as intimately related to the arts of his own time and subsequent decades as it is to the achievements of his predecessors. In theme and form, James's fiction is often as much like Rodin, or like Redon (with monstrous fantasies emerging in a familiar world) and Munch (whose stark patterns and compressed emotion in *The Cry* are a landmark in the development of Expressionism), as it is like Tintoretto or Veronese, whom James included

[27] Although the term is a comparatively recent one in the vocabulary of criticism, *expressionism* is best recognized as a generic mode of artistic expression which would embrace many distinguishable versions rather than as a convention confined to a certain period, or to the artists who first occasioned the formulation of the term, or to the painters and dramatists who display its features in purest form. Even when the particular cases of Van Gogh and Edward Munch are taken as models (as they are, along with Bosch and Grunewald, by Herbert Read in an earlier essay), the clearly representational function of their form, subordinate though it is to emotional or psychological pressures, and the prominence of the form and medium as such in the finished work, should prevent our conceiving the style wholly in psychological or emotive terms. Herbert Read defined *expressionism* in 1948 as a form "that gives primacy to the artist's emotional reactions to experience. The artist tries to depict not the objective reality of the world, but the subjective reality of the feelings which objects and events arouse in his psyche or self." ("The Situation of Art in Europe," *op. cit.*, pp. 50-51.)

Distortion is sometimes taken as the distinguishing mark of expressionism. Yet distortions are so frequent a feature of common activity, so often encountered and recognized in everyday life outside the arts (in dreams, moments of extremely intense emotion, the aberrations of nature, the contortions of birth and death), and so pervasive a phenomenon in literature and the arts (in caricature, for instance, and in the Greek classic drama), that the relations among an expressionistic work, its subjects and occasions, and its viewers or readers, are obscured if one defines expressionism as the intended or heightened *distortion* of reality. Sheldon Cheney, in *Expressionism in Art* (rev. ed., New York, 1948), treats the problem of definition on pp. 69-95. For a contrary view, see Arnold Hauser, *The Social History of Art*, 4 vols. (New York: Vintage Books, 1957-1958), IV, 229.

among his favorites. Indeed, the full articulation of James's later style which emerges in *The Spoils of Poynton* encompasses not only the bolder rhythms of expressionism but the style that Professor Arnold Hauser has called the first strictly "modern style," namely "mannerism." [28]

If the displayed contortions of expressionism derive from the interaction of the medium with the raw materials and elemental experience engaged in the creative process, and accordingly show more vividly in the sheer medium of the finished work (e.g., brush strokes and configurations of the paint, or the charged, compulsive force of images), the displayed tensions of mannerism derive from the interaction of the medium not with the raw but with the already molded, conventionalized patterns among the artist's materials, and accordingly they are more conspicuous in relation to subject, syntax, and theme. Different though the two stylistic conventions are in some *pure* cases, the one displaying more elemental realities and subconscious responses, the other displaying more sophisticated subjects and conscious intentions, they are easily compatible. And forces in American culture which have encouraged its major talents to front the essential elements of life directly and candidly in art and to make bold experiments with form—the fluid society, the process of constructing a new society, the ethos of crisis— have also encouraged the self-conscious creation of a *manner* and its perfection. In James a manneristic style encompasses the deepest impulsions of expressionistic art, and both terms are needed to define the basic conventions of James's style.

Professor Hauser's description of Renaissance Mannerism gives proper emphasis to the variety of achievement within it (he includes Shakespeare as well as Tintoretto, Bronzino, and Bosch as Mannerists) and the profound if disturbed awareness of historical transition which is its matrix. He describes it as a "completely self-conscious style," committed not only to perfect an art but "to define the artistic purpose itself"; it is the first style to see "the relationship between tradition and innovation

---

28 James's reactions to the Impressionists are in "The Impressionists" and "John S. Sargent" in *The Painter's Eye,* ed. John L. Sweeney (Cambridge, 1956), pp. 114-115, 217-218, 221, and *The American Scene,* pp. 45-46. His reaction to the later painters is recounted in Virginia Woolf's *Roger Fry, A Biography* (New York, 1940), p. 180.

as a problem to be solved by rational means." It sees tradition as a "bulwark against the all-too violently approaching storms of the unfamiliar," recognizing ambivalent prospects in the "unfamiliar," which is "felt to be a principle of life but also destruction." The "over-straining" of its forms expresses the fear that form might fail in the struggle with life, and art fade into soul-less beauty." It replaces established norms "by more subjective and more suggestive features." At times it deepens religious experience, at times it becomes "an exaggerated intellectualism, consciously and deliberately deforming reality, with a touch of the bizarre and the abstruse; sometimes, however, it is a fastidious and affected epicureanism, translating everything into subtlety and elegance. . . ." The "real connections" among things "are obscured and things are brought into an abstract relationship to one another . . . but the individual objects themselves are described with the greatest exactitude. . . ." The style is constructive rather than simply indulgent or defensive, and the "over-straining" of its forms, whether *deformations* or *translations* of reality, establishes a scale, a measure of relevance, which does not inhere wholly in its subject: "motifs which seem to be of only secondary significance for the real subject . . . are often over-bearingly prominent. . . . The final effect is of real figures moving in an unreal arbitrarily constructed space." [29]

It is so measured an act of construction that is figured in James's style, the forms rendered taut under the double pres-

[29] Arnold Hauser, *The Social History of Art*, 4 vols. (New York: Vintage Books, 1957-1958), II, 100-103. Wylie Sypher's *Four Stages of Renaissance Style: Transformations in Art and Literature, 1400-1700* (Garden City, N.Y.: Anchor Books, 1956) includes a brilliant treatment of Mannerism in Renaissance literature and the other arts, although it over-emphasizes the defensive strategy, and the subjective inwardness, of the style. See pp. 100-180. The same author's *Rococo to Cubism in Art and Literature* (New York, 1960) includes James, along with Proust and Impressionist painters who emphasize "atmospheric light and color," under the category of "neo-mannerism," pp. 192-193. But in this work his terms and analysis are less perceptive and judicious.

Both Herbert Read and Giorgio Melchiori have termed James's style manneristic, but confine the mode to his prose style in the narrow sense, the textures of his fiction. Melchiori's remarks, though suggestive, found the style too exclusively on the psychology of uncertainty and divorce it from the actualities of historical crisis which bear so directly on American culture and James. See Read, *The Tenth Muse* (New York, 1958), p. 190; and Melchiori, *The Tightrope Walkers: Essays on Mannerism in Modern English Literature* (London, 1956), pp. 13-33.

sure of historical change and nascent vision, the seeming trivia within its subject, even the seemingly irrelevant or ornamental among its motifs, given coherence by the vividness of pattern, the firmness and later the contortions of insistent movement, and the firm structure which James's usage of the novel form displays. And it is this style that *The Portrait of a Lady,* with the consistency of its emphatically visual form, verges into and that *The Spoils of Poynton,* with its distinctly dramatic logic, fully displays, different though the representational aim of *The Portrait* is from the more boldly expressionistic aim and more prominent manner of the later work.

It was the dramatic potentiality of the style which was most striking to historians of painting in the nineteenth century. But if its dramatic effects were what struck them most favorably, what disturbed them in the style was the affectation which seemed to accompany it. The Manneristic style which Hauser defines is one which nineteenth-century writers regarded as marking a crisis in the history of European painting and as a mode fraught with danger, if it were not indeed the very symptom of pretense and decay. For them, as for us, the distinctive features of Mannerism as a particular Renaissance style or as a basic style known in versions of different artists and periods, were fascinating because of their relation to fundamental problems connected with any style; indeed, it is the stylistic convention (as Hauser's analysis makes clear) whose basic function is to articulate the conscious concern with manner, with form, and with the very definition of art itself.

In 1890 in *The Tragic Muse,* immediately before James began writing for the stage and a few years before he began *The Spoils of Poynton,* he expressed his concern about the risks entailed in any "personal manner" and suggested a close and disturbing association among a "manner of expression," the very nature of the drama, and "affectation." In that novel Nick Dormer asks Gabriel Nash: " 'Don't you think your style's a trifle affected?' " and Nash replies that the charge of affectation is always brought against " 'a personal manner: if you've any at all people think you've too much.' " In the revised text Nash was to add that affectation is inescapable in any articulation of experience and " 'must have begun, long ago, with the first act of reflective expression—the substitution of the few placed articulate words for the cry or the thump or the hug.' " Inescapable or not, affectation seems to one character to be the very definition of acting on the stage; speaking of actors, he asks: " 'Isn't their whole art the affectation *par excellence?'* " (II, 173, 203.)

Later in the preface James was to associate the "histrionic temperament" with the public fabricated " 'personality' " of the stage performer which diverts attention from the authentic "drama itself," but in that preface, as in the novel itself, he was to associate the "histrionic temperament" also with his heroine, the actress Miriam Rooth, who redeemed the "histrionic temperament" and epitomized not merely "the poor stage *per se*" but the generic nature of " 'art' at large." James's concerns about the interconnections of a mannered style, affectation, and the histrionic talent centered in these instances in the drama and in the manner of the aesthete Nash, but the problems were posed also by mannerism in any form and had long fascinated James, and fascinated the art critics whose writings on painting were most familiar to him.[30]

He used a familiar vocabulary in a review of 1876 when he remarked on the tendency toward mannerism in literature and castigated the extreme it had reached in the drama criticism of Janin, whose "juggling with thought" was a substanceless show of irrelevancies. He had read Hawthorne's remarks in *The Marble Faun* which may first have brought the issue to his attention: the statement that the disturbed atmosphere of Miriam's paintings, haunted as they were by her mysterious demon, struck her rival painters as "a case of hopeless mannerism, which would destroy all Miriam's prospects of true excellence in art." James regretted the "touch of mannerism" in Hawthorne's own late romances, and was even more harsh on the lapse of the Goncourt brothers into "curiosity and mannerism." But while James and important nineteenth-century historians whom he read spoke disparagingly of the excesses of mannerism and of the style itself, they were nonetheless responsive to it in the canvases of its best exemplars beyond what their disparaging remarks might suggest. Much as they con-

[30] *The Art of the Novel,* pp. 81-82, 91.

tributed to the definition of the historical style in the Renaissance paintings they discussed, their writings did something
more: they revealed the wider-ranging response of their imagination to the complexities of the style and to the generic features which gave it current relevance for the nineteenth century. Their remarks about certain painters who developed the
style reveal their understanding of the resources of mannerism
while at the same time disclosing some of the literary sources
in Europe which entered the matrix of James's own style.
An observation which James made in 1873 shows how the term
mannerism and more importantly the style itself dramatized
the problematical relation between art and life which was of
intimate concern to him. He published these notes: "The light
today magnificent; the Alban hills of an intenser broken purple
than I had yet seen them—their white towns blooming upon it
like vague projected lights." It was "like a piece of very modern painting," he concluded, and "a good example of how Nature has at times a sort of mannerism which ought to make us
careful how we condemn out of hand the more refined and affected artists." [31]

In *The Renaissance in Italy,* John Addington Symonds wrote
of the "inexpressibly chilling" portraits of the Mannerist Bronzino and pointed out that the painters who followed Michelangelo merely imitated the defects of their master's later style,
but in the case of Michelangelo himself, Symonds found the
late style of *The Last Judgment* a "mighty mannerism," a triumph despite his judgment that in that work Michelangelo's
style had "hardened into mannerism" and that the "difficult
posturing" and the "strained anatomy" were now "wilfull." [32]

Symonds' judgments were more sure than the troubled reactions of Ruskin earlier in his more seminal writings which, significantly, encountered Mannerist painters in connection with
what Herbert Read has recognized as the first attempt to define
expressionism, in the paintings of Turner, and to find prece-

31 James, *Parisian Sketches: Letters to the New York Tribune, 1875-1876,* eds.
Leon Edel and Ilse D. Lind (New York, 1957), p. 96. Hawthorne, *The Marble
Faun* in *The Complete Novels and Selected Tales,* p. 607. James, *The Shock of
Recognition,* p. 518; *Partial Portraits,* p. 208; *Italian Hours* (Boston, 1909), p. 209.
32 Symonds, *The Renaissance in Italy: The Fine Arts* (New York, 1888), pp.
365, 361, 310-311.

dents for it. Indeed, it was when defining the "penetrating," "grasping imagination" in *Modern Painters* that Ruskin summoned up the example of Tintoretto, and he discussed him again along with Michelangelo in the course of defending the "penetrative imagination" against the charge of distortion and against the claim that such an imagination does not need a recognizable subject at all. Between his assertion that the imagination penetrates into the essentially "true nature of the thing represented," and his assertion that the imagination does need a subject to penetrate, lies a long and troubled footnote solemnly warning young painters against using Michelangelo or Tintoretto too early as models.[33]

Ruskin returned to the pair in 1872. He admitted that both painters made concessions to bravura that brought on stylistic decay among the Mannerists in the next period, but he insisted that the two masters were different from each other (Tintoretto being the greater), and in his contrast of the two he presents a distinct image of the artist conceived as a theatrical performer. Michelangelo, he said, was the superbly ambitious, competitive artist, envious of rivals, acknowledging no limits to his talent, goaded to further effort by his failures. "Always in dramatic attitudes, . . . appealing to the public for praise," he and Raphael are "the leading athletes in the gymnasium of the arts." Tintoretto, by contrast, is supremely content with the limitations of his art, and indifferent to the attention of his audience, one who performs with "ease" and "the simplicity of a wild animal."[34]

The athletic prowess of a performer that Ruskin attributed to the artists, Taine had attributed to the figures depicted, in a discussion of the Mannerists which placed equally strong emphasis on the mode of dramatic performance and underlined also the drama of historical crisis as its matrix. In the late sixteenth century, Taine wrote, society in Venice and elsewhere found itself "on the confines of the feudal and modern ages," a "final moment" of historical transition when the relatively

[33] Read, *The Philosophy of Modern Art,* p. 82. Ruskin, *Works,* III, 173-174, 183, 188-189.
[34] Ruskin, "The Relations Between Michael Angelo and Tintoret," *ibid.,* XIV, 141-142.

"primitive impulse and energy" of the earlier age combined with the "worldly ease," the "gentlemanly elegance" and "urbanity" which would soon replace it. The Italy that produced Michelangelo was in a transitional stage when the medieval and modern epochs were "at their confluence, each penetrating the other in the most wonderful manner and with the most surprising contrasts," which were epitomized by Michelangelo's *The Last Judgment*. In that painting the master had lapsed into mannerism but was nonetheless triumphant. Copying and exaggerating his own style, he "enlarges" and "inflates" the human figure; "prodigal of foreshortenings and violent postures," he presents figures who are like "athletes" in a "gymnasium" seeking to attract attention. Yet the huge work is a triumph and "We cease to feel the abuse of art, the aim at effect, the domination of mannerism. . . ." [35]

Tintoretto likewise, in Taine's estimation, had proven his detractors wrong and thoroughly justified his indulgence in the "disproportionate" and "extravagant." Granting his impetuousness and improvisations, granting the "exhaustion and the mannerism which sometimes lead him to introduce old metal into his new casting," he has the power of one who is seized "by an image which takes possession of him." He paints as one who is "impelled" to depict "not this or that man" as a subject but a larger action or event, "a moment in nature or in history." [36]

It is such a larger action and moment of historical transition that is figured in the bickering over furniture and fiancés in *The Spoils of Poynton,* and its drama is created within the strained gestures, and the taut structure, of a manneristic style which is inherently dramatic and compatible with the deepest impulsions and compressions of expressionistic art. In André Malraux's terms, the "forms are discrepant from appearance," and they render in their contortions the rhythms of historical actuality as well as inward anxieties and concerns. And the style encompasses not only the surface but also the basic structural foundations of James's fiction, the "sacred mystery of structure," as he called it when working out the preliminary notes

35 Hippolyte Taine, *Italy: Rome and Naples: Florence and Venice,* tr. J. Durand, 2 vols. in 1 (New York, 1871), II, 340; I, 183, 194-195.
36 *Ibid.,* II, 317, 319.

for *The Spoils,* which he had learned or tested in the 1890's when writing for the stage. It is the deeper impulsions of the style which help explain why *The Spoils of Poynton* manages to display the fragile or even brittle conventions of the well-made play in combination with the more compulsive power, the stronger pressures, of Ibsen, whose plays were exercising a profound impact on James in the year preceding the publication of *The Spoils* (1896). James had been steeped in the well-made play, despite his early awareness of its hollowness, since his early days in Paris, when he had "thoroughly mastered Dumas, Augier and Sardou"; and the basic materials of *La Dame Aux Camélias* or *Le Mariage d'Olympe* are apparent in the novel— secrets withheld from important characters but shared with the audience, contention over physical objects, the sequence of sudden reversals of fortune, the striking intervention of parents to impede one courtship and favor another. But the dramatic cohesion and moral pressure of the novel owe less to the facile stagecraft of the well-made play than to the "bewildering incongruities," the "strangely inscrutable art," of Ibsen, particularly to the later plays when Ibsen's "later manner" became "the very prose of prose." Whatever relevance James's remarks have for Ibsen (they concentrate on the more enigmatic and symbolic later works), they illuminate immensely James's own creative process, his concern about the limitations of a provincial culture, and his conception of the resources of the dramatic mode.[37]

James confessed that the strong sense of life in Ibsen produced "inward strife" in the beholder, an "irritating spell," rather than merely pleasant composure, and James's tone is often that of stunned fascination in expressing admiration for Ibsen's "angular irony" and "mingled reality and symbolism," for his moral rigor and intensity, and for the mastery with which he converts the " 'middle-class' " austerity, the "bare pro-

---

[37] André Malraux, *The Psychology of Art,* tr. Stuart Gilbert, 3 vols. (New York, 1949-1950), III, 123. James, *Notebooks,* p. 208; *Parisian Sketches,* pp. 49-50; *Letters,* I, 60; *The Scenic Art: Notes on Acting and the Drama: 1872-1901,* ed. Allen Wade (New York: Dramabook, 1957), pp. 246, 258. Wade's collection reprints the important essays, including "On the Occasion of Hedda Gabler" (1891) and "On the Occasion of The Master Builder" (1893), as well as "John Gabriel Borkman" (1897) which James reprinted in *Notes on Novelists* (1914).

vinciality of life" in his community, into a "substitute . . . for charm"—in sum, for the dramatic compression that "converts his provincialism into artistic urbanity." In the last of James's essays on the playwright, he dissociated himself from those who regarded Ibsen as merely a "pictorial monster, a grotesque on the sign of a side-show," yet described the dramatist nevertheless as a "provincial of provincials" who was a "monstrous rarity" in his literary excellence. What he went on to describe was a prodigy of symbolic construction which was congenial to his own ambitions and conception of structure. Ibsen remained an "extraordinary curiosity" whose miraculous combination of "violence" and "insidious form" was not easily explained. Part of the mystery was that the "violent substance imposes, as it were, his insidious form; it is not (as would have seemed more likely) the form that imposes the substance." Whichever came first, substance or form, it was "his rare mastery of form" that James sought to define as a rigorously pruned, starkly efficient combination of symbolic abstraction and vitality.[38]

Ibsen's figures in the later plays were striking because they lacked what James called the *"signs"* of any derivation from "observation"; they lacked the referential indices of observed detail. Ibsen's solemnly austere dramaturgy avoided the comically familiar and his characters showed none of the "signs" of literally actual life that Englishmen might recognize. Granting that perhaps the figures displayed Norwegian "signs" instead, James nevertheless inferred that one characteristic of Norwegian figures must be this "very lack of signs." The figures displayed, he found, "no tone but their moral tone." They were "highly animated abstractions" with the power, when represented on stage, of becoming "at once more abstract and more living." Indeed, the plays themselves are like lamps of the spirit "glowing through what the world and the flesh make of us as through a ground-glass shade": the figures dance and burn "with the flame practically exposed. There are no shades in the house, or the Norwegian ground-glass is singularly clear." In Ibsen's "lonely provincialism," in the "bareness and bleakness of his little northern democracy," the "deficiencies" become themselves "a sharp value in the picture." There is, James said,

38 *The Scenic Art*, pp. 257, 247, 259, 245, 247-249, 252, 291-293.

"no small-talk, there are scarcely any manners." In *John Gabriel Borkman* the "sturdy old symbolist" had brought a perfect example of his dramaturgy "down from that [Norwegian] desolation," and James described a powerful, baldly abstract symbolism, enlarged in scale beyond the "meagreness" of the materials, powerful in part because of the contrast between the admirable "economy" of its "civilized" form and the bareness of the bleak community it presents: "Well in the very front of the scene lunges with extraordinary length of arm the Ego against the Ego, and rocks in a rigour of passion the soul against the soul—a spectacle, a movement, as definite as the relief of silhouettes in black paper or of a train of Eskimo dogs on snow." [39]

While no such rigor of passion and movement was to rock James's fiction until the three late novels, and while there were always in his case elaborations of form to qualify the austerity he found in Ibsen, James's remarks in 1897 define pressures bearing on his imagination which left their imprint the year before on *The Spoils of Poynton* and were to become more pronounced in the later phase of his career: the pressure toward a dramatic "economy" in which the bareness of materials and the perfection of form, in their contrast, set off the action of the characters with heightened clarity and present them with the sharp "relief of silhouettes," however inscrutable the figures and the art might remain; the aim for an extension of scale and moral urgency beyond what the meager appearances, the ostensibly bare materials, suggest; a pressure toward symbolic extension so strong that customary "signs" are abandoned or remade, and the very foundation of the art, its structure, becomes symbolic. The manner characterizes not only the surface textures of the prose in its energetic twisting and distended tautness—but also the extended reach of his themes and characterization and the foundation of the fiction's movement and architecture. The author, like the dramatist, is screened from view in the wings, but the movement of the drama, its objective presence and style, become conspicuous, stand in bold relief. The style becomes an instrument for the rendering of characters and themes which range in import beyond what was

[39] *Ibid.*, pp. 292-293.

customary in the novel of manners, even though the occasions and settings are those of polite society and though the squabble over household furnishings seems trivial. They have this extended import and scale because the manner is basically symbolic in function, though implicitly so: its manner is symbolic without being founded on a rhetoric and nomenclature of emblematic signification. His form is distinct and tangible yet more plastic than generically denotative or emblematic prose, aiming beyond the given specifications of actuality, emblems, and types toward a new reality which is the offspring of what it finds and what it makes.

It is the articulated pressure to mold and reshape the world it finds that renders the manneristic style, with stronger rhythms of the expressionistic mode, an appropriate stylistic convention for social conditions and personal concerns which are in the throes of crisis. Yet the assets of the style were employed at the peril of risks which James and his contemporaries were keenly aware of. Indeed what is most revealing in the writings of Symonds, Ruskin, and Taine about Renaissance Mannerism is their feeling that the style by its very nature creates a crisis for the art of anyone who uses it; it opens the way to decay, falsification, and affectation as well as to enlargement of effect and dramatic power; the style itself, to a degree that differentiates it from other conventions, is at once a threat and an opportunity. Michelangelo's "mighty mannerism" or Tintoretto's "disproportionate" and "extravagant" effects were achieved not by avoiding the risks but by running them. The style was at once an instrument and a challenge whose mixed perils and assets called for a kind of commitment on James's part which could not be simply neutral or coldly utilitarian: it called for a more intimate engagement with form which involved his moral and imaginative life more intimately with his materials, and implicated his drama more thoroughly in the life it depicts. *The Spoils of Poynton,* which first clearly displays the reorientation of James's style that was to be completed in the later phase of his career, is not one of James's masterpieces; its texture is not resilient enough to bear the attention it demands, and its form remains too slight to support the full weight of substance and import which it seeks to accommodate.

Yet it is a brilliant innovation of that order which does not simply describe a subject already given but helps create one. The institutions of courtship and marriage are central, as they were in *The Portrait of a Lady,* but they are not so much *represented* as scrutinized under a pressure more intensely analytic than that in the *Portrait,* and under that pressure fused with the institution of ownership—the possession of "things"—in a process which is generically dramatic. Indeed, the processes of art—including the composition of painting but chiefly the enactments of the drama—are dimensions of the subject being analyzed imaginatively as well as models for the form. The novel's import is best revealed in the mannered contortions of its form, where the drama of word and action becomes "overbearingly prominent" in its motives, where the style, in sporadic phrases or insistently in larger patterns, presses beyond the apparent confines of its given subject to establish a larger scale of relevance and create a world by symbolizing it. The *Spoils* becomes the process of historical renewal which it enacts. It helps create the process and the community of vision which opens up in and around "the little drama" of James's own " 'Spoils.' "

[II]

THE SPOILS OF POYNTON

THE story lay germinating in a report whose fossil facts are discernible in James's first manipulations of them in notes dating from 1893. A mother, who had collected "valuable things—pictures, old china, etc., etc." and whose son had recently married, was cut off in her widowhood by the English custom (James thought it "ugly") which settled the entire inheritance (land, house, furnishings) on the son. Moreover, custom stipulated that the son reside in the family house and the mother live in a dower house elsewhere. The mother disliked the new wife, moved the furnishings from the house, took the case to court, raised a "public scandal." Her latest maneuver—James did not record, if he knew, how the case came out—was to declare that her son was illegitimate and therefore had no rightful claim anyway. In saying that the mother had been "deposed" by institutions of inheritance which are designed to be guarantors of stability instead of sources of violence, and twice calling her counteraction "rebellion," James was already dramatizing the crisis that moves so swiftly in the first chapter of the finished novel, impelled through sudden shocks by the vehement feelings and aggressive "management" of Mrs. Gereth. And in calling the furnishings "things" he was beginning the treatment of his subject by abstracting the implications of the objects under dispute: those "things" which, as Emerson had written in the "Ode to Channing," are "in the saddle / And ride mankind," and which James later spoke of in the preface as "exerting their ravage" with a "merciless monotony." [40]

James's preface points also to another relation between the "things" and modern behavior, namely modern Britain's economy and its relation to its cultural past which James had commented on in 1877. The English, he wrote, are not "the greatest artistic producers of the world" but "the greatest consumers"; the "rest of the world has painted for them"; "English gentlemen have bought—with English bank notes—profusely, unre-

[40] *Notebooks,* pp. 133-137; *The Art of the Novel,* p. 129.

mittingly, splendidly." As the preface puts it later: the "row" between the mother and son evidenced "that most modern of our
current passions, the fierce appetite for the upholsterer's and
joiner's and brazier's works" which were the products not of
contemporary England but "of the more labouring ages." The
preface goes on: "A lively mark of our manners indeed . . . ,
and full of suggestion of their possible influence on other passions and other relations." [41]

The connection—and eventually the symbolic fusion—of the
"things" with manners, with the past, and with "other passions"
is what the first chapter of the novel begins to achieve in proceeding from Mrs. Gereth's anxious irritability to Fleda's firm
anticipations; in presenting the stroll about the Brigstocks'
grounds when, thanks to Mrs. Gereth's "management," the
mother is seen "possessing herself of her son," and when Fleda
and Owen are paired temporarily as partners; and finally in
moving to its last sentence: "Her [Fleda's] meager past fell
away from her like a garment of the wrong fashion, and as she
came up to town on the Monday what she stared at in the suburban fields from the train was a future full of the things she
particularly loved." It is significant that before the novel's
"things" are identified as the "Spoils," they are introduced
first as a sheer verbal form associated with Owen (the characteristics Owen lacks are called "things") and then used in the
sentence just quoted as a form fraught with a wide, not a narrow, range of implications: a "future full" of "things." And it
is further important that the "things" are involved in an action
which already, in other connections, suggests acts of possession:
Waterbath is described as "possessing" the "advantages that are
usually spoken of as natural," and there is a glimpse of Mrs.
Gereth "possessing herself of her son." The act of possession
comprises the first of three motives which launch the novel's
drama and are projected by James's mannered style in the opening paragraphs in curiously insistent phrases which seem at once
charged with import and pointlessly irrelevant to the subject,
but which in that seeming irrelevance gain prominence as
forms engaged in shaping the novel's nascent drama. Each mo-

41 "Picture Season in London," *The Painter's Eye*, pp. 133, 137; *The Art of
the Novel*, p. 123.

tive may be distinguished separately in the early stages of the novel, although it is their interaction, and the complex ironies they entail, that create the crisis which becomes distinctly dramatic in Chapters Fifteen and Sixteen. (10-11, 3.)

The act of possession was familiar to James's imagination as part of the everyday experience which he shared with well-off inhabitants of the nineteenth century; moreover, he had written in *The Portrait of a Lady* of Caspar's "act of possession," of Daniel Touchett's purchase and "careful keeping" of his mansion, and was to write, in the preface later, of the *Portrait*'s subject which he had held in "complete possession." In *The Spoils*, the action centers first on Owen and the increasingly imminent possibility of his being possessed by his disdainful, domineering mother, or of his being possessed in marriage, either by his increasingly demanding fiancée, Mona, or by Fleda, who before his engagement relishes the prospect of leading him around by the nose with her condescending "cleverness" and pronounced sense of "direction." (10-11.)

It is this action, already quickened in the first chapter, which is enlarged to encompass the crisis of the spoils and Poynton: their fate and status are joined with Owen's, and they add an urgency to the conflict, for the rare objects in the Jacobean house (itself preserved for over two centuries) are old, and once were lodged in the hands of the Chinese, Florentines, Frenchmen, Spaniards, and Maltese who originally made or possessed them. More recently they have been bought and transported, by an "imperious" Mrs. Gereth, to the seat of empire, the hodge-podge of modern England, comprised of new-fangled Waterbath, old Poynton, and London, where the gaping heir-apparent (costumed like an actor but redolent in Fleda's opinion of both "nature" and the peasantry) rides to the hounds, collects rifles and whips, and, when in London, stops by his club and carries a spear-like umbrella. Implicit in the "things" is the artful past, the labor and craftsmanship and history, which modern imperial England has appropriated and whose possession is now at issue. (14, 59, 150.)

Different modes of possession also are at stake in the action. Owen's casualness and Mona's perfunctory manner in respect to Poynton and the "things," unappreciative and legalistic, prefigure a proprietorship which would neglect their merits and violate their integrity with tasteless new additions (notably a "winter garden"). Mrs. Gereth's manner, founded originally on the affection, taste, and resources which she shared with her late husband, is a combination of passionate devotion to high standards and predatory acquisitiveness which amounts to "loot" and theft. Early in the novel she commits outright theft from her son; her violence to Poynton in removing the "things" is called "revolt" in the unrevised version,[42] even before she commits the act of rebellious usurpation which is figured in her declaration: " 'I've crossed the Rubicon; I've taken possession.' " Fleda's manner toward them is responsive rather than grasping, while being appreciative of the Poynton she hates to see violated. Yet in her dependence on friends and relatives she is thought, notably by her sister, to be a "leech." (34, 147, 61, 60.)

The action of possession is fraught with significant conflict. Customary institutions which favor the continuance of dynasties and the dominance of males, while permitting their affiliation with families and mates of lower taste and status, are at odds with familial harmony and intimacy, with the rising assertiveness of women, and with standards of taste or the appeal of culture. A courtship, institutionalized in Mona's and Owen's engagement, is used as a weapon and challenged, stretched and strained, almost destroyed. The middle class' interest, whether perfunctory or consuming, in the comfort and status of having "things" is enforced by the middle class' aggressiveness which, in the behavior of Mrs. Gereth, would shake the local foundations in open rebellion to guard and use her valuables and beauties. Another middle-class girl is drawn into the crisis from a position on the periphery; all but cast out by her father, a welcome but unsettled guest in the spare room of her sister, she is utterly dependent on her father's meager contribution to her support, on the acquaintances whom she visits, and on a yet unproven talent for Impressionistic painting. The viability of the action derives from the fact that it sustains and deepens simultaneously two perspectives which are in dramatic conflict: one is the fear that the act of possession in an acquisitive society is

42 The Spoils of Poynton (Norfolk, Conn., n.d.), p. 53.

unavoidably predatory and divisive, turning "things" into mere items, and turning persons (even relatives and fiancés) into mere tools and "things"; the other is the feeling that only through acts of full possession could the conflict be satisfactorily resolved and Poynton with its treasures, Mrs. Gereth, Owen, Fleda, or Mona come into their own.

A comparable ambivalence surrounds the prospect of marriage, arousing conflicting anticipations in the reader which correspond to the main impulsions of the dramatic movement. Owen's submission to either Mona or Fleda early in the novel would stamp marriage as a fiasco, a constricting form devised by domineering scheming women. Yet the novel presents the senior Gereths' marriage as a "perfect accord" and it aims toward Owen's marriage with either Mona or Fleda as a form within which the fruits of intimacy and trust might be actually enjoyed, a welcome alternative to loneliness for Fleda, subservience to his mother for Owen, or the intermittent, tentative delights of romping and scrambling up embankments which engage Owen and Mona when they appear in the first chapter. The action moves dialectically: it gives rise to suspicions, increasing enmity, and friction among the characters, yet their very conflict brings them into closer association than prevailed at the start. But in bringing Fleda into the center of the action, as the novel does in moving from Mrs. Gereth's consciousness to Fleda's in the opening chapter, it brings into prominence another action which is fused with the first. The act of possession is joined with another motive, the act of communication or expression, which is introduced by the remarks in Chapter One about Mrs. Gereth's professed scorn for "advertised" passions, Mona's manner of communication "without signs," and Owen's simplicity and naturalness of expression. (6, 9.)

Besides being an accumulation of "things," the Jacobean house is a "canvas" and Poynton is termed "a complete work of art." The passion for "things" which characterizes manners in the modern imperium also characterizes modern taste, as James had suggested when writing of the tendency of French fiction to "resolve its discoveries into pictorial form," its "analytic consideration of appearances," the "new sense" of "the associations awakened by things." Accordingly the novel's "things," which are " 'works of art' " to begin with, become the raw materials—all the more raw for being "loot"—of Mrs. Gereth's art. They are the "record of a life," indeed "great syllables of colour and form, the tongues of other countries." Arranged and composed at Poynton, they are a triumph of art, the result of the late Mr. Gereth's "generosity," the "perfect accord" which he and Mrs. Gereth shared, and her "genius." While weighing her predatory "infernal cunning," one must recognize in her acts the passion of the writer whom James thought the greatest since Shakespeare, and whose talent for marshalling objects, he said in the preface, he admired: Balzac.[43] (13, 43, 22, 13.)

Late in his career James became even more eloquent in his praise of Balzac than he had been earlier, granting firmly in 1913 the power even of his "vulgarity," and registering in 1902 reactions to Balzac which correspond to Fleda's response to Mrs. Gereth's actions and the Poynton she has created. James noted the oppressive sense of confinement resulting from Balzac's immersion in his immediate *milieu* and from his undeviating struggle with his mammoth subject which left him " 'caged,' " indeed "locked," in his medium. Balzac was the "man of business doubled with an artist" whom Taine had described, and the tangible *"things"* which fill his novels "are at once our delight and our despair" when their "enchanting aspects" are weighed against the oppressive "over-crowding of the scene." As James had written in 1878, Balzac was an artist with "a mighty passion for things," for "material objects, for furniture, upholstery, bricks and mortar." He was a "profound connoisseur in these matters"; with his "passion for bric-a-brac," Balzac's "tables and chairs are always in character." So, in the novel, Mrs. Gereth has an "almost maniacal disposition to thrust in everywhere the question of 'things,' to read all behavior in the light of some fancied relation to them"—to feel that they are " 'living things,' " that " 'they return the touch of my hand.' " So likewise, in building his novel around the "things" at Poynton, did James interpret his characters' behavior by their relation to the precious objects, and accord to the "things" the presence and power of virtual life in rendering them a cen-

43 *The Art of the Novel*, p. 124.

tral motive in his fiction. At stake in the novel's acts of expression are the creation and appreciation of art—indeed the very definition of art which is characteristic of a manneristic style.[44] (24, 31.)

This is not to say that Mrs. Gereth *stands for* either Balzac or James, nor that the process of seizing and treating a subject pictorially with analytical insight into a world of "things" is the subject for report in *The Spoils*. Rather it is to say that the activities which James and Balzac in some measure share with other writers are figured in Mrs. Gereth's predatory actions, and that, while they need to be purged and redeemed, these actions are acknowledged to be necessarily involved in the process of historical renewal which produced *The Spoils* and which *The Spoils* helps to create.

Poynton figures most prominently in this action, and its effects as art are double when recorded in Fleda's response. It is a high standard, the answer to "the need to be faithful to a trust," the sacred altar Mrs. Gereth has made of it once she has unearthed and laid hands on her materials. It alone, not Waterbath, constitutes "the imagination of a bond" of affection. Yet its grandeur, like Waterbath's vulgarity, stifles Fleda's fragile creativity; she cannot paint there in the constricting *prison* which permits only a "Buddhistic contemplation." Yet oppressive though the estate is, Fleda imagines to her despair that without it as a habitat Mrs. Gereth would appear like Marie Antoinette reduced to the Conciergerie, or like an exotic bird dropped onto "a frozen moor to pick up a living," or like an emaciated and "unnatural" ghost sinking into quicksand. (46, 170, 148, 146.)

Poynton, however, is not the only example of a work of art. There is the dower house, Ricks, in its original state, with the unpretentious charm that Fleda and even Owen and Mona appreciate. Then there is Ricks later, stuffed with the furnishings Mrs. Gereth has hauled away from Poynton, become a painful "torment of taste" which has "exterminated" the maiden aunt who once lived there, leaving "no trace . . . to tell her tale." There are also the small paintings in the shop window—

[44] *Notes on Novelists*, pp. 159, 126-127, 118-120; *French Poets and Novelists*, pp. 90, 93.

"brought . . . forth in sorrow" and regretfully never "snapped up"—which Fleda is looking at appreciatively when Owen finds her in London. Finally there is Ricks later, after Mrs. Gereth has returned *"the* things" to Poynton and brought out and re-arranged the maiden aunt's belongings—" 'fished her out' " of the " 'empty barn' " of her obliteration—as if resurrecting the aunt herself. Without knowing it, Mrs. Gereth has composed in smaller scale the masterpiece which Fleda recognizes. (43, 54, 79, 148, 248.)

The effects of Poynton as art on Fleda and others, and the effects of the other works on the various characters—the inspiration and the stifling confinement, the shared concern and the violence, the displayed offer in the shop window and the regrettable neglect, the extinction and the resurrection—are matched by their effects on the action of the narrative. Poynton causes strife verging on warfare, giving rise to camouflage and serving as its instrument, yet the very contention brings the principal characters, even Mona and Owen, closer together in revealed communication and acquaintance than they were at the start. All the separate expressive powers of the principal characters remain imperfect but are heightened as the novel advances, and all contribute to bringing the novel to the turning point in Chapter Sixteen. This includes Mona, with her kept secrets and calculated silences, her featureless but increasingly felt power, which blooms late in the novel in what Fleda calls her "natural charm." It includes Mrs. Gereth, whose scorn of advertising does not prevent her from indulging in it with all her blatancy and whose combat with her son and Mona eventuates in her artistic triumph at Ricks. And the process of drawing out expressive power and achieving more intimate communication engages Fleda, who, by keeping her love for Owen hidden in secrecy, consents to becoming, this impressionistic painter, what Mrs. Gereth first, then Owen, and finally Mrs. Brigstock make of her: a go-between, a "medium of communication," or, in the revision, a "messenger and mediator." [45] (255, 47.)

The act of mediation in art and expression entails a third motive in the novel's movement, the act of salvage or redemption which James spoke of in the later preface, saying that, as

[45] *The Spoils of Poynton* (Norfolk, Conn., n.d.), p. 54.

against the inexorable wastage of life, art "rescues" and "saves," in fact "hoards and 'banks,' investing and reinvesting [the] fruits of toil in wonderful useful 'works' and thus making up for us, desperate spendthrifts that we naturally are, the most princely of incomes." [46] In the novel the motive is introduced by the remarks in Chapter One that one Mrs. Firmin is "redeemingly" married and that the Brigstocks could not exercise the "saving mercy" of leaving the decor of Waterbath alone. Mrs. Gereth's determination to protect Poynton and prevent first Owen's engagement, then his marriage, to Mona by enlisting Fleda and using her as a "thing" or tool becomes the more ambitious effort to *save* Owen, to save the priceless estate, and to save Fleda from spinsterdom. This is the process for which Fleda becomes the mediating and transforming agent. (8, 7.)

The novel reveals in every facet that the process entails a double effort which is precisely analogous to Mrs. Gereth's effort originally to unearth and acquire the "things" and then compose Poynton: the effort to discover, salvage, and restore; and the attempt to transform and make new. Fleda will attempt, on the one hand, to restore the integrity of Poynton after Mrs. Gereth's theft of the "things"; she will help "reinstate" Owen in his rights; she undertakes "to help him to live as a gentleman and carry through what he had undertaken." This is the saving mercy of her help, founded in part on protective and maternal instincts. Yet we find her hoping not only that Owen maintain his stature but that he change, that he rise beyond any level of independence yet displayed and, without being subservient to either Mrs. Gereth or Mona or even to herself, accept the full burden of his maturity, including his plighted word. He has, she feels, no "right to get off easily from pledges so deep and sacred." As the action develops, Fleda extends her vision to the hope that Owen might become even "sublime." The discovery of her passion for him entails the expansion of her vision and her demands upon him: "She never knew the extent of her tenderness for him till she became conscious of the present force of her desire that he should be superior, be perhaps even sublime." In a word, Fleda's condescending affection has become a transforming passion. It refuses to leave things as they

[46] *The Art of the Novel,* p. 120.

are, her love being recognizable to herself only in the light of the desire it creates, the desire for the transformation of Owen. (95, 106, 180.)

That the novel's action becomes a process of transformation is owing not only to Fleda's given ideals, imagination, and capacity for experience but also to the pressures generated by contention over the "things," the attempt to communicate and express, and the effort to win Owen. Fleda's love releases a vision of mutual love which is new in the novel, which grows in and is nourished by its movement. That vision of love governs the novel finally, surviving and taking the measure of the catastrophe which ensues, only after it is created by the pressures of the action and brings them to the final crisis which, in Chapters Fifteen and Sixteen, is constituted as an archetypal drama. The complex vision, and the dramatic scenes in which it is created, demand attention in detail, but they are understandable only in the context of the larger patterns of the crisis which precede and follow them and must be considered first.

The ironies which characterize the crisis illuminate its dialectical nature, for they inhere in the fact that the process of salvage and transformation engages all the antagonists whose conflict helps bring it about. The plot, instead of taking the form of a conspiracy which deceives and traps its central figure (as in *The Portrait of a Lady*), engages all the characters in combat; in *The Spoils,* all the principal characters become contestants, and all are involved, though in varying measure, in the redemptive process which Fleda deepens and extends. Mona, too, wants Poynton restored and insists that Owen assert himself, and she exerts pressure toward that end. Mrs. Gereth, confessing her grossness and modifying her contempt for her son in tender praise of him, becomes gradually more concerned for Owen (while still cherishing the "things") and begs Fleda on her knees to " 'Save him.' " Even Mrs. Brigstock finally seeks Fleda's mediation. And Owen's plea at the novel's turning point is simply: " 'What I want you to say is that you'll save me.' " In making Fleda the mediator and savior, they contribute to the dialectical process of salvage and re-creation. (126, 186.)

The crisis and the irony are complicated by the fact that the process is actually fulfilled in large measure, as are the aims for full expression and possession, even though balked of complete fulfillment in a tragic resolution that culminates in the destruction of Poynton, which is not only caused by but figured in the fire and ruinous winds of a " 'cruel cruel night.' " There is a measure of success despite the tragic wastage. Owen is restored to the rights of custom, the "things" are returned, and Poynton is restored for a time to the imperium. With Fleda at any rate, Owen is more eager and able to initiate action: he seeks her out, twice in London tracks her down, and does propose marriage to her. Yet the engagement to Mona holds; Owen keeps his pledges of love, and a civil marriage, then a church marriage, follow; husband and wife, despite Owen's temporary revulsion against Mona, finally are living together. Fleda's condescending affection for Owen has deepened, and despite her reluctance she is brought to the point of sending the telegram in hopes of possessing him in marriage. Later, after that effort has failed, she is ready to take " 'immediate possession' " of the Maltese Cross which Owen offers her as a present. (265, 258.)

Moreover, Owen, who had some "natural art" to begin with and whose appreciation of Poynton was awakened by the theft of the "things," becomes more passionately articulate in personal address and written letter; Fleda has become more revealingly so in speech and telegram and act. Mona's power and charm have communicated themselves to Owen and to Fleda's imagination, and Poynton is again, for a time, the "complete work of art." Fleda can imagine that Mona even "had taken [Poynton] in"; in her limited way "she felt when it had been touched." Correspondingly, Mrs. Gereth, though no more than resigned to Owen's marriage, has become more interested in him and in Fleda than in the " 'accursed vanities' "—the "things" which late in the novel comparatively bore her. And in resurrecting the maiden aunt in the form of her furniture, Mrs. Gereth has again created, if on a smaller scale, a masterpiece. In a measure, the world through Fleda's sacrificial mediation has been salvaged and remade. (19, 104, 255, 223, 232.)

The process has its characteristic rhythm, the pattern of movement which constitutes the structure of The Spoils of Poynton and, more firmly than anything else, defines the action as the sacrifice and rebirth of the imagination in its desperate but redeeming commitment to the contingencies of contemporary life which are imaged as the "London labyrinth," the life to which Fleda returns at the end of the novel. Fleda's sloughing off the past and returning on a train to London at the end of the first chapter set the direction and launch the movement. For five chapters the action involves the characters more closely together in affiliation and opposition, finally impelling Fleda again to London where Owen finds her outside the shop on Oxford Street. The action comes to a tentative resolution which prefigures Owen's gift at the end of the novel: it is an act of purchase which Owen initiates and Fleda shares in completing and which becomes a gift and an expressed tribute of esteem. He determines to buy Fleda a present—a lap rug, a bed table, a "massive clock," or "a set of somebody's 'works.' " However awkward or unsure, it is a purchase and an expressive gesture which is presented and accepted after being scaled down more appropriately to a pin cushion marked with Fleda's initial. (262, 64.)

For another five chapters the action aims through minor crises toward the point where Fleda entrains again for London —now "advertised and offered," indeed "ticketed, labelled and seated" like a "thing" herself in Mrs. Gereth's usage of her, fleeing Mrs. Gereth's demand that she actively solicit Owen's affection. The chapter's closing gestures mark the completion of Fleda's engagement, now inescapable, in the action, as the train for London pulls off slowly while Fleda "leans inscrutably forth" from a window and Mrs. Gereth, running alongside on the platform, grasps Fleda's hand and enjoins her to " 'let yourself go.' " But these strained gestures, so underscored by James's manner, exert a pressure beyond their immediate import. For the trip which Fleda mistakenly thinks an escape takes her to her final encounter with Owen and to the "London labyrinth" which she prepares to confront at the end of the novel. And the grasp of Mrs. Gereth's hand and her injunction to "let yourself go" prefigure the action Fleda will take later in sending the telegram to win Owen; but paradoxically they prefigure also Fleda's surrender to her love, the sacrifice to that love, which she is made to undergo and consents to enact under the pressure of the dramatic crisis which culminates in Chapter Sixteen. (140-142.)

The next four chapters (all in London but the last, when Fleda takes refuge at her sister's house nearby) open with the scene where Owen, informed shrewdly by Mrs. Gereth of Fleda's whereabouts, tracks her down and finds her in front of the art shop looking at paintings born "in sorrow" and regrettably never purchased. The section ends with the two chapters where Fleda is forced to reveal her love to Owen, the scenes which are the novel's turning point and constitute its drama.

The first (Chapter Fifteen), set in Fleda's father's house, opens with the unexpected arrival of a caller who interrupts Owen's profession of love for Fleda. It proves to be not Mrs. Gereth, as Fleda had first surmised—the parent whose interventions have been habitually bold and embarrassing—but Mrs. Brigstock, whose character Fleda has never had occasion to measure. The felt presence of one parent and the intervention of another, along with the plea Mrs. Brigstock comes to make for Mona, are reminiscent of the intervention of Armand Duval's father in the affair of his son with Marguerite Gautier, Camille, in *La Dame aux Camélias,* and his request that she break off the affair so as to protect her lover's reputation and thus permit the marriage of his sister to her fiancé whose family disapproves of Armand's alliance. Though the details do not of course correspond exactly, in James's novel and Dumas' play, the very basis of the incident, as well as the brittle neatness and striking theatrical manner with which this scene prepares for the next, are among the indications that the well-made play had shaped James's mannered style and contributed to the conversion of the narrative into drama. (172.)

The account hovers about and probes the enigmatic motives of Mrs. Brigstock, captures, with the fastidious attention that marks James's mannered style, the postures and facial expressions of the three characters while they cautiously explore for information, and while Owen takes sides more openly with Fleda, and Fleda, letting herself go, tries to impress Owen with her own "simplicity and tact." The scene opens by isolating for remarkably exaggerated and strained attention an object on the carpet, a broken tea biscuit, and other "sprawling tea-things" which produce "a vivid picture of intimacy." Come to seek Fleda's mediation in the " 'dreadful quarrel' " and to ascertain the extent of her and Owen's friendship, Mrs. Brigstock gradually recognizes the signs of intimacy in the remnant of biscuit which Owen hastens to pick up, in Owen's determination to defend Fleda, and in his and Fleda's willingness to provide explanations for each other. So completely does the scene depend on the characters' postures and forms of behavior that it is not until a later chapter that Mrs. Brigstock's deepest motives are fully brought out. Then (in Chapter Seventeen) Mrs. Gereth discloses that Mrs. Brigstock, after apparently failing with Fleda, turned to Mrs. Gereth for " 'mercy' " and " 'fair play' " toward Mona, wanting " 'not to get the old things back, but simply to get Owen,' " protesting that Owen had been " ' "misled" ' " or, as Mrs. Gereth translated it, " 'bedevilled' "—it was Fleda who had *bedevilled* him. (170, 169, 207-209.)

Mrs. Gereth's substitution of the term *bedevilled* reflects her delight in her new conviction that Fleda has been close to intimacy with Owen, but it has greater significance for the novel's drama. It clarifies the moral implications of an earlier remark, seemingly gratuitous, which is the culmination of the crucial interview with Mrs. Brigstock and which precipitates the drama's crisis. It is a remark in which Fleda assumes, in her own words, a form: the promise, appearance, burden, and risk—that is to say the form—of responsibility for the novel's action. The act —adoption of a form of responsibility—is at once histrionic and moral and constitutes the very life of both the drama and moral commitment because it creates the double possibility of success and failure, moral triumph and culpability; the assumption of responsibility as a formal *office* or *mission* or *role* is prior to incurring either guilt or credit for the commitment and the deed. It is the adoption of a form which renders a contingent act neither surely good nor patently evil but precisely questionable and renders the agent *responsible* in the sense of *answerable* for it. It stirs at the center of both the dramatic and the moral traditions of the West when, for instance, Jesus shoulders the burden of his father's and Adam's responsibility and undergoes his crucifixion, revealing the form of both loving god and criminal, so as to redeem that responsibility; or when Plato's Socrates adopts the form of his commitment to reason and virtue which is also the form of guilt when consenting to drink the hemlock prescribed as punishment by the Athenians, then does so in the deed which authenticates the responsibility of the dangerous and inquiring mind. It stirs also, in the most famous of well-made plays, when the courtesan Camille, in the interview with Armand's father, is moved to protect her lover's reputation and permit his sister's marriage. She does so in commitments which constitute the prospective form of both sacrificial renunciation and faithless prostitution, then enacts the deeds which (by accepting another liaison) separate her from her lover but pay tribute to the institution of marriage and consecrate her and Armand's love.

Fleda is brought to a comparable questionable act when Mrs. Brigstock, looking "more deeply and yearningly" than Fleda had thought possible, prepares to let Fleda explain her association with Owen. Mrs. Brigstock makes a declaration which is simple, halting, and genuinely felt: " 'I came, I believe, Fleda, just—you know—to plead with you.' " Fleda's reply—superior and sophisticated but nonetheless genuine—is in the form of an ironic and hypothetical question on which the scene turns. She replies: " 'As if I were one of those bad women in a play?' " The reply wounds Mrs. Brigstock, who breaks off the interview and proceeds to seek Mrs. Gereth's help in simply getting Fleda out of the way. (177.)

But its ironies, thrown into relief by the hypothetical status of the question, suggest the ramifications of the action in which Fleda's relation with Owen threatens to break the engagement which binds him to Mona. As regards Mrs. Brigstock, the ironies impute to the older woman both a moral claim and a presumptuous, self-righteous condescension toward Fleda and suggest that her behavior is not only stern but unjust and propped and footlighted, costumed and cued. As regards Fleda, the remark suggests that Fleda is an outsider and *bad,* that she stands in the moral position of Camille and, further, that she is the sacrificial protagonist of a play and knows it. Yet the remark in its stunning irony suggests with equal clarity that Fleda is not *bad,* that her motives, as well as the degree of her intimacy with Owen, have been misunderstood, and that she stands not on stage but in the colorless surroundings of a house in London. The ironies are not mutually exclusive and probe to the depths of the dramatic action. They reveal the kind of event (internal and histrionic, whether on stage or off) which James had described in the actress Miriam Rooth in *The Tragic Muse* when she says goodbye to Peter Sherrington but expresses gratitude for his friendship: "the expression of this was already . . . a strange bedevilment: she began to listen to herself, to speak dramatically, to represent." While making the declarations "she felt as if they were snatches of old play-books, and really felt them the more because they sounded so well," but "they were as good feelings as those of anybody else" and she seems to Peter to have "the truth of gentleness and generosity." Fleda's remark—like Miriam's farewell, it is equally genuine and histrionic—presents the form or *role* which defines the moral agent, dramatic protagonist, and sacrificial figure that Fleda becomes in assuming the burden of the action which she did not originate but which, through her involvement with the Gereths and the Brigstocks, she helped to create. And the remark establishes the drama as the governing analogy both for the action in which Fleda takes part as mediator and for the narrative medium and mannered style which present it. (II, 251-252.)

The scene prepares for the crucial scene following it with the staged efficiency of a well-made play and suffers the chief risk of its conventions, that of producing more in theatrical effect than is redeeemed in dramatic action, more in stylistic finish and self-conscious manner than is redeemed in the complete fusion of symbolic form. But the manner of *The Spoils* is sustained by the firmest rhythms of its action, which moves from Fleda's adoption of the form of responsibility to the symbolic action, in the next scene, which redeems it.

Here in the *scène de passion* the novel penetrates to the depths of the experience it reveals and presents the boldest challenge to its dramatic irony: that of presenting the experience which unites Owen and Fleda, the vision of love to which it gives birth, while simultaneously revealing that their union is not yet the utterly reciprocal harmony which Fleda has envisioned and that it is impossible of full attainment yet in marriage with Owen, the marriage to Fleda which he feels would save him, the marriage which even Fleda later, by sending her telegram, tries to secure. The vision is not founded simply on renunciation, for it is infused with intensely possessive longing. It is not an exclusively personal love, for it puts pressure on the social forms which prepare for it or hinder it. It does not consist simply of a retreat from intimate experience but, though it falls short of or postpones full consummation, it is the product of intimate communion and expression. The emergence of the vision, and Fleda's commitment to it, hazard the separation of Owen and Fleda and the triumph of Mona, but they create also the possibility, the symbolic vision, of redeeming love.

In three particularly compressed passages the action shows vividly the passion which unites Owen and Fleda while suppressing, in image, tone, and texture, the division between them which emerges clearly only toward the end. The unattainability of Fleda's vision of utter reciprocity and full possession in love, the "sense of the IMPOSSIBLE" which the *Notebooks* stipulated for the "unarrested drama" of this scene, sounds in the note of jarring violence and the indications of Fleda's fears, shows in the still immature dependence of Owen on Fleda's direction and in his visible "sadness" and "terror" at recognizing it, which prefigure not happiness but anguished sacrifice. Yet the passages present an embrace and a communion in love. The language and action are steeped in the gestures of seizure, grasped and clasped hands, possession; the incident is the culmination of an act of expression; the communion between Owen and Fleda becomes, in the second passage, the symbolic form of salvation.[47] (189.)

The first passage moves in quickening strokes to the intensity of an embrace which joins possession and surrender in the rhythms of passion, then terminates in the ominous discord of violence, crumbling stone, and severance:

"The words had broken from her in a sudden loud cry, and what next happened was that the very sound of her pain upset her. She heard her own true note; she turned short away from him; in a moment she had burst into sobs; in another his arms were round her; the next she had let herself go so far that even

[47] *Notebooks*, pp. 254, 251.

Mrs. Gereth might have seen it. He clasped her, and she gave herself—she poured out her tears on his breast. Something prisoned and pent throbbed and gushed; something deep and sweet surged up—something that came from far within and far off, that had begun with the sight of him in his indifference and had never had rest since then. The surrender was short, but the relief was long: she felt his warm lips on her face and his arms tighten with his full divination. What she did, what she *had* done, she scarcely knew: she only was aware, as she broke from him again, of what had taken place on his own amazed part. What had taken place was that, with the click of a spring, he saw. He had cleared the high wall at a bound; they were together without a veil. She had not a shred of a secret left; it was as if a whirlwind had come and gone, laying low the great false front that she had built up stone by stone. The strangest thing of all was the momentary sense of desolation." (188-189.)

The passage which follows, using the gestures of courtly devotion and religious chivalry, presents the very form of saving devotion; yet Fleda's elevation and Owen's prostration before her on his knees present also the form for Fleda's recognition of the distance, now by this act widened, which still separates them. The combination of elegance and devotional intensity, the contortions which mark the compulsive rhythms as well as the surface tension, are the epitome of James's mannered style:

"It was easy indeed not to speak when the difficulty was to find words. He clasped his hands before her as he might have clasped them at an altar; his pressed palms shook together . . . while she stilled herself in the effort to come round again to the real and the thinkable. He assisted this effort, soothing her into a seat with a touch as anxious as if she had been truly something sacred. She sank into a chair and he dropped before her on his knees; she fell back with closed eyes and he buried his face in her lap. There was no way to thank her but this act of prostration, which lasted, in silence, till she laid consenting hands on him, touched his head and stroked it, let her close possession teach him his long blindness. He made the whole fall, as she yet felt it, seem only his—made her, when she rose again, raise him at last, softly, as from the abasement of it. If in each other's eyes now, however, they saw the truth, this truth to Fleda looked harder even than before—all the harder that when, at the very moment she recognized it, he murmured to her ecstatically, in fresh possession of her hands, which he drew up to his breast, holding them tight there with both his own: 'I'm saved, I'm saved,—I *am*! . . .' in the tone he so often had of a great boy at a great game." (189-190.)

In the face of his boyish confidence and his prostration before her, and in the knowledge that his and Mona's engagement has not been settled between them, Fleda breaks away after kissing the hand that Owen "brought . . . down hard on her wrist" and which during the scene still "held her fast." She insists that " 'the great thing is to keep faith' " and that instead of merely provoking Mona to break the engagement, or cruelly breaking it himself, Owen must " 'settle' " the matter with her or " 'at any rate be utterly sure.' " Just as Fleda's kiss of Owen's hand is virtually simultaneous with her break away from him, the very declarations which express the nature and form of her love are those which hazard her own betrayal and defeat by enforcing the formal engagement to Mona and by honoring Mona's feelings. (196-197.)

What moves within Fleda's demand that Owen and Mona mutually "settle" their affair is a vision of utterly reciprocal possession in a loving engagement which is so complete that Fleda, though genuinely desiring Owen, is apprehensive when gripped by it. She is now not so much timid as determined, though her rigor seems stone-like to Owen and later her scruples seem "perversity" to Mrs. Gereth. Her hard, stone-like stare, which earlier accompanied a temperamental timidity, calculated inaccessibility, and a virtually maternal care, is now a manner more intensely articulate, intimate, and firm. It images not only her timidity in the nakedness of exposure but a passionate determination founded on her vision of love, a vision in which engagements are made or terminated through faithful and mutual exchange, not through neglect or manipulation and force, and in which the given form of marriage is transformed into a redeeming one, joining firm independence with protective care (the capacities Owen has begun to display and which

Fleda commands now in heightened intensity) in a harmony of
mutual possession. The vision is beyond Isabel Archer's recognizably traditional conception of marriage in *The Portrait of a
Lady* as subordination of the wife to the husband. Fleda is so
seized by her vision that she can imagine the cruelty of its violation and she can see the possibility that Mona is genuinely in
love: " 'You must be utterly sure. She must love you—how can
she help it?' " (186, 219, 177, 196.)

Moreover, Fleda can imagine the fierceness with which she
would grasp the engagement and the marriage if they were
hers: *never* would Fleda renounce or relinquish her hold.
Her act of renunciation, which she now risks and virtually insures, is matched by a vision of possession which is embodied in
Fleda's hope for marriage, in the possessive gestures of this
scene, and in the denouement when Fleda sends the telegram
and later goes to Poynton to take possession of Owen's gift. The
novel accordingly turns on the paradox that the renunciation
and the hope, the sacrifice and the vision, virtually create each
other; the act of renunciation and the vision of possession are
the source and image of each other.

Neither is complete until Fleda writes her telegram and later
confronts the fire at Poynton. Yet both the sacrifice and the vision
are constituted by or founded on this chapter, including the exclamation and gestures which bring it to a close. Fleda's cry,
" 'Never, never, never!' " sustains in its irony both the vision
which, if realized, would never let her renounce her love, and
the somber impossibility of its actual fulfillment in marriage
with Owen. " '*I* wouldn't give you up!' she said again. He still
had hold of her arm; she took in his blank dread. With a quick
dip of her face she reached his hand with her lips, pressing
them to the back of it with a force that doubled the force of her
words. 'Never, never, never!' she cried; and before he could succeed in seizing her she had turned and, flashing up the stairs,
got away even faster than she had got away from him at Ricks."
(197.) The reference to Ricks is ominous, yet it defines Fleda's
final crisis, for it recalls the unmarried and not-yet resurrected
aunt whose "things" are stored there.

The last chapter presents Fleda with the crisis which tests in
virtual torture her mediation. She has lost Owen in fact, for the

"bribe" that Mrs. Gereth offered to persuade Fleda to act to get Owen—reinstalling the "things" at Poynton in all their splendor—acted too on Mona, and Mona, with her strong will and "natural charm," moved successfully at precisely the same moment when Fleda, refusing to track Owen down in some more direct fashion, sent her telegram instead. Yet Fleda takes pleasure in knowing that Poynton is restored, that her "love had gathered . . . in" the spoils, and in recognizing the triumphant resurrection at Ricks when Mrs. Gereth transforms the aunt's furnishings into a masterpiece. And she is happy in imagining the growing warmth of Owen's and Mona's quickened life together, despite the " 'great accepted pain' " of her own loss which links her to the maiden aunt of Ricks. Though the resolution is imminent as the chapter opens, the situation of the characters and Poynton is new and not fully worked out; the state of affairs at Poynton is not known to Fleda and Mrs. Gereth, the degree of intimacy of Mona and Owen since their marriage is uncertain, Fleda's resignation is not fully tested, and the relation between Mrs. Gereth and Fleda has become "a new one," with Fleda uncertain whether the events have made them "strangers or yokefellows" and anticipating that only now in a final confrontation would they know each other. (212, 235, 253.)

After renewing her admiration for Mrs. Gereth, and paying tribute to Mona's vitality and the promise of Mona's and Owen's marriage, Fleda confronts the final crisis when she receives the letter from Owen which gives the measure of his devotion to her; he offers again a gift, not the whole of Poynton but the most " 'beautiful and precious' " thing in it that nineteenth-century Britain has salvaged from its past, which she is to choose for herself. Owen is still respectful of his mother's and Fleda's taste, but he speaks now from informed, mature experience: he hazards the surmise that the " ' "gem of the collection" ' " is the Maltese Cross, actually a crucifix dating from "the great Spanish period" which Mrs. Gereth, hearing of its "precarious accessibility" at the British possession of Malta, had tracked down and "unearthed." The pin cushion with Fleda's initial, the offer of his hand in marriage, have become another gift: the "thing" made expensive and sacred by the craftsmen of old who fashioned and kept alive the image of sacrifice and passion. It is

Fleda's intention to accept it, as it had become her intention to marry Owen, and she anticipates taking "possession" of the rooms in imagination as she visits Poynton in December to take possession of the gift. And she anticipates cherishing the gift as a "symbol" of what is "finest" in Owen, discovering in the immediacy of possessing it "just what her having it would tell her." (258, 74, 260-261.)

That vision and love are challenged and denied fulfillment, and even their proffered symbol is destroyed, by the neglect of the Gereths and their caretakers, and by the fire and winds of the "cruel cruel night." The disaster intervenes too suddenly at the end and is not sufficiently prepared by ominous undercurrents of the action and by the imagery of fire which begins in the first chapter to play sporadically and too feebly in the texture of the prose. (7, 19, 211, *et al.*)

But Fleda's crisis is nonetheless desperate. A sudden lurch, in the face of the smoke which stuns her on the railroad platform, almost throws her in the path of the departing train. Moments later, after stepping outside the waiting room directly into "a great acrid gust," she meets the temptation of abject surrender to death: She hears "a far-off windy roar" which in her terror she "took for" the roar of "flames a mile away." But they are more pressingly within her, and they "acted upon her as a wild solicitation. 'I must go there.'" But "the same omen" turned into an "appalling check," matching the restraining hand of the station master who holds her back. "Limp and weak," she feels herself "give everything up," but feels then "the raw bitterness of the hope that she might never again in life have to give up so much at such short notice." The challenge is presented again in stark clarity: she asks "'Poynton's *gone?*'" and hears the station master's answering question: "'What can you call it, miss, if it ain't really saved?'" But in the world where everything, like breakfast at Waterbath, is punctual, Fleda looks up from the dark of her despair to distinguish in the "thick swim" of "things" the face of a clock and asks if there is an up train. She is quickened into life to return to modern London, in the era of Waterbath, and to the somber contingencies, the next challenge to her will and imagination, to which the novel impels her. (264-266, 3.)

To her tipsy, indifferent father's apartment? To the spare room at her sister's to turn out paintings? To Ricks? The future is imaged as the "London labyrinth" and is left uncertain and unknown. But Fleda is in possession of the past in the only way finally it can be known and redeemed: in memory and in art; in the things which are its records and in the life and imagination which can confront and cherish the past while accepting the uncertain future in the willingness to live and shape it. The past is embodied now most enduringly in the triumph which Mrs. Gereth makes of the maiden aunt's things at Ricks and which is revealed in Fleda's recognition of it: the "impression somehow of something dreamed and missed, something reduced, relinquished, resigned: the poetry, as it were, of something sensibly *gone*." And she has the memory embodied in the letter Owen sends her, his devotion articulate in the offer of a gift which is a symbol of the sacrifice he now shares in recognizing, can cherish, and now can name. And as the novel moves to join with the future opening up beyond it, Fleda's will and imagination stand in expressed possession of the saving strength to live. (249.)

The Spoils of Poynton enacts James's tribute to the beauties of the past but along with that, as Wright Morris has been almost alone in insisting,[48] James's somberly firm commitment to the conditions and prospects of his own time. In his "London Notes" of 1897, reporting on the triumph of modern vulgarity and the "commercial instinct," common to Britain and America but epitomized in Victoria's Sixtieth Jubilee, James wrote explicitly of the historical crisis which he had dramatized in *The Spoils of Poynton,* and he personified in Poor History the sacrifice made by anyone who must pay loving tribute to the past while coming to accept the conditions of the present, the sacrifice of which Fleda Vetch was made the mediating agent. It is possible, James wrote, that the "triumph of vulgarity" was the "triumph of the inevitable" and that vulgarity, instead of being an excrescence on social reality was "the show" itself "pushed aloft by deep forces" which had to be confronted and acknowledged. "We miss, we regret the old 'style' of history," he wrote, but "the style would be there if we let it," despite the fact that the present age "has a manner of its own that disconcerts, that

48 Morris, *The Territory Ahead* (New York, 1958), p. 190.

swamps it." Poor History must meet "these conditions. . . .
She must accept vulgarity or perish." "Some day doubtless," he
continued, "she *will* perish, but for a little while longer she
remembers and struggles." Poor History "becomes indeed, as
we look up Piccadilly in the light of this image, perhaps rather
more dramatic than ever—at any rate more pathetic, more
noble in her choked humiliation. Then even as we pity her we
try perhaps to bring her round, to make her understand a little
better." [49] Fleda's sacrifice, James's mannered style, and the
drama of which they are the instruments, encompass that crisis
and understanding and create the vision which authenticates
them.

[49] *Notes on Novelists,* pp. 432-433.

CHAPTER THREE

The "Religion of Doing"

The priest departs, the divine literatus comes.
Walt Whitman, *Democratic Vistas*

Inquiry occupies an intermediate and mediating place in the development of an experience.
John Dewey, *Essays in Experimental Logic*

Analyzing then consists in expressing a thing in terms of what is not it. All analysis is thus a translation, a development into symbols, a representation taken from successive points of view. . . . In its eternally unsatisfied desire to embrace the object around which it is condemned to turn, analysis multiplies endlessly the points of view in order to complete the ever incomplete representation, varies interminably the symbols with the hope of perfecting the always imperfect translation.
Henri Bergson, *The Creative Mind*

THE "RELIGION OF DOING"

TOGETHER the *Portrait* and the *Spoils* help define the crisis for the imagination which was the matrix of all James's master-pieces but which emerged with sharpened intensity in the 1890's, when first the failure of *The Bostonians, The Princess Casamassima,* and *The Tragic Muse* to gain critical or popular approval after 1886, and then James's failure as playwright on the London stage in the early '90's, gave special urgency to any reformulation of his role or any reorientation of his craft. Complex though the sources of the crisis were in James's personal and professional life, its impingement on his fiction is best revealed in the challenge, at once stimulating and threatening, which it presented to his form.*

His expectations for the creativity of form in actual life and for its creative function in art were never single, and the *Portrait* and the *Spoils* both show with what force James questioned the validity of form even in works which display brilliantly his devotion to form in the novel and moreover associate form intimately with responsible commitment and moral action. It is the interaction of two pressures which defines the crisis for his imagination: the impulse to challenge form against the determination to create and perfect it. The one impelled him to recognize not only the possible corruptions of form but the limits to the effectiveness of any form. The other impelled him to affirm the necessity of form for the achievement of creative purpose and suggested, for the art of fiction, still untried opportunities for formal experiment in the resources of the novel and those of painting and the drama.

Two works which span the decade of the '90's, *The Aspern Papers* (1888) and *The Sacred Fount* (1901), project the crisis in its boldest outlines, not only because they display the conventions of Gothicism but because they do so in a way—namely the mode of parody or caricature—which heightens their display of form and accentuates James's self-conscious con-

---

* References enclosed in parentheses in the text are to James's fiction and, unless otherwise indicated, to the New York Edition. Other footnotes appear at the bottom of the page.

cern about his relation to his fiction and his form's relation to what goes on there. These tales, like the *Portrait* and the *Spoils,* show that James's detachment and objectivity—whether that of the watcher and painter, or of the collector and dramatist, or of the historian—are not the index of severance from his world but of engagement with it, an engagement deriving from the fact that the form of his fiction implicated him in its action, however disturbing the motives or outcome, however tortured James's feelings in recognizing the interpenetration of his commerce and his art, of predatory acquisition and the triumph of form. The intimacy of his involvement is all the more close for being implicit in the tales, and all the more stunning for associating him with strikingly odd companions. One is the nameless editor (the "publishing scoundrel") who vainly courts a diffident middle-aged woman and bargains deceitfully with her aged aunt so as to get hold of the valuable papers which record the older woman's affair with the dead poet Jeffrey Aspern. The other is the nameless "I" of *The Sacred Fount* who spends an entire novel in a guessing game about other persons' affairs of passion, only to have his structure of hypotheses—his " 'houses of cards,' " his " 'creation' "—challenged if not shattered by the woman who had helped him construct it.

The final test for the intimacy of these associations is, of course, the two tales themselves when considered within the field of relevance which they establish in the surrounding data. Within that field of relevance, James's criticism yields access to the tales and helps gauge the urgency of the crisis which challenged his imagination, as his art moved in the direction indicated by the *Spoils:* from a mode of representation to the more expressionistic form of the three novels of the "major phase," from an art which *projects* a representational vision to one which more boldly *constructs* a vision and enacts a sacrifice. *The Aspern Papers* is best understood in the light of two groups of critical essays. One includes those written in the 1880's and gathered as *Partial Portraits* (1888), where James explores the relation of pictorial and analytic strategies to the generic act of representation. The other group comprises three later essays (published in 1897, 1899, and 1914) on George Sand, that veritable paramour of the Muse whose fiction first and later her "papers" presented to James the most problematical case of the relation of autobiography to art. *The Sacred Fount* is best seen in a perspective which includes this same background but encompasses also the later critical essays (the Prefaces, James's essay on Shakespeare's *Tempest* in 1907, and items collected in *Notes on Novelists* in 1914), where the vision worked out in *The Sacred Fount* is worked into James's mature criticism. In *The Sacred Fount* itself James reduced his art to its elemental absurdities by creating an abyss between the world of art and the actualities beyond it, yet in the act of revealing these absurdities he reconstituted his art as a radically creative process. It became more a *structure* than a representation, reconstructing the world in its mockery of it and founding creative form on an enacted sacrifice which at once measures and becomes the expense of vision.

[I]

THE ART OF REPRESENTATION

WHETHER the novel should be a "structure built up of picture cards" rather than an imitative transcript or "excision from life" was precisely the question, James wrote in 1884, which agitated French writers in the nineteenth century. The question in effect was whether fiction was founded on an act of *imitation* or on an act of *construction*—whether the intent and effect of representing reality in the sense of imitating it were paramount, or whether the aim to make or construct reality was dominant. James raised the issue in his essay on Turgenief in the course of distinguishing Turgenief's novels, founded on character, from novels founded on a plot, a formal architecture, or an imposed choreography; he distinguished Turgenief's practice from fiction founded on a *construct* of "picture cards." James felt that in England and America the question was too seldom asked. With some show of diffidence, he declared his preference for Turgenief's manner.[1]

It is the question, however, not James's preference, which governs the collection of essays, *Partial Portraits*. James no doubt genuinely preferred Turgenief's fiction, but he knew that the two options were not mutually exclusive; before stating his preference he had held up the examples of Balzac and Scott as combining the transcription of life with "architecture" or "composition," and his own *Portrait of a Lady* showed that plotted story and materials taken from life were compatible in practice.

Moreover, James's opposition of a transcription to "a structure" is ambivalent, for James's concerns are polarized not along one axis but along two. One opposition sets the *realism* of the new continental writers against the storied *romance* which builds pleasant "picture cards" at the expense of confronting life as closely as Turgenief and others did. A second and more important polarity, however, is that displayed *among* the new continental realists themselves: the opposition between Turge-

[1] *Partial Portraits*, pp. 315-316.

nief's "air of reality," which deferred to character portrayal, and the novel in which pictorial "composition" or "structure" took precedence. James's distinctions were founded not on clear-cut genres but on processes of creation whatever the genre employed; it was in *Partial Portraits,* in the concluding essay, "The Art of Fiction," that he cautioned against overemphasizing the distinction between the *novel* and the *romance,* envying the French because they had only one name for both and declaring that "I can think of no obligation to which the 'romancer' would not be held equally with the novelist. . . ." In opposing an imitative transcription to novels displaying an imposed "composition," which he gathered loosely under the notion of a "structure of picture-cards," James did not define a choice between available alternatives but dramatized two pressures bearing on his art. *Partial Portraits* is founded on the tension between James's commitment to the priority of form and his desire nonetheless to portray the actualities of experience, and the essays display his effort to work out the ramifications of his commitment to form in the vocabulary of representational pictorial art. The pressure behind the essays is generated by James's admiration for Turgenief's "air of reality" but also by his tacit recognition of his own manner and what his shared with the method he called "analytic" in two of the "new votaries of realism," Daudet and Maupassant. In their art the acts of observation and construction were joined in a distinctly pictorial form, the representational mode which is the subject of scrutiny in *Partial Portraits.*[2]

James used the term *representation* for the generic act of rendering reality in the arts, despite the fact that on one important occasion in *The Portrait of a Lady* he had, in Ralph's words, opposed "representation" to "expression," associating "representation" pejoratively with dramatic pretense, the forced appearances of satisfaction kept up by Isabel after her marriage, the "mask" that amounted to an "advertisement" for the Osmond whose delegate or "representative" she had become.[3] James's play with the word in the novel indicates his awareness of the complexities involved in its usage. But in *Partial Por-*

2 *Ibid.,* pp. 298, 394, 106.
3 *Novels and Tales,* IV, 143-144.

traits, as in *The Portrait,* he holds particularly to representational painting—in the narrower sense of three-dimensional or illusionist painting—as a governing model for literature, rather than to specifically dramatic representation; the cast of his vocabulary is predominantly pictorial. Yet he aimed, within that particular vocabulary, to explore the *generic* mode of representation in the arts and in doing so James gave increasing emphasis to the constructive act entailed in the artistic process—to caricature, analysis, and dramatic projection as against imitative strategies.

From the opening essay about Emerson's "search for . . . a manner" to "The Art of Fiction" at the end, the volume affirms the importance of form in art and asserts the priority of form over moral preoccupations. The tribute to the "magnificence of [the novel's] form" is based on the novel's openness to a variety of moral points of view, whether already manifest or promised in the history of the genre, but the tribute is based also on the sufficiency of formal perfection as a legitimate end in itself. Moreover, the volume consistently summons up representational painting as a model for writing, as when criticizing Emerson's failure to give a full portrait of his Aunt Mary within her "frame" and when criticizing George Eliot for presenting a "moralized fable" instead of "a picture of life," allowing ruminative "meditation" to blur "the sharpness of portraiture." [4]

The vitality of the essays derives, however, from divergent conceptions of the nature of representation. The opening essays, the later pages on Turgenief, and "The Art of Fiction" are governed by one conception, the familiar view that representation is fundamentally an act of imitation, at odds though this conception is with James's practice in *The Portrait of a Lady.* The intensely personal and "direct impression of life" which James claimed for the novel is an imitative correspondence to life. Trollope presented a "picture" rather than a "story," but he avoided compositional effects and his artifices, subordinate to verisimilitude, present a "replica" of a society or a class. Turgenief's pen, in effect, *traced* a given figure; the novelist, with the historian, aims to transcribe actuality; the writer's

4 *Partial Portraits,* pp. 33, 407-408, 15, 50-53.

method is perfectly analogous with that of the painter and through "solidity of specification" renders the "look," the "surface," and the "substance"—the full "illusion" of actuality. This argument culminates in "The Art of Fiction" in the protest that the novel is indeed a form but is an organic rather than "a factitious, artificial form" founded on mere "ingenuity" and the alteration or "rearrangement" of actuality—that it need not be a "substitute" or mere "convention" but can be a form which is "a living thing" in close and full "correspondence with life." [5]

Counter to this imitative conception of representation is another, founded on the act of construction or manipulation. This second conception emerges at times tacitly in brief remarks—as when James takes Trollope to task for throwing aside the "mask" and costume of historian by making explicit reference to the inescapable "make-believe" he is presenting, the "arbitrary thing" he is contriving and telling.[6] But the second conception appears most fully in the volume's more extended discussions of the relation of morals to art, the function of form, and the relation of the artist to his work.

Time and again in the essays there are clear suggestions that art is morally dangerous, irresponsible, or immoral, either because of its content or because of the very nature of artistic manipulation. The painterly "plastic" manner of composing is "irresponsible." Maupassant's triumphs, "so licentious and so impeccable," are truly alarming; they are tolerable only because in the happily pluralistic world of the novel some other "point of view will yield another [*viz.*, wholesome] perfection." The famous statements near the end of "The Art of Fiction" that "the moral sense and the artistic sense lie very near together" in the "quality of the mind of the producer," and that the quality of the work of art will depend on the quality of its author's mind, define the dramatic ambiance, the moral ambivalence, of the creative imagination. Indeed, the preceding paragraph concedes the possibility that moral corruption inheres necessarily in the conscious practice of art and derives in fact from the nature of moral courage. Insisting that the diffidence

5 *Ibid.*, pp. 384, 106, 131, 380, 390, 397-398, 402.
6 *Ibid.*, pp. 116-117.

prevailing in the English novel was debilitating and that it evidenced the absence of moral courage in the novel, James declared that the continental novel by contrast was morally courageous because "the essence of moral energy" is to confront "the whole field" of behavior. James then added: "To what degree a purpose in a work of art is a source of corruption I shall not attempt to inquire; the one that seems to me least dangerous is the purpose of making a perfect work." In sum, there are purposes that are morally dangerous, perhaps corrupting, including even the aim of formal perfection, to say nothing of more risky objectives. James's position in *Partial Portraits* encloses a moral drama, at best only tentatively resolved, with James endorsing a position but feeling compunctions about it, and with the prospect of moral complicity on the artist's part still vivid to the author of *The Portrait of a Lady*.[7]

Clearly James's moral anxiety in these essays has connections with his insistence on the priority of form. For while James could easily praise his friend Stevenson's "essential love of style" and defend his "manner" even if some thought it "a manner for manner's sake," he recorded in his essay on Turgenief that the Russian did not take to James's own fiction because "the manner was more apparent than the matter." This is to confess that for all James's respect for Turgenief's example, and similar though their fiction might be, James's fiction was too architectural or mannered, too conspicuously composed, to measure up. In fundamental ways, their strategies diverged. Moreover, there were differences in style and strategy among the continental writers, joined though they were in opposition to the prevailing moralism of English fiction. James gave protracted and admiring attention to two of them, Daudet and Maupassant, whose methods contrasted even more than did his own to Turgenief's and clearly ran the very risks which "The Art of Fiction" endorsed while minimizing: the moral energy which might corrupt, the pictorial method which was irresponsible, the perfection of visual form which could become too conspicuously "apparent." What is significant is that James's discussion of their form, and of their authors' relation to the fiction, taxes the terminology of imitation and reveals a formal strategy

7 *Ibid.*, pp. 49, 51, 287, 406.

124

which is more dramatic though it can be nonetheless visual and lies within what James called "the arts of representation." In discussing the "analytic" method of Daudet and Maupassant, James reveals a conception of form which is simultaneously an intimate expression of the author and a constructed vision.[8]

The principal fascination in Daudet's case was also a source of danger: he was a "master of composition" whose very proficiency risked "the factitious"; his was a "pictorial point of view" that often settled for the conventional and produced "a mechanical doll," a "clever water colour" instead of a complete illusion. It was in discussing Daudet's mastery of the novel of manners as his mastery of analytic perception that James defined the new literary modes of continental literature: "the analytic consideration of appearances" or the "tendency to resolve its discoveries into pictorial form" which called for "a closer notation" of the world of appearances. It was Daudet's triumph that he "writes with a brush" and "has caught . . . a particular pitch of manners . . . the picture shines and lives." He could balance " 'in happy equilibrium the qualities of observation and the qualities of style' " (James quoted Zola's encomium). In *Les Rois en Exile* he achieved indeed "a finished picture." *Le Nabob,* by contrast, lacked total effect: it was a "series of almost diabolically clever pictures." Yet Daudet's style in both the finished and the diabolical pictures was one which James admired fervently even though he would not choose to write in so transparently self-revelatory a manner. And while the *style* and the *form* of a work need not be identical (James had written earlier that George Sand's mistake had been to think style a substitute for form), he saw that in Daudet's fiction the style was a direct function of the analytic and pictorial form.[9]

Although Daudet remained "more an observer than an inventor," his style was remarkably active; James was impressed by what he called Daudet's "gymnastics of observation" and found them difficult to describe. The difficulty lies in the fact that these "gymnastics" elude the terminology of imitation be-

[8] *Ibid.*, pp. 140, 299, 206.
[9] *Ibid.*, pp. 197-198, 206, 214-215, 203, 234, 212-213; *French Poets and Novelists*, p. 180.

cause they relate not so much to the subject observed as to the author who performs with the subject and to the reader who must be enabled to see it. When describing the style, James did not abandon pictorial terms but did reach for more dramatic metaphor: the style "defies convention, tradition, homogeneity, prudence, and sometimes even syntax, gathers up every patch of colour, every colloquial note, that will help to illustrate, and moves . . . triumphantly along, like a clever woman in the costume of an eclectic age." This "mode of expression" is not "the old-fashioned drawing in black and white" because it "never rests" but is always "panting, straining, fluttering, trying to add a little more, to produce the effect which will make the reader see with his eyes, or rather with the marvelous eyes of Alphonse Daudet." [10]

Such a style renders a subject but not so much by imitating it as by constructing a lens for seeing it; the prose does not simply reveal patches of color but gathers them up and builds up effects upon them; "solidity of specification," and black and white contours, even the syntax of the idiom are being consumed in a constructive effort to engage the reader in an act of vision through the medium of Alphonse Daudet.

This conception of representation is impressive, as an anticipation of James's own stylistic development but also in its own right as a theory of representation in art. But its reminder of Daudet's intimate presence has profound implications when set against the two preceding sections of the essay, which draw attention to the "personal note" in Daudet's "eminently expressive manner." For James had discerned in Daudet a complex fusion which he thought "modern": a combination of ingratiating "sociability" and "light comicality" with the depiction of "the miseries and cruelties of life." And James had gone on in the next section, with Daudet's charm and the reader's pleasure in mind, to conceive representation in art as the exploitive and sacrificial fount of entertainment, a conception which governed James's attitude toward the effect of his own art.[11]

He took note of Charles Dudley Warner's contention that entertainment should be the novel's purpose and countered with

10 *Partial Portraits*, pp. 217, 232-233.
11 *Ibid.*, pp. 210, 219-220.

a double assertion: "the main object of the novel" is *not* to entertain but "to represent life," yet "the *effect* of a novel" or of "any work of art," *is* "to entertain." To produce an illusion in art, he went on, is to create a "miraculous enlargement of experience" for the reader: "The greater the art, the greater the miracle, and the more certain also the fact that we have been entertained—in the best meaning of that word at least, which signifies that we have been living at the expense of someone else." The "someone else" proves to be the characters in the fiction who undergo the miseries and cruelties of life, and pay for the entertainment of those who watch. The expressed charm of Daudet's prose, and the "enlargement of experience" and entertainment of the reader, are derived from the victimization of the figures depicted in the fiction.[12]

In the next essay James pursued the connections among author, form, and characters in the case of Maupassant, the "impersonal" master in whose pictorial art James found the action of analysis—and a form of entertainment gained at its characters' expense—even though the techniques of enumeration and explicit explanation were ruled out. And James not only discerned the action of analysis but the presence of the author who practiced it. Maupassant did not utilize explicit explanations nor did he employ the "selective comparative process" that characterizes the analytic mode in other cases, but this fact did not justify Maupassant's own theory (James quoted the preface to *Pierre et Jean*) that the writer should present the illusion of life as he sees it without " 'complicated explanations' " and " 'dissertations on motives,' " and that " 'psychology should be hidden in a book, as it is hidden in reality. . . .' " James countered by pointing out that what is hidden in life and in art—and what is taken for substantially real—depend on the aims and expectations of the observers. For one observer, motives will be on the surface of life, from another they will be hidden; for one person, the "relations, and conditions" of an "incident" or "attitude" will be virtually a part of the thing itself, while for another the thing itself will be discrete and isolated from its motives. In Maupassant, sexual motives are neither disconnected from character and incident nor hidden: "peeping behind the

12 *Ibid.*, pp. 227-228.

curtain," Maupassant engages in analysis even though analytic enumeration and explanation are missing. He seems simply "unscrupulously, almost impudently" to catch his subject because he expresses it so swiftly "by an admirable system of simplification" that his style lacks the *ostensible* techniques of deliberate analysis.[13]

The analytic process was nonetheless visible and James discussed the phenomenon in terms of dramatic projection, or self-dramatization. If one argued (as Maupassant did) that the analytic novelist could do no more than cloak "his own peculiarities" in the "costume of the figure analysed," this was equally true, James claimed, of "any other manner of writing," including Maupassant's own "objective" method of "painting from the outside." It is more difficult to "convey the impression of something that is not one's self," but James suggested that the effort is "delusive at bottom" and that Maupassant, "remarkably objective and impersonal though he is, has not kept himself outside of his books. They speak of him eloquently. . . ." [14]

The impersonal manner, accordingly, as well as the ingratiating "personal note" of Daudet, evidenced an analytic penetration of experience and yielded the dramatic presence of the writer, though the evidence in style and form was strikingly different. Instead of the sociability and charm, there was the "hard, short, intelligent gaze," the "bird's-eye view contempt" of Maupassant's "artful brevity"; instead of the "gymnastics of observation" in Daudet there was the "studied sobriety" of Maupassant's diction, and there were his phrases so "ingeniously cast" that every epithet is "a paying piece." Maupassant's art did not depend on " 'plot' " and rendered "the uncomposed, unrounded look of life, with its accidents, its broken rhythm," yet the "picture" is characteristically "dominant" over the material, and the form to an extreme degree is manipulative and constructive. Maupassant's form includes the rigid economy of means which it gains at the cost of excluding the ethical dimensions of experience, suppressing or bypassing some conditions of life so completely as to give the form the "tinge of the arbitrary." And the form includes a rigor of observation that is de-

13 *Ibid.*, pp. 251, 256-259.
14 *Ibid.*, p. 259.

cidedly cruel to its victims. "The author fixes a hard eye on some small spot of human life . . . , takes up the particle, and squeezes it either till it grimaces or till it bleeds"; when he came nearest to geniality (in *La Maison Tellier*), it is the "geniality of the showman exhilarated by the success with which he . . . makes his mannikins (and especially his woman-kins) caper and squeak, and who after the performance tosses them into their box with the irreverence of a practiced hand." [15]

In the essays on Daudet and Maupassant, moral insights and pictorial considerations join to define an art of manipulation and deliberately constructed effects within the aims of representational art. While neither James's intentions nor his practice should be identified wholly or exclusively with those of Daudet or Maupassant, his response to their example is intimate, and it is more complicated and profound than the relatively set reaction to Stevenson and Turgenief and to the caricaturists who are the only graphic artists treated directly in *Partial Portraits*. Yet the essay on Du Maurier and the caricaturists has an importance which is given emphasis by its position in the volume: it follows the essay on Turgenief (which is thus sandwiched between those on Daudet and Maupassant and the essay on caricature) and is the last chapter on specific figures before the concluding essay on "The Art of Fiction." In the essay on George Du Maurier, James distinguished the good-natured deftness of pictorial representation in Du Maurier and the artists of *Punch* from the "strangely expressive" caricatures of the French, admiring the English draughtsman's "rare pictorial character" (memorable long after the "morality" was forgotten) and preferring his "quiet gradual movements" to the "violent action" in the caricatures of Cham and "his wonderful colleague, Daumier." The Frenchman's art is characteristically "farcical and grotesque"—"at bottom it is almost horrible." Indeed, "it has been claimed that Cham's drawings prove the French to be a cruel people." Yet there is more than perfunctory concession in James's recognition of the power of these grotesque French caricatures: their "rare pictorial character" is but an extension of the visual mode they share with Du Maurier, the strategy of caricature in which formal contortions and

15 *Ibid.*, pp. 251-252, 262-263, 278-280, 285, 279, 266, 269.

analytic simplifications are dominant. James's inclusion of the essay on caricaturists in a volume which explores the nature of "representation" is his recognition of the role which the formal strategies of caricature play, as Professor Gombrich has shown, in the perfection of representational techniques in art. James's tribute to the power of the French is as significant as his preference for Du Maurier. And while James's essay on Turgenief is a moving memorial to an admired master who placed characterization above constructive form, the same essay includes near its end a compassionate tribute to Flaubert. He, unlike Turgenief, failed, in James's estimation (with the exception of the masterpiece *Madame Bovary*), but his failure was heroically tragic and sprang from his "passion for perfection of form." [16]

The double tribute to Turgenief and Flaubert reminds the reader, as the essays do more assertively elsewhere, that there is more than one legitimate strategy within the art of representation, including those wherein readers are entertained and the form is wrought at the expense of the characters and materials. The essays define an art in which form is prior to subject, in which form becomes involved with moral problems not only because it treats given moral issues but because it creates them in the very process of artistic manipulation, and in which "representation" is founded not on imitation but on composition, construction, expression, dramatic projection, analysis. James's scrutiny of the "gymnastics" of effect in one writer, and the "objectivity," the deliberately constructed sentences, and the "artful brevity" of another, reveals in both cases the intimate presence of the author. And it reveals in James's own case a consideration of important components of his own craft and manner which were to become more pronounced later in his career. The *Partial Portraits* are an intimate part of James's own autobiography.

No case, however, posed so intriguingly the interrelation of autobiography to art as the case of George Sand. She was an admittedly extreme case (for she lived "in all her chambers—not merely in the showroom of the shop"), yet James found that

16 *Ibid.*, pp. 352, 372, 358, 336. Gombrich, *Art and Illusion*, pp. 330-358; see especially pp. 343, 345, 350, 355. James, *Partial Portraits*, p. 319.

her procedures typified "the relation between experience and art at large." She wrote countless novels but obliged also with a memoir, *L'histoire de ma Vie;* she had illicit affairs with talented men and made novels out of them in *Indiana* and *Elle et Lui.* In other words, she supplied abundant materials. In the essay on Sand in James's *French Poets and Novelists* (1878), he treated the aspects of her career that had fascinated him for decades: her knack of improvisation and her "peculiar want of veracity"; the candor and fluency which protest so much as to be implausible; her combination of masculinity and femininity; her need and desire for money which led her to the career of writing; her glorification of passion while being too "explicit" and "business-like" in tabulating it; her devotion to style; and her paradoxically distant relation to the experience she drew on so transparently: "we imagine she outlived experience, morally, to a degree which made her feel . . . as if she were dealing with the history of another person." When James had written a brief notice on her death in 1876, he did not express his often strong diffidence about the "painful side" of "emptying table drawers after an eminent writer's death," nor anticipate "feeling as one who has broken open a cabinet or rummaged an old desk"; he simply wondered at her "fertility" and stated that "her admirers will be anxious to learn whether it has not bequeathed some documents—memoirs, reminiscences, or narratives more explicitly fictitious—which are yet to see the light." [17]

Two decades later, such papers, bequeathed by George Sand and gathered by editors of the *Revue de Paris,* did see the light, and in the face of her letters to Musset and Sainte-Beuve James wrote three protracted essays which are among his most brilliant on the mysteries of "the relation between experience and art at large." Her letters, he said, reawakened an earlier admiration for the woman, indeed "stirred . . . the ashes of an early ardour," and while his reactions as reader were a mixture of warmth and "chill," he confessed enjoying the "renewal" of his fascination. Her case inspired derision but

[17] *Notes on Novelists,* pp. 182, 161; *French Poets and Novelists,* pp. 155-156, 160-161, 166, 175, 180, 184; *Parisian Sketches,* p. 134; "Balzac's Letters," *French Poets and Novelists,* p. 119; *Parisian Sketches,* p. 177.

horror and compassion as well by being both grotesquely comic and tragic, and James's comments are all the more illuminating of his own fiction for the fact that by 1897 he was patently reading Sand's case in the light not only of her novels and papers but of his own tragi-comedy, *The Aspern Papers*. That story had been occasioned by the effort of an American sea captain to get some "Shelley documents" from Byron's mistress, the aging Jane Clairmont, in Florence; but James had carefully shifted the setting for his story to Venice, which had been not only a favorite haunt of Byron but the scene of the love affair between Musset and Sand, the one episode of her career that most fascinated and appalled James. James had commented on the affair in the essay on Musset which opens *French Poets and Novelists,* but his later remarks are more pungently revealing. In her letters, she had bequeathed "to the great snickering public" the "shreds and relics of unutterable things." [18]

James asked in stunned amazement what could be the motive for using her affairs in her fiction, and for publishing her letters, but in a clever dialogue with himself he dismissed sheer promiscuity and egotism as major considerations; her material served instead "for the encouragement of the artist nature," showing that no tragic suffering is so great as to preclude its assimilation in art, and presenting "a frank plea for the intellectual and in some degree the commercial profit . . . of a store of erotic reminiscence." If she " 'used' " her affair with Chopin, she did use it "brilliantly"; and "the artist in general," though anyone but Byron would acknowledge "limits" to what he will divulge, customarily "arrives at a sense of what he may have seen or felt, or said or suffered, by working it out as a subject. . . ." [19]

One detail was particularly striking to James: the ease with which one lover (Musset's physician) replaced another (the ailing Musset himself) with the latter's endorsement: Dr. Pagello became "a lover in the presence and with the exalted

18 *Notes on Novelists*, pp. 160-161, 207, 211, 177; *The Art of the Novel,* pp. 162-163.
19 *Notes on Novelists*, pp. 162, 223, 229.

approval of an immediate predecessor—an alternative representative of the part. . . ." [20]

Outright reversals and mixtures of roles, however, received closer attention from James. Musset was younger than Sand by six years, and by comparison was somewhat feminine; George Sand was the epitome at once of masculine domination and maternal supremacy. As the male she was like the "great statesman and the great poet" who are applauded by history as they exercise a prerogative of "free appropriation and consumption" of female consorts. Yet as female she was strangely "maternal" in nursing along her affairs; she was indeed the "supersensuous grandmother" of the affair. Possibly she felt the "duty of avenging on the unscrupulous race of men their immemorial selfish success with the plastic race of women." [21]

Revealing though the materials were, the letters remained mere "shreds and relics" of the "unutterable things," and significantly James found that the actualities of Sand's affairs remained shrouded also in the fiction which used them. Her "manner" derived from the experience yet paradoxically obscured it. It "confounds itself with the conditions in which it was exercised," and in the fusion the "liberality and variety" of her temperament and experience do "overflow into beautiful prose," but the manner does so at the expense of the actualities which inspired them. Her fictional account of her affair in *Elle et Lui* is "told as if in a last remove from the facts, by someone reporting what he has read or what he has had from another." The difficult, unpleasant facts are forgotten or blurred; "everything but feelings" remains dim. "We recognize that we shall never know the original narrator and that the actual introducer is the only one we can deal with . . . we can never confront her with her own informant." Her manner, then, becomes a revealing screen between her imagination, which has outlived the experience, and the experience on which it draws: the actualities of experience are kept from sight by the very artistry which exploits and partially exhibits them.[22]

20 *Ibid.*, p. 174.
21 *Ibid.*, pp. 169, 172, 178-179.
22 *Ibid.*, pp. 173, 184.

James spoke regretfully of this situation, as if it challenged the reader's legitimate curiosity but also as if it arose from a sadly unavoidable gap between the person who underwent the experience and the "introducer" who later recounted it—a chasm which remained unbridgeable even when the two were the same person and when (as Mérimée was astonished to discover) the original experience and the task of writing were close in time because the writer was wont to leave her lover's bed at dawn to resume writing. Yet James also expressed revulsion at her utilizing the experience at all, as if the methodical "worker" at six A.M. should be obliterated or expiated; and he suggested that the enterprising worker could be "drowned" only in the "oceans of ink" that Sand's pen produced. What James's remarks suggest, whether accurately or not with respect to George Sand, is an expiatory art that dissolves the utilitarian practices of its maker in an ocean of prose which introduces recognizably the intimate experience of its author yet fails to reveal it fully.[23]

James remained mystified finally as to how "the graceless facts . . . confound themselves with the beautiful spirit." In referring, however, to her art as itself "a second echo" or second "edition" of the subject, instead of the first edition that one hoped for, he revealed the deep if tangential connection he saw between the process *within* the craft of George Sand and the struggle *outside* it between the artist and the editor or critic who might (like James) confront and try to penetrate her art: art itself is an "edition" of experience; artists are editors. It is because in this view art is an "edition" that James's comments on the predicament and aims of the editor and historian not only refer to their actual editorial tasks but have a bearing also on the craft of imaginative writing; he described a struggle between editor and artist which is at the same time a dialectical process within the creative act itself. Though it was regrettable that Sand's style cut loose from its subject like a "balloon" or "soap bubble," there was further compensation beyond the fact that it dissolved the crudities of its execution in ink: there was the possibility that it might become a fortified refuge for the author when and if he were besieged by editors or historians.

23 *Ibid.*, p. 185.

This prospect James first outlined as a program for the future, then declared that it was George Sand's triumph to have achieved it already.[24]

Encounters between denuded writers and the public will remain accidental, he predicted, but they cannot be avoided, should be regularly organized, and should "take their place among the triumphs of civilization." James insisted that there *are* "secrets for privacy and silence" but demanded that they, like efforts to betray or reveal them, be put to the test of dramatic and mortal combat: let the privacy "only be cultivated on the part of the hunted creature with even half the method that the love of sport—or call it the historic sense—is cultivated on the part of the investigator"; under these conditions, he went on, "the game will be fair and the two face to face." He concluded: "Then the cunning of the inquirer, envenomed with resistance, will exceed in subtlety and ferocity anything we today conceive, and the pale forewarned victim, with every track covered, every paper burnt and every letter unanswered, will, in the tower of art, the invulnerable granite, stand, without a sally, the siege of all the years." George Sand did answer and publish letters and did make rash sorties outside the tower, yet it is "in the citadel of style" that "she continues to hold out." [25]

It is such a struggle between craft and precaution—such a ferocious game and such a sacrifice of pale forewarned victims —that launches *The Aspern Papers*. And if James's imagination was enlisted in that story to protect the artist's privacy and the intimacy of passion from editorial encroachment, it was enlisted too in the editor's or historian's effort to use them and bring them to light. In fact it is the role of piratical historian that James assumed in writing the preface to the story for the New York collection which he helped edit. In that preface James was clearly raking over his own past as writer (to say nothing of Jane Clairmont's), and when acknowledging the "vicious practice" of inventing an American Byron, he compared his illicit fictive trick to "smuggling." When he wrote that he was glad he never actually met the aging Miss Clair-

24 *Ibid.*, pp. 186, 183-184.
25 *Ibid.*, pp. 168-169.

mont, though with luck he "might have seen her in the flesh," the reason he gave was as callously utilitarian as anything declared by the narrator, the Publishing Scoundrel, in the story itself: the "fount of waters" certainly would already have "run dry." Some parts of his own past, he wrote, are injured when reconsidered: they respond "with agitation and pain" to the "re-visiting, re-appropriating impulse" while the recalling imagination "heaves as with the disorder of drinking it deeply in," as if the historical imagination, at work in the preface, were desecrating a grave, a crime charged against the narrator in the story. Indeed, the opening remarks of the preface pretend to boast of having penetrated some provinces of the Italian past, but acknowledge that the conquest amounted to a mere glimpse into a very few chambers of the past because of a combination of tact and incapacity on the part of Caesar. Offered ostensibly everything in our intercourse with the past we politely neglect, anxiously fail, to take it up; "we have entered, we have seen, we are charmed" by the Italian setting but we Caesars do no more than "peep" into a paltry "two or three chambers . . . with the rest of the case escaping our penetration"; before "the great historic complexity at least—penetration fails." James's act in writing *The Aspern Papers,* as he acknowledged in the preface, is analogous to the deeds of the Publishing Scoundrel who narrates it; for the ambition of both to penetrate, and their failure completely to do so, is revealed by the Narrator who rented rooms in Juliana's house.[26]

It was James's concern with his own art—and with what George Sand's, Daudet's, Maupassant's, and the caricaturists' revealed generally about the workings of the imagination— that gave authenticity to the first-person narrative technique and to the Gothic conventions which are utilized in *The Aspern Papers.* James's avoidance of the fictive first-person narrator later in his full-length fiction, and his warnings against the autobiographical method early and late in his career, do not rule the method out as a vital resource of fiction but define hazards accompanying its use. Though he warned against "the terrible fluidity of self-revelation" in the preface to *The Am-*

[26] *The Art of the Novel,* pp. 166, 168, 160-162.

bassadors and in a later letter to H. G. Wells, it was the long novel he had particularly in mind. James's remarks in the earlier essay on Maupassant about self-projection and his discussion of the autobiographical technique in an unpublished review of 1865 are more suggestive. In the review James warned that while "the autobiographical form of composition" was particularly strong for childhood reminiscence and "retrospection," it is dangerous because it is essentially dramatic, "the most dramatic form possible." The writer "puts off his own personality" and "assumes" another character, a task so difficult when the character is "different from himself" that none but a genius should dare attempt to portray his utter opposite.[27]

But in the essay on Maupassant two decades later James suggested that some measure of self-projection is probable in *any* narrative strategy, and even in the late letter to H. G. Wells, where James spoke most severely against the method, he acknowledged its "persuasive or convincing force" in the tale of horror or "the fantastic." [28] *The Aspern Papers* is no less a horror story for being a subtle caricature, a deft but fantastic parody of the creative process, the process of confronting the historical past, and the very Gothic conventions it uses. And the tale is no less tragic for the Scoundrel's success in acquiring a painted portrait of Jeffrey Aspern and presenting an entertaining one in prose to the reader: because the painted trophy of his success is also the haunting image of his abysmal failure, and the portrait, like the story itself, is gained at the cost of the aging Juliana's betrayal, the sacrifice of middle-aged Miss Tina, and the loss of "the precious papers." *The Aspern Papers* displays those features of the "arts of representation" which fascinated James in *Partial Portraits:* the moral courage which risks corruption, the imaginative act which composes pictures and plays roles by seizing experience through analytic penetration, the entertainment which is founded on careful manipulations and deliberately constructed effects, the displayed but subtle contortions (cruel in connection with Miss Juliana and the Scoun-

---

27 *Ibid.*, p. 321; *Letters*, II, 181; review of Bayard Taylor's *John Godfrey's Fortunes*, published by Leon Edel in *Harvard Literary Bulletin*, XI (Spring 1957), 245-257, quoted remarks, pp. 255-256.
28 *Letters*, II, 181.

drel, more generous in connection with Miss Tina) of caricature. And whatever was latently dramatic in its materials, or
technically and psychologically dramatic in the autobiographical convention and the analytic mode, James made dramatic
in execution by an act of construction at the end, where the
narrative is converted into a sacrificial drama and where
James's art in 1888 advanced beyond the criticism collected in
the same year and established the priority of the dramatic over
the compositional mode of painting.

[II]

THE ASPERN PAPERS

BOTH the comedy and horror of the tale are sustained by the paradoxically double perspective which is created for the reader by the Scoundrel's first efforts, with the help of his friend Mrs. Prest, to launch his " 'plot,' " as it is called, his " 'kind of conspiracy.' " (112.) * One perspective is that of utterly bland yet bold candor which is the Editor's unabashed manner with Mrs. Prest and through her with the reader. The other is that of cagey duplicity, exercised at first with Juliana and Miss Tina and through them with the reader as well, the reader being prevented by the Narrator from knowing even the alias which he uses, let alone his real name, which he manages to divulge later to Tina without giving the reader even his initials. In such close and unremitting proximity are the candor and the duplicity that each becomes outlandish, and they are ludicrous and starkly shocking both in the bold contrast they afford and in the fantastic oddity of their conjunction. (111.)

When the Scoundrel announces to Mrs. Prest that " 'Hypocrisy, duplicity are my only chance,' " and when he opens the second chapter with the transparently Satanic declaration " 'I must work the garden—I must work the garden,' " he is rehearsing a fraud before our eyes: acknowledging it nakedly while beginning to practice it, naming his role while playing it, confessing his artful disguise while donning it. Part of the somber comedy inheres in the fact that his conduct never loses this quality of a rehearsal even when he begins the performance of his plan and moves closer to its achievement. Whatever may have been his motives and reactions originally (we have access only to the "introducer" of the experience and cannot confront him with his former self), the recollection which he begins to gather in his narrative is colored by his knowing in advance the main outlines of all he discovered and underwent in his negotiations with the Misses Bordereau. When he recalls that "I was beating about the bush, trying to be ingen-

* *The Aspern Papers* is in volume XII of the New York Edition.

ious, wondering by what combination of arts I might become
an acquaintance [of the Bordereaus]," he displays not only the
anticipations of an unscrupulous historian and opportunist but
also the tone of a bemused spectator, after the fact, of his own
conceit and futility. (12, 15, 3.)

A different attitude, anxious and disturbed, is revealed in
fusion with these by the time he has finished the first paragraph.
He declares that the decisively "fruitful idea in the whole business"—that "the way to become an acquaintance was first to
become an intimate"—was Mrs. Prest's clever contribution to
his scheme, and he shortly recalls that Mrs. Prest had once offered help to the Bordereaus when old Juliana was sick so as
not to have the guilt of neglect "on her conscience." The moral
implications of these remarks are complicated when the Editor
recalls "laying siege . . . with my eyes" to Juliana's "citadel"
and feeling that the sound of Jeffrey Aspern's "voice seemed to
abide there by a roundabout implication and in a 'dying fall.' "
In these remarks are embedded the waking nightmare which
is the Editor's stunned recognition not only of his own lurid
deeds but of a collaboration, in which his partners include Mrs.
Prest (the helpful onlooker, eager for amusement) and the
poet Aspern himself. (3-4, 16, 5.)

Mrs. Prest's patience is limited—to the Publisher's relief,
she leaves Venice in June, having "expected to draw amusement from the drama of my intercourse with the Misses Bordereau" but being "disappointed that the intercourse, and consequently the drama, had not come off." She had for weeks
"reproached me for lacking boldness" and for "wasting precious hours in whimpering in her salon," for, while she "hadn't
the nerves of an editor," my "eagerness amused her" and she
relished my "fine case of monomania." The tale's horror derives partly from the fact that Mrs. Prest, fruitful idea and all,
defines not only her own but the reader's engagement with the
Scoundrel's project: the reader's interest in the Editor's curiosity, the entertainment provided *him* by the Publisher's monomania, the reader's amused disdain for the strange ineffectuality which accompanies the Narrator's boldness of plan, the
dawning recognition that the Scoundrel's "intercourse with the
Misses Bordereau," and the consequent spectacle, have not yet

proved to be the intimacy and drama that his plan leads one to expect. (38-39, 9, 5.)

Aspern's collaboration is of longer duration and more intimate, for in the Publisher's haunted recollection his deeds summon up (by a roundabout implication, to be sure) the poet whose papers he seeks to possess and publish, and whose relation with Juliana Bordereau was at once the redeeming intimacy and the betrayal which the Editor's affair with Juliana and Miss Tina ludicrously, grotesquely reenacts. The Scoundrel's tendency to associate himself with his idol is the measure not only of his vanity but of real connections which exert their pressure on the story's diction. The "critic" and "historian" is nonetheless " 'a poor devil of a man of letters,' " who has "always some business of writing in hand." By the time Miss Tina finally asks him " 'Do you write—do you write?' " and " 'Do you write about *him*—do you pry into his life?' " the ironic analogy between the Publishing Scoundrel's affair and the writer's is clearly projected in the weird hallucinations which are the product of the Editor's original scheme and his haunted recapitulation of it. The Editor remarks early that Aspern "had been kinder and more considerate than in his place—if I could imagine myself in any such box—I should have found the trick of," and the "combination of arts" which he eventually employs to negotiate with the Bordereaus places himself in precisely that box by the time he invades Juliana's apartment and rifles her desk. The analogy is deepened later when he confronts the prospect of marriage with Miss Tina and brushes against a plan for an alternative which crosses his mind ("I mightn't unite myself, yet I might still have what she had") without bringing him to identify the alternative as either theft or an illicit affair. (88-89, 45, 65, 7, 141.)

The ironic association between the publishing Editor (on his "eccentric private errand") and the publishing poet on the errand of art, which is completed later in the story, is anticipated in the imaginary conversations which the Scoundrel constructs with the poet whom he calls his "prompter" in the drama. "Invoked" and hovering, Aspern's ghost accompanies the Scoundrel as if "he regarded the affair as his own no less than as mine" and assures him that Juliana " 'was very attractive in 1820. Meanwhile, aren't we in Venice together, and what better place is there for the meeting of dear friends?' " When Tina first displays signs of love, Aspern's painted portrait seems "to smile . . . with mild mockery; he might have been amused at my case," and when her touching, desperate invitation to marriage is tendered, the portrait, with an "odd expression" on its face, seems to taunt: " 'Get out of it as you can, my dear fellow!' " (42-43, 131, 133.)

This is the voice of the poet who had met Juliana (so the Editor concludes) on the errand of art while sitting for a portrait in her father's studio, and who had had the boldness and passion to enter into an affair with her in the 1820's, but who (so the impression was in 1825) "had 'treated her badly' " and left her with the deeply ingrained suspicions which Miss Tina thinks stem from " 'something—ages before I was born—in [Juliana's] life,' " namely the love affair to which the papers are thought to allude. Although Aspern's published poems are less ambiguous than Shakespeare's sonnets, it is difficult "to put one's finger on the passage in which [Juliana's] fair fame suffered injury"; yet it is pertinent to ask if the rumors about Juliana's "impenitent passion" and tarnished respectability are substantiated by the poetry of the American who wrote when "our native land was nude and crude" and who in that enviable freedom was able "to feel, understand and express everything." Were the rumors "a sign that the singer had *betrayed* her, had *given her away*, as we say nowadays, to posterity?" The phrases (which I have italicized) transform each other into puns, and suggest that Aspern both commemorated his beloved and exposed his mistress, that he both immortalized and victimized his Juliana in betraying or giving her away to posterity. (96, 7, 80, 48-50.)

These rumors, hypotheses, and queries are all parts of the Editor's mere theories about Aspern's life and Juliana's past conduct (he had "hatched a little romance" about her expatriation), and along with his constructed conversations with Aspern are part of his twisted recollection. Yet in them emerges an authentic picture, though a fantastic image rather than a strictly accurate portrait, of Jeffrey Aspern. The painted miniature portrait, executed by Juliana's father, which the Editor accepts as a gift from Miss Tina and then pays a huge price for, is at once a Rorschach blot for the exercise of the Historian's imagination and a speaking image of the strange Orpheus who loved Juliana and used her to the profit of art. (47.)

Orpheus as a prototype for Aspern occurs to the Scoundrel early in the tale when thinking of the throngs of women who had "flung themselves at his head" and when excusing the injuries that were bound to occur "while the fury raged"; the Editor exclaims: " 'Orpheus and the Maenads!' " The shade of Orpheus emerges again momentarily when the Editor speaks of Aspern hanging, like Orpheus' lyre, "high in the heaven of our literature" and when he raises the question of Aspern's loyalty to Juliana. The Editor mentions Aspern's return to Europe and his claim in one poem "that he had come back for her sake"; the Editor hopes that the voyage was for her sake and not "just for the phrase." (7, 5, 47.)

While in these instances the figure of Orpheus, seeking to be reunited with his love, is ironically associated with Aspern specifically, it functions more allusively and pervasively in the tale because so circumscribed an identification is impossible under the pressure of the story's action and form. The introduction of Orpheus proves to be apt for the very reason that it seems, on first encounter but also subsequently, to be oddly farfetched. Introduced in the third paragraph, the legendary associations are in keeping with the contortions, the multiple refractions of association, the proliferation of displacements and substitutions, which characterize the Gothic form; they serve to precipitate out the ambiguities of the Orpheus legend and scatter its implications in stark and twisted versions. The result is that the legend of Orpheus, the Maenads, and Eurydice does not so much separate opposing sides in a tragic struggle as shape an action in which characters are mutually engaged, define the process of their interaction, and suggest the contingent possibilities, frenzied and controlled, destructive and creative, of their interaction. The legend's relevance is all the more weird for the fact that the Historian's information is and must be rife with conjecture, hearsay, and evidential inference, including the "very strong presumption" (but little more) that any papers exist at all. The tale hovers, to its peril but with its corresponding boldness, on the brink of utter historical uncertainty which is ludicrous and terrifying. And in the negotiations among Aspern, Juliana, Tina, and the Scoundrel the ghost of Orpheus—so passionate for his Eurydice yet so distant from her and from all other women afterward—is crossed with the masculine femininity of George Sand, the devotee of passion who outlived but used and celebrated it, a pale victim nonetheless triumphant against the siege of all the years. (12.)

If the divine Aspern was the supreme lyricist and may have made a second trip across the waters for Juliana's sake, he is seen now in the company of a male friend, having replaced the Editor's collaborator Cumnor as a companion; his voice is present now in a " 'dying fall.' "

Yet this Orpheus never married, and Juliana is an oddly unspliced Eurydice. And if she is passionate in devotion to the memory of their love, pitiable in her tomb-like isolation from the present, and pathetic in her attempt to honor the relics of their love by keeping them in a trunk and planning to burn them finally rather than to violate their privacy, there is also an uncanny strength and a weird craft in the feat which the battered woman performs on her deathbed to balk the predatory maneuvers of the Editor, whom she has discovered rummaging her desk: single-handed she removes the papers from the trunk, thrusts them into her bed, and sews them up between the mattresses. Her motive is to secure the papers, but her logic is an extension of the Scoundrel's, who suspected that she had "consigned her relics to her bedroom," perhaps to "some battered box that was shoved under the bed, to the drawer of some lame dressing-table" or to her desk, a "receptacle somewhat infirm but still capable of keeping rare secrets." The infirm woman's act is in strange keeping not only with her now desperate attempt to protect the integrity of her love but with the strategy she has been pursuing since renting rooms to the Soundrel, the scheme of using the papers and the affair they image to entice from him the favor of money. (100.)

The Editor early found it unnerving that "these women so associated with Aspern should so constantly bring the pecuniary question back," and whether Juliana is teasing him with allusions to her "rapture" or keeping Aspern "buried in her soul," the signs of her "acquisitive propensity" loom large in the Editor's recollection. When he agrees to pay, three months in advance, the huge rent she has long managed to live without, Juliana exclaims "almost gaily: 'He'll give three thousand—three thousand tomorrow!'" It is she who thinks the Historian should sell the surplus bloom of the garden he has grown to beguile his hostesses and who proposes to sell the portrait of Aspern for a staggering thousand pounds. Indeed, with her (as with George Sand) the "vision of pecuniary profit was most what drew out the divine Juliana." Behind the green eye-shade which screens her actual attitude from the Scoundrel, the old woman is "full of craft." (James had been told that "George Sand looked a great deal on the ground . . . that one felt shut off from her by a sort of veil or film.")[29] And while her conversation (like the Scoundrel's narrative) permits glimpses of the bliss she recalls, it yields occasionally also the "old-time tone" or "caper" of the shrewd bargainer which the Editor's idolization has obscured, the incipient shrewdness that has become more pronounced and justified since Aspern left her and since the well-heeled Scoundrel, presenting the occasion for profit, has appeared at her door as a possible "victim" and virtually "taught her to calculate." (29, 69-71, 86, 88.)

What the Editor comes to see gradually is that Juliana seeks money for Tina's sake, and that her maneuvering behind her green shade in her combat with him is as cagily strategic as his siege, and that it is founded, like his tactics, on the "fruitful idea" of gaining acquaintance through intimacy. Coaching Miss Tina and luring on the Editor, the "supersensuous grandmother" who has "outlived passions and faculties" nevertheless shows signs of her "adventurous youth"; she is not only engaged in combat that is partly defensive and partly vindictive but is nursing along an affair, as her fears and hopes are transferred to the plight of her niece. Miss Tina, middle-aged but "amiable and unencumbered," is a *"parti"*; and Juliana, disdainful though she is of her ward's shyness and her lodger's bower of bloom, seeks to secure happiness for Tina in love. Her last encounter with the Editor is the one that renders her speechless and precipitates her death, but she manages on her deathbed, through " 'signs' " as Tina explains later, to suggest to Tina the import and pressure of Juliana's desire: despite the fact that she should burn the papers, Tina clearly favors the Historian and his idea of publishing them, and consequently Juliana would consent, for the sake of her niece, if the Scoundrel were to become " 'a relation.' " Whether or not the "relation" Juliana had in mind were necessarily marriage (the marriage she had done without but may have learned to hope and bargain for), marriage becomes the aim of Tina; and while the Editor stands "pensively, awkwardly, grotesquely" declaring " 'It wouldn't do, it wouldn't do!' " he recognizes that in the affair he has undertaken, marriage has come to be "the price." (71, 92, 129, 133-136.)

It is the Historian, first and foremost, who has undertaken the Orphic task of retrieving the papers from their tomb and resurrecting the dead in reawakening Juliana and quickening Tina to an interest in life. And it is he, though he is without "the tradition of personal conquest" and must now protest his manliness, who gets caught in the dream of marriage which had been Orpheus' bond of love. The courtship of Tina was, to begin with, the unscrupulous expedient which the Editor proposed half-jokingly to Mrs. Prest as the means he might employ to get the papers. But it has been transformed into the desperate commitment which he faces as the dream of marriage comes to life across the chasm of the years to become the pathetic hope of Tina's waning future. Marriage becomes the instrument by which the Editor may not only redeem his campaign to capture the papers but make good on the antic courtship which his scheme, Mrs. Prest's fruitful idea, and his courtly conduct have turned into.

In the course of his affair he is haunted by examples of other heroes—lovers and warriors whose careers are echoed in his imagination and in the painting and statuary he consults for advice, and whose success exacerbates his self-consciousness. The painted ghost of Orpheus beams encouragingly, then taunts his strangely unmaniacal devotee. The Editor's servant Pasquale enjoys the frequent visits of a "young lady with a powdered face" and is friendly also with the household maids, and during a visit with one of them to Juliana's sick chamber "Pasquale

peep[s] over the doctor's shoulder" while the physician eyes
the Editor, an odd Musset, as if "taking me for a rival who
had the field before him." The equestrian statue of Marcus
Aurelius, benign and bestride, is far away in Rome, the Editor
recalls, but in Venice one of "the finest of all mounted figures,"
a statue of the *condottiere* Colleoni, stares indifferently past the
hesitant Historian, engrossed probably in "battles and strategems" of "a different quality from any I had to tell him of."
Yet the preoccupations of that mercenary mounted warrior—
like those of the Maenads and George Sand, Orpheus and de
Musset—do define the complex irony of the Narrator's courtship-siege, which penetrates far into the buried past and cham-
bered present he seeks to enter but winds up finally balked, in
actual deed and in the Historian's compulsive reconstruction
of it. (41, 106, 139.)

As in the displacements of a fantastic dream, the Historian's
anticipated expenses, lavish but vaguely budgeted, recede behind Juliana's demand for a huge rent; the papers (first hidden
in a trunk) are shifted to the mattresses of Juliana's deathbed,
to reappear, locked up by Tina, in the desk where the Scoundrel had first rummaged for them, then disappear in flames;
the coveted papers, the relics of love, are displaced by the "careful," "elegant" portrait; and Aspern's presence, presumably
mediated by his poetry, is mediated also by the green shade
and wily craft of Juliana, to be echoed finally, in a dying fall,
in Tina's and the Scoundrel's awakening to the dream and
the entanglements of love. (28, 94-95.)

Both that awakening and its betrayal are entailed in the
courtship-siege which takes form as the Historian's plans are
translated into performance, as his actions and motives are
recapitulated in memory, and as the stunned recognition which
his deeds and recollections yield is presented in the fantastic
account which he constructs and renders with such finesse. The
vocabularies of war and love and commerce are joined in a
grotesquely ironic suspension. The boldness of the delineations,
and the contrasts of character and motive, which are intensified
under pressures which force them into closer contact and even
fuse them, mark the narrative as a parody—in visual terms, a
caricature. When the Narrator undertakes to " 'work the gar-

den'" and recalls that "I would batter the old women with lilies—I would bombard their citadel with roses. Their door would have to yield to the pressure when a mound of fragrance should be heaped against it"—his outlandish declarations project at once the love affair which his conduct simulates and increasingly approximates, the campaign he wages as he invades Juliana's room and desk, and the acquisitive enterprise which resembles increasingly the burglary he denies intending when he presses the button of Juliana's secretary, intending "not to do anything, not even . . . to let down the lid" but solely "to test my theory, to see if the cover *would* move." The images, with the actions and motives they express, take the measure of each other, suggesting at once the Editor's cross-purposes, the extent of his success, and his final ineffectuality. His engaging tactics bring him closer to, but fail to culminate in, the marriage Tina longs for; his courtly siege reaches the fortress but terminates in embarrassed retreat; his expensive suit brings him closer to the papers he would gladly buy but results in their permanent removal from the market. (45, 117-118.)

His is a compound recognition of his ineffectuality as warrior, lover, and bargaining historian, and of his guilt for the deeds he *has* perpetrated. His recollections avoid the easy dichotomies of credit and condemnation, and the blatant antitheses of radiant innocence and utter depravity, but the tale is founded on an intimate confession which is the more effective and vivid because it takes account of the complexities of the experience which the Narrator and the others undergo. Accordingly the tale is permeated by the "moral sense" and moral courage which James dwelt on in *Partial Portraits* and located close to the "artistic sense" in the artist's mind. From the earliest paragraphs of the story on, for all the Editor's bland decorum, the feelings of guilt are apparent even when showing faintly beneath broader strokes of reckless, unscrupulous editorial enterprise. In the course of the narrative these feelings become pronounced and more nakedly revealed until, in crucial moments, they match in vivid intensity the grotesquely evil intentions he displays. His violations of Juliana's privacy and Tina's trust become increasingly outrageous, yet he becomes more candidly conscience stricken about them, welcoming the opportunity to divulge his aim and his identity to Tina while enlisting her as a cohort.

If the bald contrast of these conflicting emotions reveals the form of caricature, the effect is enforced by pressures bearing on the action for which the Narrator is not alone accountable, though his recognitions and re-enactment bring them into the narrative which he constructs. The figure of Aspern rises from the past to haunt the narrative: a model of love, profitable conquest, and expressive power which images both the consummations of love and art and their betrayals which the Scoundrel's efforts render in debased and antic form. Juliana emerges from her tomb-like isolation, affording the prospect of entertainment to Mrs. Prest and profitable success to the Historian, and risks the gambits of love and commerce for Tina, with all the craft of an artist and the bargaining power of an extortionist. Tina emerges from seclusion, pathetically but ludicrously helpless in her innocence, coached and thrust before the Historian by her shrewd aunt, liberated by the Historian's intrusion in her life which culminates when (at Juliana's cruelly blunt insistence) he takes Tina to St. Mark's Square; her "return to society" is marked by her "theorising about prices" of merchandise, her "spirits" are "revived" by "the sight of the bright shop-windows." It is she finally who acts on the proposition that the Editor might gain acquaintance with the papers through the intimacy of marriage and bargains to that end in her next-to-last interview with the Scoundrel. The motives which impel the Historian are not peculiar to him, and accordingly the contortions of caricature are features of the story's action as well as of its portraits. The fantastic delineations, the bold strokes, mark the lines which divide but also visually join the area of willed action to the realm of inescapable conditions which impinge on the effort to " 'rake up' " and resurrect the past, " 'violating a tomb' " to penetrate and take possession whether in the art of entertainment or the commerce of love. The fantastic proliferation of lovers, the mounting payments of rent, the multiplying series of mediators between the Editor's present and the past, between him and the love, possession, and expressive power which are imaged in the coveted papers

—these respond to pressures which pervade and lie deep within the story and press its incidents into a drama founded on caricature. (78-79, 90, 134.)

The combination of the ludicrous and the horrible are piercingly comic in one crucial incident which joins the gestures of love and utilitarian transactions to those of the historical imagination. The Editor hopes to reach Aspern's past by shaking Juliana's hand, sealing their verbal contract for rent. But when his "desire to hold in my own for a moment the hand Jeffrey Aspern had pressed" is balked by Juliana's refusal, he turns to Tina instead, exclaiming " 'Oh you'll do as well' " and Juliana demands coolly: " 'Shall you bring the money in gold?' " Compressed into the incident is the very crux of the drama, the transference of the Historian's effort from Juliana to Tina and the ironic analogy between his expedient affair and that of Aspern. (30-31.)

The caricature is less relaxed, more cruel in the scene where the Scoundrel, pressing the button of Juliana's desk, turns to find that the aged woman is watching him. The "pale forewarned victim" and the Editor with the "historic sense" are at last "face to face." The confrontation is unrelieved, and the Narrator's confession is stark in its candor, as he recalls that Juliana, in her nightdress with her hands raised in condemnation, "had lifted the everlasting curtain that covered half her face" and that "for the first, the last, the only time" he "beheld her extraordinary eyes." Her glaring eyes "were like the sudden drench, for a caught burglar, of a flood of gaslight; they made me horribly ashamed." Memory is no safe refuge from the pathos and dignity of her emaciated figure: "I never shall forget her strange little bent white tottering figure, with its lifted head, her attitude, her expression." Nor is his stammered excuse that he "meant no harm" a protection from the force with which she "hissed out passionately, furiously: 'Ah you publishing scoundrel' " and fell back "with a quick spasm, as if death had descended on her, into Miss Tina's arms." (118.)

The mode of caricature has become the instrument of tragedy by the time Tina, who prevented Juliana from burning the papers before she died, tries to redeem her effort and the gambits of both Juliana and the Editor in her last interviews with the Historian. Her "cry of desolation" when faced with separation from the Editor, the sobbing which resounds "in the great empty hall" after she has offered " 'everything' " to him, are tragically genuine. Yet her awkwardness, though touching, is pronounced, and the aim of her efforts is clearly calculated. When she suggests that if he were a "relation" he might see the papers, she talks in quickening phrases with a compressed subtlety of implications which combine heartfelt intensity with the sureness of a desperately rehearsed performance, "as if speaking words got by heart." She pursues her pathetic aim with "transparent astuteness" and after giving the painted portrait of Aspern to the Historian as a present and proposing " 'Couldn't we sell it?' " her proposal that they join in the commercial traffic is a ludicrous but touching parody of the dream of marriage she clings to: " 'We can divide the money.' " (132-135.)

The Historian's precipitous flight from "the poor deluded infatuated extravagant lady" is an embarrassed, nerveless retreat, an abdication of his mission; he seeks refuge in an opportunism sanctioned by Aspern's example (" 'Get out of it as you can, my dear fellow!' ") and in the comfort of moralism ("my predicament was the just punishment of that most fatal of . . . follies, our not having known when to stop"), but neither the equestrian statues which haunt him nor the importunities of his own mind during sleep will let him rest in the certainty that "I couldn't, for a bundle of tattered papers, marry a ridiculous pathetic provincial old woman." The very atmosphere of Venice prepares for the transformation into drama which the closing pages accomplish. Piazza San Marco now resembles simultaneously a domestic residence (a "splendid common domicile, familiar domestic and resonant") and a "theatre with its actors clicking over bridges," a "stage" with the Venetians becoming the "members of an endless dramatic troupe." The drama hinges finally on two events which take place in the same house on the same night: Tina's secret burning of the papers and the sudden resurgence of the Editor's determination to acquire them. (136-137, 140.)

The Scoundrel recalls jumping from bed in the morning, instantly aware that during the night his determination to see

Tina again had revived, and feeling like one who has "left the house-door ajar or a candle burning," wondering "Was I still in time to save my goods?" His "passionate appreciation of Juliana's treasure" has returned, and he begins to ponder some way of gaining possession of the papers without marrying Tina. He is still trying to invent or name an alternative when Tina admits him to Juliana's "forlorn parlour" for their final interview. (140-141.)

The Miss Tina whom he confronts has undergone a "rare alteration" which the Editor's preoccupation with "strategems and spoils" had prevented his anticipating, although ironically his machinations, and his failure to press them to completion, have helped produce the transformation. Unknown to him and to the reader, she has burned the papers, we learn later, consumed by the "sense of her failure" to win the Editor's love and consent to marriage and convinced that she has no reason now to keep them. What is significant about the form of the story at this point is that three events, on three different occasions, are made to coalesce by the story's form: the burning of the papers, the Historian's and Tina's separation the next day, and the Historian's recapitulation (some weeks or months later) of the incidents in memory and in his account. The act of burning the papers is made inseparable from the Editor's reconstruction of his discovery of their loss, and both the destruction of the papers and the Editor's account are rendered through the drama of Tina's transfiguring performance in the closing interview. The sacrifice which she performed and suffered when she burned the papers and the drama later of her separation from the Historian, are inextricably fused; the story is so constructed that together these occasions become the sacrificial foundation of the Scoundrel's narrative enactment. As a consequence, the burning of the papers is made an image of the betrayals and wastage which recur in the story—but also an image of the intense passion which produced the "shreds and relics" of Aspern's affair with Juliana, and produced the dream of love which is consecrated by Tina's pathetic sacrifice and commemorated by the Historian. (141.)

Tina has done not simply the *right thing* (too long delayed) nor the *wrong thing* but, as she puts it, the " 'great thing' ": the only gesture—ruinously, regrettably destructive, intensely expressive, faithful to the passion the papers symbolize, and certain to be gripping in its impact on the Historian—the only act which is now adequate to the tragic experience which has ensued. The burden of Tina's final interview with the Editor—she might have refused to see him, and left him in the dark—is to redeem her act in the drama of their separation. That she does so is owing to the new "force of soul" created in her by the experience she has undergone and to the firmness of her sustained performance. She becomes, with "every paper burnt," the "pale forewarned victim," triumphant in the "tower of art" and the "citadel of style." And it is her last look back at the Editor, and her acceptance of his money for the painted portrait of Aspern, that frustrate and complete, distort and express, betray and reveal the denouement of Orpheus' mission. (141-142.)

She "had strung herself up to accepting" their separation, and the "rare alteration" in her spirit enables her "in her abjection" to "smile strangely, with an infinite gentleness" at the Scoundrel. The "look of forgiveness, of absolution" which she gives him is the "magic" of her spirit, the effective "trick" of "her expression." The effect is to transfigure Tina—"she was younger, she was not a ridiculous old woman"—and simultaneously to bring the Scoundrel farther than he has yet come on the voyage of love—to the brink of marriage and (he thinks) success: "I heard a whisper somewhere in the depths of my conscience: 'Why not, after all—why not?' It seemed to me I *could* pay the price." Yet the whisper is supplanted by the stronger note of Tina's voice, sounding her farewell with wishes for his happiness; she is acting out the separation she had "strung herself up to accepting," the tragic anticipation which had transfigured her and stirred the Editor's will and conscience. (141-142.)

Her smile is part of a deliberately controlled performance. With her "gentleness" she tells him nonetheless firmly that " 'I shall not see you again. I don't want to' " and finally divulges the information in a piercingly effective sequence that she had not only destroyed the papers but that she did so " 'one by one, in the kitchen,' " and that the process " 'took a long time' " because " 'there were so many.' " In the harsh glare of this exposure of his baseness and futility, the Editor recognizes that Tina's transfiguration is over and that she is again a "plain dingy elderly person." Her last remark is both an expression of moral revulsion and a recognition of tragic necessity: " 'I can't stay with you longer, I can't.' " In a strangely twisted version of Orpheus' separation from Eurydice, *she* turns her back on *him,* but then pauses to look back once, giving him the "one look" that marks their separation but grips his memory: "I have never forgotten it and I sometimes still suffer from it, though it was not resentful." The Scoundrel's last effort is to pay for the portrait of Aspern which Tina gave him, a substitute for the papers and his hopes but an image of them which he possesses and keeps above his desk. Pretending to sell the painting, he sends Tina a sum much larger than its market value in an effort to compensate for his deeds and to express his gratitude. Her last gesture is to keep the money, "with thanks." (142-143.)

These transactions parody the experience they supplant, yet like the painted portrait of Aspern, they recall the exploits and the sacrificial drama which brought the portrait to light, recall *all* that is implicit in the Historian's closing declaration: "I can scarcely bear my loss—I mean of the precious papers." Thanks to the sacrificial drama which Tina's action constitutes, the painted portrait is resurrected and acquired, the transactions are completed, and the entertaining narrative is constructed and presented, but these are accomplished at the expense of a more complete vision, a more intimate communion, and a more appropriate form, which the story's brilliant art can create as possibilities only in the torment of betraying them.

[III]

THE PREFACES

IT IS the torment, along with the exhilaration, of witnessing and creating such an experience as that dramatized in *The Aspern Papers* which James expressed with comparable intensity in the Prefaces of 1907-1908. These essays on his own fiction are James's brilliant contribution to the theory and criticism of the novel. To place them, as I have done, in the immediate context provided by *The Aspern Papers* and *The Sacred Fount* (both Gothic tales and both parodies) is to risk suggesting a more narrow relevance for them than they are known to have, but the context outlines sharply their most modern features and the problematic depths of imaginative experience which informed them: the obsessive concern with the assets, hazards, and limitations of the imaginative life, the attempt to validate the institution of the novel in a culture which ignores, debases, and assaults the arts, the double concern for *objectivity* and *intimacy* in the arts, the experiential, strenuously activist, orientation which replaces the more contemplative and categorical aims of traditional aesthetics, the importance accorded to technique and an expressive medium, the tenor of crisis, the awareness of process and change, the concern for the writer's responsibility and the grounds of his authority. The Prefaces are a landmark in the history of expressionism.

This is not to say that the Prefaces lack the coherence and certainty, the range and profundity of relevance for the art of fiction and indeed the imaginative life in general, that Professor Richard Blackmur and James's most rewarding critics have claimed for them. It is to suggest that "calm" and order of the kinds which characterize most earlier literary theory and which Professor Blackmur claims for James's Prefaces, are as absent from the essays as is the belligerency of controversy—that the strength as well as the tenor of the essays derives rather from the euphoria and anxieties of James's intimate involvement with his fiction, from what he called, in the preface to *The Ambassadors*, "the thrilling ups and downs, the intricate ins and outs, of the compositional problem" which kept "the author's heart in his mouth." His heart was there located, at that point in the essay, because he was fascinated by two problematical relations at once. One was the conversion of his protagonist's adventure in the novel into a technical adventure for the author executing it, the adventures being intimately if mysteriously connected. A second disturbing relation was that between the vivid revival in memory of ambitious intentions for the novel and the disappointing recognition that these ambitions had not been fully achieved, even in the novel which James thought his best. The Prefaces confront repeatedly the inseparability of the two adventures and they dwell on the paradoxical interconnection of masterly success and artistic failure. And it is the torment (the profound doubts as well as the satisfactions) of these encounters, and the articulated pressures behind them, that give the essays their force.[30]

James's certainty was a sureness of tact and of commitment rather than a certainty of formulated conclusions, his Prefaces were the celebration of a process, a mission, and a form rather than a statement of theory. The Prefaces have their commanding stature as explorations of the imaginative life and the forms of fiction because they probe to the problematical depths of the process with intimacy and candor, and overtly obsessive concern (qualities they share with *The Aspern Papers* and *The Sacred Fount*), employing often grotesque metaphors which are neither incidental nor symptomatic of a narrowed range of interest but reveal the essays' profundity and daring. Whether treating Gothic tales or masterpieces in other genres which express less compulsively but nonetheless intimately the process which produced them, the Prefaces illuminate the works because they draw on the same resources of experience and metaphor as do the creative works themselves. If the Prefaces run the risk of making artistry resemble a "problem in mechanics" and yet avoid that pitfall, as F. W. Dupee has suggested,[31] it is because they are impelled at profound levels by more viably problematic motives than pride in technical ingenuity. They draw on the myths, with their respective vocabularies, of religious sacri-

30 *The Art of the Novel*, pp. xxxviii, 319.
31 *James* (New York, 1951), pp. 278, 280.

fice and exploitive capitalism. And they fuse sacramental actions with the basic transactions of capitalism (loaning and repaying, keeping accounts, shopping and keeping shop, appreciating value) and with the enactments of the "grasping" or "penetrating imagination."

When James recalled his relish for the difficulties of artistic creation, he could write of being charmed by his task and of the "golden glow" of his assurance; but he could in the same preface confess being "delightfully and very damnably" intrigued by his difficulties, "enjoying" a "costly sacrifice" just as "ogres, with their 'Fee-faw-fum!' rejoice in the smell of the blood of Englishmen." When he contemplated searching the "shrunken depths of old work" to revive the creative process, he wrote of dragging a river: "the long pole of memory stirs and rummages the bottom, and we fish up such fragments and relics of . . . the extinct consciousness as tempt us to piece them together." Earlier sections of this study have drawn attention to the Prefaces' confession of complicity in the commerce of his plots, James's acknowledgment of his own " 'Spoils,' " the piracy and exhuming he acknowledged responsibility for in *The Aspern Papers*.[32]

Yet these fantastic metaphors are not the only indications of the problematical nature of imaginative creation in the essays. Others are the metaphors of parenthood and marriage which are important also, as metaphors as well as themes, in his other major novels. The subject of one novel becomes a child watched by its fond parent; in another the subject, in a cradle, is threatened with strangulation; in yet another case the imagination itself is the favorite "hope of the family." In the instance of *The Tragic Muse* (slighted by the reading public), James refers to it first as "a poor fatherless and motherless, a sort of unregistered and unacknowledged birth," then even while defending its merits expresses the chagrin and sorrow felt by a parent for "the maimed or slighted, the disfigured or defeated, the unlucky or unlikely child." At the point where he confronted most directly the question of the relation of form to substance in the finished novel, he described their indissoluble fusion as a "marriage" achieved in "the sacrament of exe-

[32] *The Art of the Novel*, pp. 310-312, 318, 26.

cution." So responsive is his criticism to the many contingencies he knew in the practice of art that even this commanding metaphor suggests two possibilities, including the prospect that the *marriage* subsist in a state of crisis: for one, the possibility that within the fusion of marriage no separation of the partners exist; for another, the possibility that no separation be *displayed*. The marriage "has only to be a 'true' one for the scandal of a breach not to show." [33]

Such remarks define the contingencies as well as the aims and achievements of the artist, and center all of them in the *ado* which the writer makes, the act of "doing" or executing his works. So crucial is this act of execution in James's conception of his craft that his terms for it must be the governing metaphors for our consideration of his Prefaces: he called it the "sacrament" which "marries" form and substance in the preface to *The Awkward Age,* and, in the final preface to *The Golden Bowl,* he included it as part of the "religion of doing." [34] It is the Prefaces' focus on this "religion of doing"—for all their complexity and their necessarily scattered though fruitful attention to specific cases—that gives them their profound coherence. The "sacrament" of marrying or the "religion" of "execution" proves to involve given conventions and forged techniques, the instruments of artistry, in the very sacrifice that they constitute. They become intimately engaged in an act of devotion which involves them with the life they depict and the drama they enact. But they become subject themselves to the process of which they are the instruments, capable of transformation into the achieved marriage of art because they are subject to the costs which the process imposes and the ruinous waste which accompanies it. And in the crisis of creation which the Prefaces explore, the exercise of authority by the writer becomes an act of mediation, a torment of participation in the "religion of doing" which absorbs him in the process. It renders him the vicarious participant in the created drama and the life it images. And it renders him the vicarious witness of the marriage of art which he helps create by administering or executing its sacrament, both betraying and celebrating it.

[33] *Ibid.,* pp. 293, 121, 183, 79, 81, 115-116.
[34] *Ibid.,* p. 347.

To the definition of this process all the roles and analogous offices which James suggests for the novelist contribute. Besides those already mentioned—the watcher, architect, and plotter; the employee and employer and shop-keeper; the painter, purchaser, and dramatist; the smuggler; the parent—there are the "conjurer," the "accountant," the puppeteer, the governess or nurse, the "seer" and sayer and "poet."[35] In these varied roles the Prefaces present an apology for the "morbid imagination," a confession in a series of "shrines and stations of penance" of his "immoral" interest in probing the characters of his subjects, while at the same time celebrating the "sense of 'authority'" of the "master-builder," the "modern alchemist" possessed of "the old dream of the secret life." And the Prefaces present for fiction (whether comic or tragic) a strategy of *representation* in which the compositional strategies explored more tentatively in *Partial Portraits* take precedence over imitative modes, and the fusion of analytic and dramatic modes takes precedence over the strictly pictorial manner which governs the vocabulary of *Partial Portraits* and the design of *The Portrait of a Lady.* The "closeness of relation" to life that James had insisted on in "The Art of Fiction" as the distinct asset of the novel is rendered in the Prefaces as a combination of dramatic construction and intimacy of rapport which avoids direct reportage or "merely referential" narrative. And the "magnificence" of the novel's form, which had made other arts seem constrained by "rigid" conventions in *Partial Portraits,* is founded in the Prefaces on a sacrificial enactment which absorbs the strategies of painting and the drama and even builds on the friction between them, becoming an art whose forms are unusually intimate and expressive of the pressures, social and personal, bearing on the imagination which produced it.[36]

The crisis which the Prefaces present as the matrix of art appears repeatedly as a dangerous exploration, "with no harbour of refuge till the end," in which the writer takes part once his "strange unrest" launches him on the adventure which, like that of Columbus, is to precipitate an *unexpected* encounter and call for the enterprise entailed in "'making land.'" The

[35] *Ibid.,* pp. 116, 312, 74, 337-338, 340-341.
[36] *The Art of the Novel,* pp. 155-156, 123, 321; *Partial Portraits,* pp. 397, 407.

wider social context for the Prefaces, barely but tellingly sketched in, is an unsettled horizon dominated by broken engagements and ruptured marriages, the "bastard vernacular" of communities debased by intrusive journalism, slang, and clashing dialects, the "down-town" world of business, and the names on shipping lists of American tourists which are foreign to the Anglo-Saxon tongue and ominous to James. The names are "exotic symbols" scarcely more readable than those on "the stony slabs of Nineveh." Virtually unintelligible, the names are at odds with the habitual "communities," the recognizable "tradition," which were expressed by the names formerly encountered in banks and tourist attractions, and which were founded on "settled premises." [37]

In connection with the institution that most concerned him, the novel, the Prefaces describe more thoroughly its immediate social context, though they bring up in piecemeal fashion these conditions: the temptations and opportunities, the pressures and confinements, afforded by the reading public or the impact of publishers' demands and schedules.[38] If James's attitudes toward these matters suggest the boundaries of his habitual sympathies, they do not indicate that in the face of them he drew back into the indulgent complacencies of the given tradition in his commitments as a writer. The Prefaces consistently present the novelist as welcoming a challenge and creating, not taking refuge in, a tradition, preferring "dramatic analysis" as a mode of discovery to the *"a priori* judgment" which a novel might demonstrate.[39] Accordingly, the Prefaces do not bolster their claims by citing precedents already conveniently established for the novel but range widely through painting and the drama as well as fiction in *search* for them; the Prefaces establish precedents themselves in the course of the quest, sometimes constructing illustrative dialogues to do so.[40]

For an imagination which relishes conflicting "impressions" because they are more interesting to alert minds, preferring them to the "complacent conclusions" congenial to the closed

37 *The Art of the Novel,* pp. 21, 159, 264-265, 189-190, 279-280, 274, 208-209.
38 See, e.g. *ibid.,* pp. 20, 53-54, 57, 79, 106-107, 226, 295, 317.
39 *Ibid.,* p. 265.
40 See, e.g. *ibid.,* pp. 20, 49-50, 62, 84, 112-113, 129, 323, 340, 343.

minds of more vociferous citizens, the experience of life was an encounter, and the act of rendering it in art a crisis. The burden of the preface to *Roderick Hudson* (the first of the essays, and one which shows clearly James's concern to give coherent shape to the entire series) is to give preliminary definition to that crisis by noting the "ache of fear" or "anxiety" that always accompanies the development of a subject, the "beauty of the constructional game" which is also a "torment of interest" when the artist faces the "variable process" of executing his subject. The preface establishes immediately that rendering life in art, even delimiting a subject, is a process without settled precedents, and that the artist substitutes for patterns which he might prefer to find given him, a preliminary order which does violence to the network of the subject's "relations," the texture of experience and the wider fabric of actuality which includes it. This process James called a "crisis" and a "sacrifice." [41]

For either comedy or tragedy, life is an unbroken "continuity" of relations which the artist must both "consult" and "ignore" while trying to ascertain "where, for the complete expression of one's subject, does a particular relation stop. . . ." But no "fond power disposed to 'patronize' " art has provided "conveniences" or a "visibly-appointed stopping-place," and accordingly the artist must "invent," "establish" them by the radical exercise of his own authority: his "expertness" consists in the "courage to brace one's self for the cruel crisis from the moment one sees it grimly loom." The "dire process" of delimiting a subject by cutting into the fabric of reality James called not simply a process of selection but a "surrender and sacrifice." The "sacrifice" was more extreme in the case of the *romance*, James made clear in the next preface—in a *romance* the rope tieing the "balloon of experience" to the ground of actual life is cut; the romancer should minimize the "sacrifice" of the network of relations and keep it comparatively hidden; the violence should not "flagrantly betray itself," and readers should be kept if possible "from suspecting any sacrifice at all." But the sacrifice of the "community" of relations to gain intensity and created form is not peculiar to the *romance* but is an inescapable condition of art, unavoidable to the painter who

[41] *Ibid.*, pp. 213-214, 4-6, 16, 8-9.

"wishes both to treat his chosen subject and to confine his necessary picture." [42]

Outright "elimination" of material is no solution for the authentic artist, though in the "terror" of execution "abject omission and mutilation" of materials are tempting. Accordingly, when discussing an example of the process of treating the actualities of life, James described the process not as the selection of some and the elimination of other materials but as a sacrificial transformation of materials which gives "all the sense" of actuality at the expense of "all the substance or all the surface." Art foreshortens and compresses its materials to gain "values both rich and sharp," with the result that the observed phenomena, "the mere procession of items and profiles," is not only "superseded" but "almost 'compromised.'" So close does the practice of art necessarily come to mutilation, and so certain the risk of violence, that its exercise is indeed a problematic "case of delicacy," and James could define it only in terms of the threatened compromise, the possible distortion and betrayal.[43]

The fact that the "principle of simplification" in *Roderick Hudson* had been the logic of a dramatic "Action" multiplied the "horizons and abysses" of artistic construction, for dramatic "compactness" had always been "factitious." Nevertheless, the preface endorses a basically dramatic action and discusses at length one feature of James's dramaturgy, the center of consciousness or "centre of interest," which was the basis of his "constructional game," whether he used the strictly autobiographical convention of first-person narrator as in *The Aspern Papers,* or, as in *Roderick Hudson,* narrated the story himself but kept a narrative focus on events and reactions as registered in the mind of one or more central characters. Familiar though this principle in his criticism and fiction has become, James's remarks in the first preface bear further examination in the light of the unusually intimate connection between form and substance in the "marriage" of James's art.[44]

The "subject" of *Roderick Hudson* is the young sculptor of

42 *Ibid.,* pp. 5-6, 33, 14.
43 *Ibid.,* p. 14.
44 *Ibid.,* p. 15.

that name, but the structural basis of the novel is the mind of his friend Rowland Mallet, whose "view and experience" of Roderick and other friends are at once part of the action and the instrumental medium for dramatizing it. The novel's "drama" is precisely "the drama of that consciousness," Mallet's mind, which has a movement of its own that is important in its own right as part of the action; his mind must be the limited mind, "sufficiently pathetic, tragic, comic, ironic, personal" to be plausibly human. Yet his mind must also be "a sufficiently clear medium to represent a whole," to make "intelligible" the entire story, serving "like a set and lighted scene" to contain the "play" which is comprised of others' actions. What these remarks indicate is that Mallet is at once a spectator, the stage for the play, an actor in it, and a figure who serves to represent the entire play. He is part of the action, a witness, and one who also represents it. He not only presents a drama but dramatizes and symbolizes the formal act of mediation, performed by James and all his characters, which constitutes it. Accordingly he becomes a structural feature of the novel which renders its structure both symbolic and conspicuous or prominent. Without being at all a simple spokesman for the author—and without being the *only* measure of James's participation in the novel, an equivalent for James himself—his reactions reveal and accent the mediating form of James's projected presence and of all that is implicit in the fiction. The intimacy of an art (as a revelation of the author or of the other actualities it images) is the intimacy of a form and derives not directly from an encounter with life but indirectly from an encounter which is mediated by the imagination and by a form.[45]

James was to insist later in his essay on Browning's *The Ring and the Book* (1912) that the novel was the most intimate of forms. Poets, by contrast, seem always to be across the street from their readers; there "we mostly see the poets elegantly walk" and we greet them from a distance with no chance of bumping into them. "It is on this same side, as I call it, on *our* side, . . . that I rather see our encounter with the novelists taking place. . . ." Our "brush of them, in their minor frenzy" is a more intimate, "a comparatively muffled encounter."

[45] *Ibid.*, p. 16.

Browning's unprecedented triumph had been to achieve this novelistic intimacy in verse. The "convulsions" in the texture of his poetry are the birth throes of the creative process, and he presses close upon his readers in the effort to "express his inner self . . . and to express it utterly. . . ." James praised Browning's "energy of appropriation" of materials, which required "not to be shaped . . . but rather to suffer disintegration, be pulled apart, melted down," and admired Browning's power to scrutinize life from a "point of view . . . almost sublime" and to "smuggle" as many "points of view together into that one" as he wished. A comparably analytic and dramatic act of construction, and a correspondingly intimate form, are claimed for the novel, and for James's fiction, in the Prefaces, notably in those to *The Princess Casamassima* and *The Awkward Age*. And James acknowledged one risk which his absorption of the dramatic strategy into fiction entailed, the danger of overtreatment, the danger of displaying the consistency of form at the expense of subject and content.[46]

The penetrating and analytic act of the imagination (the "creative effort to get into the skin" of a character, the "act of personal possession of one being by another") and the " 'histrionic temperament' " (displayed by theatrical performers but typifying " 'art' at large") together produce the dramatic strategy which governed the novel's structure, based on the governing center or centers of consciousness which included, in James's lists, Isabel Archer, Fleda Vetch, and the Publishing Scoundrel, Densher in *The Wings of the Dove,* Strether in *The Ambassadors,* and the Prince and Maggie in *The Golden Bowl.* The center of consciousness in *The Princess Casamassima,* Hyacinth Robinson, is described as sustaining the "assault" of London and responding appreciatively to it in a measure that permits an intimate involvement with the author, who describes himself as sustaining that same "assault" and probing it with the "penetrating imagination." [47]

James's remarks on his relation to his protagonist are dense because the intricate relation involved *both* (author and fictive

[46] "The Novel in the 'Ring and the Book,' " *Notes on Novelists,* pp. 398-399, 388.
[47] *The Art of the Novel,* pp. 37, 91, 70-71, 329, 59-60, 77-78.

character) in the double task of watcher and builder; both take part in observing the action and constructing its image. The two activities are scarcely distinguishable, and the intimacy between fictional agent and author is so close that remarks about the one seem to apply to both. The preface insists that the distinction between "doing" and "feeling" is unreal in connection with both the experience of observing life and that of treating it in art. And it describes the center of consciousness, Robinson (a revolutionary anarchist who chooses to commit suicide rather than perform the destructive mission he had accepted), as one who must not only act as protagonist in the story but respond to the action he is engaged in, "appreciate" it— that is, *augment* it as well as respond with understanding—as a witness. The more sensitive the observing consciousness the better, James argued (with Lear and Hamlet in mind), but the basic process, to a degree that varies from character to character, matches the imaginative act of the author. James's discussion hinges finally on perplexing assertions about "the *imputing* of intelligence" to the actualities he observes, the "projected light" he throws upon and thus *adds to* the life he treats in fiction, and his insistence that the process depends on his intimacy with the fictional agent who is the center of consciousness. Indeed, the act of imputation and projection creates the intimacy between the author and his agent that enables his account to yield any image of actual life at all.[48]

James points out that the author of a story is the attentive "listener to it" as well as the "reader of it," but suggests that even this act of witnessing life's "story" entails the active effort to "make it out, distinctly, on the crabbed page of life," to extract it from "the more or less Gothic text" of actual life in which it appears, and that this very process posits an actively intelligent mind which is both attentive to and caught in the "imbroglio." The crux of the writer's "affair" is the *"imputing* of intelligence"—creating the intelligence in the center of consciousness as part of the "constructional game" which not only expresses the artist's effort to give an intelligent account of life but enables him as reader and listener to do so. The imputation of intelligence by the artist, burdening and crediting his

[48] *Ibid.,* pp. 63-66.

THE "RELIGION OF DOING"

action with the lens of consciousness, is the basis for any capacity his art may have to image life.[49]

The artist's concern, James explained, is necessarily not the immediate report on life but an act more indirect and intimate, a more finely measured evaluation (capable of creative enlargement) which James called appropriately an "appreciation" of life; his "report of people's experience," altering but augmenting life, is his "appreciation of it." And intimacy with his center of consciousness was the necessary condition for James's appreciation of the experience, just as the projection of light by the imagination was the necessary condition for rendering actuality in art: "I can't appreciate save by intimacy, any more than I can report save by a projected light." The "projected light," then, is an increment of value in James's dramatic "economy," the constructed center of consciousness with a plausibly limited intelligence imputed to him. In him the burdens of "doing" and "feeling" are joined. He is the image and instrument of the artist's mediation as well as an actor and witness of the drama who can best render the action "dramatically and objectively." [50]

The strategy is objective in that it exposes the main instrument of measurement, with its limitations, to view, and it is the "guarded objectivity" of his dramatic strategy which James examined in the preface to *The Awkward Age,* where he discusses the structural function not of character but of dramatic "scene," illuminating further the translation of the analytic mode into a more fully dramatic one which is adumbrated in *Partial Portraits* and displayed in *The Spoils of Poynton* and the later fiction. Insisting strenuously that even with a superior subject the artist must *"build,"* that the dramatic form commits him "to construction at any cost," James described the basis of dramatic construction as an arrangement of artifices, a "cabalistic" ritual, which isolates its central action as a mystery and breaks it up into its aspects. The drama renders its central action an enigmatic mystery by penetrating and revealing it in the refractions of its "distinct aspects," each facet illuminated by a distinct "Occasion" or "scene" or "Act" which serve as

49 *Ibid.,* p. 63.
50 *Ibid.,* pp. 65-67.

distinct "lamps" to illuminate aspects of the central subject. The "guarded objectivity" of dramatic construction derives from the absence of narrative explanations by the author, the "imposed absence of that 'going behind,' to compass explanations and amplifications, to drag out odds and ends from the 'mere' story-teller's great property-shop of aids to illusion. . . ." The drama demands this "special sacrifice" but gains by being "more of a projected form than any other," challenging and "coercive" in its appeal because it must be struggled with, strained, and stretched. The "presented occasion" of the dramatic scene is "thoroughly interesting" and "thoroughly clear" but must "tell all its story itself, remain shut up in its own presence." With the self-contained "logic" of a mathematical construct (the compactness that is dangerously "factitious"), the drama depends on "cross-relations, relations all within the action itself." It gains its objectivity and its force of authority from the very condition that threatens the writer's authority by excluding his own voice and explanations: namely that "references in one's action can only be . . . to each other, to things on exactly the same plane of exhibition with themselves." This is the constriction which challenges the novelist to test and strain the form to the utmost while keeping to its exacting consistency.[51]

On reconsidering the logic of his plan for *The Awkward Age*—the isolation and enclosure of the central subject, its division into many "aspects" and the corresponding number of dramatic scenes, and the need to strain the form to the utmost to make up for the narrative techniques sacrificed to the logic of a stage play—James feared that his subject was doomed to "appreciable," even "preposterously appreciative," "overtreatment." While he left the question open to subsequent critical consensus, he insisted that the "high consistency" of his dramatic treatment was itself an "exhibition" of form worth achieving and doubted whether a line between appropriate treatment and overtreatment could be drawn (though the difference could be felt and insisted on by any reader). In *The Awkward Age*, he felt, as in any "really wrought work of art," no discontinuity between form and content was apparent. De-

51 *Ibid.*, pp. 109-111, 114.

THE "RELIGION OF DOING"

spite the striking consistency of its form, despite the "exhibition" of its structure in the finished work, the marriage of form
and action had been achieved in the "sacrament of execution." [52]

The marriage of art described in the Prefaces is one that invites and withstands the strong pressures it must sustain,
whether of subject and action or of artifice and convention;
and to the achieved display of these interacting pressures—the
energy and the form of crisis—the essays return time and again.
At times they draw attention to resulting "deformity" and disproportion—the unequal halves of novels, the misplaced center
and "makeshift middle"—at times they claim the triumph
when the novel openly displays its mastery of "treatment" by
formal contrasts, or preserves its form while it "strains, or tends
to burst, with a latent extravagance, its mould." Whether the
crisis is created by tensions between the strictly formal conventions of the fiction or between the form and the actual life
it treats, the Prefaces insist on the displayed prominence of
form and the conflicts among formal strategies which produce
it.[53]

The convention of spoken dialogue on which the stage play
is constructed, for instance, is so alien to English popular taste in
fiction and to the *narrative* basis of fiction, and so foreign to
James's device of the center of consciousness (with its capacity
for revealing *unspoken* response) that dialogue must be repressed, held forcibly in subordination to narrative presentation. The effort "to surround with the sharp black line . . .
that helps any arrangement of objects to become a picture," to
rival painting and accent its contours in fiction, is firmly sanctioned, although the Prefaces relegate the pictorial strategy to a
subordinate role of preparing for fully dramatic scenes. And
the achievement of dramatic compactness and objectivity, the
"building up" of scenes and centers of consciousness, is another
means of constructing compositional "blocks" which are ex-
hibited, "squared to the sharp edge," in their formal neatness
and solidity. Yet the strategies of painter and dramatist are at
odds with one another: "picture . . . is jealous of drama, and
drama . . . suspicious of picture . . . each baffles insidiously

[52] *Ibid.*, pp. 114-116, 118.
[53] *Ibid.*, pp. 85-87, 302-303, 158, 320, 46.

168

the other's ideal and eats round the edges of its position. . . ." One of the triumphs of form is achieved when, "under certain degrees of pressure," several centers of consciousness are compressed into "a represented community of vision" and the "boundary line" between painted "picture" and dramatic "scene" shows the "weight of the double pressure." [54]

The friction between techniques, the pressure generated by the interaction of formal conventions—the agon *within* the form—is part of the process in which life and art exert pressures against each other in fruitful if problematical conflict. Life "strains ever" to "justify its claim" to attention, James wrote in the preface to *Daisy Miller,* it "struggles at each step, and in defiance of one's raised admonitory finger, fully and completely to express itself." The "real art of representation" rests not on avoidance but on "controlled and guarded acceptance, . . . a perfect economic mastery, of that conflict." The "expansive, the explosive principle in one's material" challenges the form, which in turn suppresses the expansive "space hunger and space-cunning" of the subject; yet the material is "thoroughly noted," its explosive force permitted "to flush and colour and animate" the energetic form which it threatens and thereby quickens. It is in such a "marriage" that the form becomes, again in Malraux's terms, "discrepant from appearance" yet continuous with the surfaces and depths of actuality which it encounters and images in the "deep-breathing economy," as James celebrated it, of his "organic form." [55]

The torment of crisis, engaging his fiction's form along with its creator's imagination and the actions his novels depict, and the exploitive sacrifice enacted in undergoing it, James made the foundation for the novel's supremacy as a form in the last three prefaces. They bring to a culmination the central conceptions which emerged from James's attempt to "live back into a forgotten state" of artistic creation, reviving the "dead reasons" of intentions "buried" in the work, reawakening the "creative intimacy" of the original occasion and reconsidering the work in the light of it, extending the "religion of doing" into visions of new creation by converting the "first stir of

[54] *Ibid.,* pp. 106-107, 320, 101, 322-323, 296, 298, 300.
[55] *Ibid.,* pp. 278, 84.

life" of an earlier work into "the glorious birth . . . of still another infant motive." Whether possessing in the "back-shop" of the imagination the figure of Isabel Archer, remaining in "intimate commerce with his motive" in *The Spoils of Poynton,* or engaging in the "vicious practice" of smuggling in *The Aspern Papers,* the imagination acknowledged in the Prefaces is one which must "borrow" its material from actual life but then "lends and gives, . . . builds and piles high" in return and shares in the victimization of its characters.[56]

In its "intimate commerce" it probes "with the longest and firmest prongs of consciousness" to "grasp and hold the throbbing subject. . . ." It possesses and gets into the skin of Christopher Newman to leave him vitally alive but confined within "a medium 'cut-off' and shut up to itself." It finds "charm" in a "dramatic struggle" which involves the brutality of a young girl's "exposure" to the duplicities of adult society and the "sacrifice" of freedom suffered by the adults. The imagination is pleased because young Maisie, suffering "the strain of observation and the assault of experience," is so able to sustain the additional "tax" (James called it "monstrous") which his form imposes on her, that "we get, for our profit, . . . by an economy of process interesting in itself, the thoroughly pictured" rendition of her vulgar mother. In the case of Hyacinth Robinson, it is the "sharpest of his torments" that provides the crux of the drama; "staggering" under the weight of the intelligence imputed to him by the author who must confess his "immoral" interest in "personal character," he "collapses, poor Hyacinth, like a thief at night, over-charged with treasures of reflexion and spoils of passion of which he can give, in his poverty and obscurity, no honest account." As in the case of actual figures used as prototypes—as in the case of *any* of his materials, James declared—characters are "passed through the crucible of his imagination" and cooked in his "intellectual *pot-au-feu.*" They are not "boiled to nothing," to be sure, but gain a "final savour" from their "new and richer saturation" in the stew, the "genial medium." In that process the character's "prime identity" is "destroyed" but its "final savour" is constituted and it becomes a "different and, thanks to a rare alchemy, a better

56 *Ibid.,* pp. 11, 183, 122.

thing." The materials are consumed in a sacrificial process which is the foundation of art.[57]

The sacrifice encompasses even the plans for the novel and the vision which inspired it. The "sacrament of execution," with its "surrenders" and "compromises," creates the finished work only at the expense of the "best thing" it sought to achieve. The attempt to portray a painter's triumphs in *The Tragic Muse* necessarily fails (because the triumph lies not in the painter but in his work), and accordingly the rendition of the painter Nick Dormer falls short, remaining as "flat as some mere brass check or engraved number," the storage check or pawn ticket which is the "symbol and guarantee of a stored treasure." The triumph of art builds on its own failures and betrayals.[58]

This is the insight which governs the preface to *The Wings of the Dove,* including its remarks about the work's "deformity" and about the author as a "wary adventurer," endangering a subject which threatens him—"standing off" from his subject, then "coming back to it," walking "round and round" his "formidable" theme or subject with its "possible treacheries and traps," expecting the "offered victim" to give a great deal but to exact "equal services in return" and to "collect this debt to the last shilling." The failure of intentions to "fructify," James wrote, the artist's failure to realize in execution his "first and most blest illusion," is "far from abnormal": it is the very basis of creation. The "artist's energy fairly depends on his fallibility," his capacity for error and for being deceived. He must be the "dupe" of his plan in order to be "measurably the master" of what he produces, which is a mere "substitute" for the original vision. He bases the foundation for his bridge surely enough on the original design, and the finished work *does* bear traffic; but the span does so "in apparently complete independence of . . . the principal grace of the original design." The "substitute" becomes real at the expense of the original design, the vision being an "illusion" for the "necessary hour" which serves the fallible artist's imagination. The triumphs which this preface proceeds to claim for *The Wings of*

---

[57] *Ibid.*, pp. 258, 37-39, 105, 102, 146, 150, 147, 72, 156, 230.
[58] *Ibid.*, pp. 126, 97.

the Dove, wrought from the destructive friction between "picture" and "drama," are a flawed substitute for the original vision, salvaged by the "Angel" and "Demon" of "Compromise" from the glories, now "lapsed," which had been originally imagined. The creative process, accordingly, embraces a ruin within it. The Prefaces do not simply admit that art shows evidence of its imperfections. They suggest that the very necessities of form, the artistic process itself, contribute to a ruinous wastage on which mastery depends. The process accordingly entails not simply the attempt to fulfill aspirations and realize visions but to redeem them from the betrayals and corruptions which the creative imagination has helped to enact. It becomes of necessity a process of salvaging the vision and materials it wastes, a process of redemption.[59]

The succeeding prefaces describe more amply the nature of the sacrificial process. When the watchful author, the "handler of puppets," encounters the "germ" for a story, he thrills at "the business of looking for the unseen" as if he held the "gage" of a challenge in his hand or were following "bloodhounds" in pursuit of a "hidden slave." After deciding "where to put one's hand on it," he does not transplant it but forcibly "plucks" it from the garden of life, he shops for his materials in stores until deciding on a purchase or "capture." Then ensues the *"process"* of making, of "expression, the literal squeezing out, of value . . . ," the "ciphering" comparable to that of a bookkeeper or "accountant." The preface goes on to describe the "costly sacrifice" for "composition" and the "amusement of the . . . difficulties" which his form entails, including the subordination of dialogue and the elimination of the "terrible *fluidity* of self-revelation" of the autobiographical technique in fiction. Both are sacrificed to his technique of the center of consciousness, who is "encaged" in the strictness of the narrative's dramatic logic, the "exhibitional conditions" which enforce on the character "proprieties" which are unusually stiff.[60]

The preface closes with the confession that *The Ambassadors'* young hero, Chad, by being deprived of the chance for "direct presentability" in one important episode, has been

[59] *Ibid.,* pp. 302-303, 288-290, 296-298.
[60] *Ibid.,* pp. 308, 311-312, 318-321.

"compromised" and "despoiled" by the "treachery" of the form, though the form in that incident achieves admirable "representational effect" in accordance with a pictorial rather than a fully dramatic strategy. The novel is filled with comparable triumphs which, though they "compromise" the subject and betray one of the novel's formal strategies, redeem another logic of the novel's form. *The Ambassadors*, James wrote, is filled with these "repaired losses, these insidious recoveries, these intensely redemptive consistencies." Indeed, the "oppositions" among the formal strategies it absorbs—the "expressional change and contrast" of formal effect—give the genre of the novel an intensity matching, if not exceeding, the intensity of the stage play. The novel is the "most independent, most elastic, most prodigious of literary forms," and it is founded on a process which is both treacherous and redemptive, betraying and redeeming its materials in the act of creation.[61]

So consuming is the form's redemptive power that it can transform the less substantial of its instruments, convert them into substantial figures in their own right and so fuse the "matter" of the subject with the "manner" of its treatment that the two are left distinguishable but inseparable in the marriage of art. The distinction insisted upon in the preface to *The Portrait of a Lady* between elements which belong directly to the subject and other elements which relate "intimately to the treatment" is restated in the preface to *The Ambassadors,* where the character Maria Gostrey and the final chapter of the novel are declared to have no essential relation to the subject, to relate instead wholly to the "treatment" and "form." Miss Gostrey is in effect a useful actress hired by the author "at a high salary," a wholly subordinate and instrumental character with only a "false connexion" to the principal character, Strether; the final chapter (Strether's farewell to Miss Gostrey) adds "nothing whatever" to the action but is "an artful expedient for sheer consistency of form," serving to make more vivid, to "express," certain values that have already been established by other incidents. Yet James reintroduced this distinction only to make a profound shift in its relevance, orienting it toward the preliminary rather than the final stages of the compositional proc-

[61] *Ibid.,* pp. 325-326.

ess. The context in which it is introduced is governed by a concern for the problematic role of artifice and "dissimulation"—for the "treacheries," and "the redemptive consistencies," of the creative process—and by James's tacit recognition that the function of Miss Gostrey and of the final scene, in being subordinate to more urgent matters, is not incidental to the practice of his craft but central to it. It is "part and parcel," indeed the very basis of the act of *mediation,* the act of expression, in art. To speak of using Miss Gostrey and the final scene so as "to express as vividly as possible" something "quite other than itself," something *else,* is to define the very function of art: the remarks define not only the function of *minor* instruments in their relation to major characters and events but define the relation of *all* of art's instruments to the actualities they image or the vision they reveal. James declared: "all art is *expression*" and went on to describe the process whereby the mere hiring and employment of instruments turn into veritable "ecstasies of method" and Miss Gostrey's "false connexion" is made to "carry itself . . . as a real one"; she takes on not only the dissimulated appearance but "something of the dignity of a prime idea." The scene which has "nothing to do with the matter" and "everything to do with the manner" of treatment is rendered "for fully economic expression's sake, as if it were important and essential. . . ." The *substantial* materials and vision, and the *as if* deriving from formal construction, are joined by the "sacrament of execution" in the marriage of art. And the craft which redeems the *as if* of Miss Gostrey's merely instrumental role and joins it with the more urgent action of other characters epitomizes the very basis of the creative imaginative act, which the preface to *The Golden Bowl* founds on the fusion of the poet's " 'taste' " with his "active sense of life." [62]

The preface to *The Golden Bowl* completes James's celebration of his art in an essay which commits him to the "religion of doing" despite a profoundly apologetic concern that must be actively countered by the thrust of "doing"—the burden of revising or "re-doing" and the commitment to further creative effort. Despite the fact that one's art may appear "ragged" be-

[62] *Ibid.,* pp. 53, 322-325, 340.

cause it "perpetually escapes our control," mere "gaping contrition" is contemptible. Though at liberty to abandon his connection with his work to the "desolation" which unavoidably dissolves so much human effort, though free to "disavow" his performance, he may, by examining and endorsing his work, establish "the tradition of his behavior" and find his "responsibility reconstituted." This James did in the preface to *The Golden Bowl*. There he acknowledged "all the possible sources of entertainment" in his fiction—the " 'fun' if we but allow the term its full extension"—and insisted that for the artist "to 'put' things" is "to do them" and that the deeds which give "expression" to life are part of the responsible exercise of freedom and contribute to the "religion of doing." He undertook to establish "the tradition of his behavior" in a celebration which not only defines the viability of his art and of the novel—claiming them to be instruments worthy of "the seer and speaker" who "under the descent of the god" is the " 'poet,' " whatever his form—but which confesses also their limitations, the precarious footing of their authority in a world where authority is problematical and is acknowledged to be so, where authority is challenged on all sides and where responsible authority is that which acknowledges the challenge, recognizes the claims, and incorporates the challenge in its constituted forms and enactments. The preface to *The Golden Bowl*, the last of the "shrines and stations of penance," begins by returning to the question of the center of consciousness, the structural basis of James's fiction, and revealing a specifically vicarious imagination: one which participates in the reality it helps to form and make sacred, by creating a flawed substitute for it only to become a mere surrogate and mediator for the process itself.[63]

The essay risks redundancy to make clear that the fictional center of consciousness is a deputed agent of the author, functioning to establish a "painter's or poet's" access to the subject, no matter how little the character's ostensible imaginative power. James singled out as examples his first-person narrators (like the Publishing Scoundrel) before citing central characters who serve the function without actually performing the task of narration; but the essential function is the same in both

[63] *Ibid.,* pp. 345, 347-348, 340.

175

cases. The narrator, he said, is the "deputy" or "delegate" of the author himself, a "convenient substitute or apologist," a "confessed agent" of the writer. Through him or her the fiction gains a "more or less detached, not strictly involved" observer, but also a "near" exposure to its action which is so close that James disliked calling the method "indirect and oblique." The story also gains a "personal" response instead of the author's own "impersonal account"—his mere "cold affirmation or thin guarantee," at once "gross" and "bloodless," which James had disparaged in the preface to *The Wings of the Dove*. And the fiction gains an objectively embodied delegate for "the creative power otherwise so veiled and disembodied." [64]

Yet the method entails so complete a delegation of authority that it verges on outright abdication by the writer, and accordingly the essay hastens to emphasize the issue of responsibility and to suggest the complexities, indeed the "embarrassed truth," surrounding James's commitment to his craft.[65] It explores the issue with a sense of urgency that links it with Emerson's "The Poet," Hawthorne's *The Blithedale Romance,* or Whitman's *Democratic Vistas* and other American classics which make the responsibility of the artist a matter of pressing concern, and joins it with Melville's "Benito Cereno," "Bartleby the Scrivener," and *Billy Budd* in exploring the problematic relations between the exercise of authority and either the abdication or the delegation of it. Brief though James's remarks are, in the context provided by the preceding prefaces and by his own fiction they can stand beside such profound explorations of the problem as Shakespeare's *Measure for Measure* and *The Tempest,* where the issues are raised (whatever their solutions) in connection with the actions of the Duke and Prospero: the Duke's reluctance to "stage" himself, his delegation of power to Angelo, his surveillance of Angelo in disguise and his continued exercise of power under the protection of deceit, his gradual involvement with his populace, the exposure of his disguise and his public resumption of authority at the end— and in *The Tempest,* Prospero's retirement from the active

64 *Ibid.*, pp. 327, 301.
65 *Ibid.*, pp. 327-328.

rule of Milan to devote himself to his books, his overthrow and banishment, his practice of his art with Ariel's help on his island domain, the drowning of his book, and the projected return to his dukedom.

In James's final preface, he declared that not his, but an alternative form, is irresponsible: "the muffled majesty of irresponsible 'authorship.' " Authorship is irresponsible when it is concealed without being confessed, as James's concealed presence is confessed in the structure of his fiction; authority is irresponsible that is comfortably scarved and remote in majesty from its figures rather than being implicated itself in the "torment of interest," as James's art is implicated by the "cruel crisis" of its composition. The "painter of the picture or the chanter of the ballad" can "never be responsible *enough*," and James took responsibility not merely for some parts of his "doing" but for "every inch of his surface and note of his song," whether to his credit or his shame, finding in the adoption of his particular form the "most instead of least to answer for." It is that responsibility, acknowledged in the Prefaces, that is confessed implicitly in the fiction by being embodied in the form.[66]

In *The Golden Bowl* itself, James explained, the "manner" in which the "embarrassed truth" of his responsibility "betrays itself" is unusual, because in that work "the muffled majesty of authorship" which he declared irresponsible does *"ostensibly* reign," that novel (like *The Ambassadors* and *The Wings of the Dove*) being narrated directly by James himself while focusing with exceptional closeness on its two centers of consciousness, the Prince and Maggie. But it is precisely that willed dependence on, that deference to, his centers of consciousness that redeems an otherwise irresponsible artistry, renders his craft a responsible act because it enables him to create the fiction and become a vicarious participant in it while acknowledging that he cannot literally be an actor in it, that his characters suffer under the imposition of his form, that he cannot "appreciate" or "construct" the action, cannot create the novel, single-handed. The Prince "virtually represents to himself everything that concerns us" although he does not "speak in the

66 *Ibid.*

THE "RELIGION OF DOING"

first person"; Maggie's mind reveals as much, while "playing her part" in the drama, as either the Publishing Scoundrel or Fleda Vetch, and thus serves as an instrument, a "compositional resource," as well as a "value intrinsic." It is they, and the function of mediation which they both symbolize and perform, that redeem James's artistry from the irresponsibility which he risked in assuming the deceptive pretense of "majesty" which *"ostensibly"* governs *The Golden Bowl.* The "bleeding participants" redeem the craft by expressing completely the contingencies of his "constructional game": they give form to James's hazard of abdication as well as to his determination to create an intimate form and to engage in the encounter with life. Others share the function (James named Mrs. Assingham), but the Prince and Maggie bear the larger burden.[67]

If they reveal James to be more nearly detached than they from full immersion in reality, they do not disengage him from the action but draw him into it, enabling him with his "penetrating imagination" to become a vicarious participant and to assume responsibility for all the action as a consequence of his commitment to his form. For in the light of his form James could see himself "shaking it off," that "muffled majesty of authorship," indeed "disavowing the pretence of it" in the act of so constructing his novel as to "get down into the arena and do my best to live and breathe and rub shoulders and converse with the persons engaged in the struggle," the characters who spend out their lives for the entertainment of those who watch, in the "struggle which provides for the others in the circling tiers the entertainment of the great game." The preface need not name the Roman Colosseum to suggest an entertainment enjoyed at the "expense of someone else," a community of martyrdom and exploitation and art. The author makes clear, however, that he is not an actual or full participant: "There is no other participant, of course, than each of the real, the deeply involved and immersed and more or less bleeding participants. . . ." It is they who pay the larger price. Yet he has achieved his mastery because he has held firmly to his form in the "sacrament of execution"; he has "held" it both "fast" in his grip and "fondly" by constructing the novel, building his

[67] *Ibid.,* pp. 328-330.

art on the sacrificial struggle of "bleeding participants" in the arenas of life and art.[68]

The conjunction of ritual sacrifice, exploitive commerce and combat, and the act of artistic construction which the Prefaces reveal in such ample detail has a special relevance, of course, for James's own art, but the motives singly or together appear in James's late essays on other figures and reveal how commanding they were in his conception of the creative process. George Sand's profitable use of her erotic affairs, the combat within her art between the "victim's" desire to protect her privacy and the "inquirer's" determination to betray it, and her eventual triumph in the "citadel of style" provide a case in point. Zola affords another, for while he relied on thorough-going "imitation" in depicting the commonplace and sordid, his "design was from the start architectural" and his is "one of the few most constructive achievements of his time." He "inordinately sacrifices" to the vulgar commonplace and pays by being overwhelmed by it, but in *Germinal* and *La Débâcle* "the sacrifice is ordered and fruitful for the subject. . . ." It is Balzac who fully demonstrates that great artists "really *bought* their information," there being "no convincing art that is not ruinously expensive," and who shows that "his spirit has somehow paid for its knowledge" and moreover, that "he had more to spend." His rare genius is a trust fund which has survived "the extravagance of . . . his twenty years of royal intellectual spending," because the "original property—the high, prime genius" was safely "tied-up from him" and the original capital has "steadily, has enormously, appreciated." [69]

It is an essay on Shakespeare's *The Tempest,* however, published in 1907 when James was writing his Prefaces, which best displays how intimately the essays on other writers impinge on James's own imaginative life, and how deeply he was concerned about the artist's involvement with his creations and his responsible commitment to the "religion of doing." He apologized to those interpreters who unlike himself were sanguinely certain of their "triumphant pointings of the moral" in the face of "one of the supreme works of literature," and confessed that

[68] *Ibid.*, p. 328.
[69] *Notes on Novelists*, pp. 60, 34, 29, 54; *The Lesson of Balzac*, pp. 94, 101, 116.

he stood "baffled" in "strained and aching wonder" before the "serenity" of the play's subject. The subject remains "unwinking and inscrutable as a divinity in a temple, save for that vague flicker of derision, the only response to our interpretative heat . . ."; our only solace is the satisfaction of "having crossed the circle of fire, and so got into the real and right relation to it. . . ." Then James proceeded to take issue with two claims that most disturbed him: one was the assertion of Halliwell-Phillips, in his *Outlines of the Life of Shakespeare,* that Shakespeare's plays, unlike such meager records as his will and unlike his lyric poems, reveal nothing about the author because the dramatist necessarily obliterates himself in assuming the personalities of his characters; the other was the view of Brander Matthews that *The Tempest* was Shakespeare's farewell to the stage.[70]

James insisted that instead of being obliterated the dramatist is in effect enclosed and diffused, still present, in his art. The citizen is "effectually locked up and imprisoned in the artist," and the artist is "steeped in the abysmal objectivity of his characters and situation," but he survives in the depths where the "great billows of the medium itself play with him," and we, looking over "a ship's side, in certain waters," can see him much as we see, "through transparent tides, the flash of strange sea-creatures." Usually the reader encounters violence at the depths to which the artist has plunged in the succession of his works, but in *The Tempest,* though he "sinks as deep as we like," what Shakespeare "sinks into, beyond all else, is the lucid stillness of his style." [71]

Such a plunge *could not* be an act of abdication or imaginative suicide—James's conviction has the force of intimate concern and the thrust of a commitment made in the face of the uncertainty of its foundations. If Shakespeare deliberately said farewell to the stage in *The Tempest* and then, despite the "amplitude and perfect control" of his powers which are displayed in that play, kept to his decision, he had chosen to

[70] James's essay appeared as the introduction to *The Tempest* in the *Complete Works of Shakespeare,* Renaissance Edition, ed. Sidney Lee, XVI (1907). It is reprinted in *The Appreciation of Shakespeare,* ed. Bernard M. Wagner (Washington, 1949). For the quotations above, see pp. 475-476.
[71] *Ibid.,* p. 477.

" 'elect,' as we say, to cease, intellectually, to exist. . . ." Why would he choose suicide, choose "not to be," when his power seemed undiminished? Would not that creative energy, if diverted to another field, break the dams to "ravage" another country? The answer lies in the work itself, in the "figured tapestry, the long arras" that "hides" Shakespeare but leaves him within reach of the desperate inquirer, the Hamlet with "the finer weapon, the sharper point, the stronger arm, the more extended lunge." [72]

James had made that lunge, and also suffered and survived the onslaught, in the work published in 1901 but omitted from the New York Edition, *The Sacred Fount*. It precedes the bulk of James's later criticism, including the Prefaces, and the three finished masterpieces of what the late Professor F. O. Matthiessen has named "the major phase." It presents boldly and nakedly the crisis for the imagination that James's later essays were to describe as the matrix of art and defines, in its lurid extremity, a turning point in his career when he probed the resources of his artistry to their seminal absurdities and reconstituted his art on his deepened recognition of both the power and the limits of its perilous authority. The work presents a caricature or parody of James's art, as Wilson Follett discerned three decades ago, though it is a more profoundly creative parody than he suggested. It is a lunging attack on the authority of art which is at once a critical examination of the constructive foundation of James's own craft and the challenge of life itself to the validity of *all* imaginative creation. Yet the attack is a profoundly creative one; it joins the challenge to authority with the redemptive power of his art which together construct a vision from the materials which the imagination shatters and plays with. Moreover, both the lunge and the redemptive effort are directed also toward forms of behavior of English drawing-room society and the actual middle-class world implicit in it, the marriages and liaisons, the decorum and the commerce, of a world in the throes of change. *The Sacred Fount* presents an image of life and art which is at once a grotesque mockery of their actual interaction and a hypothetical vision of their redemptive possibilities. It enacts the "miracle"

[72] *Ibid.*, pp. 479, 481.

of entertainment—the "miraculous enlargement of experience," the "appreciative" transformation of actuality which a "penetrating" and constructive imagination helps bring to life—while celebrating the absurd folly, the sacrifice of passion, which it makes the sacred fount of both life and art.

[IV]

THE SACRED FOUNT

THE PLAY of fantasy which characterizes *The Sacred Fount* is not confined to the actions of the nameless Narrator, the "delegate" and "confessed agent" who is used by James to present the narrative, but characterizes also other inhabitants of Newmarch. Both the exercise of his imagination, and the Newmarch which stimulates and challenges it, are fantastic exaggerations, ludicrous and unnerving in their extremity but none the less relevant to the realities they parody. The " 'searchlight of irony' " as an instrument of self-scrutiny, which Wilson Follett credited to James but which Professor Leon Edel would withhold from him, probes the imagination's attempts to "read" experience and construct hypotheses about it, but scrutinizes also the world of Newmarch which that imagination confronts, making a somber mockery of its needs and institutions. The parody is severe and compelling in its fascination, not only because it is scrupulously controlled but because it moves with a compressed energy which challenges all control; the form of parody is assumed, like Hamlet's "antic disposition," to control the unintended parody that James's art threatens to become and to measure the pressures that motivate it; and it embraces simultaneously the activities of the Narrator's obsessive imagination and the diversions (some idle, some desperate) of the other house-party guests who, like readers of entertaining novels, are literally "living at the expense of someone else"—their weekend host who is never named.[73]

It is not the authority of the Narrator alone, but also the authority of James's imagination (which is engaged with the Narrator in creating the fiction) and the authority of the enigmatic novel itself which is challenged by the parody, the presentational form which renders an account in this case only to

[73] Wilson Follett, "Henry James' Portrait of Henry James," *New York Times Book Review*, August 23, 1936, pp. 2, 16; Leon Edel, "An Introductory Essay," *The Sacred Fount* (New York, 1953), p. vi. Subsequent references to the text of the novel are to Professor Edel's edition, a reprint of the first American edition (New York, 1901), and are included in parentheses in the text.

call into question its own validity. Yet its light is so searching, the parody so profound, the challenge so integral to the creative act itself, that the novel's authority is redeemed in the act of recognizing the perils and limits as well as the powers of its authority, taking their scrupulous measure, and founding the novel on a constructive act which authenticates them. The Narrator's failure, the collapse of his " 'houses of cards' " which is dramatized so vividly at the end, is not dissociated from James's mastery in the novel but is instead one of its sources. The Narrator's failure is made the basis for the weird and inventive novel which his absurd folly enabled James to create.

One condition under which the Narrator's imagination operates is an isolation so extreme as to render his loneliness unsettling and his access to experience dubious, with an effect for the reader which is terrifying and funny. His first gesture as he boards the train for the country house is to shy away from a companion whom he fears will pay him no attention, and much of the time at Newmarch he spends in lonely speculation about the relations among the other guests: he strolls down empty wooded paths; he walks down a long corridor, avoiding two married friends but desperately curious about them, then hears "the closing of the door furthest from me" and turns around "to find the Brissendens gone"; he stands anxiously exposed beneath an electric light in a vacant hall at midnight, watching through a window, as if from across a void, the figure of an acquaintance who "seemed as lost in thought as I was lost in my attention to him." He drifts from deserted room to deserted room after others have gone to bed, seeking Mrs. Briss in response to her summons to the midnight rendezvous that closes the novel. The effect is consistently eerie, at once chilling in the sense of isolation and oppressive in the sense of enclosure. (2, 199, 202.)

Within the lengthening corridors of this surrealism, the musing Narrator scrutinizes his fellows in silent isolation—a psychic isolation which persists even when the effect is comic as well as weird, and even when he converses with other guests. They seem as wrapped as he in a shell of privacy and to be joined to him by no more than the curiosity they share, or the interest in his hypotheses that he manages to arouse, and by the

skein of language which they wind around it. While each
engages in the double task of telling things to another and
reading the remarks of his partner, virtual miracles of communication take place—as when the Narrator exclaims with
glee and pride " 'Then . . . you *could* tell what I was talking
about!' " But these miracles appear (when they do) in exchanges which are haunted by what is dropped unfinished or
left unsaid, bristle with nightmarish abstraction and enigma,
and are subject to absurdly protracted improvisations or to
sudden ruptures and dissolutions. In one of the questions put
by the Narrator at the end, the language, become linear and
abstract, balloons off from the ostensible trivia of the action
toward the verge of nihilism: " '*Was* this "something" your
conclusion, then and there, that there's nothing in anything?' "
Earlier, the painter Obert, who so pleases the Narrator by understanding him, asks " 'How on earth can I tell what you're
talking about' " and proceeds to break off the conversation
abruptly with the complaint that " 'I think you ask too much of
me.' " In an earlier conversation the Narrator has managed
to detain Obert by adding one question to an already long
string of them, but as Obert strains to get away the discourse
spins out to the edge of inconsequence since the dialogue is
serving to parody the sheer task of keeping the novel going; his
added question has accomplished no more than to move the
figures indoors and "so far up our staircase as to where it
branched toward Obert's room." (205-206, 286, 20.)

Comically unimportant though that accomplishment is made
to seem, the remark defines two grimly serious purposes, one
being to parody the process of building intrigue on the sheer
talk and ruminations of house-party guests, the other being to
present the significantly odd community in which the Narrator
is placed. Obert's willingness to play along with the Narrator's
interest up to a point, yet break away from it; the Narrator's
attempt to build a community of interest while holding back
some of his private notions or deepest suspicions; the terraces
and staircases where these figures converse along with the private chambers into which they disappear—these serve to define
the weird community which the novel presents in revealing detail. Trivia may burgeon into Gothic obsessions, or intriguing

conversation dissolve into inconsequence, but the resulting disproportions reveal a brilliant caricature of a distinctly modern community where change and immanent transformation are the norms and where both privacy and sociability are compulsive goals of the inhabitants.

On the opening pages, the Narrator's compounded memories and anticipations present a world of shifting contingencies—"possible friends and even possible enemies," distinctly genial acquaintances and equally unsociable persons who within a day were to prove to be the reverse, fellow railroad passengers "on whom one built with confidence" only to find that they were not going to Newmarch at all—and the community at Newmarch emerges as a fantastic combination of old acquaintances, merely reassembling on one of many similar occasions, and a group of persons so jumbled together, so profoundly altered, that many friends cannot so much as recognize each other. (1-2.)

On the one hand, characters are separated by abysses and the group seems singularly unsettled. Settled traditions and new conventions appear together in a shifting mixture. While there is nothing essentially new in the relation between Mrs. Froome and Lord Lutley, they display "the wondrous new fashion" by traveling openly together—"and their servants, too, like a single household." The institution of marriage is being flouted if not challenged by another institution (Mrs. Froome's liaison), while being exhaustively *used* by Mrs. Briss. Couples married and unmarried, aristocrats and middle-class persons, appear "mingled and confounded, as might be said, not sorted by tradition." (4, 15.)

Indeed, it is a world of fantastic, almost directionless change. Guy Brissenden has become aged since his recent marriage while his wife, though older than he, has become more youthful; she so thrives as to be " 'bloated' " while he has become " 'shrunken,' " and the Narrator can recognize neither. Gilbert Long, once a handsome dolt, now possesses such wit and eloquence that neither the Narrator nor Mrs. Briss easily recognizes him. If people seem to be changing, one is later said to be changing " 'back.' " Mrs. Briss later denies that Long's change for the better ever took place. We are told of swift "cessations and resumptions of life" in swift, almost throbbing, succession, by the widow May Server. (67, 212, 151.)

In the play of language take place changes as extreme as any asserted to be true. The age of Mrs. Briss (about forty-three, though she now looks only twenty-five) is advanced to fifty in the banter of one guest, then advanced to ninety-three by Mrs. Briss herself (who feels " 'as if I changed every seven minutes' ") only to be told that if she would dress for the age of twenty-five she would look a mere charming fifteen. The effect is to create a shifting perspective (patently fictive in some of the banter, presumably actual in the lives of some of the guests) which is governed by the immanence of change, unpredictable contingencies in a state of crisis whose very pattern and direction are called into question by the fantastic proliferation of wrinkled or rejuvenated faces, bulging or shrinking torsos, and verbal exchanges which seem to enclose at once a real mystery and a hollow void. (5, 8.)

While isolation and change verging on chaos characterize the community, relations at Newmarch paradoxically seem at times unusually close and members of the community oppressively interconnected. The local habitation, for the duration of the party, is made to seem more self-contained and cohesive than the vague locales from which its separate guests were drawn, all selected for the contribution each would make, all assigned to rooms (with name plates affixed), and all mutually involved in unrelenting games of prying inquiry and artful maneuvering. The Narrator who at first avoids Gilbert Long on the railroad platform is nevertheless already subject to longings for companionship and also recollections of it, and he has been building, in his anticipations, the miniature society which is beginning to form at Newmarch. His expectations are part of the constructive process by which the party takes form. So also are the motives of Long, who, though he makes a habit of avoiding the Narrator elsewhere, now seeks to renew their acquaintance; he moves his baggage into the Narrator's compartment and brings along Mrs. Briss, his companion for the train trip. These actions define one of the pressures bearing on Newmarch and on *The Sacred Fount:* the determination, whether for idle or profound motives, to form a society. Newmarch being "a place of a charm so special as to create rather a bond among its guests," the Narrator soon finds himself talking with Long "quite as with the tradition" of "prompt intimacy." (2-3.)

Throughout the novel the Narrator's pursuit of fellow guests, his attempt to engage them in conversation and enlist them as cohorts in his speculations, his compulsive effort to establish social intercourse and prolong it, are ludicrous yet gripping attempts to form the elemental basis of a community. His attempts are comparable in kind to the careful planning of Lord Lutley and Mrs. Froome, of the Brissendens and other guests, and of the nameless host who occasions the party and assigns the guests to rooms; and the Narrator's efforts are the basis for his involvement, as observer and participant, in the action. Moreover, they are the basis for the "near" exposure to the action of the novel which engaged James, through his "deputy or delegate," in the act of creating the novel and which establishes a community of interest with the reader who is entertained while reading it. *The Sacred Fount* is a parody of all these communities simultaneously and constitutes their inseparable fusion. It becomes the attempt to found a community—for characters, author, and reader alike—on the basis of intimacy and to transform the novel into a fully intimate form, one which might court its readers with tact, veil the privacy of its characters and so achieve communion with them, penetrating their forms of behavior to the reality harbored in them and, for the reader, intimating the actualities it images and the vision it creates.

One way the novel parodies the process in which formal relations emerge as intimate ones, while also parodying the Narrator's attempt to discover and understand them, is by presenting its figures repeatedly in pairs of which one partner only is visible: the Narrator's awkward effort to identify, or even discern, the second partner has the effect of completing a pattern and adding to his store of information while calling into question his supply of data and the adequacy of his interpretation of it, suggesting that he imputes to the relation something that may not be there. Yet the felt presence of veiled intrigue and of authentic enigma is as pronounced as is the suggestion of the Narrator's delusion, with the result that the same episodes which mock his reliability present a possible pattern of relationships and establish it as hypothetically or tentatively valid, a pattern which may actually be unfolding before his eyes, almost independently of his attempt to *read* or interpret it. One instance occurs when the profile of Mrs. Server is turned "as if for talk with some one" beyond the range of the Narrator's and Mrs. Briss's view; it is more than two pages before the observers—discerning first "a brown shoe, in a white gaiter" then no more than "the shoulder and outstretched leg" of a man—can ascertain that the hidden companion emerging from behind a tree is not the Gilbert Long they had hypothesized but Mrs. Briss's husband. (82-84.)

Antic though this behavior is, it suggests the reality of clandestine relations of some sort which have been implied, though not conclusively demonstrated, from the moment the Narrator learns that Mrs. Briss is being escorted by Gilbert Long, that her husband is arriving with Lady John, and that Lord Lutley and Mrs. Froome have pooled servants and baggage in a "single household." One of the most enigmatic relations is established when the Narrator enters his own chamber to find that someone else, mistakenly thinking the room his own, had entered it from the other end and called out the Narrator's name. The "stranger," whom the Narrator cannot at first recognize, is a married man, the "hero of his odd union," who had been "put by himself, for some reason, in the bachelor wing" and, "exploring at hazard, had mistaken the signs." The man, aged almost beyond recognition, proves to be Guy Brissenden. The encounter presents "poor Briss" as an alter ego for the Narrator (who likewise makes hazardous explorations and makes mistakes) and establishes an intimate relationship between the two which is central to the novel. The Narrator adds Briss to his "little gallery . . . the museum of those who put to me with such intensity the question of what had happened to them," taking him as a figure in the "play," as he is to call it later, "that had so unexpectedly insisted on constituting itself for me. . . ." When they part toward the end of the novel, they shake hands in a darkened corridor, "while things unspoken and untouched, unspeakable and untouchable" stand or pass between them, and after watching Briss "retreat along the passage," the Narrator returns with tears in his eyes to resume conversation with the painter, Ford Obert, in a lighted room. (20-22, 168, 227.)

The "relations" which take shape in *The Sacred Fount* are tenuous and hypothetical, enigmatic and fantastic, but they image a significant community in which elemental human activities are at once constrained and given release, veiled and given room to play, by forms. The forms which are central in the novel are marriage (whether formalistic or intimate), the liaison (whether founded on promiscuity or more lasting bonds), and the arts (an enigmatic painting, a piano recital, and the art of conversation). Together these adumbrate a distillation of civilized refinements and conventions.

The characters live at Newmarch in the realm where the Narrator feels that they live: namely, "in a beautiful old picture, we were in a beautiful old tale." Poor Briss peers from the frame of a Velasquez portrait and leans over the "rigid convention" of his clothing much as some defunct ruler "at the opera looks over the ribbon of an order and the ledge of a box." The forms which emerge are at once social and artistic in these "halls of art and fortune," and the environment at once stimulates and challenges the imagination. (130, 156, 158.)

It releases the wildest fancies in Obert, Mrs. Briss, and the Narrator, yet its bland decorum and affluence, the felicitous "harmony and taste," check the fantasies it helps produce; Newmarch closes the door on the "most finely poetic" sense with the disdain accorded an "univited reporter" or "the newspaper-man kicked out." The occasion of the piano recital shapes the group of guests into a "dispersed circle," and the music embraces "the infinite." The concert, whether or not colored by "an hallucination" of the Narrator, presents a complex image of the function of art, creating a community of listeners whose anticipations of some important "experience" have been aroused but whose postures ("composed" and "receptive") reveal the determination to impress each other, the mere desire of the "imagination to be flattered, nerves to be quieted, sensibilities to be soothed," along with the authentic "thirst for the infinite to be quenched." Both "beauty" and "terror" inhere in the "conditions so highly organized" which protect at the cost of concealing May Server's "lonely fight with disintegration," providing a rare moment of rest while the occasion and the music help her sustain the appearance of tranquil "amenity." (156-157, 165-167.)

In the Narrator (and in the reader) Newmarch occasions "intense obsessions," a "strained vision" which at once stimulates his ingenuity and oppresses him so that (like Ariel or Prospero finally in Shakespeare's *Tempest*) he longs for "liberation." The dense "thickness" of the "medium" at Newmarch is unnatural, a "crystal cage" which separates from "the summer stars" the absurdly civilized inhabitants, "the ladies in particular at once so little and so much clothed, so beflounced yet so denuded." Only his inveterate curiosity keeps the Narrator from acting on his determination to leave abruptly, and "escape all reminders" of Newmarch by "forswearing all returns." Yet oppressive and deceptive though the forms of intercourse are at Newmarch, they harbor more than one "dim community" of intimacy which the principal characters foster, shield, and talk about. And although the Narrator at the end does leave the premises abruptly, his remembered account of his weekend is testimony that he could not, if he did indeed want to, "escape all reminders" of it. (193, 199-201, 169.)

Three pressures begin to build up within that community in connection with arrangements for the party. One is the pressure of actuality: needs and desires, both social and personal, for erotic love or companionship, curiosities of mind and feeling, hazards of experience which extend beneath the exposed surface of actuality but spread out upon the surface also, whether because they occasionally erupt and partially emerge on the surface or because (as in the case of Lord Lutley and Mrs. Froome) they openly pervade its forms of behavior. The many arrangements, chance encounters, and planned rendezvous of social intercourse at Newmarch repeatedly suggest a network of "relations," clearly formal within the fabric of the fiction and equally formal within the characters' decorum, which suggest "relations" which either are already more dense and intimate than their mere surface alone, or are becoming so as the party continues.

A second pressure is generated by both the attempt to understand these "relations" and the efforts to foster and protect them. This is the desire to ascertain *facts,* to establish those bare and confirmable redactions of actuality—those forms of thought and discourse into which we shape our information and knowledge of complex events and motives and which are called *facts*—a procedure which entails the assigning of names, the discovery of identities, the allegations that definable deeds did or did not happen, the determination that distinguishable causes did produce the distinguishable results and that certain persons do or do not know tangible items of information. The search for *facts* is subject to a condition which Obert and the Narrator agree upon: that they will pursue their inquiry without resort to two avenues of factual certainty, the " 'detective and the key-hole,' " the professional spy or the voyeur's means of direct (though protected and concealed) observation. This restriction virtually confines them to "relations" of sheer public contiguity and to the pace, apparent direction, and displayed manner of the characters' behavior. (66.)

The third pressure—one which, like the search for *facts,* implements the attempt to conceal actualities as well as the effort to discover them—is the impulse of the "penetrating imagination" to probe and cope with actuality by constructing hypotheses about it, theoretical constructs which comprise an image of the world in which the imagination functions and which govern or guide the imagination's concurrent conduct in it. The instrument used in building these hypotheses or images, which serves in place of the disreputable detective or the prurient keyhole, is the form of " 'analogy.' " The constructive scrutiny which employs this instrument of analogy risks error, utter folly, and cruelty, but it renders the actual world amenable to insight and to participation in its activities while appreciating them or adding to their price and value and so altering the world it watches. Yet the searching irony of *The Sacred Fount* rests on the paradox which it exaggerates by parodying: the fact that the same constructive scrutiny which reveals and shapes the actualities of personal and social experience serves also to shield and obscure them, bringing the imagination closer to the experience it longs to share but erecting barriers to certain knowledge and full participation. This drama of the

amused myself with making out that he had found her." Count-less *if* clauses and rhetorical questions confirm his disclosure that his "imagination" was adding "touches . . . to the pic-ture" and that he "easily multiplied and lavished them." At times he gives rein to the "constructive joy" he finds in his inventiveness, feeling "as inhumanly amused as if one had found one could create something," and while he has scarcely begun his task, "created nothing but a clue or two," he warms with "a mild artistic glow." At times he is even less cautious, declaring of one character that " 'I must, with an art, make him not want to' " and proceeding to secure this effect in the next sentences with such success that he remembers feeling "that joy of determining, almost of creating results, which I have already mentioned as an exhilaration attached to some of my plunges of insight." Speaking as if he were literally the author of *The Sacred Fount*, he says later of another character: "I felt somehow the wish to make her say it in as many ways as possible—I seemed so to enjoy her saying it." At other times he cautions himself against his "extravagant perceptions" and his "idle habit of reading into mere human things an interest so much deeper than mere human things were in general pre-pared to supply." (54, 140, 96, 221, 104, 213-214, 267, 156.)

The perspectives established by these remarks of his own render fearsome and ludicrous the game of observation which occupies him at Newmarch, where he finds that the mere sight of a man drawing up a chair suggests "the real existence in him of the condition it was my private madness (none the less private for Grace Brissenden's so limited glimpse of it) to be-lieve I had coherently stated," and he goes on to ask: "Is not this small touch perhaps the best example I can give of the intensity of amusement I had at last enabled my private mad-ness to yield me?" Even when he seeks refuge from the New-march group, determined *not* "to see" and roaming in isola-tion to avoid "hovering personally about them," he finds that the very atmosphere of the place keeps alive the "sense of play" and that "if one wanted something to play at one simply played at being there"; whether actually there in their midst or (like James, like the reader, and like himself after he has left), simply *playing* at being there, he helplessly thinks about the others and fixes what he has seen more firmly in his memory. (162, 90-91.)

So anxious is he about his additions and constructions that he draws the reader's attention to his role and not only raises the issue of his responsibility but defines it with increasing precision. He points out that his "cogitations" would be "as stiff a puzzle to interpretative minds" as other people's conduct had become for his own and indeed that the pattern of his own conduct at one point—his "tell-tale restlessness," his deliberate "detachment" from the figure, May Server, who most interests him—is precisely analogous to *her* restlessness and her avoidance of him and her apparent avoidance of the presumed lover in whom she is most interested. His "discretion" seems "odd" in his own eyes because though separate from her he is absorbed in her case, and his absorption leaves him "more attached, morally," not less, to his "prey." (91-93.)

These remarks reveal that even when "detached" in his observation, his conscience and imagination are involved in the action which he depicts—that his behavior is analogous to the behavior of others which he puzzles over and that it is part of the action which his account invites the reader to scrutinize. On a crucial occasion when he and Mrs. Briss discover that Guy Brissenden's hidden companion is May Server, the Narrator is gripped by moral compunctions which define his responsibility. Mrs. Briss's "eagerness" in identifying Mrs. Server (" 'We have her, . . . we have her; it's *she!* '") moves him with an "odd revulsion" to question his "curiosity" and, for a brief moment, to think May Server's affair "none of my business." But his further reflection, although it returns him to his "amusing" inquiry, is not so much an evasion of his responsibility as a complication of it: it is not his inquiry that is dangerous to May Server, he declares, but his sharing it with Mrs. Briss. His "anomaly" is that he feels "as disgusted as if I had exposed Mrs. Server" while feeling certain, with justification, that he has "yet *not* exposed her" for they have simply seen her chatting with a friend. He returns to his "business" determined to "take care" that he not " 'compromise' " the woman whom he observes. And to protect her he begins to deceive

Mrs. Briss, separating her from May Server and hoping to throw her off the scent while leaving the way open to exchanging information later. The glance with which he leaves Mrs. Briss—"a look in which I invited her to read volumes"—and more particularly the look of assent which she returns him establish "the first note of a tolerably tight, tense little drama, a little drama of which our remaining hours at Newmarch were the all too ample stage." When, "for the effect I desired," he leads Mrs. Server away to view paintings, it is to reveal what is at stake in the enigmas of *The Sacred Fount* as well as in the painting of " 'the man with the mask in his hand' " which they look at. (45-49, 54.)

The painted figure in black, "with a pale, lean, livid face and a stare, from eyes without eyebrows, like that of some whitened old-world clown," holds an object which is at first unidentifiable but resembles "some ambiguous work of art," then appears on closer scrutiny to be the mask of a human face made of "some substance not human." May Server, asking " 'what in the world does it mean?' " and speaking apparently of the entire painting, hazards a title for it: the " 'Mask of Death.' " The Narrator, however, thinks it " 'rather the Mask of Life' " and concentrates on the contrast of the two faces in it, declaring that " 'It's the man's own face that's death' " while the mask is " 'blooming and beautiful,' " indeed " 'extremely studied.' " Without actually contradicting him about the mask Mrs. Sever insists that she sees nothing but the grimace in the mask and that the man himself (whether or not the image of death) is indeed " 'dreadful.' " The Narrator adds another issue when he questions whether the figure is about to don the mask or has " 'just taken it off.' " The characters proceed to look for resemblances among the guests, displaying a combination of playful curiosity, intense interest in what the resemblances might lay bare, and careful caution lest the correspondences prove embarrassing. When Obert suggests that the mask " 'looks like a lovely lady,' " the Narrator agrees emphatically and Mrs. Server, with a combination of resentment and bemused interest, suggests that the figure's face must then resemble one of the male guests. Obert is certain that it does but either cannot place or will not name the man; the Narrator declares that he sees the resemblance but will not divulge the identity; Gilbert Long declares that the resemblance is obvious. And Obert—whether because pleased to find his reading of the picture confirmed, surprised at a friend's error, or relieved to have an erroneous identification divert attention from a telling resemblance—jumps with surprise when Long declares that the figure resembles Poor Briss. May Server says that she sees the resemblance to Briss, but says so in a voice which may, as the Narrator thinks, indicate mere politeness. And the Narrator declares that Briss was the man he had in mind. (55-59.)

It is the mixture or suspension of these various possible meanings in the painting, and the full range of possible relevance to the lives of its viewers, that the episode establishes in the novel. It embodies the multiplicity of its implications, in their tentative suspension, rather than establishing the certainty of some identifications while concealing them with the feigning appearance of others. Significantly, the mask in the painting hides nothing, though it may recently have concealed the face or may soon cover it. And the painting is a profoundly suggestive image of the fiction in which it appears as well as of the characters' actions. The staring face, which may be the face of life or the face of death or the face of both, is a *painted* "representation of the human face," as much a "representation" as is the fabricated mask held in the figure's hand. The mask is a painted mask, a distinguishable object whose ambiguous presence and form are visible before its identity is revealed; yet it is an image which is as relevant to human experience as the painted representation (a costumed performer with eyebrows removed from his "pale" and "livid" face) of the "whitened old-world clown" who holds the mask. The painting and the speculations which it provokes image the drama of *The Sacred Fount* itself: the hazard of smothering life's face with the death-like grimace of artifice; the chance of removing a death-like mask to reveal the features, at once pale and livid, of life itself; the prospect of covering the face of death with a mask of life and beauty; the hope of so composing the grimace and the beauties of masking artifice, and so presenting the drama of using it, as to protect life while revealing its intimate presence and constructing imagined possibilities for it.

It is within the context of such multiple contingencies that the Narrator challenges the validity of his own musings, or invites others to do so, and defines his responsibility for the effects of his scrutiny which he risks. He points out that his "theory" (as he prefers to call his "tangle of hypotheses") remains unconfirmed by Lady John, and when she finally taunts him for not telling precisely what he is inquiring about—and for boring her by playing a groping providence whereas a " 'real providence *knows*' "—he clings, with all the excess of mockery, to the "undiluted bliss" of his "superior vision," the intoxication of being "magnificently and absurdly aware" while others were "benightedly out of it," but he recognizes, looking back on it, that this superiority may have been a "frenzied fallacy" for which he was "all to blame." Although two pairs of people balance like "bronze groups at the two ends of a chimney piece," he warns himself against imagining that they do in fact so balance and reminds himself that "Things in the real had a way of not balancing." He displays " 'notions of responsibility' " which Obert, more relaxed and casual, thinks excessive or " 'extraordinary.' " By the time Obert begins to lose interest, or thinks it best to pull out, the Narrator invites the challenge of Obert, asking " 'what havoc will [he] play' " with his " 'superstitions,' " and " 'how many panes' " will he smash in the " 'great glittering crystal palace.' " (174-177, 182-183, 210, 205.)

The final threat to his glass house is the challenge of Mrs. Briss at the end, but her challenge is in keeping with his own strategy of questioning his hypotheses, and as he confronts her in their midnight interview, he finds himself welcoming the contest that their game has become, as each prepares to test the certainty and vision of the other. When the issues are finally joined between them, the Narrator is virtually "paralyzed" by the recognition that in the amusement of his game he has become responsible for awakening Mrs. Briss and possibly Gilbert Long to "consciousness" of his inquiry and for creating the brassy cruelty which she now displays in combating him. But his paralysis has the effect of preventing his surrender to sympathy for his antagonist; only by "the sacrifice of feeling" can he steel himself to continue his inquiry, and with a clear sense of his responsibility for the risks this inquiry entails, he determines to repress any consideration for Mrs. Briss and Long: "I was there to save my priceless pearl of an inquiry and to harden, to that end, my heart." As the interview proceeds, each proves to be trying to protect someone's privacy and to be challenging the allegations of the other. And it is on the combat of the two—each still collaborating in a cagey game yet trying to penetrate and destroy the fortress of the other—that the drama of the closing chapters depends. (241, 243-244, 295-296.)

The " 'houses of cards,' " the " 'creation,' " that are at stake in their interview have been built up gradually in the course of the weekend. The structure derives from four observations which the Narrator thinks important and which are confirmed by other characters, though one is later denied: Gilbert Long's astonishing improvement in volubility and wit (first insisted on but later denied by Mrs. Briss); the fact that the Brissendens are married; the fact that Briss had aged in appearance since his marriage while Mrs. Briss has regained a lost youth; and the change in the lovely widow May Server, her conspicuous sociability which has appeared since Obert last saw her when painting her portrait. With these and subsequent observations to build on, the Narrator brings to bear his theory of the transforming power of intimate passion and constructs his "glittering crystal palace." (9-10, 296.)

It is "intimacy," the "pressure of soul to soul," that has transformed Long; some lover loyal to him has applied the "seal of passion" which left its "tell-tale traces" in his new brilliance; Long and his benefactor hide their affair, as Mrs. Briss insists, by avoiding each other in public except for seemingly casual encounters. The Narrator begins to search for Long's lover. (16-17, 9-10.)

He is guided by an analogy with the Brissendens' marriage, which he is also scrutinizing. Their marriage, no matter how seldom they are seen together, is founded on intimacy, and (as in any case where the partners in intimacy are widely separated in age) one partner is rejuvenated at the expense of the other;

Poor Briss is " 'the author of the sacrifice' " to passion who must " 'pay' " for so " 'expensive' " a " 'miracle' " and "tap the sacred fount" of passion to sustain the affair of love. Accordingly, Long's lover must correspond to the wasted Guy Brissenden. Though Mrs. Briss first declares that it is Lady John who has given Long "a mind and a tongue," so shallow a woman as Lady John cannot account for Long's transformation. She does have a shop but while she advertises her wares, she never parts with a thing that would account for Long's new garb; the woman in question, unlike Lady John, would have sold things, parted with them and closed up shop for her lover. (41-42, 29-30, 9-10, 17-18, 35-36.)

It must instead be May Server. Her extravagant manner is not the sheer promiscuity that Ford Obert first suspects; indeed Obert, once handed the " 'torch' " of the analogy, is certain that Mrs. Server must be loyal to a lover in their midst and that she thrives at his expense. Obert is wrong, however, the Narrator feels, to think Mrs. Server the thriving partner; without disputing Obert, the Narrator privately thinks her the exhausted partner whose sociability is a mask (like that in the painting) shielding her abject exhaustion. When he and Mrs. Briss discover her alone with Briss, and Mrs. Briss exclaims " 'we have her; it's *she!*' " the Narrator concludes that they have identified Long's lover. As Mrs. Briss insists later, on what the Narrator calls "fantastically constructive" grounds, Mrs. Server's lips have been worn dry in the service of Long's cheek. And when May Server is discovered again with Briss, Mrs. Briss applauds " 'this invention of using my husband,' " explaining that Mrs. Server is using her husband, among others, to mask her affair with Long. Buttressed accordingly by Mrs. Briss, the Narrator rounds out his theory with the notion which he does not disclose to Mrs. Briss: the notion that Briss and May Server, the authors of the sacrifices respectively for Mrs. Briss and Long, seek refuge together in a community of abjection, finding relief from the need to wear a mask and solace in their mutual recognition of the loyal devotion they sustain, the one for his "blooming" wife, the other for her thriving lover. They support each other in their "resistance" to the "doom" which their sacrifice threatens for them. As Obert later puts it (even

though he now asserts that May's lover is probably not present
at Newmarch), Mrs. Server is drawn to Briss by " 'pity . . .
the sight of another fate as strange, as monstrous, as her own.' "
(17-18, 85, 79-81, 220, 224.)

When the Narrator encourages Poor Briss to seek out Mrs.
Server at the end of Chapter VII, it is for the " 'sympathy, the
fellowship, the wild wonder' " of such shared commiseration—
for the intimacy of confession and compassion—that he sends
Briss to join her. Together they conserve their strength for the
sacrifice each performs, the sacrifice which the Narrator has
made the basis for his creation. The sacrificing person who
pays for the "miracle," he imagines, might "give much more
than she had." Indeed "pure beauty," not present to begin
with in the "resources" of the " 'sacrificed' " person, might
emerge as an increment in the process, might be created in the
course of the sacrifice. The Narrator imagines that in the
"strange relations" which he thinks he has glimpsed, the resources "might really multiply in the transfer made of them; as
if the borrower practically found himself—or herself—in possession of a greater sum than the known property of the credi-
tor." The transaction which entails this sacrifice and the increment of coin and beauty is the basis of the Narrator's "creation,"
his House of Fiction, as it is the basis of Henry James's art.
(126, 30, 53.)

If this "creation" has the tentative status of an hypothesis
and the fascination of a speculative game, the game becomes a
desperate one because the creation is constructed and main-
tained, chiefly by the Narrator but also by Obert and Mrs.
Briss, against a pressure which is strong, though not emphatically talked about, early in the narrative, and which is intensified by Mrs. Briss in the midnight interview. It is the pressure
of certain anticipations, based on observed facts presented in
the opening sections but then suspended, most of them, in a
solution of comparative silence. These include the fact that
Mrs. Froome and Lord Lutley are openly carrying on an affair; that Mrs. Briss traveled to Newmarch with Long, while
her husband accompanied Lady John; that the Brisses (Mrs.
Briss herself makes a point of it) are not often seen together;
that Briss, "for some reason," has been assigned a room in the

bachelors' quarters; that Briss is seen on crucial occasions with May Server; that Obert, when first seen by the Narrator, is almost "sequestered" with May Server, and that she is last seen, at midnight, strolling again on the arm of Obert. The clandestine relations suggested by these observations are no more confirmable than the others on which the Narrator's House of Fiction is built, but they establish possibilities which challenge the accuracy or the completeness of the Narrator's conception on crucial points. Perhaps May Server, when the Narrator first sees her, *is* "making love, possibly," as he first thinks; perhaps she is as promiscuous as Obert first surmises. Perhaps, when Mrs. Briss exclaims of May Server " 'We have her, . . . it's *she'* " she is jealously identifying her husband's lover or discovering a calculating seductress, not his tragic confidante. (40-41, 14, 19-20.)

Moreover, the Narrator's "creation" may be aiding those who help him construct it by concealing instead of revealing their intimate relations just as he intends to protect May Server from the scrutiny of those who up to a point share in his inquiry. The "crystal palace" in which Obert shows an interest, sometimes eager, sometimes casual, sometimes aghast, may be satisfying his personal interest in "pretty women" as well as his professional curiosity as a portrait painter. The Narrator's "creation," however unnerving in its proximity to the actual state of affairs, may in effect be protecting Obert when he names Poor Briss as Mrs. Server's confidant and leaves her lover unidentified. Mrs. Briss may be more concerned for the ostensible respectability of her marriage than for fidelity and marital intimacy; her occasional conversations with Long may indicate that she is carrying on an affair with Long (or would like to be), and Briss's encounters may indicate that he is carrying on an affair (or trying to). If so, the Narrator's structure which Mrs. Briss helps him construct is screening, from his view at least, the shambles the Brisses' marriage has become, her own relation with Long, and Briss's philandering. (14.)

It is some of these possibilities that are made explicit with all the bluntness of factual assertion by Mrs. Briss after summoning the Narrator to the midnight interview which closes the novel and which not only determines the Narrator to leave

on the next train but prevents his attaining any further degree
of factual certainty in his inquiry. Her challenge is based on the
assertions that the Narrator is " 'crazy' " and that the crucial
transformation of Gilbert Long, which she earlier had agreed
was so striking, never took place: Long is " 'the same ass' " he
always was. Her challenge culminates in her assertions that
Lady John is Long's lover, and that Mrs. Server—" 'sharp' "
and promiscuous behind the " 'extravagant' " behavior they
had once termed the mask of a hidden loyalty—has made love
to Briss himself. (278, 305, 316-317.)

Though Mrs. Briss throws stones from her " 'fortress of
granite' " with real force and speaks with a "tone" which the
Narrator grudgingly envies, her assertions cannot be taken as
confirmed. They remain allegations of fact, not their irrefutable demonstration, for the thrust of her claims is so integral to
James's novel, and so closely joined in the combat which now
brings her and the Narrator face to face, that her " 'system,' "
the combination of factual assertions with their implications,
is given the same hypothetical status as the Narrator's " 'palace' " which she challenges. And her challenge, resting on information allegedly supplied by her husband, brings back into
prominence the question of marriage—the question of the
actual relation between the Brissendens within the form of
their marriage—which is central in James's major fiction and
in the marriage of art which he was to celebrate in the Prefaces. She withdraws within the citadel of her marriage after
asserting the facts presumably told her by her husband, leaving
the Narrator with no means of testing her assertions since he
still eschews detectives and keyholes and does not seek out
Briss or Mrs. Server later to question them. And the Narrator
is left with the crisis, which her challenge creates, to consider
when gathering his recollections of the weekend. (311, 318-
319.)

But the uncertainties of the Narrator's position are matched
by the hazards of hers. So complicated is her predicament that
she speaks with the anger of a reader who has been misled by
the Narrator's "tangle of hypotheses." She complains that with
his " 'art of putting things, one doesn't know where one is, nor
. . . do I quite think *you* always do,' " that he mistakenly

thinks the power of "penetration" in others is equal to his own, that he had " 'talked [her] over' " to the view that Long was cruelly " 'sacrificing poor May.' " At other moments Mrs. Briss sounds like a character in an analytical novel who objects to being scrutinized and used by its author. She resists when the Narrator seeks to " 'catch' " her, to " 'focus [her] under the first shock' " of a particular discovery; she complains that " 'I cudgel my brain for your amusement' " and protests the discomfort when admitting that " 'You focussed . . . I felt your focus.' " She declares resentfully: " 'You've made of me . . . too big a talker, too big a thinker, of nonsense.' " And indeed, James's center of consciousness, the Narrator, has admitted wanting to perplex his listener, wanting her "perplexity . . . to result both from her knowing and her not knowing sufficiently what I meant." Moreover, he has felt toward Mrs. Briss the responsibility of her creator, reflecting that it is he who has "spoiled" her equanimity; it is he who has "given" her the consciousness which now impels her to resist his efforts. (262-263, 266-267, 289-291, 301, 254, 295.)

The import of the clear parody in the final scene is that Mrs. Briss is not the antithesis of James's art but a participant in it as reader and an instrument of it in her contest with the Narrator. Her challenge has the flair of triumph as she withers the Narrator with her assertions, leaving him first with the ruins of his structure, which he is confident he can reassemble; then in the assertion about May Server and Briss administering so telling a blow that he feels even older than Guy Brissenden, feels indeed a thousand years old and expects that he will "never again . . . hang together." But the fascination of the closing scene derives from the fact that her victory is not an utter triumph. Her eventual victory, such as it is, comes after her own confession of failure in being forced to divulge items she was trying to hide. And while her effort does succeed finally in stopping the Narrator's inquiry on the spot and sending him off the premises, it does not establish the certainty of her assertions. In the searching irony of the closing chapters Mrs. Briss's very assertions give support to the basic tenets of the Narrator's theory even while seeming to shatter the superstructure, indeed they give his theory a wider and more somber extension than he has heretofore made explicit. (311-312, 318-319.)

The authenticity of Mrs. Briss's assertions is undermined by her manner during the interview and by the melodrama with which she has staged the " 'so intensely nocturnal' " confrontation. Her force is unmistakable—the Narrator feels it displacing the more fragile power of the "tragic lady," May Server, as Mrs. Briss's "brass" bumps against "the weaker vessel" until the "shock of the brass told upon the porcelain" and May Server's beauty lay "in pieces" with the Narrator and Mrs. Briss facing each other over the "damage" their game has entailed. But Mrs. Briss's power is not the impregnable authority of established fact. As in George Sand's case, her "fortress of granite" is the "citadel of style." Her "grand air" is a compound of the "fine dishonesty of her eyes" and the "light of a part to play," as she burgeons with what she keeps suppressed and talks openly about other things. Like the Narrator, she is trying to penetrate through his talk to discover precisely what he has learned or imagined since she last saw him. Each knows the other "to mean, at every point, immensely more" than either openly declares. And she is, as the Narrator thinks, "suffering and stammering and lying" in an effort to put an end to his inquiry. She is not genuinely interested in replacing error with fact but in stopping the inquiry and demolishing the dangerously intriguing structure he has erected, as if it were painfully close to the truth. She denies that "Long's metamorphosis" has taken place with the needlessly sweeping declaration " 'I don't believe in miracles.' " She insists that she wanted to divulge no information at all that night, that indeed she had ruled out Lady John as Long's lover earlier simply to protect Lady John's name as if she, like the Narrator, were trying to protect certain actual relations that she knows or claims to know. (242, 245-246, 272-273, 269-270, 301-303.)

When she finally recognizes that she is in " 'too deep' " to get out, her predicament approximates the desperation which the Narrator has defined in his own case, that of being no longer able to "save" Mrs. Server or Poor Briss and being able only to salvage his "understanding," his "precious sense of their loss." And to salvage what *she* can, she relies finally on the very kind of "personal confidence" which the Narrator has posited as the only firm evidence, since even a "confession" by any participant would be possibly a lie: she relies on a mere report which she claims to have from her husband and which she claims she has not tested even by asking how he found out. That her claims rest on nothing more—and nothing less—than the confidence and intimacy shared by a married couple, and that their intimacy lies beyond the reach of the Narrator's instruments, is presented at precisely the point where Mrs. Briss declares that Long's affair with Lady John has been " 'confirmed.' " The Narrator remarks that "My eyes had been meeting hers without . . . hers quite meeting mine, but at this there had to be intercourse," and Mrs. Briss adds that the confirmation has been made " 'By my husband.' " If her eyes and the Narrator's do meet in this chaste exchange, the community of vision is feeble before the intimacy with Briss to which she lays claim. She retreats behind the closed door of her intimacy with Briss in the simple statement: " 'I take his word.' " When she adds that " 'if one uses Poor Briss—by which, I mean, if one depends on him—at all, one gains . . . more than one loses,' " her remarks do not shatter but enforce the Narrator's theory that in their marriage Mrs. Briss thrives and " 'profits' " at the expense of her husband. And when Mrs. Briss adds other remarks about Briss's amusements, both her entertaining report and her husband's activities present a strange image of James's own art which is also, paradoxically, an image of an art beyond his own. (273, 302, 310, 306-307, 30.)

Briss, she declares, enjoyed encouraging an innocuous flirtation between Long and Lady John to " 'amuse himself' " and was happy to bring Lady John to the party on the train; after all, he has a right to his " 'amusements.' " What is more, he shares them, " 'dear old Briss,' " providing Mrs. Briss with a store of information which he freely divulges without even being asked. Once he " 'does wake up' " to what is going on " 'he'll go through a house.' " While he did not know all the consequences of what he was revealing, in disclosing that Lady John was Long's lover, he did aim " 'to give her away.' " Despite a "natural revulsion" to what he may see, he has an eye for seeing and (so the Narrator completes "the picture") when Briss

" 'sees . . . he luckily tells.' " Indeed, in the intimacy of their marriage the "hero of his odd union," Briss himself, confides in his wife as a matter of course—he " 'regularly' " tells. He has told Mrs. Briss that May Server made love to him and that she is calculating or " 'sharp.' " In this way—and without asserting whether Briss accepted or rejected Mrs. Server's alleged offer—Mrs. Briss has come to know more than she herself can vouch for, she has learned " 'more than I saw.' " " 'I thank God,' " Mrs. Briss exclaims, " 'for dear old Briss tonight.' " (306-307, 309-310, 316-317.)

Whether Mrs. Briss's remarks about her husband are true or not, they suggest a degree of knowledge, and an intimacy of communion, beyond the Narrator's own powers. Yet they also suggest the actions which are the foundation of James's own novel: an exploitive scrutiny, an entertainment, and an increment of information gained at the expense of others, with Mrs. Briss using "dear old Briss" and gaining more than she knew from him, and Briss finding his amusement in the flirtations of others and at the expense of May Server. Even if the Brisses marriage is a mere expedient convenience, a base of operations for gossip and philandering and illicit affairs of passion, or if it is a genuinely loyal bond which is threatened by temptations at Newmarch and their sophisticated tolerance, Mrs. Briss's strategic use of her marriage and of her husband confirms the Narrator's theory that within their marriage Briss is being used and sacrificed to his vigorous wife. And even if Mrs. Briss's allegations about May Server are a fabrication designed to put a stop to the Narrator's inquiry, they enforce, indeed magnify cruelly, the effect they have if true: they present a situation in which Briss's casual entertainment and his sharing of the information with his wife are gained, as are the reader's entertainment and James's novel, at the expense of the woman they speak of, whether consciously to slander or reluctantly to expose.

Accordingly, the effect of the final interview is a paradoxical one: it suggests the failure of the Narrator's " 'houses of cards' " as an instrument of truth and as a protective defense of May Server's integrity—while yet suggesting the authenticity of his theory, giving it relevance to possibly tawdry fact as well as to

the more exalted passions and forms of intercourse which he
had taken to be real. And in the context of Mrs. Briss's calculations and anxieties, her "system" suggests for Poor Briss a role
which she has not named, the role of lover to May Server,
whether in a casual affair or in a more enduring passion; it
may be one which he perfunctorily acknowledged or under
pressure confessed, or one which his wife may simply suspect
with whatever certainty she has mustered. Because Mrs. Briss's
allegations by implication add hypotheses to the novel and add
undemonstrated assertions of fact instead of supplanting the
Narrator's structure, the closing interview does not conclude
the Narrator's experience or even fix a final ambiguity, but
rather intensifies the pressures which have built up during the
weekend and leaves the Narrator with the unresolved crisis he
faces in gathering afterward the memories of his sojourn.

What he makes out of the experience, embodied on reconsideration in *The Sacred Fount,* is implicit in his rendering of
Mrs. Briss's scornful farewell ("'You poor dear, you *are*
crazy'"), for it places the Narrator in a position analogous to
Poor Briss, the presumed fount of her strength and the "'author'" of the "'sacrifice,'" which is the basis postulated for
their marriage: her farewell withers the Narrator, as she presumably withers Briss, to an age of a thousand years while
gathering in herself "the strength of twenty-five." (318.)

The Narrator proceeds to construct a version of the weekend
which redeems that authorship, on Briss's part and on his own,
acknowledging the possible validity of Mrs. Briss's allegations
while yet, in the face of the possible truth of her "system," committing himself to the transformations *he* had envisioned and
now reconstructs. The novel is not so constructed as to demonstrate in retrospect that the Narrator's speculations were wrong,
by presenting clear contrasts between earlier delusions and
later certainties in the light of irrefutable evidence; it is so constructed as to support the possibility that *both* structures
which haunt his narrative are relevant to what took place and
hypothetically true, and to make them the basis for James's
commitment to the form of his own novel and to a tragic
vision harbored in the antic nightmare. The Narrator defines

with stunning clarity his own double role as a celebrant of a transforming passion which may actually exist within the Brissendens' marriage and within the form of May Server's liaison with a faithful lover, and as the creator of a passion which he may have imagined to be there and projected onto the comparatively common forms of their behavior. In both roles, the Narrator appreciates and augments the measure of devotion they actually display while he pays, in his mad folly, the price for the "miracle," rubbing shoulders with the participants in his drama while he pays as " 'author of the sacrifice.' "

But while shouldering the responsibility for that authorship, he makes vividly clear that he is a vicarious witness when compared to the participants who observe life more closely from within the form which shields their experience, and that even as creator of the forms which shape their passion he is cut off from the passion which they know. He is cut off not only by the citadels which his characters erect to protect their privacy but by the very hypothetical form into which he has cast his investigation after leaving Newmarch. That form testifies to a double failure: the failure to protect May Server from the observation of Mrs. Briss and even Grace Brissenden's failure to protect Lady John and herself from the view of the Narrator; and the failure to establish with utter certainty the actual "relations" at Newmarch. But the Narrator's account presents too the effort to redeem that inquiry by devising a form which reveals yet protects the intimacy of passion, whether tawdry or transforming, from unrelieved exposure to his scrutiny. For all its vividness, it shields, rather than brutally exposes, the realities it presents (even Mrs. Briss's actual motives). And for all its uncertainty, the form successfully presents a range of experience which it will not and cannot encounter directly; it *intimates* the realities which his penetrating scrutiny has made vividly present to himself and brought within the reader's presence. The novel accordingly is founded on an act of construction which not only supports both the " 'palace of thought' " and the "system" Mrs. Briss has opposed to it but confesses the possibility that the Narrator's " 'palace' " of beauty and fidelity has been derived from the commonplaces of intimate experience and social behavior—ordinary pretenses of decorum and the ordinary furtive diversions—which Mrs. Briss's assertions make paramount.

When the Narrator last sees Gilbert Long, whose transformation is so much at issue, his reconsideration of Long's case induces him to revive his theory, despite the determination he had reached moments before to abandon his "obsession" and leave Newmarch; this reconsideration at the time bears the weight also of the Narrator's later reconsideration of the event in memory when he authenticates his final commitment to Long's transformation. He recalls merely that Long had sought the refuge of privacy and was prolonging "his soft vigil." For whom Long waits—or of whom or what he thinks—the Narrator does not stipulate; he recalls indeed that he "scarce knew" what Long's gestures "proved," but that he was as moved by them "as if they proved everything." In the face of this uncertainty, Long's presence holds its force in memory as it had on the original occasion and revives the theory that the Narrator had been about to abandon: the incident "had for my imagination a value, for my theory a price, and it in fact constituted an impression under the influence of which this theory, just impatiently shaken off, perched again on my shoulders." (202-203.)

When the Narrator encounters the Brissendens together for the last time, he concedes that he "*did* know nothing about them" and that "whatever might be . . . the deep note of their encounter" was "wholly their own business," and he leaves them in the privacy to which Mrs. Briss returns again at the end of the novel. But his rendering of their "encounter" acknowledges many possibilities, including the drab one that Mrs. Briss was no more than bluntly dressing Briss down for whatever neglect of duty or decorum. But when the Narrator says that "I recall how it came to me . . . that I mustn't think anything too grossly simple of what might be taking place between them," he goes on to give again the full force of what he had imagined: that Mrs. Briss was at once challenging Poor Briss with her youthful vigor but also longingly "making love to him with it as hard as she could"; and that her husband, already "back in hand," was "feeling afresh in his soul, as a response to her, the gush of the sacred fount." (198-199.)

Whether as passionately loyal husband of Mrs. Briss, as philandering spouse now got back in hand, as passionate lover of May Server, or as Mrs. Server's chaste confidant, Briss's role is crucial in the Narrator's drama, and when the Narrator recalls his last sight of Briss, still not sure what he murmured in greeting him, his recollection acknowledges the high cost of marriage for Briss and the Narrator's own dependence on Briss's fount. Briss looks in abject envy at the apparently relaxed, contented clusters of men in the smoking room, and the Narrator confesses his profit at the expense of Briss's abjection. The shock of Briss's appearance "renewed my sources and . . . spoke all, in short, for my gain"; as the Narrator imagines Briss's "humiliation," the "twists and turns" through the corridors, carrying a message from his wife, the Narrator finds that Briss's errand to *him* is "the final expression" of his "sacrifice." They part with the handshake that is an image both of the barrier which separates the Narrator from Briss's experience and of the tacit confidence they share: "things unspoken and untouched, unspeakable and untouchable, everything that had been between us in the wood a few hours before, were between us again." The encounter in the wood to which the Narrator alludes is the occasion when, after sending Briss to a rendezvous with May Server, he had left them alone together. (225-227.)

Their rendezvous is never observed. But in leading up to it Briss displays some indications that he already knows May Server better than he is willing to divulge; yet he also gives some indications that he has only begun an acquaintance that troubles him, so bewildering is the lonely widow's façade of happiness and so keen the sense that she might " 'break down.' " He confesses that while he is not " 'thoroughly pleased' " with her (or " 'in love' " as the Narrator puts it) he does want to be " 'kind' " to her. Briss declares: " 'I do—for" her—help to keep it up.' " Briss's kindness, which falls short, he claims, of either the perfection of pleasure or the fulfillment of love, is precisely analogous to the feeling of the Narrator, whose "telltale restlessness" leaves him nonetheless "attached, morally," to his "prey," and "far gone" in mere "pity" for May Server. He had said that he was "too sorry for her to be anything but sorry" and that his recapitulation of his story, "my recital of the rest of what I was to see," would "in no small measure" account for this "odd feeling." (119, 121-122, 92-95.)

It is because Briss's professed feelings are so precisely analogous to the Narrator's while Briss's actual *exposure* to experience (as husband, lover, or confidant) is so much closer than his, that the interview between them in the wood is crucial to the novel. For then, feeling that Briss has become "plastic wax in my hand," the Narrator dispatches him to see Mrs. Server so that Briss might actually " 'know' " what the Narrator has " 'divined' " about May Server—"launching him," as it seems later, on an experience which May Server will allow Briss to " 'know' " " 'for the wild wonder of it' " while making every effort to keep the Narrator from apprehending it directly. If Briss speaks at times in this interview not only as a participant in the action but as a *reader* of the Narrator's proposal—asking for a " 'clue,' " in vain requesting the Narrator to " 'tell' "—it is because in these passages James has defined the hazards and limits of his art and confessed responsibility for it: he has launched Briss, as reader and as participant in the arena of life, toward an experience and a degree of knowledge which are beyond the immediate access of James's own and of any art. The Narrator has enlisted Briss, who had mistaken the Narrator's room at Newmarch for his own, as his "delegate," as the instrument of his desire to participate in May Server's experience without violating it and to help sustain her effort. And whatever the Narrator may have anticipated at the time, his memory and the account governed by it are taut with the tacit recognition that the companionship he encouraged, perhaps launched, in fact may as well have been an assignation or seduction as the chaste exchange of confidences which he has either glimpsed or imagined. (124, 126-127.)

When in the next chapter the Narrator himself comes upon May Server, resting in a glade alone, he presents an account which is so composed that it does not rule out the various possibilities that his weekend has brought to light. This chapter, rather than the concluding one, is the scene on which the entire novel depends, because it is here that the novel confronts most directly its own ambiguities, defines the Narrator's vicarious role, and establishes the constructive basis on which the

novel is founded. The scene does not rule out a casual amatory rendezvous between May Server and Briss—indeed, it is
haunted by that possibility. Yet it does not rule out the contingency that May Server may be Gilbert Long's loyal lover who
shares mute confidences with Briss, the correspondingly faithful husband who is the fount of his wife's reinvigoration. Nor
does it rule out the possibility that Briss and May Server are
joined in an enduring, erotic liaison as well as in the intimacy
of confidences and confession. These several possibilities the
Narrator's recapitulation both intimates and shields through
the mask—at once the antic "grimace" and the "studied charm"
—of its hypothetical form. Besides, the account redeems even
the lowest abasements which the characters' experience may
entail and James's art risks exposing, and it redeems the failure
of his art either to reveal completely or completely to protect its
figures and their passions; it does so by constructing and
celebrating a fusion of transforming passion, intimacy of communion, and the fidelity of lovers within the form of a "relation," whether within the form of an affair, the form of marriage, or the form of art. By celebrating simultaneously the
transforming power of an illicit affair and the viability of a
marriage founded on sacrifice, and by bringing into such intimate proximity a communion of confidence (shared by Mrs.
Server and Briss) and a communion of passion (shared by
each with a corresponding lover or spouse), James holds within
the measure of his art the pressure which "strains, or tends to
burst, with a latent extravagance," the "mould" of form, threatening to mar the "sacrament" which "marries" form and content; and he contains within that measure as well the pressure
of passion which would cling even to a factitious marriage or
convenient affair and transform them through sacrifice.

The Narrator's private interview with May Server begins
just after he has dispatched Briss to find her and closes when
Briss arrives in the wood and the Narrator leaves them alone
together; the very framing of the scene serves to define the
Narrator's role as mediator in the relation he encourages, observes, and shields. And while his discovery of Mrs. Server in
the glade is an observed scene, the Narrator's musings under-
line the extent to which his imagination is contributing to what

he presents and heighten the sense of creative power which, if nothing else, is his gain from his encounter with Mrs. Server. He comes upon her at a time when he is elated because "the more things I fitted together, the larger sense . . . they made." The strengthening coherence and "beauty" of his structure justifies his "indiscreet curiosity"; it "crowned my underhand process" or "wizardry." He is pleased because to have "thought it all out" was "to have brought it" into being. May Server incarnates for the Narrator the very thing he had been hoping for, emerging "exactly as if she had been there by the operation of my intelligence, or . . . of my feeling." Confessing the clumsiness of the term, he names the feeling "tenderness" and proceeds to describe a combination of tender care and predatory scrutiny. (128-130.)

He openly watches her but waits for her to approach so that he will not seem aggressively intrusive, yet he admits that he is "waylaying her in the wood," and when taking a few steps toward her to reassure her he feels "as if I were trapping a bird or stalking a fawn." The bower where they take a seat, on benches arranged symmetrically in a circle where two paths cross and enclosed by "arching recesses in which the twilight thickened," bespeaks the "beautiful old picture, the beautiful old tale" in which the Narrator places them; it suggests the "influence of the grand style" and the conventional setting for intimate rendezvous in the realm of painting and musing reminiscence. There in a communion of virtual silence, and in passages which are among the most delicately beautiful James ever wrote, the Narrator celebrates the sacrificial fount of passion and redeems the effort to give it form. (130-131.)

It is the failure of his own inquiry and the breakdown, the tragic failure, of May Server's efforts at expression which paradoxically reveal the fount of passion to the Narrator. The action reveals fully the complex process which James was to explain in the preface to *The Wings of the Dove,* the process whereby the artist's triumphs are produced not by his abandonment of formal artifices but by their breakdown under the strain of continuing use; his triumphs are produced from the very failure of his original plans, from the wreckage of his aspirations which his effort to express them helps bring about.

The Narrator provides the tender attention which leaves Mrs. Server "relieved and pacified" after her desperate pretenses in public; once he serves her by providing words for her, "putting the thing to her so much better than she could have put it to me." But while there is an "equal confession" in their tacit communion and the Narrator takes "no advantage" of her beyond the advantage he had originally intended, he admits learning "more than I had bargained for" from the exchange. (134, 150, 143, 137-138.)

Wandering " 'on the muse' " and taking " 'stock of my impressions,' " the Narrator recognizes that although he approaches "nearer to her secret" he remains "still not in possession of it"; yet he feels that he is "near enough . . . for what I should have to take from it all" and surrenders to the sheer presence of the woman, relegating the mere details of her relations, the facts and identifications, to the limbo of the relatively unimportant, the "vulgar," the uncertain, the unspoken. As she "gave herself" to his "intenser apprehension," becoming to that extent *his* fount, Mrs. Server "went through the form of expression"; and it is her failure, along with the effort she still persists in making, that reveals the ravages of passion: "what told me everything was the way the form of expression broke down" as her fixed "lovely grimace" began to tremble and to blur. She strives to maintain a blank silence but "her exquisite weakness simply opened up the depths it would have closed," bringing to light her abject abasement as the "victim" of passion and revealing the tragic consciousness of her abasement which drives her to "struggle and dissemble." Moved to compassion by the sight of "what consuming passion can make of the marked mortal on whom, with fixed beak and claws, it has settled as on a prey," the Narrator resolves to "keep clear" of any other secrets; "identifications" become "vulgar" before her "admirable state," her "wan little glory." (133-137.)

Accordingly, the Narrator claims to know "now with a vengeance" who her lover was but avoids naming him. In this way he manages to shield Mrs. Server from the full glare of explicit exposure, and shield the name of whichever man may be her lover, veiling at once the complete details of his hypothesis and the uncertainties which still permeate it, as he confesses that by being "so fatally meditative about poor Long" he has now "learnt more than I had bargained for." Compared with his understanding of her tragedy now, "the other vision" of the affair was "gross" and "grosser still was the connection between the two." The Narrator is gripped instead by the consuming passion he has glimpsed and moved by the thought that he and any others might fall as far as Mrs. Server. (137.)

But it is the very act of being moved to compassion and contemplating a common fate that implicates the Narrator's imagination in the very usage of May Server that has ravaged her. He is joined with her in his vision, yet he relegates her momentarily to oblivion in imagining their common fate. And just as she has been reduced to "a sponge wrung dry and with fine pores agape" by the passion that has consumed her, so she is reduced now to the mere "symbol" of intimate passion, the mere instrument of the vision which she stirs in the imagination of the Narrator once he has probed "near enough," while trapping his bird or stalking his fawn, to be in the presence of the sacred fount. He declares: "I for a while fairly forgot Mrs. Server, I fear, in the intimacy of this vision of the possibilities of our common nature." She then becomes what he helps to make her: "a wasted and dishonoured symbol" of those common possibilities. In turning from her and reducing her to a mere symbol by virtue of taking her as part of his medium, converting her into an instrument of expression, he has "almost 'compromised' " her, in the language of the later Prefaces, giving "all the sense" of her tragedy "without all the substance or all the surface," and the Narrator goes on to redeem his strange involvement, shielding though revealing the sacrifice to passion she is making, blurring or suppressing the bare facts as George Sand did while intimating them nevertheless, presenting her as a "wasted and dishonoured symbol" in his account and constructing on the basis of her sacrifice the vision of loyalty and love he affirms and the very art he uses to celebrate it. (136.)

His art matches the "frantic art" she musters "to make her pretty silences pass, from one crisis to another, for pretty speeches," and the "heroic grin" that he will recall feeling in his own "facial muscles" is the "glittering deceit" of May

217

Server's "smile" with which she covers up the virtual nothingness to which passion has reduced its victim. But as his own
account verges on a corresponding nothingness, he takes her
hand to comfort her and, feeling that she seeks an even "deeper
relief" than what he can afford, he goes farther than he has
yet and imagines the "softer ease" which she hopes to find
with the man she awaits. He builds a vision of the "common
fate" that she and Briss share, whatever the facts of their relation: "the simple revelation of each other" in "some intimacy of unspeakable confidence, that no one else in the world
could have for either." (139-140.)

Defining his own relation to her as "a rough substitute for
Guy's," he imagines her enjoyment of the confidence he himself provides and the even deeper communion to be afforded,
presumably, by Briss. He could not at the time put her feelings
into words, but looking back now he redeems that failure (for
himself and for James) by turning Mrs. Server's "pretty silence"
into a "pretty speech," presenting now "something of the sense
that I should have made [the words] form" earlier in an imagined speech of Mrs. Server:

" 'Yes, my dear man, I do understand you—quite perfectly
now, and (by I know not what miracle) I've really done so to
some extent from the first. Deep is the rest of feeling with you,
in this way, that I'm watched, for the time, only as you watch
me. . . . It does help my strange case . . . to let you keep me
here; but I should have found still more of what I was in need
of if I had only found, instead of you, him whom I had in
mind. He is as much better than you as you are than anyone
else.' "

The passage redeems the possibility that he has attained an intimate communion with a reader (who by some "miracle" now
understands him) and that his watchful scrutiny has become a
welcome support to the victim of passion, while defining his
role as that of a vicarious substitute for the more intimately
shared communion she knows or seeks. (141.)

The scene suggests that Mrs. Server awaits a chaste communion and that her companion is Briss, but the Narrator's re-

flections are tense with the suggestion that the "intimacy of unspeakable confidence" anticipated is the erotic communion of lovers and the dialogue strains with the uncertainty as to whom, if anyone, she awaits. The interview comes to a crisis when the Narrator, thinking of Briss, refers to "him" without naming him, and it becomes uncertain whether Mrs. Server understands him to mean Briss or Long (or even someone else) and what connection with her she thinks the Narrator attributes to him. When in obvious apprehension she delays replying, her beauty is intensified by her "peril" and becomes so touching to the Narrator that he foregoes testing his suspicion that she is covering up her alliance with Long by refusing to acknowledge him. Instead he clarifies his remark, naming Briss explicitly, and is surprised when Mrs. Server, self-consciously as if on public display, denies any concern with Briss, indeed "quite repudiated poor Briss." Whether she is speaking candidly or covering up a relation, chaste or erotic, with Briss, her confusion and her repudiation of Briss challenge the Narrator's structure: "the whole airy structure I had erected with his aid might have crumbled down at the touch she thus administered if its solidity had depended only on that." But he does not found the structure finally on identifications, and imputes to May Server the "nobleness" which would refuse to "incriminate" her partner. On this basis he reaffirms his conviction that a relation between May Server and Poor Briss exists and that it is not casual but intimate and loyal and kept sacred in privacy by Mrs. Server—that it *"was,* for its function, a real relation, the relation of a fellowship in resistance to doom." (143-146.)

While the Narrator's conviction remains that their fellowship is chaste, the possibility persists that it is *not,* and moreover, the logic of his imaginings enforces the suggestion that the utter communion he posits must already rest on, or soon become, a consummated sexual intimacy. His " 'extraordinary interest in my fellow-creatures,' " he tells Mrs. Server, " 'has bred for me the idea that Brissenden's in love with you.' " The direction of his imaginings is unmistakable and goes beyond anything he has so far made clear. For the reader, who knows that the Narrator has earlier *sent* Briss to find Mrs. Server, the force of his remark that Briss may be "in love" is multiplied when the Narrator asks her, " 'I daresay you wonder . . . why, at all, I should have thrust Brissenden in.' " It is at this point that May Server, with her "heroic grin," establishes the enigmatic foundation for the Narrator's "palace of thought." She insists that Briss is in love with his wife and has produced in her the splendors which everyone notices, and on the suggestion that nevertheless Briss might temporarily be in love with her she protests that she has " 'never *been* in love.' " These statements testify that Briss is a faithful husband at the cost of marking herself as one who either has been denied the fulfillment of love or who is incapable of it. But the widowed Mrs. Server makes these declarations over her objection that the Narrator should not "make her talk" and does so only with the aid of her "heart-breaking facial contortion" and an "exaggerated" formal exclamation which move the Narrator again to compassion. (147-150.)

So fearful is he that she may break down, he holds back from forcing her to talk further. And so moved is he by her beauty that he is impelled to imagine, as he has not yet done, the more complete passion known to "the man—whoever he was—to whom her sacrifice had been made." Like her lover, he is stunned by the "wonders" of "her passion and beauty," and he imagines, as a "blinding light" in the "eyes of her lover," the passion to do what he himself does in his account: the passion to keep her beautiful and "to have made her more so." Yet he acknowledges that his mind is not completely filled by her wonders because he lacks the "direct benefit" of the graces which she reserves for her lover, though the Narrator himself stands now in the presence of her desperate passion and sees the nothingness and the reality, the "absence" and the "presence," the very "cessations and resumptions of life" which play in the masking contortions of her facial expression. (150-151.)

When, at that point, Briss himself appears on the scene, the Narrator is moved by compassion to "spare them both and to spare them equally." Acknowledging his responsibility for his "providential supervision," he determines to protect their intimacy, whether confessional or erotic, trusting them with the privacy he insures them. He exercises his "providential super-vision" paradoxically by delegating it to them while confessing responsibility for it, the gesture which *The Sacred Fount* (like the later Prefaces and the essay on *The Tempest*) makes the paradigm of James's art. The Narrator's last look at Briss assures him that Briss has recently been with his wife and that she has again impressed upon him "the intimacy of their union." (153-155.)

It is impossible for the Narrator to ascertain with utter certainty, at the time or later, the full nature of Briss's and Mrs. Server's relation—whether indeed they have defined it for themselves before he encounters Mrs. Server or whether they have yet to be joined in the intimacy he encourages when he leaves them alone in the wood. But the triumph of his account is to render the several possibilities (even the vulgar relation) which their behavior would confirm while giving the full force of his imagination to the redeeming passions which may transpire within the forms of the affair and the marriage and which are celebrated by his account. And James celebrates these forms and passions by so constructing the novel that they govern it even if they are built on the basis of a tawdry affair and an empty marriage, on the wreckage of a woman who has " 'never *been* in love' " but is *made* its "wasted symbol," and on the attentions shown her (perhaps kind, perhaps designing) by Long, Obert, Briss, and James's center of consciousness, the Narrator, who so "appreciates" the raw materials of common experience as to create an imagined community of intimacy and love from the ruins of his attempt to find one given and to possess it. It is this vision which is reawakened later when the Narrator last sees Long and which is quickened when he shakes hands with Briss and "things unspoken and untouched, unspeakable and untouchable," stand or pass between them. It survives the midnight interview with Mrs. Briss when she blasts the Narrator's mad folly from the citadel of her marriage, and her brass bumps the delicate porcelain of May Server, only to confirm by aggravating the sacrifice. May Server, by providing the multiplied "resources" and the increment of "pure beauty," pays for the "expensive miracle" beyond what was "bargained for," becoming along with Briss the "wasted symbol" through whose mediation the Narrator and Henry James redeem *The Sacred Fount.*

The Sacred Fount, though banished from the republic of the New York Edition, occupies the place in James's career which Professor Blackmur defined—"the very nexus between his later middle work and his three late great novels" [74]—because it brings into a painfully sharp focus, indeed brings to a crisis for James's imagination, the powers and limitations of the imagination which had engrossed him in the decades since *The Portrait of a Lady.* It reveals what were to be the complex relations between James's rendering of the actual world and his involvement in it as penetrating observer and vicarious participant, between his profound if reluctant assent to the human condition in the middle-class world he knew and the determination to help transform that world through the rituals of commitment which his major works enact. The incidents of the house party are trivial, the isolation of the community is extreme, and the novel's engagement of its reader is a perilously risky game. Yet the fictive world presented—the world which includes the painted "Man with the Mask," the piano recital, and the Narrator with his vocabulary of "paying," "beauty," "drama," and "sacrifice"—is a fantastic distillation of actual conditions with which James came to terms: crassly utilitarian, vulgar, and conventional forms of behavior in and out of marriage; predatory, exploitive manipulations in everyday commerce or intercourse; the compulsive search both for cohesive communities of interest and intimacy and for impregnable privacy in a society where persons and classes are unsettled and not "sorted by tradition"; the ingenuity and desperation with which persons cling to forms or seek to establish them when their experience verges on "nothingness" or when they resist a "common doom"; the all but utter uncertainty and the all but utter confidence (James could muster both) which accompany the attempt to grasp and share in the experience of another person or the mystery of passion, and which accompany

[74] Richard Blackmur, *"The Sacred Fount," Kenyon Review,* IV (Autumn 1942), pp. 328-352, 330.

the attempt to confront and participate in an imminent future which emerges but remains by definition yet unknown.

Both the hazardous uncertainty of outcome and the thrust of firm commitment characterize the final actions of Isabel in *The Portrait* and Fleda in *The Spoils of Poynton.* And if a comparable uncertainty becomes a weirdly comic nightmare in *The Sacred Fount,* when the Narrator gathers his recollections of the weekend, the thrust of commitment becomes correspondingly desperate and James's commitments—to liaisons, marriages, and even predatory transactions and the intimacies harbored in these forms, to the "penetrating imagination" and to forms of art including the form of *The Sacred Fount* itself, and to the act of sacrificial mediation in life or art—are founded less on the actual life he finds than on the vision he creates (the constructed form and the vision created in it), which seeks to transform that life. But the actual world imaged in *The Sacred Fount,* for all its seeming inconsequence, is the same acquisitive society which the three late masterpieces confront and accept in the process of attempting to transform it. It is the society in which Chad Newsome of *The Ambassadors* takes up painting and then later considers "the art of advertising," the society in which Milly Theale in *The Wings of the Dove* makes her "last counter-move to fate" by the "use of her wealth," the society in which Adam and Maggie Verver in *The Golden Bowl* buy works of art, acquire a new wife for Adam, and purchase a husband for Maggie.

James's tormented involvement in that world and his assent to it are acknowledged in *The Sacred Fount,* as in the earlier *Portrait, The Spoils of Poynton,* and *The Aspern Papers.* The three late novels likewise reveal that James is implicated in the actions he depicts by his own transactions as a publishing novelist and by the forms he adopts or creates, which involve him (through his "delegates," plots, pictorial arrangements, and dramatic strategies) in the process of transformation which he helps bring to a crisis and helps to enact in his fiction.

It is the process of transformation—emergent in the world he knew, compulsive in his imagination, and congenial to the style he developed and to the genre of the novel with its capacity to make things new—which joins James's art to the world it depicts, and it is that process, with the wastage and sacrifice it entails, which impelled him to transform the given materials he depicts and even the novelistic instruments he uses in *The Portrait of a Lady* and, more boldly, in *The Spoils of Poynton*. James's exercise of power in the genre of the novel became a radically bold one, notably in the three late novels, because the crises of transformation which he depicted in the lives and social destinies of his characters were joined to a crisis within his art, involving the formal conventions he used in the throes of transformation. The friction among the pictorial, the dramatic, and the novelistic which he emphasized in his later criticism, the corrosions, compromises, and sacrifices, the dialectic of combat within the imaginative process which he wrote of in the essays on George Sand, are dramatized in *The Aspern Papers* and more baldly in *The Sacred Fount*, where the governing perspective on James's late career is most clearly, if perilously, established.

The later novels run the risks which Dorothea Krook, in her incisive essay, has defined as the imminent threat for James of absolute " 'idealism,' " the divorce of consciousness and creative form from reality, the rendition of a world of mere "appearance" at the expense of severance from the reality behind it. Yet *The Sacred Fount* reveals that the world of "appearance" is not distinct from reality but that appearances and the dense mysteries surrounding them are integrally part of the reality which art must confront. And it suggests, as do the Prefaces later, that James's art does not define the hazards of a philosophical position so much as perfect a form of tact in dealing with the personal and social relations which inhere at once in the conduct of an author's characters, in his conduct with them, and in his behavior with his reader. If James's constructive imagination threatens severance from his world, it more firmly provides the basis for an engagement with it; and *The Sacred Fount* defines precisely the vicarious or mediating role of the imagination and its created forms which enable the artist to penetrate reality and, in the achieved intimacy of his involvement with his materials and with his readers, to shape the world he helps to make. In *The Sacred Fount*, indeed, as Ezra

Pound declared, James achieved "perfect form, his form," though perfection became, as perfection can, a fantastic aberration in the act of its achievement. In the later fiction, as in *The Sacred Fount*, the intimacy of James's address to his subject, the intimacy of his vicarious involvement in his medium, is confessed in the actions of Strether, of Kate and Densher and Milly, of the Assinghams and the more important characters in *The Golden Bowl*. The representational novel, with its increment of beauty and entertainment gained at the expense of "bleeding participants" in the fiction, became the intimate novel—the novelistic construct described later in the Prefaces with "picture" and "drama" conjoined under pressure in jealousy and suspicion, each eating "round the edges" of the other to produce the distinctly narrative drama, the "exquisite treachery" and "redemptive consistencies," of James's expressionistic form.[75]

As the aim to help transform life, to help redeem it through the exercise of the imagination, became paramount for James, the role of memory became crucial in the enactments of his imagination. The confrontation of the past in memory, its possession in memory and imagination, were part of the crisis for Isabel Archer and Fleda Vetch which stirred each of them, under the pressure of Caspar's embrace in Isabel's case and the reawakening of the impulse to live in Fleda's, to make their commitments to life in a somber present. In *The Sacred Fount*, the crisis for the Narrator's imagination is completed in memory after the events at Newmarch, and his recollections become a stage for the imagination's final commitments—not a stage for the indulgent nostalgias which characterize much of the *fin-de-siècle* after Pater but a stage for a radically creative process in which the commemoration of an old life is integral to the effort to constitute the basis for a transformed one. Strether's memories in *The Ambassadors*, Kate's and Densher's in *The Wings of the Dove*, and Maggie's in *The Golden Bowl* become a stage for the process of transforming Chad, redeeming the

---

[75] Dorothea Krook, "The Method of the Later Novels of Henry James," in *The London Magazine*, I (July 1954), pp. 55-70, 59. Pound, *Make It New* (London, 1934), p. 292. James, *The Art of the Novel*, pp. 298, 325-326, 328.

commerce of Kate's and Densher's world, and forging anew at the culmination of James's career the marriages created in *The Golden Bowl* and the flawed artistry of the novel which celebrates them.

CHAPTER FOUR

The "Affair of Life": *The Ambassadors*

The real hero, in any of James' stories, is a social entity of which men and women are constituents.

T. S. Eliot, "Henry James"

The French Revolution rounds off the spectacle and renders it a picturesque service which has also something besides picturesqueness. It casts backward a sort of supernatural light, in the midst of which, at times, we seem to see a stage full of actors performing fantastic antics for our entertainment. But retroactively, too, it seems to exonerate the generations that preceded it, to make them irresponsible and give them the right to say that, since the penalty was to be exorbitant, a little pleasure more or less would not signify. There is nothing in all history which . . . "composes" better than the opposition, from 1600 to 1800, of the audacity of the game and the certainty of the reckoning. We all know the idiom which speaks of such reckonings as "paying the piper." The piper here is the People. We see the great body of society executing its many-figured dance on its vast polished parquet; and in a dusky corner, behind the door, we see the lean, gaunt ragged Orpheus filling his hollow reed with tunes in which every breath is an agony.

Henry James, "Madame de Sabran"

[I]

CHAD'S TRANSFORMATION AND THE VICARIOUS IMAGINATION

" 'Do I STRIKE you as improved?' Strether was to recall that Chad had at this point enquired." The quoted question (in the first chapter of Book IV) presents literally the first words spoken in *The Ambassadors* by the younger protagonist, Chad Newsome. The larger sentence which renders the recollection of Chad's query by the older protagonist, Strether, is set off by the drama enacted in *The Ambassadors* and the demands it makes of the language in which it is presented. The sentence condenses the drama of Strether's embassy to Chad, defining the novel's main axis of movement, and epitomizes the transformation of prosaic prose into the particular poetry which dominates *The Ambassadors*, the poetry of musing recollection. (I, 148.)*

The phrasing yields something close to rime when the sound of "Chad" is echoed instantly in the verb "had," and once the quoted question is included in the larger declarative sentence, the words seek to settle into regular meter yet move in a suspension which attains coherence without congealing in the fixity of order, buoyed up in a resilient medium which permits subjects, for the moment, to exchange places: the subject of the question, "I," fuses momentarily with the subject of the larger sentence, Strether, before being distinguished from him and identified as Chad. In bringing Chad and Strether together, then setting them distinguishably apart, the prose performs the ambassadorial mission which is the novel's action. Indeed, the medium's rudiments, its tenses, are converted into style, for within a syntax that defines a world as *past,* a character presents himself, in dialogue, in the syntax of the *present,* and then the sentence presents a *future* that is at once anticipated as fu-

---

* References enclosed in parentheses in the text are to the New York Edition, *The Ambassadors* being volumes XXI and XXII of that edition. Other footnotes appear at the bottom of the page.

ture and already known as past. By presenting Chad through the medium of Strether's anticipations and recollections, the prose brings actual experience to a density beyond what can ordinarily be mustered because it has been given a sustaining form beyond what can ordinarily be imagined and made.

The Ambassadors projects a world where a present is made viable by being made utterly subservient to a reconstituted past and a projected future. The double action of resurrecting and anticipating the possibilities of life—revealed chiefly through the vicarious imagination of Strether, but realized chiefly through the transformation of Chad and founded finally on the sacrificial passion of Chad's lover, Madame de Vionnet—is the drama which *The Ambassadors* is constructed to enact.

That the relationship between the older man and the younger becomes the main orientation of the novel is a triumph of its execution, for the situation between them is implausible. It is not believable, on the face of it, that a fifty-five-year-old widower would accept, as a virtual condition of his marrying Mrs. Newsome, the mission of journeying to France beforehand to free her son from an illicit affair, nor is it credible that he would persist as long as Strether does in thinking that Chad's and Mme. de Vionnet's affair is an attachment without sexual consummation. Neither is it plausible that a twenty-eight-year-old man would make his decision whether to leave his mistress and return to a family business in America contingent on Strether's decision whether to leave Paris and himself return to Massachusetts, and to the fiancée (Chad's mother), and the editorship of the magazine she subsidizes, which await Strether there. Each man faces a crisis in his amatory, familial, and occupational plans, and the complications of the crisis for each of them and the interdependence of their situations are brought into analytical focus by the novel's form.

The interdependence of Strether and his younger friend, and what comes to be a deepening sense of responsibility for both of them, is one feature of the formal construct which is the basis for *The Ambassadors*. In constructing the form, James created in it as full an illusion of actuality as his materials and art permitted, but the novel is governed by the "stiffer proprieties" of its form which James was to mention in the preface as burdening Strether while becoming "suffered treacheries" for Chad. These "proprieties" with their "redemptive consistencies" display the patterns which are dominant in *The Sacred Fount,* which was yet to appear in print when in 1900 James sent the prospectus for *The Ambassadors* to the publisher: a relation between two men, one of whom actually undergoes experience while another participates in it vicariously (Poor Briss and the Narrator in *The Sacred Fount,* Chad and Strether in *The Ambassadors*), and a relation in which renewed vitality and an increment of beauty are gained from intimate passion and a lover's sacrifice. In the institution of an erotic affair between a man and an older married woman, and the conventional expectation that the young man would gain in refinement and be prepared for marriage, James found material he could use for an ambitious confrontation of " 'the affair of life' " in his contemporary civilization and the somber prospects of a middle-class culture for the future. (I, 218.)

James's form enabled him to define the urgency of Chad's future by concentrating Strether's attention on it and to define Strether's and Chad's responsibilities by measuring their cost in the sacrifice of others who are devoted to them. The assumption of the burden of sacrifice, by Chad and Strether themselves and the younger girls who grow fond of Chad, but chiefly by Mme. de Vionnet and Miss Maria Gostrey, is the culmination of the action, but that sacrifice is made redemptive by being made subservient to the ambivalent prospects of Chad's future, the crisis which *The Ambassadors* does not resolve but adumbrates at the end when Strether will leave Paris for America and Chad and Mme. de Vionnet will face the approaching end of their affair.

The tenor of reverie which dominates the prose of *The Ambassadors* and the formal "treacheries" which leave Chad at one remove from the reader while placing in the foreground the mediating imagination of Strether, should not obscure the fact that Chad's destiny is as crucial to the novel's significance as is Strether's deepening vision which the novel presents more directly, nor the fact that the action is rendered distinctly as a crisis. As *The Ambassadors* approaches its culmination, it defines precisely what is both a formal and a thematic relation between Strether and Chad when it declares that Strether, on the verge of going to pieces himself, keeps his equilibrium by holding "his personal life to a function all subsidiary to the young man's own. . . ." The crisis for each is intensified under the impact of the other, and the history of each proves to match in important respects the history of the other and to relate both characters to the central issues of *The Ambassadors* and to James's artistry in executing it. (II, 231.)

The displayed textures of Strether's mind, the modes in which he encounters experience, project a state of crisis which pervades the novel, confirming scattered statements of James that the state of crisis is generic to imaginative activity and to Strether's situation. In his autobiographical *Notes of a Son and Brother* in 1914, James said that a "strong imaginative passion" might be an interesting subject not because of the crucial *consequences* it might have but because, for the man who is "its subject or victim," the "play of strong imaginative passion . . . constitutes in itself an endless crisis." And while the preface to *The Ambassadors* carefully differentiates Strether from the artist whose "imagination in *predominance*" commands his life, it attributes to the Massachusetts editor "imagination galore" along with an intensely "analytic faculty" and describes "the revolution performed by Strether" in Paris where his mind, sustaining "unexpected assaults," undergoes "a change almost from hour to hour." Yet if it is Strether's role to undergo this crisis, with Chad "transforming" him "beyond recognition," he plays a constructive part in helping to create a more expansive crisis which the prospectus for the publisher defined: Strether "revises and imaginatively reconstructs . . . civilization." There are limits to Strether's capacity to accomplish this or even to conceive the task, but this redemptive charge of reconstructing civilization is imputed to him, and the effort engages the two facets of his mind on which the novel is constructed, his memory and his imagination. (II, 306.) [1]

The novel defines early Strether's burdensome "double consciousness," his combination of "detachment" and "zeal"; but even more important are the two operations of his mind in

---

[1] *Henry James: Autobiography*, ed. Frederick W. Dupee (New York, 1956), p. 454; *The Art of the Novel*, pp. 310, 314, 316-317; *Notebooks*, p. 396.

which both his zeal and detachment are exercised, namely the memory and the imagination, which are so intimately fused that Strether's experience is simultaneously a recapitulation of past experience and an anticipation of new experience, for himself or for others and indeed his entire society. The emissary from Woollett, Massachusetts, who lingers at Chester on the opening page is anticipating the *renewal* of friendship with an old friend, Waymarsh, and unexpectedly making a *new* friend in Maria Gostrey. As his eye follows the outline of the city's ancient wall—a "girdle, long since snapped, of the little swollen city, half held in place by careful civic hands"—the memory of a visit thirty years before is the first of a pattern of memories which become part of Strether's burgeoning consciousness; the reawakened memories help him to measure the sense of profound change, the sense that he was "launched" on some new experience which was "disconnected from the sense of his past, and which was literally beginning there and then." (I, 5, 15, 9.)

The novel simultaneously reawakens a past, about which Strether feels guilty concern, and builds a challenging future as Strether's memory and imagination interact to alter and enlarge his vision. Indeed, "nine-tenths of [Strether's] current impressions" are "recalls of things imagined," and when he makes finally his profound surrender to Mme. de Vionnet's integrity and beauty, it is because "memory and fancy" were irrevocably "enlisted for her." Earlier in Notre Dame Cathedral, both the "museum mood" and the example of Hugo's imaginative fiction are enlisted in Strether's attempt to "reconstitute a past," and both memory and imagination are enlisted in the mission he undertakes, "the work of redemption" or the "process of saving Chad." Both are shaken by uncertainties which arise when Chad, asking in Book IV whether he strikes Strether as being improved, presents the "case of transformation unsurpassed": the "sharp rupture of an identity" which leaves Strether facing "an absolutely *new* quantity," the strikingly "made over" Chad. (II, 6, 276, 7; I, 88, 112, 137, 150.)

The issue of Chad's changed identity which strikes Strether so forcibly when Chad enters his box in the theater and later in their first interview is complicated by the fact that, whatever may actually have happened to Chad's manner and character, Strether's recollections and current impressions are necessarily in part a construct of his imagination. Confronted now with "a phenomenon of change so complete," Strether's imagination is virtually at a loss because it had "worked so [strenuously] beforehand" in constructing Chad's early history. But while Strether may have misgauged the " 'horrors' " Chad suspects Woollett has attributed to him, Strether has also pieced together a past for Chad which is significant because it reveals a problematic interrelation among Chad's familial, occupational, and amatory plans and suggests for Chad a pattern of moral deterioration which shadows his character even after his presumed transformation. (I, 136, 156.)

Chad's recent past establishes an important connection between himself, his family, and its business which is tangible, despite the fact that Chad has been living abroad and avoiding a career in the family enterprise. He has a large independent income from his maternal grandfather which, in case his mother should cut off his allowance, would secure his independence and enable him to escape the mission imposed by his dead father and enforced by his mother—the obligation to enter the Woollett business and add to his and the family's fortune. But he still enjoys a large allowance from the Newsomes' own coffers which supports his sojourn abroad and whatever affair he is indulging in. Chad feels no compunctions about using the money, though his independent income may derive from the " 'not particularly noble' " practices (as Strether puts it) of Chad's grandfather, and the Newsome money may derive from comparable " 'infamies' " as Maria Gostrey imagines them— common practices of the business world, as Strether sees it— and the capital which has accumulated through appreciation. For Chad, the money does not burden his conscience and the loss of part of it is no desperate threat. (I, 59, 62-63.)

What produces the crisis for him are the expectations associated with his inheritance: that he will break off his affair with the presumably " 'base, venal' " woman in Paris and return to marry (the likely girl being Mamie Pocock, the charming young sister of a brother-in-law who is active in the family business) and that he will take a position in the business himself, that he will be " 'on the spot' " for a new phase of the enterprise which, thanks in part to his father's foresight, has opened up recently. The Newsome family business is of portentous scale and social consequence—a " 'roaring trade,' " a " 'great industry' " manufacturing a " 'ridiculous' " but widely used domestic product, " 'almost a little industrial colony' " which may soon become a " 'monopoly' "—and one statement enforces the association of the business with familial concerns and creative activity: Strether speaks of it as if it were a baby, " ' a big, brave, bouncing business.' " The particular occupation which Chad is to consider is defined when Jim Pocock speaks of Chad's returning " 'to boss the advertising' " and when Chad, much later, points to the attractions of "the art of advertisement" and declares that promotional art to be " 'infinite like all the arts.' " (I, 55, 70, 59-60; II, 84, 315-316.)

It is these prospects which Chad has been avoiding for over five years. During Chad's first trip, as Strether reconstructs it, Chad had indulged for a while in sheer idleness, but then, showing signs of serious purpose, lived with students, relieving the family with the announced intention of enrolling in "some *atelier*" as a student of painting. But a vocation never materialized, and Strether imagines a series of increasingly tawdry liaisons, presumably the worst being the one that detains Chad when the novel opens—the affair with Mme. de Vionnet which, as Strether is to discover, has so strikingly improved him. (I, 90-94.)

Strether's history relates directly to Chad's own in ways which complicate the connection between them. For Strether, at the age of fifty-five, is not only separated from his immediate family, as is Chad, but stands in a tenuous relation with a new family that includes Chad as a prospective son-in-law, and he is presently engaged on a mission which promises either to secure his professional career or to imperil its continuance. He looks back on professional failures "in half a dozen trades" though he still has a strong sense of vocation, and he had had the ambition to do some service to Letters, to erect a "temple of taste" in America. But his sole " 'scrap of an identity' " is his name on the cover of a magazine devoted not to the arts but to the earnest solemnities of "economics, politics, [and] ethics," so that while he has come closer to a literary career than Chad did to the atelier, his occupation remains a substitute for the one he aspires to. (I, 83, 87, 65.)

The young wife who had shared Strether's first trip to Europe died shortly afterward, and he had so "insanely" indulged in grief that he "banished" his young son, selfishly thought him "dull" and sent him off to school where he died of diphtheria. Strether's guilt over the "young son he had stupidly sacrificed" remains a buried ache which revives habitually "at the sight . . . of some fair young man just growing up" and makes him "wince with the thought of an opportunity lost." Such a young man is Chad, and when Strether's current errand to Europe warms the buried seeds, the "subconsciousness," of his professional ambitions as an apostle of Letters, it stirs too his feeling for the family he has lost. His recognition that he failed to detach himself from the memory of his wife, his feeling of guilt about his son, and his longing to atone for that neglect give the force of intimacy to his interest in Chad's case. They establish a virtually subconscious basis for his involvement with Chad's future, whatever the outcome of his mission—an involvement which Mrs. Newsome has made the virtual condition of her marriage to Strether by insuring that Strether's consent to rescue Chad be virtually part of their engagement. (I, 84, 86-87.)

Strether's mission to Paris not only reawakens unfulfilled ambitions for a career as a *literateur* but also protects the job he does hold, for the Mrs. Newsome who has made him Chad's "prospective stepfather" also subsidizes and guides the policy of the Review which Strether edits, providing " 'all the money' " and " 'three-fourths' " of the faith in the idealistic causes which the Review espouses. Strether does not " 'touch the business,' " he tells Maria Gostrey, but professionally he gains his " 'scrap of an identity' " from the " 'large beneficence' " with which the Woollett enterprise backs the magazine. When Miss Gostrey exclaims that such beneficence must be " 'a kind of expiation of wrongs' " and that Strether, as editor, does in effect " 'assist her to expiate' " even though he himself is not guilty, Strether insists that it is he who has sinned by virtue of being " 'where I am' "—that is, as editor and emissary, dependent on the

Woollett money and its Review, with little to show for personal or professional achievement. (I, 164, 63-67.)

Against the pressure of all these recollections, buried obligations, and acknowledgments, Strether's admission to Maria Gostrey gains its moral and dramatic urgency: that he does " 'stand to lose,' " if he fails in his mission to " 'save' " Chad, that he stands to lose " 'everything.' " Moreover, the novel's pecuniary vocabulary, the terminology of spending or paying and being paid, ceases to remain merely ornamental and assumes under these pressures a definitely structural function, measuring the extent and the limitations of Strether's experience. (I, 73, 75.)

The ambivalence of Chad's and Strether's relation to the Woollett enterprise (dependent on its resources and profits but detached from its operations), their tentative relation to the same family and its interests as represented by Mrs. Newsome, and their still unresolved occupational patterns bring the two men's situations so close that they are veritable refractions of each other, though Strether's history emerges in greater amplitude because he is better informed about his own case, because the contours of his life have been more firmly fixed, and because Strether's conciousness and conscience are given prominence in the narrative medium. Indeed, Strether's consciousness so governs the novel that motives clearly important in Strether's own case and the pressures he intends to apply to Chad have a double effect: they color or distort Strether's first impressions of Chad as well as Strether's reconstruction of Chad's recent history, yet they also anticipate or project motives which are already at work in Chad or bearing down on him from other directions; they exaggerate the scale of Chad's "transformation" while suggesting the nature of the transformation. The disproportionate expectations which Strether projects onto Chad's case, along with the profound relevance to Chad's case that his anticipations prove to have, together form the basis for the comedy of *The Ambassadors*. At the same time they dramatize the problem which Strether's experience must resolve, the question of Chad's "transformation," the "process of saving Chad."

Though Strether and Chad are scarcely acquainted when

they finally meet in Paris, their relation becomes an intimate one in precisely the sense James was to define in the preface to *The Princess Casamassima* as inhering in his own relation to his centers of consciousness and inhering in those characters' relations to the figures they observe. Strether encounters Chad in the "projected light" of Strether's own concerns and can encounter him at all only by virtue of "appreciating" him in the double sense of appraising and enlarging Chad's value. Strether is so intimately involved with Chad's situation, and so clear an index of James's involvement with his own medium, that James used to designate Chad a phrase—the "son and brother"—which he was to use later for himself in the title to his second autobiographical volume, *Notes of a Son and Brother*. The phrase is drawn simply from the facts that Chad is Mrs. Newsome's son and Sarah Newsome Pocock's brother, but beyond that, it suggests important dimensions of Strether's feelings: Strether looks on Chad, as James was later to look on himself, in the role of son and in the role of close and competitive brother, directing toward Chad the aspirations and expiatory sense of responsibility which he felt for his own lost son and projecting onto Chad the unfulfilled aspirations of his own experience.

The phrase appears in the long section (one James insisted be added to the magazine version for inclusion in the first edition) [2] in which Strether reconstructs Chad's two trips to France, recalls Chad's incipient interest in painting, and worries that he might compromise his "authority"—that Strether might "give [his] authority away"—if he were to be too beguiled by "entertainment" in Paris, yet decides that it might be possible "to like Paris enough without liking it too much." Strether's reflections on his "authority" add a dimension to the moral issues of the novel, for they make clear that he is measuring the relation between authority and entertainment which James had discussed in *Partial Portraits* and that he is running the moral risks which James had defined in *Partial Portraits* as the only authentically moral basis for an author's conduct in his

---

[2] Professor Edel, in restoring the definitive edition of *The Ambassadors*, has remarked on this addition in his "A Note on the Text" (Boston: Riverside Edition, 1960), p. xvii.

art as well as for conduct outside art: that Strether is not only pursuing Chad but embarked on a risky adventure strictly analogous to his. The analogy becomes more complete later when it is suggested that Chad, too, is in search of a way "to like Paris enough without liking it too much" and moreover that some of Strether's basic moral assumptions—the propriety of marriage, the need for an occupation—are shared by Chad. Indeed, the scene in the café when Strether and Chad have their first talk provides the basis for their accord. Yet it so unsettles Strether's imagination as to challenge his authority, the adequacy of his language even, to appraise Chad's situation. And the scenes in Book IV which follow it, with Chad's friend Little Bilham and Maria Gostrey, strain the language to establish the half-truth that Chad's affair is a " 'virtuous attachment,' " the " 'technical lie' " as Strether much later calls it, the perilously authoritative fiction on which the characters proceed and on which James built *The Ambassadors*. (I, 88-92, 180; II, 299.)

Strether's first words to Chad in the café are to blurt out: " 'I've come, you know, to make you break with everything . . . and take you straight home. . . .' " Instantly he recognizes that his words, "breathlessly" delivered with a runner's virtually sweaty determination, are wide of the mark. In the mirror of Chad's calmly "receptive attitude" and his shy reticence, Strether recognizes his own "disordered state," and while he proceeds to spill out his demand for "an immediate rupture and an immediate return," he begins to back away apologetically from the " 'arguments and reasons' " on which Mrs. Newsome's demands are based. When Chad responds with the question " 'Do I strike you as improved?' " Strether retreats into what he recognizes immediately as a labyrinth of confusion; by declaring " 'I haven't the least idea,' " Strether lies in the face of the "transformation unsurpassed" which he has noticed, but expresses in the same statement the uncertainty he now feels in facing the "absolutely *new* quantity" in Chad. (I, 147-149.)

By the end of the scene his confusion is compounded, for Chad's protestations against the vulgarity which the " 'low mind' " of Woollett has attributed to him have brought home to Strether that, in the poverty of his own experience, he has no sure basis for recognizing even the "good," let alone the "bad" which he has never claimed to know in other than theoretical terms. At the core of the scene is the first detailed picture of Chad which the reader encounters, along with Strether's first groping attempts to clarify his impression of Chad —attempts which establish a discrepancy between Strether's language and his behavior which is to last through to the end of the novel. And the divergence of Strether's language from his behavior establishes for the reader the profound though delicate irony—the felt discrepancy among modes of apprehension—which pervades *The Ambassadors*. (I, 160-161.)

The Chad who confronts him with pointed questions and the gentle taunt that Strether counts on " 'bringing me home in triumph as a sort of wedding-present to mother' " to throw on a ceremonial " 'bonfire,' " possesses a manner which Strether attempts to describe. Combining assurance with a touch of "shyness" which bespeaks tactful respect for the privacy of others, Chad is distinguished by good looks and the marked streaks of gray in his hair which Strether notices repeatedly. The crudities of his "past did perhaps peep out" of his visage but they "merged" into the refinement of his handsome appearance, and the jaunty informality with which Chad pushes back his hat and his "strong young grizzled crop" present the combination of youthful vigor and mature experience which strikes Strether "almost with awe" and clearly with envy. Strether recognizes the appeal of a man "marked out by women," Chad's "massive young manhood" which suggests to Strether some viable "self-respect" and "sense of power, oddly perverted" which is both "ominous" and "perhaps enviable." It is a Chad so endowed who provides the basis for an agreement with Strether: he acknowledges readily that in the past " 'I've let myself go' " but declares that " 'I'm coming round—I'm not so bad now,' " and he insists (whether with moral independence or indifference) that, while he could not callously " 'give people away,' " he has never been so bound to a woman that " 'as against anything at any time really better' " he could not act on his own. (I, 151-158.)

Chad's tactful intelligence, his professed concern for others and his professed independence, as well as his "massive young manhood" are displayed in a manner which gives him "a form and a surface, almost a design," producing a combination of features which James habitually found fascinating, the characteristics at once of a finished work of art and of the expressive actions and instruments which produce it. Chad seems to have been "put into a firm mould and turned successfully out," and, whereas he "had formerly, with a great deal of action, expressed very little" he "now expressed whatever was necessary with almost none at all." One reason why the scene is crucial is that it establishes a relation between the function of James's style and the interaction of Strether and Chad: for between them they dramatize James's attempt to minimize the inescapable failure of an idiom to render the realities it shapes, figured chiefly in the comedy of Strether's speech and James's recognition of both the assets and the still uncertain reliability of his own reticence and the refined manner of his later phase, imaged chiefly in the expressive power of Chad's manner. (I, 152.)

Against this display of assured power and expressive form, Strether's attempts to phrase his demand that Chad "break off" and his reactions to Chad's character stand in distinct and antic relief. The sole effect of his opening thrust is to be "disconcerting" to himself, and his show of aggressive tactics, with the demand for a violently sudden "rupture and an immediate return," raising his "flag at the window" and waving it "straight in front of his companion's nose," have all the visible signs of preposterous make-believe, of melodrama. Strether is relieved to have got it all out at the start because he senses instantly that anything afterward is bound to be "undone" by the unexpected circumstances. His mixed feelings complicate the ensuing drama. For while Strether retains something of the momentum of his opening assault, he begins to feel, with some relief, that his mission is over, that he has "already acted his part": having merely delivered the message, he has completed his errand. Moreover, in his admiration of Chad's "transformation," he glances at a fact which might be a stumbling block to his "work of redemption": Chad is no longer malleable because the "transformation unsurpassed," has been completed. With his "confounded gray hair," Chad is not only enviably young but mature. Strether faces, in the new Chad, "the finished business": his errand is over not only because he has delivered his lines but because his mission is now irrelevant and too late. The "possibilities" he has counted on pursuing have "melted away" and there remains no way of "computing at all what the young man . . . would think or feel or say on any subject whatever." (I, 147, 149-150.)

Chad's replies have the effect of widening the novel's focus, already fixed sharply on his presumed affair, to include an affair which proves to be analogous to it, Strether's engagement with Mrs. Newsome, and to expose the comic melodrama of Strether's demands. Chad's manner has the immediate effect of altering Strether's own manner. The next time Strether makes his request he does so in a more subdued tone, and from that time on the touches of melodrama in his imagination are vestigial and, though there remain discrepancies between his idiom and the realities it tries to render, his imagination is now embarked on a more careful adventure in defining terms. (I, 150-151.)

At pains to define Chad's new appearance, Strether has recourse to a relevant phrase which is also an archetypal cliché —Chad is "a man of the world"—and the novel calls into question the adequacy of the phrase by noting the "relief" Strether feels in having found a "formula" for Chad's appearance. When a bit later Strether is struck by Chad's masculinity, another stock phrase springs conveniently to mind which Strether clings to because it so "gratified his mental ear": Chad is a "Pagan," he *is* because he "would *logically* be" and "must be." Yet the puzzle in Chad's case is that he is both a "pagan" and a "gentleman," with the disturbing consequence that Strether can "scarce speak to him straight." When they separate for the night, Strether is left with a still unresolved problem of terms and forms of perception which is posed not only by Chad's new identity but by his affair and by Strether's relations with the women Strether knows. (I, 150-152, 156-161.)

The last two chapters of Book IV sharpen the focus on the relation between Strether and Chad, not only by describing how favorably Strether is affected by Chad's acquaintances, their taste and "freedom"—and correspondingly suggesting how responsibly Chad seems to be considering the prospect of his future in Woollett and "trying to live . . . into the square, bright picture" which that prospect affords—but by enforcing the analogies between Chad's affair and Strether's relations with both Mrs. Newsome and Maria Gostrey. Chad's pointed question about Strether's engagement parallels Strether's pointed question about Chad's entanglement, and the last chapter opens by remarking on the fact that Strether writes less frequently now to Mrs. Newsome and confides "with scarce less earnestness" in Miss Gostrey, the expatriate whom he had met in Chester and who guides his initiation into Europe. Strether's fiancée is being displaced by his newly found confidante; lest Chad should write home and distort the situation, Strether insists on explaining his "funny alliance," and the exaggerations (uninhibited for Strether) in which "the wild freedom of his original encounter with the wonderful lady" is described heighten the analogy with Chad's illicit affair in comic relief: Strether and Miss Gostrey had "picked each other up almost in the street." (I, 162-165.)

The correspondence between their two situations becomes more exact when Maria Gostrey predicts that the Newsomes and Pococks, who have sent Strether after Chad, will themselves come over in pursuit of Strether because he has confessed that life for him has become a compelling " 'doom' " that is both " 'paralyzing' " and " 'engrossing,' " that like Chad he is transfixed in Paris because " 'one wants to enjoy anything so rare' " as the " 'miracle' " of Chad's transformation and whatever lies behind it. Chad's alteration is proving to be a " 'plant' " concocted by " 'fate.' " Like the novel which is its image, life itself is proving to contain, in Strether's words, " 'a plot,' " and the *plot* of the novel is figured in the complex of analogies which shape the interaction of the characters. Another important likeness between the situations of Chad and Strether is fashioned when Strether learns that Chad's affiliation involves him with a Parisian mother and her marriageable daughter, just as Strether's affiliation in Woollett involves him with a Massachusetts mother and her still marriageable son. (I, 167-168.)

The analogies inhering in the relation between Strether and the "son and brother," with their alliances in Woollett, Massachusetts, and Paris, France, are the very foundation of *The Ambassadors,* and they so infuse the novel as to constitute its implicit form and the revelation implicit in it of the authority which James exercised in writing it. The second chapter of Book IV gives prominence to the declaration which embodies the express form of these analogies, a remark which is the culmination of an important conversation between Strether and Chad's young friend Little Bilham, in which Little Bilham recasts the image of Chad and reveals a crucial dimension of his transformation.

The conversation with Little Bilham, carefully centered in the chapter, has been just as carefully prepared from the moment (in Book III) when Strether, ascending the stairs to Chad's apartment after seeing the "young man" on the balcony, had found him to be Bilham instead, temporarily residing there while Chad visits in Cannes. Bilham serves Strether as a substitute or preliminary version of Chad; he is Chad's "intimate and deputy," exposing Strether to Chad's taste and his circle of acquaintances (including the *femme du monde,* Miss Barrace), and presenting in himself what is, as Miss Gostrey points out, a case of specifically American intensity, a devotion to Europe and the study of painting so "intense" that his only occupation is an "occupation declined," the study of painting having supplanted any determination to produce it. Accordingly, like Chad without a job, he has stayed in Paris, and it was Strether's invitation to Bilham, delivered to Chad's address, that brought Chad instead into the box at the theater precisely at the moment when Miss Gostrey and Strether were discussing Bilham's utility to Chad in molding Strether's expectations. When Strether has his first confidential talk with Bilham in the café, the reader expects illuminating details and is not disappointed. (I, 98, 113, 125-126.)

Bilham divulges that Chad's affair is already unsettled by Chad's feelings and that his "transformation" has not yet jelled or revealed its full consequences. Quite " 'changed' " though Chad is, he is not " 'happy' "; there is " 'a lot behind' " the striking manner which Strether has mistaken for a tranquil and fixed " 'equilibrium.' " The "finished business" either is not finished or is too burdensome to bear. Bilham states that

Chad actually " 'wants, I believe, to go back and take up a career' " and that he not only " 'ought to get married' " but " 'wants to.' " The former Chad—the " 'well-rubbed old-fashioned volume' "—has been " 'revised and amended' " and " 'isn't used . . . to being so good,' " so carefully polished and edited. Bilham does not think that Chad might return to his unedited state, but suggests that Chad not only wants a career but also is " 'capable of one . . . that will enlarge and improve him still more' " and that he wants to marry so as to be " 'free' " of the burden of being as " 'good' " as he now is. Bilham's remarks adumbrate both an enlargement or improvement of Chad and a falling off from his recently attained virtue, an extension of his transformation and a lapse. Bilham's revelations are a challenge to Strether precisely because they confirm the validity of Chad's transformation but also suggest that it has stirred earlier ambitions and created the contingency of further change. (I, 177-178.)

When Strether pays the bill at the café and considerably over-tips the waiter, Bilham exclaims " 'you give too much' " and leaves the café, preparing, "as if the transaction with the waiter had been a signal," to divulge the nature of Chad's predicament and to shape Strether's reaction to Chad's affair. When Strether asks " 'why isn't [Chad] free if he's good?' " Bilham explains: " 'Because it's a virtuous attachment.' " The phrase *virtuous attachment* is as excessive as Strether's tip to the waiter, yet it provides a governing definition for both the facts of Chad's affair (which it glosses over) and for the standards of loyalty and moral conduct by which the affair is to be judged, whether by Bilham and Chad, by Strether, or by the reader. (I, 179-180.)

The phrase is crucial in part because its terms are subject to interpretation by various characters and to the revision of events: *virtuous* clearly means one thing (sexual abstinence) to Strether and another to Bilham, and an *attachment* (as against, say, a marriage or a bond or an engagement) may conventionally be expected to be more or less close and more or less lasting. But the phrase has, by virtue of its abstractness, an even greater structural importance, for it brings into sharpened focus the numerous attachments which have been forming since Strether encountered Maria Gostrey and indeed since he became engaged to Mrs. Newsome. The remainder of the chapter draws the reader's attention not only to Bilham's "revelation" but to his phrase for it, to the similarity between Chad's affair and Strether's attachments and to the hypothetical status of Bilham's assertion.

For Strether has no sooner begun to digest Bilham's announcement than he feels uncertain of its implications, and while his "imagination" has already "made something" of the remark which he mulls over in memory, he consults Maria Gostrey instantly about the disclosure and the phrase in which it was framed; and although she will, at the end of the novel, make clear that she soon suspected the facts of Chad's affair, she does not yet know the identity of Chad's friend, and her suspicions must be expressed tentatively while accepting *virtuous attachment* as a usable term. But before the novel presents that *first* interview with Maria Gostrey, it presents *another* with her that transpired two days *later,* after Strether had talked directly to Chad and learned that Chad wanted him to meet his " 'two particular friends, two ladies, mother and daughter' " who, Strether infers, must together comprise the virtuous attachment. The effect of the novel's form at this point—splicing both interviews with Maria, virtually remembering the first while rendering the second, infusing the later with the earlier in flash-back—is to splice Bilham's insistence on the virtuous attachment with Chad's disclosure that he is attached to *two* friends, a mother and daughter, and thus to extend the notion of a virtuous attachment to include the familial relation which pertains between Chad and his women friends. (1, 180-182.)

The narrative form in this way enforces Chad's design of winning Strether's approval by displaying his mistress as a responsible parent, and it makes Strether's delusion as to the sexual innocence of the affair more plausible, for, as Maria Gostrey says jokingly, in the second interview, " 'an attachment to them both then would, I suppose, almost necessarily be innocent.' " But the narrative form affects the novel's structure more profoundly. It gives to the daughter (Jeanne de Vionnet) a prominence comparable to Pansy's in *The Portrait of a Lady* and to the relation of mother and daughter an importance corresponding to that between Mrs. Newsome and Chad and to that between Strether and both his dead son and his prospective stepson. (I, 180-182.)

Moreover, Maria's tentative agreement in the first interview that the " 'word,' as the French called it," for Chad's new circumstances *was* virtuous attachment, that Bilham's phrase "would serve as well as another," that "after a pause . . . the more she thought of it the more it did serve," has the effect of underscoring the hypothetical status not only of the phrase but of the later speculation about the mother and daughter. In sum, the effect of the narrative form is not simply to lend credence to Strether's delusion but to give weight—the weight of a complex hypothesis entertained tentatively and seriously —to Strether's inferences that the attachment is somehow to both women and that the attachment somehow involves marriage. These inferences, in ways not expected by Strether, are later borne out by the action of the novel when Chad's parental concern for the daughter is brought to light. And while in the ensuing conversation the contrast is clear between Strether's overly eager assurance that Chad plans to marry one of them and the "deeper well" of Miss Gostrey's tacit suspicions, the function of their queries together is to open up possibilities for the action, to extend the range of its significance and deepen it. (I, 180-183.)

For Strether has held back from asking Bilham the name of Chad's friends and this decision makes their speculation about Chad's affiliation necessarily hypothetical, and Strether has avoided asking the name for a profoundly revealing reason: so as to keep from interfering, from seeming "interested," to show that Chad's "virtuous attachments were none of his business." His attitudes toward the Woollett business (which, like Chad, Strether draws on but never "touches") and toward Chad's love affair are similar, and this scene in Book IV makes the enterprise in Woollett and the affair in Paris together the objective of its controlled reticence, its strategy of silence. Strether feels a "delicacy" about naming Chad's friend which is comparable to the delicacy he had felt earlier, but no longer feels, about naming "the quite other article," the article manufactured in Woollett. And just as Maria Gostrey, faced with the silence about the Woollett article, found that in "ignorance she could humor her fancy," so now she and Strether give play to fanciful speculation about whether Chad plans to marry the unnamed daughter, whether he is attached to the younger or the older woman, and whether or not the mother is a widow. (I, 181, 61.)

The consequence is that the intrigue of the novel is heightened and the possibilities encompassed by the action are multiplied. Enlightened by Little Bilham's declaration, Strether feels "almost a new lease of life," and when Strether reveals his own uncertainty by charging Miss Gostrey with not believing in the " 'innocence' " of Chad's attachment, she replies that she does not " 'pretend to know,' " that " 'Everything's possible. We must see.' " It is the multiple possibilities which are harbored in the many attachments and embodied in the resemblances among them that become the subject of *The Ambassadors,* and it is the combination, in Strether's "new lease of life," of action and vision, the mission to "do" straining under the obligation to "see," that makes his adventure a tragicomedy of the vicarious imagination. (I, 188.)

His experience proves to be the measure of both his success and his failure, for the "new lease of life" stirring at Chester permits him to take part in the saving of Chad but forces him to recognize the limitations of his power. And it enables him to appreciate more deeply Chad's new potentials and to recognize more clearly the importance of his destiny, while forcing him to reduce in scale his conception of the "transformation unsurpassed" which he had thought he witnessed, to adjust, that is, the melodrama of his expectations to the viable drama he helps to make. By the time he meets Mme. de Vionnet in her house where "everything . . . made her immeasurably new, and nothing so new as the old house and old objects," witnesses Chad's conduct with Mme. de Vionnet and her daughter, and confronts the imminent sacrifice sustained by Mme. de Vionnet as she and Chad approach " 'the point where the death comes in,' " he has paid in kind, but paid even more vicariously, for the knowledge that the "miracle" of Chad's transformation is inseparable from the "suffered treacheries," the exploitive and sacrificial process, of making it. (I, 246; II, 317.)

[II]

VIRTUOUS ATTACHMENTS

THE full variety of virtuous attachments in *The Ambassadors* —whether existing in fact or fancy, whether actual in finished form or latently prefigured in such preparatory forms as engagements—are projected against a background which is selected and designed to show off their analogies or likenesses: James's model of Europe, where life is a visual spectacle and where social arrangements impress one (as they impressed Christopher Newman in *The American*) as a theater, with characters behaving as if in " 'a regular old play,' " in a staged drama. (II, 111.)

The streets of Paris, the "vibrations of the air, human and dramatic," a voice "calling, replying, somewhere . . . as full of tone as an actor's in a play," constitute a theater as much for Strether as for the less sensitive Americans, the Pococks, who come over as a second phalanx of ambassadors later and await "the performance of 'Europe.' " Strether's first encounter with Chad in a Parisian theater is fitting in a projected world where, as earlier in London, the "figures and faces" of spectators are "interchangeable with those on the stage" and Strether feels "as if the play itself penetrated him with the naked elbow of his neighbour." In *The Ambassadors* life itself is a drama, and the drama encompasses life on stage but life behind the painted scenes as well, as when Strether and Miss Barrace silently compare notes in the wings while discussing the plight of Sarah Pocock and the performance of Marie de Vionnet at Chad's reception for the Pococks. The Paris of *The Ambassadors,* as Strether asserts, is a world where the " 'visual sense' " threatens to stifle any moral sense or seems to have obliterated it already, where, as Miss Barrace concedes, " 'we all do, here, run too much to mere eye.' " But, as she goes on to insist, it is " 'in the light of Paris' " that " 'one sees what things resemble.' " And it is the light precisely of the likenesses which Paris and Strether's imaginings afford that defines Strether's mediating role as the center of consciousness in the novel and defines the action as a break with both the recent and then the immediate past which produces the increment of Strether's vision along with a viable tradition and future for Chad. (II, 24, 105; I, 53; II, 174; I, 206-207.)

When Strether lingers at Chester in the opening chapter with "more money than usual" in his pocket and "pleasantly chinks it before addressing himself to the business of spending" —or when later Strether delays seeking out Chad's apartment and feels that some "fate" has made him "hover," indeed "advance and retreat, feeling half ashamed of his impulse to plunge and more than half afraid of his impulse to wait"— the language has a paradoxical effect: it defines a preparatory stage in Strether's experience which he will move beyond once he does begin to spend and comes closer to plunging, yet it also defines a circumference of conditions which he will never escape, a *plot* which will lead him, even at the end, both to "advance" and to "retreat." His function in the novel, implicitly symbolized by his imagination and behavior, is to serve the action as vicarious observer and participant and to serve James as the instrument and structural center of his novel. The culmination of Strether's vision in Book XII has the authentic impact of shock and insight, but it reveals that Strether, while perhaps feeling "hot or shy" as the "secrets of others, brought home to us, sometimes do make us," is held close but nevertheless distant from a revelation which is for him also "grim." For the reader and sometimes for Strether himself, there is amusement along with pathos in Strether's anxiety about sacrificing his "authority" to entertainment, his confessing to a "depraved curiosity" when sniffing Chad's apartment during his absence or, as Waymarsh puts it, " 'nosing round' " Chad's affairs, when it is clear that the feelings "hot or shy" are principally for others, that the affairs remain Chad's, not Strether's, and that the "authority" is Strether's only as a delegate and surrogate for Mrs. Newsome's and James's authority. When Waymarsh taunts him that he is " 'being used for a thing you ain't fit for. People don't take a fine-tooth comb to groom a horse' " or when later Strether feels that he is being "used" by his young friends, their allegations enforce the irony of the role as mediator which Strether is assigned in James's dramaturgy, the "stiffer proprieties" imposed on him by James's novelistic form. (I, 5, 86; II, 285; I, 88-89, 105, 109, 256; II, 179.)

Strether's early suspicion that he was "too late" to take part in the literary movements of his youth which were now "already spent," that even if the "playhouse" were still open, "his seat had at least fallen to somebody else," becomes a more profound recognition under the pressure of one of the novel's most brilliant scenes, the party in the garden of the sculptor Gloriani, when Strether is introduced to luminaries of current Parisian society in the cloistered garden where the surroundings bespeak the "survival" of the traditional past, a "persistent order" which converts the "open air" into a "chamber of state." There, under Chad's careful stage management, Strether is introduced to Marie de Vionnet and, later, to her daughter Jeanne. He is so stunned by the beauty and "common humanity" of Mme. de Vionnet that after she moves away from him he withdraws into virtually private meditation, but he does so under the impact of two particular matters which enforce his sense of alienation and his inclination to stand aside: one is the fact that Mme. de Vionnet exchanged pleasantries with a friend in his presence but intentionally failed to introduce Strether, then walked away on the arm of a man whom Strether, an amateur, feels must be "one of the [professional] ambassadors"; the other is the fact that he has just learned from Bilham, the fact that Mme. de Vionnet's husband is still living. Though the "want of ceremony with which he had just been used" is rapidly suppressed by the information about her husband, both fill the "reservoir" of insight which has been widening in Strether's consciousness. Both—the fact of his unceremonious exclusion, and the fact that her husband still lives—produce Strether's recognition that the possibilities which *this* ambassador now encounters have come, for him, "simply too late," that he has been excluded from them by the plot of fate; and his recognition prepares for the commitment which Strether makes irrevocable much later when he declares that he is " 'making up late for what I didn't have early' " but that he will and can do so only by living vicariously through the experience of younger people. (I, 88, 195-196, 213-217; II, 51.)

The first overt expression of this commitment—the with-

drawal from experience transformed into the confrontation of
it vicariously—is the long exhortation to " 'live,' " delivered
to Little Bilham, which James had based on the actual exclamation of his friend Howells to a younger artist, Jonathan
Sturges.[3] Forceful and genuine though the exhortation is—
that in the full vigor of his youth Bilham should " 'live all you
can' " so as to avoid Strether's mistake of side-stepping the
" 'affair of life,' " or " 'missing the train' " and hearing only its
" 'faint, receding whistle miles and miles down the line' "—
the core of its message is no more important than the dramatic
ironies which qualify its import. It is more authentic than
Strether's frantic injunction earlier to Chad to "break off" his
affair, but his uninterrupted "quiet stream of demonstration,"
delivered "with full pauses and straight dashes" to an increasingly "solemn" Bilham, is equally rhetorical, and the thrust of
the rhetoric obscures the ambivalence of the perspective which
Strether's speech maintains. Indeed, Strether's aphorism " 'Better early than late' " is not an answer to but an evasion of the
familiar advice from Little Bilham which prompted it: " 'Better late than never.' " His speech, splendid and moving though
it is, is not the purely "active and positive" declaration which
Professor Edel has found it,[4] for in context it reveals the limit-
ing conditions to human endeavor as well as the opportunities
and illusions which enhance it, the painful deprivations of a
life devoted to seeing as well as its claims to redemptive charm
and insight. Strether urges Bilham to choose to live while the
time is ripe, yet declares that one's mind is a " 'helpless jelly' "
in the " 'mould' " of circumstances and that one has only " 'the
illusion of freedom.' " He speaks as if the life he urges upon
Bilham were more active than the task of mere "seeing" yet
speaks also as if the failure even to *see* life's possibilities early
enough had been part of his failure to live, and he is gratified
that " 'I see it now. . . . Oh, I *do* see, at least; and more than
. . . I can express.' " Strether's speech is a slightly foolish surplus of advice delivered to a young man already familiar with
its ostensible import and most apt to respond to its ironies, to

3 *Notebooks*, p. 226.
4 Professor Edel's remarks on this scene are in the excellent "Introduction"
to *The Ambassadors*, p. ix.

state (as he later does) the claims for seeing, and to live life in large part by watching the spectacle presented by others, the mode of experience which Strether expresses rhetorically in turning from the lost opportunities of his own case to a concern for the prospects still open, he hopes, to Bilham. (I, 216-218, 278.)

That translation of Strether's concern, his effort to salvage something from his fate by living wholly through the lives of others, takes a nonrhetorical form in the same episode when he looks across the garden to find a titled lady conversing with the great Gloriani and wonders whether he is actually " '*in*' " their world by virtue of being thus "related to them" by the mere act of observing them. His next reflections make clear that he is in their world only by virtue of envies which place them beyond his immediate access. He senses something "covertly tigerish" in the "great world" which makes him "admire" and "envy" first "the glossy male tiger," the great sculptor Gloriani whose piercing glance earlier at the party had struck Strether as the "aesthetic torch" at its most intense, the "straight shaft" of scrutiny at its most penetrating. But before he can exclaim to Bilham that Gloriani, with his forceful masculinity and the power of his artistry, is the man whom he " 'should most enjoy being like,' " his eye is caught by the sight of Jeanne de Vionnet approaching him under the "consummate calculation" of Chad's guidance, and the ascendancy of Gloriani is displaced by Strether's envy of Chad. Chad is "better still even than Gloriani," and as Strether's feelings quicken while he imagines being " 'like' " Chad, he imagines that Chad is presenting his virtuous attachment, that Jeanne de Vionnet is the favored one, that Chad seeks his prospective stepfather's "blessing." Strether is correct in essence though wrong in the particular notion that Chad intends to marry Jeanne, but the imagined union is one of Strether's first tributes to marriage as a might-have-been for himself and a merely *might-be* for the young people who enchant him. (I, 219-221, 197.)

Strether's subservience to his younger friends, and the consequent intensification of his own renewal of experience, in combination give coherence to the fact that Strether is continuously rendered in the novel both as a parental figure burdened with authority and as a baby: he is likened to crowned rulers along with the "comedians" whom he resembles (though "not exactly") and to the child whom Maria Gostrey led "forth into the world" in his initiation to Europe, then "weaned" from misconceptions, guiding his steps as he "held on by her garment and was fed by her hand" until he is ready, as she announces at the structural center of the novel, to " 'toddle alone.' " At that point Strether can declare to her " 'I'm youth. . . . I began to be young . . . the moment I met you at Chester' " and yet make clear that his youth is not only a tardy but a vicarious one, a substituted " 'poor show' " for the " 'thing itself,' " a " 'tribute' " to youth derived from " 'the lives, the conditions, the feelings of other persons.' " Though neither Chad nor Mme. de Vionnet is so young as to be immature—indeed it is their combination of youth with maturity which grips Strether—they are, as Strether says, " 'mine. Yes, they're my youth.' " (I, 136, 13, 35; II, 49, 39, 50-51.)

Exhilarating as the resurgence of his youth is, it is cultivated by Strether in the full knowledge that it is vicarious. And Strether's experience is so molded by James that it consistently but implicitly symbolizes the instrumentation of James's art as it moves with increasing precision and insight into the depths of the realities it confronts, yet breaks away in tact and resignation from its own dubiously virtuous attachment to life and leaves life newly endowed and newly shaped in the prospect of Chad's unresolved future.

One role which Strether must play vicariously is that of lover, and his conscience and imagination are so carefully built upon, that not only do his perceptions project the actions of others, but the patterns of their action are refractions of his, refractions particularly of his relations with Mme. de Vionnet and Maria Gostrey. Little Bilham is one case: an intimate of Chad who has seen and lived in ways which Strether can envy and who helps, as Chad's agent, to initiate Strether into Paris, Bilham is nevertheless the one who has let seeing displace a career and who is proposed as a candidate for marriage only to reveal that he, the " 'little painter-man,' " is, like Strether, " 'out of the running.' " When Strether proposes that Bilham could stay in Europe if he were to court Jeanne de Vionnet—consciously substituting this particular proposition for the sweeping advice to "live" that he had delivered in Gloriani's garden—Bilham says that he must find his satisfaction in watching Chad's situation, and that he is too poor even to be considered by Chad and those who will arrange her marriage. (I, 277-279.)

Strether's next proposition is that Bilham marry Mamie Pocock, the charming Woollett girl intended originally for Chad. It is a suggestion which Strether makes for the preposterous reasons that it would be " 'practical politics' " to remove that temptation from Chad (now that he wants Chad to stay in Paris) while enabling him to do something helpful for Bilham and something " 'constructive—even expiatory' " to make up for " 'sacrificing so to strange gods' " in Europe and to express his " 'fidelity—fundamentally unchanged after all—to our own.' " Strether even offers to bequeath Bilham money in his eagerness to promote this affair. And while there are by then clear indications that Mamie and Bilham are beginning to feel fond of one another, the inconclusiveness of their friendship is an image of Strether's relations with Madame de Vionnet and Maria Gostrey until the very end of the novel. (I, 277-279; II, 166-168.)

Another pattern illuminating Strether's role as lover is the virtual parody of his trip provided by Waymarsh, whose "great political brow" contrasts to Strether's more sensitive features yet is not utterly alien to the scrupulous editor of the Review. While Bilham's prospects point in the direction of marriage, Waymarsh's diversions in Paris constitute a mockery of an illicit affair. Permanently separated from his spiteful wife, successful in business, desperately engaged in a " 'wild hunt for rest' " after barely missing a "nervous collapse," Waymarsh suspects everything European but takes the trip anyway. Though he sits uneasily as if leaning forward in a moving railroad car, he is drawn swiftly into the revel in Europe and swims with Strether in the waters of Chad's society, sharing the "deep immersion" in the "fathomless medium" of "Chad's manner" but watching Strether with a stern eye and enforcing a virtually familial pressure on Strether's conscience. He does strike up an affair of sorts with the *femme du monde,* Miss Barrace, and showers flowers on her though he sits " *'en exil'* " in the corner of her carriage and responds to her (she feels) as an expressionless Indian chief standing before a statue of George Washington. Once the Pococks come over, he even introduces Mrs. Pocock to Miss Barrace in her apartment. He clings definitely, however, to the principles of Woollett and urges Strether to go back. (I, 25-29, 172, 268, 206; II, 177.)

After the Pococks arrive in Paris, Waymarsh squires Jim Pocock's wife, Sarah, about in an incident which is rendered to the reader in virtual pantomime; it is a delightfully tender mockery of some affairs, innocent and otherwise, which Strether *thinks* prevail in Paris and of some of his own which *do*. For Strether is sure that Mrs. Pocock is caught up in the revel of Paris and " 'wonders' " whether she has " 'fallen in love' " with Waymarsh; he is also certain that she is indulging the pleasure only to give substance to the " 'ideal' " by " 'holding out,' " paying " *'her* tribute to the ideal' " by having her " 'romance' " and enjoying her fidelity to marriage too. Waymarsh, correspondingly, " 'thinks' " that Sarah is growing fond of him but knows that she will " 'hold out,' " and therefore he enjoys the " 'dear old man's own romance; the expensive kind, expensive in francs and centimes' " and innocent in sexless safety, paying " *'his* tribute to the ideal' " while helping Sarah do the same. (II, 135-137.)

Waymarsh's treatment in the novel is touching, brilliantly perceptive, and entertaining in its own right, but he serves also as a caricature of Strether who is likewise immersed but still alien in Europe and the world of the young expatriates, involved in attachments which enable him, at a cost, to pay tribute to the ideal attachment, whether in the form of fidelity in an affair or in the form of marriage. Indeed the close of the novel's first book focuses on Waymarsh's spendthrift purchases in a jewelry shop to establish the act of spending and a monetary vocabulary as the measure for Strether's own experience and obligations. Waymarsh squanders money in the shop— virtually doing what James, in London in 1888, had longed to do, namely "purchase most of the articles in most of the shops" in response to the "sense of the importance of deflowering, of despoiling the shop." [5] Waymarsh's "extraordinary purchase" is his attempt to declare his " 'freedom,' " to express his claim to be " 'as good' " but also " 'different' " from others. Waymarsh's " 'sacred rage' " to spend and purchase is associated immediately with the " 'freedom' " Miss Gostrey is opening up for Strether, the " 'expensive' " service she has begun to perform by freeing him from his past, for which he declares " 'I'll pay with my last penny.' " The remaining books of *The Ambassadors* render the account of his payments as his engagement to Mrs. Newsome gives way to the prospects of her son, and as his attachments to Marie de Vionnet and Maria Gostrey deepen but culminate in his separation from them. (I, 43, 45-46.)

Set off by the virtuous attachments, different but analogous, of Waymarsh and Little Bilham, Strether's affair with Mme. de Vionnet is revealed to be profound though distinctly vicarious. The irony of Chad's remark when he introduces Strether to her at Gloriani's reception reverberates through their every scene together through the novel. Chad says: " 'Here you are then, face to face at last; you're made for each other . . . and I bless your union.' " Only gradually does Strether learn details about her history—her opportunistic English mother, the years in a Geneva school where she displayed a marked talent for acting in every " 'part,' " whether memorized or improvised, in the curtained costumed, school repertory," the fond French father who left her the inheritance that made her the prey of Count de Vionnet, the charming but promiscuous husband from whom she is permanently separated. And though he soon learns from Chad that it is she, not her daughter, with whom Chad is involved, he thinks the affair Platonic. But gradually she reveals the qualities which make her the basis for Strether's reconsideration of civilization; and Strether's relation with her is a gradually deepening intimacy. (I, 210, 228-231, 252.)

In the " 'variety' " and " 'harmony' " of her charm and the fervor of her devotion to Chad she has the "various and multifold" appeal of "Cleopatra in the play" who can be "vulgarly troubled . . . as a maidservant crying for her young man," yet she displays another order of variety which Miss Gostrey at-

[5] "London," *English Hours* (Boston, 1905), p. 7.

tributes to a type of individual who commands many languages and harbors many minds, possessing "minds with doors as numerous as the many-tongued clusters of confessionals at Saint Peter's." When he first visits her, Strether's impressions yield a blend of "respectability" and "private honour" in a distinct relation to the traditional past—particularly the "post-revolutionary period" of the early nineteenth century—and to the world of commerce. Among the "old objects" are publications of an old-fashioned era, with the exception of the current *Review* which Chad has interested her in, and her "accumulations" of things have been garnered through passive "transmission" rather than by "any contemporary method of acquisition or form of curiosity." Predatory exploits like those of Mrs. Gereth in *The Spoils of Poynton* are unknown to Mme. de Vionnet, and Strether is certain that she never sells objects so as to acquire " 'better' " ones in the traffic of trade: if she or her family has had business in the shops, it has been to buy things out of "charity for some fallen fortune" or to sell them under "the pressure of want or the obligation of sacrifice." Hers is a tradition which is directly dependent upon the traffic of capitalism only on crucial occasions when drawn into the currents of commerce by generous motives or the pressure of economic necessities. (II, 300, 286; I, 271, 230, 244-248.)

When Strether subsequently recognizes her in meditation in Notre Dame, she becomes the center of his attempt "to reconstitute a past"; indeed, she constitutes it for him with a vividness which is beyond his own capacity. His escape in the church is authentic enough: he takes to the cathedral as "a form of sacrifice" to the desire to be a young "student under the charm of a museum," losing his anxieties swiftly as he gives a coin to the beggar at the entrance. His attention is soon engrossed by someone more surrendered to meditation than he. The woman, who has "lost herself . . . as he would only have liked to do," is an "intimate" of the rite who sits "within the focus" of the "shrine," and as Strether's consciousness swells with "recalls of things imagined," she reminds him of "something that, had he had a hand for drama, he might himself have written." It is precisely at this moment that Strether, in the "museum mood" and trying, with the aid of Victor Hugo, to "reconstitute a past," recognizes Mme. de Vionnet. He is certain that she has come not with the "insolence of guilt" in search of "absolution" but that she comes in innocence for solace and support: in any case, she has virtually become her church, with the "dull wine-colour" showing dimly beneath black in her dress, and like a Madonna or a St. Barbara in a picture, she is "so completely in possession" that she seems to Strether "as if she sat on her own ground" and greeted visitors at the gate "while all the vastness and mystery of the property stretched off behind." (II, 5-10.)

Marie de Vionnet's power of devotion before the shrine of sacrifice, her firm "possession" of her tradition, and the infinite variety of her appeal together prove irresistible to Strether when he asks her to lunch and their doing so (in "costly disorder") takes on the semblance of an affair beyond any wantonness enjoyed in restaurants with Maria Gostrey. Mme. de Vionnet's "maternal" duties might be wrecked, "but hadn't one a right to one's snatch of scandal when one was prepared to pay?" Strether's feeling that "the situation was running away with him" is quickened by a recognition which underscores another dimension of Mme. de Vionnet's appeal which is basic to his imaginative reconstruction of civilization: the parental responsibilities which she shares with Cleopatra and with her church. He can fix the moment when his relation with her became close, the occasion several evenings before when he had "interposed between this lady and her child." Their brief discussion of Jeanne's intimate feelings marks for Strether the beginning of intimacy between himself and Marie de Vionnet, and in particular the fact that he presumed to protect the younger girl's feelings from her mother's concern to inquire into them. (II, 13-14; I, 275-276.)

Strether will remain comparatively out of it, but his interposition in Jeanne's case and his growing familiarity with Marie de Vionnet are the match for Chad's hand in arranging eventually for Jeanne's marriage and for Chad's intimacy of long standing with the mother. Before Strether and his companion finish lunch, they have struck an agreement which implicates Strether in the continuance of Chad's affair (which he still thinks Platonic) and implicates James (who knows it is not).

They agree that Chad must " 'make . . . what he can' " of whatever " 'future' " Mme. de Vionnet could afford him, but she demands to know instantly of Strether " 'what *you* make.' " Strether retreats by saying that " 'I make nothing. It's not my affair,' " but she counters his abdication by insisting that " 'it most intensely becomes yours' " because " 'you've taken it up and are committed to it,' " and secures his agreement to stay in Paris to insure that Chad will not break away from her. (II, 22.)

The novel's later sections draw on the deepening intimacy, between Strether and Mme. de Vionnet, whether for pathos or comedy. When she greets him "familiarly" after the new ambassadors arrive, he is unnerved to seem "launched in a relation in which he had really never been launched at all," but finding that he has in effect stepped "into her boat," he begins pulling an oar to keep her afloat. The image of a boat is a telling measure of his vicarious involvement in her affair, for the image is to dominate the discovery scene later in the novel, and indeed, a capsule summary of her history since separating from her husband was that she had "brought up her daughter, steered her boat"; Strether recalls again later being "in her boat" when she confides in him that Chad, not her irresponsible husband, has arranged an advantageous marriage for Jeanne. The shock of witnessing something "ancient and cold" in the arrangements chills Strether, but he feels "much more intimate with her" for her having shared this knowledge. Moreover, the information illuminates Chad's character and his maturity, for it reveals him in the role of surrogate father, the role Strether has been playing to Chad and even to Little Bilham. Strether, who seeks to arrange marriage twice (for Little Bilham), finds that his prospective stepson has actually accomplished this feat, arranged the virtuous attachment of marriage, out of concern for Jeanne de Vionnet. By that time, Strether's involvement with Chad has entailed his own vicarious affair with Chad's mistress, and the analogy between Chad's and Strether's conduct extends eventually even to the intimacy of Strether's final interview with Marie and their separation. (II, 92-95; I, 231; II, 129, 231.)

Strether's relation with Mme. de Vionnet is matched by his relation with Maria Gostrey, which is crucial to the import and structure of the novel not only because she is more accessible to Strether (being unencumbered with husband or lover) but because she relates intimately to James's craft and to the reader. When they first meet in Chester, they have the air of a "brother and sister" meeting after a long absence, but that appearance is soon changed for another. James was to recall, in the preface, that one of the "ecstasies of method" was the writer's "dissimulation" in his use of confidantes, characters who have nothing to do with the substance but "everything to do with the manner" of telling the tale, Maria Gostrey being a hired actress serving as Strether's informant and friend but even more as the reader's, and serving "with exemplary devotion, from beginning to end of the book." James's "ecstasies of method," however, transformed Miss Gostrey, as the preface acknowledged, into a substantial figure in her own right, and Strether's relation with her into a more authentic "affair," implicating James's art and the reader's imagination in it.[6] (I, 10.)

After Strether stumbles on his compatriot in Chester (a welcome substitute for the "doom" of Waymarsh's companionship), she proves a happy convenience for author and reader as well as for Strether and Chad when she helps initiate Strether into Chad's virtuous attachment by guiding his introduction to Jeanne and his reactions to her mother. With a " 'fortune' " invested in calling cards, she is a convenience for the many Americans whom she funnels into, then out of, Europe, sending them back " 'spent' " so that they " 'stay back.' " And the dubious status of her ingenuity (she knows " 'all the shops and the prices' ") is brought out in Strether's anxieties about his debt to her. When she announces that she does not perform her services " 'for money,' " Strether remarks that since she feels affection for numerous "clients," she cannot be said to " 'do it for love' " either, and wonders " 'How do we reward you?' " Miss Gostrey hesitates—understandably, given the close proximity of money, love, and promiscuity which their conversation has implied—then replies: " 'You don't.' " From then on, Strether worries about his relation to her, and James's novel measures Strether's deepening intimacy with her, his responsibility for it, and his payment for it. Strether is fearful that he " 'can't' "

6 *The Art of the Novel*, pp. 322, 324.

surrender himself to the " 'thing of the moment' " but begs her to make it possible, and she agrees to " 'take the job' " inasmuch as he agrees to " 'trust' " her. (I, 21, 14, 37, 18, 20.)

Time and again he is conscious of his dependence on her and on the exchange of social favors which is her "bustling traffic, the exchange of such values as were not for him to handle." When he compares her services for him to his for her, he wonders "how on the day of their settlement their account would stand." As his sessions with her begin to replace the "commerce" of his letters to Mrs. Newsome, his kindnesses to Miss Gostrey are rendered paltry in comparison to Waymarsh's gifts of flowers to Miss Barrace; indeed, Miss Barrace wonders what Strether does for Miss Gostrey and both Chad and Mme. de Vionnet draw attention to the closeness of the friendship which their whole circle is struck by. When Mme. de Vionnet later makes her effort to win Sarah Pocock's respect, she pointedly draws attention to Strether's relation with Maria (" 'Do you know . . . about dear old Maria?' ") and Strether turns "responsively red" when Waymarsh adds that " 'there's no doubt she [Maria] does love Strether.' " (I, 128-129, 268-269; II, 4, 15, 29, 100-102.)

In so sharp a focus does the novel examine Strether's responsibility toward Maria and toward her "bustling traffic," which he profits from but feels he himself does not engage in, that the novel calls into question his assumption that he is not in Europe "for his own profit" and draws attention to the modification of that assurance which it immediately makes: "not, that is, the direct" profit; and it reveals the deep indebtedness which Strether incurs, whether direct or indirect, for the "blessing unsuspected" who has "now become his need" and for her "bustling traffic." Mme. de Vionnet's inheritance may render her entrance into the shops infrequent, but Miss Gostrey like Chad has "rummaged and purchased and picked up and exchanged" the "precious" items which fill the "museum of bargains" or "pirate's cave" which she inhabits in the Quartier Marboeuf. (I, 94, 120, 244-245.)

Book VII, the first of the second volume and the structural center of the novel, establishes the basis for the novel's symmetry by infusing Strether's crucial scenes with Mme. de

Vionnet and Chad repeatedly with the question of his attachment to Miss Gostrey, then closing on a scene with her. And the closing chapter, with astonishing subtlety, focuses on Strether's affair with Maria, suggesting that his interest in Chad and Marie de Vionnet, and his determination to relive his youth vicariously through the lives and feelings of others, are leading him not only to disobey Mrs. Newsome but to neglect Maria and betray her feelings. (II, 15, 37, 34.)

At the point where she declares that he is now able to " 'toddle alone,' " and where Mrs. Newsome's dispatch of the Pococks marks the fact that Strether's position is comparable now to Chad's, Strether seeks refuge from the vivid and "importunate" memory of Mrs. Newsome—"pure and . . . 'cold,' but deep devoted delicate sensitive noble"—in conversation with Maria, but finds that with his new assurance he scarcely need hold his once "small thirsty cup to the spout of her pail," that she has become merely "one of his tributaries." Strether's feeling that "he should never cease to be indebted" to her is mixed with the distinctly callous view that she is now but "part of the bristling total" of his experience. He feels this despite his recognition that she has made him a special case, that she has come close to giving him a home: at the hotel in Chester when they first met, she had seemed "as if she had been in possession and received him as a guest," and since then she has "kept him out of the shop, as she called her huge general acquaintance, made their commerce as . . . much a thing of the home—the opposite of the shop—as if she had never another customer," removing him ostensibly without actually detaching him from her "bustling traffic" in social intercourse. (I, 7; II, 43, 47-52.)

Her reaction combines "acceptance of the altered order" with a discreet attempt to stir Strether to a more intimate and permanent commitment. Strether, though his virtuous attachment has not reached a consummation, is in virtually the same position as Chad and is feeling the independence that Chad has earlier claimed in his affair, and Maria Gostrey is already in the perilous position of Marie de Vionnet. She concedes "repeatedly" that "she must prepare to lose him," but she tries to strengthen and prolong their attachment. When she asks if he remembers that " 'it was *I* who was to see you through?' " Strether replies with gratitude to her for playing her " 'part' " as mere listener and recalls her early declaration that she is never paid for her services in money, translating her statement of fact into a stipulation that she will not accept payment in any form. Yet she proceeds to hint at a " 'service' " which she will let him render her if his plans fail, but she declines to name it and Strether leaves without imagining the union which she has in mind. (II, 47-52.)

The chapter closes as Strether girds himself to "look his behaviour in the face," confident that, if "by an inexorable logic" he had to "pay for it," he was "ready to pay in instalments." Sarah Pocock is the bill-collector whom he has in mind, but the chapter's structure makes clear that serviceable Maria Gostrey and her shop are among his chief creditors, and Strether's obligations to her have been defined, indeed created, by the "stiffer proprieties" of James's form. (II, 53.)

By the end of Book VII, *The Ambassadors* has established the profound irony lying beneath both the comedy and the imminent tragedy which the remaining chapters bring to a conclusion. It is a more complex irony than that provided by the obvious contrast which underscores it: the fact that Chad and Strether have ostensibly reversed positions, with Chad now willing to leave, for a visit home at least, and Strether determined to make him stay, for a while at least, in Paris. In the Paris which reveals "what things resemble," the contrasts between patterns of behavior or social institutions become less important than the likenesses of analogy which illuminate their connections. One bleak separation between husband and wife permits the definitely temporary pseudo-flirtation of Waymarsh with Sarah Pocock; it matches the bleak separation of the de Vionnets which produces the passionate affair, of uncertain duration, between Chad and his mistress. Strether's tribute to the virtuous attachment (before and after his discovery of Chad's sexual liaison with Marie de Vionnet) is matched by his tribute to marriage in his plans for Bilham and Chad's tribute to marriage in his arrangement of Jeanne's engagement. Strether's dissolving engagement to Mrs. Newsome is countered by the relatively promising one arranged for Jeanne, but it is matched by the dissolution of Mamie Pocock's hope for marrying Chad; it is matched too by the suppression of Jeanne's love for Chad which Mamie and Strether discern and talk about while Mamie, her hopes gone for Chad, awaits a visit from his "intimate and deputy," Little Bilham. And if the strong attractions which have held Chad to Marie are matched by Strether's deepening commitment to her affair, they are matched too by Strether's involvement with Maria Gostrey which promises at once to become increasingly intimate and to be superseded. (II, 155.)

The institution of an affair between a younger man and a married woman is, by design of custom, expected to be temporary, with the woman suffering the pain of separation and the man, with whatever benefits, going on to marry. This is the expectation of the Pococks and Little Bilham and the gnawing fear of Marie de Vionnet, whose love is undiminished and who fears that Chad might return to Woollett " 'for the money' " and knows how attractive he will appear to other women. But against these fears and expectations, she has built the dream of a more enduring passion which is sustained by Strether's illusion of a virtuous attachment as well as by his promise to " 'save' " her and his active effort to keep Chad at hand. The pressure of her desire and of Strether's illusion is to make something more of the liaison than custom, tradition, or Chad's behavior so far will sanction and guarantee. The irony inheres in the fact that Chad's affair with her is matched by Strether's affair with Maria Gostrey, and that if that virtuous attachment foreshadows a deepening and enduring intimacy, it portends more clearly the separation which Strether's neglect of Maria's feelings at the end of Book VII dramatizes. (II, 21, 17.)

The pressure of the novel is to make something more intimate of Strether's attachments than his inhibitions, scruples about profit, and emotional resources will yet sanction. Yet while Strether's intimacy verges increasingly on the full intimacy of Chad's affair, his reluctance to make more enduring commitments, the signs of his indifference to Maria's deeper feelings, and the subconscious recollection that he once remained too attached to his dead wife to do justice to his own son—all these motives prefigure his separation not only from Mrs. Newsome but from Marie de Vionnet and Maria Gostrey as well. And that prefigured denouement measures the cost of his eagerness "to see," counters the thrust of his injunction to Chad to remain true to his passion, and establishes the irony, at once comic and tragic, of Chad's irresolution and Strether's certain departure at the novel's end.

Moreover, Strether's relation with Maria is more a matter of profitable convenience than he acknowledges, and the ambivalence of his own relation to Marie—pertinently phrased when he tells Maria vaguely that he has use for her to see him through—underscores by analogy the ambivalence of Chad's loyalties. Chad " 'half wants' " to stay and " 'half wants to go' " at the time when Strether persuades him to stay longer in Paris, and subsequent events keep alive the question of the consequences of Chad's transformation. (II, 34, 51, 41.)

Strether never considers that Chad's " 'development' " is " 'hideous' " (the conclusion finally reached by Sarah Pocock), but he does weigh Chad's " 'natural turn for business' " and his desire to see his mother against his displayed devotion to Mme. de Vionnet and her daughter, measures the "hardness" of Chad's "acquired high polish" and the "unconscious insolence of proprietorship" which Chad's manner now occasionally reveals against his resemblance to a "light, pleasant, perfect work of art." Indeed, he wonders whether his view of Chad's improvement is a "fantastic" magnification, the result of "observation, as *he* had practised observation" which the Pococks would "reduce" to appropriately scaled "plain terms." (II, 205, 85, 65, 68, 79-81.)

By the time the Pococks prepare to depart for America, Chad has shown that he is facing up to his dilemma but that he is uncertain. And in talking with him in his apartment, Strether feels closer than ever to "the youth of his own that he had long ago missed," that it is now "within reach, within touch" of his "senses," as he brings down "his personal life to a function all subsidiary to the young man's own." Chad could " 'like' " Mamie Pocock were it not for the fact that she seems no longer willing to accept him; he does " 'want' " to break away from Marie but is not certain of the strength of his desire. Strether tells him that Mme. de Vionnet has done more for Chad than he has ever seen done " 'by one human being for another,' "

and Chad acknowledges, in his plainer terms, that she has
done " 'an immense deal, certainly' " and that no more than
Strether can he see his way to the " 'repudiation' " that Mrs.
Newsome demands. But it is uncertain whether Chad can permit Strether to "lose everything" with Mrs. Newsome so that
Chad may continue his affair, and equally uncertain whether
Strether has accurately measured Chad's transformation, his
capacity for making a decision, his devotion to Marie, or his
capacity for the fidelity which Strether will urge upon him. (II,
230-231, 241-244.)

The crisis for Chad and Strether, and for James's art, is intensified in the next scene with Maria, the last before the discovery scene and the denouement.[7] For what Strether's confidante and James's hired actress does is to present her own
situation more pointedly, though still discreetly, to Strether. She
deftly points out (with a tacit contrast to Mrs. Newsome in
mind) that Mme. de Vionnet had made no attempt to break up
Maria's attachment to Strether, yet she envies the competition
of the more glamorous Marie and must ask Strether " 'Are you
really in love with her?' " She complains that " 'I seem to have
ceased to serve you' " and must literally ask Strether whether
he would " 'positively like me to stay.' " Probing into the
status of his engagement, she brushes aside the question of the
" 'opulent future' " which Strether might forego and asks
bluntly whether he is " 'indifferent' " to Mrs. Newsome herself. And while Strether goes on to declare that Mrs. Newsome
is " 'all . . . fine cold thought,' " and that her imaginings
about Chad were founded on ignorance, he refuses to agree
that, as Maria claims, Mrs. Newsome has " 'imagined stupidly' "
or " 'meanly' "; indeed, he speaks admiringly of Mrs. Newsome's " 'perfection' " and feels it " 'wrong' " to think of " 'any
change in her composition.' " In view of the "large iceberg in
a cool blue northern sea" which he has summoned up, he
"oddly" exclaims: " 'It's magnificent.' " (II, 211-212, 220-223,
225.)

Maria concludes that all Strether stands to " 'gain' " if Chad

[7] Professor Edel, in the Riverside Edition cited above, has restored chapters
XXVIII and XXIX (I and II of Book XI) to their proper sequence. See his "A Note
on the Text," pp. xvii-xviii.

should stay and Mrs. Newsome should break their engagement, is his " 'treasures of imagination.' " Strether can easily contemplate the possibility that he might " 'give [her] up' " and even " 'forget' " her. When once again she reminds him of their talk in Chester " 'about my seeing you through,' " he asks " 'will you take me—?' " but in the face of her hesitation he makes clear that he intends not the proposal which his words imply but simply the hope that she will take him through his experience. Understandably offended, she intentionally risks rudeness in telling him that if Marie and Chad leave town they might well do so to escape the pressure of Strether's scrutiny. The next scene, the discovery scene in the country, reveals that Chad and Marie have indeed left town; and that episode and Strether's ensuing farewells to Mme. de Vionnet, Chad, and Maria Gostrey present Strether's final reconsideration of civilization and his final assessment of Chad's transformation. Moreover, they enact the sacrifice on which Chad's prospects—and Strether's " 'treasures of imagination' "—depend. (II, 224, 226-227.)

[III]

THE DESTINY OF THE MIDDLE CLASS

WHEN Strether takes the train into the countryside a few days later, his adventure reaches its consummation in the translation of his rhetoric into the act of vision—"Don't miss the train," he had warned Little Bilham—and in the transformation of his relatively hypothetical version of experience into a new life which is at once more intimate, more dramatic, yet distinctly vicarious. And the statements that he has chosen his destination "almost," not completely, "at random" and that his impulse to visit the country was "artless enough, no doubt" draw attention in their irony to the far from random or artless arrangements of James which guide Strether's trip "as securely as if to keep an appointment." (II, 245-246.)

The countryside which he has heretofore known only as "the background of fiction, the medium of art" retains the shape and texture of those fictive mediums and brings to life the memory of a "certain small Lambinet" landscape, priced unbelievably low but "beyond any dream of his," which he had once seen on Boston's Tremont Street but never bought. The superseded academicism of the painting's style and the minor stature of the painter are appropriate to Strether's early enthusiasm, but more significant is the fact that he lost the chance to buy it. Hopefully, he anticipates seeing "the whole far-away hour" in the Boston gallery restored "to nature," and, in the interaction of his memory with the scene before him, "Tremont Street," "France," and the Lambinet painting with its "oblong gilt frame" do come to life, and Strether finds himself "freely walking about in it." The experience is the might-have-been of his youth come to life in the form of a *"would* have bought." (II, 245-247.)

Reminded of Maupassant's stories (licentious, analytic, and dramatic in their objectivity), he feels his own lips "emit sounds of expressive intention" for the first time without fear of being overheard or censored. And as his imagination plays over the memory of two visits with Mme. de Vionnet before leaving Paris, he indulges the fancy that he had come close to betraying Chad by encouraging Marie to become interested in Strether himself for his own sake. Strether has imagined an intimacy with her beyond what he dares and will allow himself out of loyalty to Chad, and beyond what his "function" as a mediator "all subsidiary to the young man's own" will permit. He is then prepared for his final insights into Chad's affair, and for his recognition of the extent to which the depth of their intimacy remains, still, beyond him. (II, 248-251.)

The frame of the picture, he finds, has stretched when he returns to a small village for supper, and while he feels that "his drama, with its catastrophe all but reached," is virtually "finished," he feels that he is "engaged with others" and that, in the country, instead of escaping the drama, his drama is, "oddly enough, still going on." The "spell of the picture" becomes "a scene and a stage," the "picture and the play" seem "to melt together," every "breath of the cooler evening" becomes "somehow a syllable of the text," and all the "fun" of Strether's "amusement" seems "harmless." Looking across at the "gray-blue stream," he feels that "the river set one afloat almost before one could take up the oars" and his eye is caught in a "sharp arrest" by the sight of a boat, with Chad at the oars and Marie de Vionnet "with a pink parasol" seated in it, drifting "as if . . . on purpose" to "fill up the measure" of the painting which called for them. (II, 252-256.)

What Strether sees, as he is finally drawn into Chad's and Mme. de Vionnet's boat, is that they hope to conceal their identity, that they are debating the "risk of betrayal" and planning to " 'cut' " him if it seems he does not recognize them, and that he is, with his scrutiny, "trying" them in a "fantastic crisis" which seems dream-like and "horrible." To prevent the "violence" of their cutting him, to establish his community with them, he gives "large play" to a frantic "demonstration" of "surprise and joy," and they bring the boat toward him in a comparably conspicuous and friendly gesture. The threatened violence, which Strether had known in Gloriani's garden when Mme. de Vionnet ignored him, is "sponged over" by the histrionics of their shared astonishment at the "miracle" of their meeting. (II, 257-258.)

Their exaggerated protestations of joy in the encounter, the affected display of unmitigated delight on the part of all three, set the stage for the more profound drama of Strether's deepest discoveries which would otherwise never materialize: that the couple "have something to put a face upon" and that Mme. de Vionnet is carrying the burden of doing so. His impression can "complete itself" only in memory when he spends the night filling in his vision and gouging "deeper into the matter" after they have all returned on the train to Paris. What he has seen are the clear signs of intimacy and the even more telling signs of it in their effort to conceal or dress it up. In "full possession of it, to make of it all what he could," he sees that his friends have arranged an amatory rendezvous and that there has been "simply a *lie* in the charming affair," a large "quantity of make-believe" in their attempt to cover it up or give it a beguiling appearance. Mme. de Vionnet's "manner" during their supper at the inn "had been a performance," one which "faltered" a bit because she had ceased "to believe in it" or because it began to seem a futile pretense, but one which she found it "easier to keep up than to abandon." (ii, 261-265.)

But if her performance is artful and toward the end becomes perfunctory, she performs it, Strether discerns, for Chad, and her histrionics become the instrument not only of her art but of her devotion. Chad would have been willing to proceed after supper to the inn where they had arranged to stay, but her "scruple" against going on with their plan is the basis of her "comedy," and Strether senses that she does this "rather for Chad than for herself." Mme. de Vionnet's passionate devotion and her assumption of the burden of the "make-believe," are the basis for Strether's reconsideration of civilization and for James's art. (ii, 261-265.)

Strether's other profound discovery, "the other feature of the show," is not the fact, simply, but the "deep, deep truth" of the "intimacy revealed" in their attachment, though it lies beyond Strether's willingness to follow it further. He has learned what "intimacy was *like*" and that there is nothing else he would wish it to be "like," but he confesses relief that they did not spend the night together as they had planned, that they did not elicit "his blessing for an idyllic retreat down the river," for that would have required an even larger "quantity of make-believe" than he managed to supply during supper and the train ride back to Paris. (II, 265-266.)

What strikes him most is a feature which is at once the basis and the result of their intimacy: the shared communion, tacit or expressed, on which their intimacy and Chad's transformation rest. Strether realizes that after the first moments of confusion, Chad and Marie "have communicated together all in silence," and his profoundest envy is for the fact that they can do so. He realizes also that later in Paris Chad and Marie enviably "could talk it over together," and, reminded instantly of his lesser intimacy with Maria, he anticipates that Miss Gostrey will again "come into requisition." But he postpones seeing her after receiving a request from Marie de Vionnet that he call on her and he accepts, feeling as if he, like Parisian "performers concocting their messages" in the telegraph office, were arranging a rendezvous and were, as he is not, "as much in the swim as anybody else." It is in his final interview with Marie that she assumes the burden of her sacrifice to Chad, and Strether, a witness and vicarious participant in her torment, gains the consummation of his vision. (II, 265-266, 269-272.)

Strether feels that he moves, "as in a gallery, from clever canvas to clever canvas," while Mme. de Vionnet and her surroundings enable him to indulge with "impunity" in his evening with her precisely because she pays for his "irresponsibility." He knows clearly that he is leaving the *Old World* behind and anticipates consciously looking back on the scene as his deepest saturation in history, and wanting to save for his imagination or "fancy" some meager "loaf on the shelf." The "tyrannies of history" and the "values, as the painters said, of expression," create for her the rare chance to be both "natural and simple." The atmosphere of her house and the "vague voice of Paris" outside, shaped by Strether's "sudden gusts of fancy" and "odd starts of the historic sense," provide the setting for Strether's deepest engagement with the past and for his ensuing break with it. The candles at the fireplace appear "like tapers of an altar"; then that religious image for the transformation of an old life into a new one dissolves into an image of the larger stage of historical action which is in keeping with the "post-revolutionary period" of Mme. de Vionnet's furnishings and heritage, and closer in the matrix of history to Chad's generation and the portentous industry in Woollett. Strether hears the rumblings of "revolution," the sounds of "beginnings broken out," the "smell of the public temper—or perhaps simply the smell of blood." (II, 273-276.)

The "pathetic, the noble analogy" for Mme. de Vionnet is the figure of "Madame Roland, on the scaffold"—Madame Jean Marie Roland (nee Jeanne Philipon), an active partici-pant in the French Revolution as a leader of the intellectual and middle-class moderates comprising the Gironde, who died a martyr after the Jacobins and the Terror took control. Her devotion to revolutionary republicanism, her love for her daughter, her fidelity to her older husband even after ceasing to love him, and her Platonic but confessed love for the younger revolutionary Buzot, are the striking features of her history in nineteenth-century biographies.[8] Her names are ech-oed in the Marie and Jeanne of James's novel. Her aspirations and sacrifice are refracted, through the tautly balanced irony of Strether's vision, in the different but analogous features of Mme. de Vionnet's life, her "post-revolutionary" surroundings, and the tradition which she firmly possesses. They are part of the past, still surviving in diminished form, which Strether resurrects in the process of reconstituting civilization, and part of the heritage which Mme. de Vionnet with Strether's help makes viable for Chad. (II, 275.)

Indeed, the very variety which links Marie de Vionnet both to the confessionals of Saint Peter's and to Cleopatra is what en-ables her to bridge the "intervals" between moments or epochs in time; the "violence in the change" from her appearance at the country inn ("a person committed to movement and sur-face") to her appearance now is dissolved in her presence in "harmony and reason." And she redeems for Strether (as for James) the " 'lie' " in the attempt to cover up the affair, by making Strether welcome the "comedy" of the performance as "an inevitable tribute to good taste." She could "make de-ception right," remove the "ugliness," and present things,

---

[8] See, for instance, Mathilde Blind, *Madame Roland* (Boston, 1886), and Ida M. Tarbell, *Madame Roland* (London, 1896).

"with an art of her own, by not so much as touching them," by managing to "circle about" them "respectfully, tenderly, almost piously." In her presence Strether is brought to accept the fact that Chad is passively benefiting from Marie's willingness to shoulder the burden of their affair and to accept the consequence of the fact that his own "intervention" in their affair has "absolutely aided and intensified their intimacy," that Strether is implicated in its consequences because he has "become, himself . . . almost an added link and certainly a common, priceless ground for them to meet upon." (II, 276-278.)

Before he has said farewell, he has witnessed her agony as she anticipates losing Chad yet struggles to prevent or postpone the event with Strether's aid. Strether is struck by her candor in assuming the guilt for what she has been willing to " 'take' " out of " 'the lives of others' " and by her sincerity in condemning the " 'wretched self' " that will do so, and he is struck by the resignation she displays in saying that instead of taking from others " 'the only safe thing is to give. It's what plays you least false.' " Yet while he is "puzzled and troubled" by what may remain unexpressed "behind what she showed," he neglects the passion behind her request that Strether stay on in Paris to be near her and Chad. Strether even brushes aside her "torment" in saying blithely that in view of her services and the beauty of her "performance" she should be able now to rest " 'peacefully' " and " 'to be easy.' " In the face of his terrifying underestimation of her passion, she tries to pretend to tranquillity by asserting " 'Well, then, here I am doing so. I *am* easy,' " but in a protracted moment of reflection Strether sounds the depth of her predicament and exclaims: " 'You're afraid for your life!' " He realizes that her torment stems from the uncertainty of Chad's decision, that she wants *not* to give him up, and that she clings desperately to Strether for assistance as a "source of safety she had tested." Her reason for clinging to Strether is comparable to her reason for clinging to Chad, but it is Chad whom she passionately wants and Strether has become her last desperate hope of securing him. Her resort to the safety of giving is not a penitent act of renunciation but a surrender which she makes in her devotion to Chad and which she will be willing to make as an act of final resignation only if she must.[9] She is "renewedly afraid" of Chad, and she stands, "visibly less exempt from the touch of time," in terror of advancing years and the possible death of their passion. (II, 282-285.)

She breaks into tears when Strether declares " 'You're afraid for your life!' " and, abandoning "all attempt at a manner," she sits exposed to his view and presents the abject passion which chills and appalls him as well as making him feel "hot or shy" in its presence. He feels "at a loss" for bringing on her collapse, and he stands "consenting" to her tragedy, helplessly apart but participating through the "inward irony" he feels "in the presence of such a fine, free range of bliss and bale," confronting the "passion, mature, abysmal, pitiful, [which] she represented, and the possibilities she betrayed." For Strether has grasped that in her service to Chad she is "exploited" by the "mysterious forces" which transform him, and that while Chad's transformation is genuine and tragically expensive, it is not "infinite." She and her tradition have made him "better" or "anything one would," but he remains "only Chad"; and Strether has contributed to the process by "his high appreciation" which, with whatever exaggerations, has "consecrated her work." Yet the process was "of the strict human order." The torture for Strether is to witness a woman's act of adoration and to see the "subtlest creature" he has ever known "vulgarly troubled . . . as a maidservant crying for her young man" and abasing herself further by assuming the guilt for her wrongs. (II, 284-286.)

Marie de Vionnet's collapse in the face of Strether's scrutiny and the eventual abandonment it prefigures are the ruin which she and Strether must attempt to salvage, and within a few moments she has "in a manner" got hold of herself and can mark, with telling scorn, the barrier remaining between herself and Strether and can anticipate her separation from Chad. She tells Strether that despite Strether's tolerance and " 'patience' " he would do anything " 'but be mixed up with us,' " that he

[9] Caroline Gordon has claimed that the crisis and sacrifice in *The Ambassadors* are predominantly religious and specifically Christian rather than broadly secular and social, and she has found in Marie de Vionnet's statement that the " 'safe' " thing is to " 'give' " an image of Christian charity. See her "Some Readings and Misreadings," *Sewanee Review*, LXI (Summer 1953), 387-388.

cannot be genuinely " 'tormented' " or he would express the torment as she does. She declares that he habitually pulls back from things " '*too* ugly' " or " 'too beautiful' " and that now, since she and Chad have forced him to " 'see' " the " 'appearances' " which he has played along with and which have created for him an " 'obligation' " to take a stand, his only resort will be to avoid thinking about them at all. He is moved to protest that there is " 'something I believe I can still do,' " while she points to the encroachment of old age and the " 'certainty' " that she will " 'be the loser in the end.' " (II, 286-288.)

The remaining chapters are devoted to defining the service for her which Strether performs while revealing also the limits of his power and devotion. They enact the sacrifice which has been suffered in anticipation and will be suffered eventually in even sharper form by Marie de Vionnet, and which Strether and Maria Gostrey suffer in smaller measure, while the final responsibility for redeeming all that is implicit in Marie de Vionnet's and Strether's services, and all that is implicit in his heritage, is conferred on Chad.

Strether's last scene with Chad is all the more tense in its irony for the fact that both men are rather at ease, with Strether resignedly preparing his departure and with Chad, recently returned from a trip to London, stepping out onto the balcony where Strether had first looked for him and calmly "taking up his life afresh." The closing chapters heighten the ambivalence of the new beginnings for both of them. Strether's service for Mme. de Vionnet is to insist now that Chad should not break away from the virtuous attachment, declaring that " 'you'll be guilty of the last infamy—if you ever forsake her' " and that he has hopes of " 'preventing [Chad], if possible, from so much as thinking of it.' " (II, 306, 308, 311.)

Yet he himself has just refused Mme. de Vionnet's request to stay near them, and he has suppressed the temptation to live on in Paris, "to enshrine himself" in Chad's guest room "at his young host's expense." And in his discussion with Chad he wavers between making his injunction absolute or insisting simply that Chad stay until he has ceased to benefit, though Strether virtually stammers in his embarrassment at mentioning *gain:* " 'Don't leave her *before.* When you've got all that can be got—I don't say,' he added a trifle grimly, 'That will be the proper time.' " Yet Strether is certain that " 'from such a woman, there will always be something to be got.' " When Chad asks whether it might not be " 'enough' " to " 'live on one's accumulations,' " he makes clear that his choice between Marie de Vionnet and Woollett entails living on the "accumulations" from either one so as to garner further profits from the other. When Strether parts from Chad, feeling as "depleted as if he had spent his last sou," his feelings are a mixture of assurance that Chad feels deeply his obligation to Marie and of fear that he may tire of her or feel other obligations and be simply " 'restless.' " And he accepts the patent uncertainty of Chad's decisions. (II, 306-308, 311-312, 315, 318.)

But the Chad he leaves behind in the mixture of freedom and involvement which his virtuous attachment entails, is a man who can now define the main issue which he is left to face. To Strether's distress Chad wants to "bargain" or argue in favor of "the art of advertisement," presenting a case for it as a combination of " 'art' " and business, an " 'art like another' " and a vocation for the " 'right man' " to " 'take hold' " with firm commitment, and Strether concedes its validity. Strether does not utterly reject Woollett, with its " 'big, brave, bouncing business,' " nor conclude, as Stephen Spender once urged, that "the life of Woollett and of advertising . . . is death." [10] He concedes that advertising, " 'at this time of day, is the secret of trade' " and that it is " 'quite possible it will be open to you —giving the whole of your mind to it.' " Behind his concession is the pressure of Strether's strong sense of vocation and his recognition that the combination of art and business which Chad contemplates may possibly harbor, though in sadly diminished and debased form, the energies of art and trade which his own career on the Review has never confronted directly or harnessed. But he makes his concession while protesting with greater force that Chad in any case should not betray Marie de Vionnet " 'for the money in it.' " (II, 315-317.)

Chad replies that his interest in the money is " 'purely platonic' " (an ironic reminder that he retains a good deal of money anyway, and an equally ironic echo of Strether's naïve

[10] Stephen Spender, *The Destructive Element* (London, 1935), p. 79.

assumption about Chad's virtuous attachment), and in a gesture of commitment he sets an imaginary bundle of money on the street and kicks it away. But Strether reads the "simulated kick" as an indication that Chad remains undecided and " 'restless.' " It is, however, precisely the viability of Chad's situation that Strether accepts in the full recognition of its risks, after bringing to bear on him the full weight of Woollett, his appreciation of the vitalities in America and post-revolutionary Europe, such as they are, and the passionate devotion of Mme. de Vionnet which have helped make Chad's particular new life possible. (II, 317-318.)

Under the added pressure of Strether's insight and sense of duty, Chad has been exposed, through his experience with his own family and with Mme. de Vionnet and hers, to the possibilities afforded by the America and the Europe he derives from. And they include the full range of values which are presented to the reader largely through Strether's appreciative reconstruction: the enterprise, vocation, and expiatory activities of Woollett; the possibly happy and fruitful marriages envisioned for Mamie and Jeanne as well as the grim marriage known to Waymarsh or the grim but fruitful marriages of Jim Pocock and Mme. de Vionnet; the intimate communion shared by Chad and Marie de Vionnet, and the communities with them and with Maria Gostrey and her "shop" that Strether knows; the burden of lying forms, appearances, and the drama which Mme. de Vionnet assumes and the payment for it in suffering for which she makes herself responsible; Marie de Vionnet's combination of art and nature, of form and passion, her surrender to love at the risk of being victimized and preparing her lover for a future separate from her.

Chad's last profession of loyalty to Marie de Vionnet defines the issue before him with a clarity and profundity beyond Strether's power to phrase: he asks in protest " 'What have I done, what am I doing, but cleave to her to the death?' "—then adds that one must " 'have it before one, in the cleaving, the point where the death comes in.' " For the encroaching " 'doom' " which Marie de Vionnet fears, or the death of passion which may occur before that, help define the prospect and the responsibilities which the mature Chad has the imagination to see. (II, 288, 317.)

The brilliance of Strether's two closing scenes with Maria Gostrey (one immediately before, one after his farewell to Chad) lies in their providing a fitting context for the situation of Mme. de Vionnet and Chad while presenting a drama in their own right. They underscore the uncertainty of Chad's plans, and paradoxically they both echo the action that has ensued and prefigure possibilities which lie ahead. When Strether's departure from Maria marks also the dissolution of his engagement with Mrs. Newsome, his renunciation of profit and marriage echo the comparable sacrifices which Chad's affair has entailed and will entail if he stays with Marie de Vionnet. Yet the departure prefigures the possibility which Strether fears in Chad's case, the possibility of a comparable break with the devoted woman whose services for him have remade Chad and created Chad's profoundest obligations. Strether's rejection of Maria's offer of marriage underscores the limitations of his own capacity for love and the fact that he is asking Chad to make a commitment in deed which he cannot match. Moreover, Strether's decision, made because he feels that it is too late for him to live life directly, and because he is subject (as James was to confess in the preface) to the "stiffer proprieties" of James's form, implicates James's art in the kind of alliance which Chad has profited from, and in the process which creates opportunities for Chad and an increment of vision for Strether at the expense of the enterprise in Woollett, the tradition of Europe, and the women who are sacrificed to make their future fulfillment possible. In sum, the closing scenes complete the enactment of the ritual break with the past and the sacrificial commitment to the future that begins when Strether arrives at Chester and reaches its crisis in Strether's farewell scenes with Mme. de Vionnet and Chad.

During the hours Strether spends strolling about Paris with Maria while Chad is away in London, he luxuriates in "the sweetness of vain delay," enjoying a virtual "lapse of life" in the calm silence of a "death-bed hush"; he imagines feeling as if he were "going to die—die resignedly" and, as if drifting through "caverns of Kubla Khan," he enjoys postponing either the "extinction" which awaits him or the "reckoning" he must face in Woollett. After he and Maria have discussed his farewell to Marie de Vionnet, and it becomes clear that he will not see Mme. de Vionnet again, Maria can anticipate her own separation from Strether which takes place in the final scene. (II, 293-294.)

Then Strether turns down the " 'haunt of ancient peace' " which Maria offers him, standing in her conspicuously domestic setting, surrounded by pottery which has "the dignity of family portraits" in her "Dutch-looking dining-room" that overlooks "a scrap of old garden that had been saved from modern ravage." First they talk of Chad's indecision: Mme. de Vionnet's conviction that Chad has " 'the makings of an immense man of business in him,' " the possibility that " 'Mr. Chad may, after all, go back,' " Strether's fear that Chad in professing his loyalty " 'protests too much,' " even the possibility that he may have been visiting " 'some other woman in London.' " But they both feel the irony that it is Marie de Vionnet " 'who has formed' " Chad and that whatever the consequences " 'he has all life before him.' " All the while Maria Gostrey has been inquiring about Strether's own plans, eliciting his declaration that his relation with Mrs. Newsome is " 'over for both of us,' " and asking him pointedly whether " ' "infamy" ' " were the word Strether had used for Chad's abandoning *his* Parisian friend. Strether senses that she is inviting a proposal, but he has already declared that he is " 'not . . . in real harmony with what surrounds me' " and that this condition " 'makes . . . a fool of me,' " and he persists in carrying the " 'folly' " through to its conclusion with the paradoxical combination of courage and evasion, correctness and cruelty, which his decision entails. (II, 319-325.)

He turns down her tacit "offer of exquisite service, of lightened care, for the rest of his days," determined to be " 'right,' " determined, that is, " 'not, out of the whole affair, to have got anything for myself.' " In rejecting the security of happiness with her to return to his final "reckoning" in Woollett, he knows only that there will be " 'something' " there, a " 'great difference,' " and that " 'I shall see what I can make of it.' " The future to which he commits himself is even more indeterminate than Chad's. But the final "reckoning" in Woollett is prefigured by the final accounting with Miss Gostrey, who serves both Strether and the reader (as the preface was to point out) "with exemplary devotion, from beginning to end of the book." Maria Gostrey points out that Strether *has* gained something—" 'with your wonderful impressions, you'll have got a great deal' "—and he agrees. His renunciation of marriage with Mrs. Newsome and the advantages that it would bring, and his renunciation of the security and happiness which marriage to Maria would afford, are a measure of payment for his increment of vision, but the payment is paltry when compared to the torment he has witnessed in Marie de Vionnet and the imminent sacrifice to which she consents in their last interview; moreover, the payment is paltry when compared to the lesser but genuine torment in Maria's feelings which echo those of Marie de Vionnet. Maria Gostrey's suffering takes the measure of his and measures the reader's pleasure and profit in reading *The Ambassadors*. (II, 325-327.)

The dubious rightness of Strether's folly, however right and however appropriate to the "stiffer proprieties" of James's form, is precisely dreadful, as Maria claims. And, by contrast, her devotion embraces the desire, even the discreetly firm effort, to possess him in the deepening intimacy of marriage. By profitably possessing Maria, then leaving her, in the affair of art, the affair of memory and imagination, rather than in the affair of marriage which she hopes for, Strether enacts for James the exploitive sacrifice on which the novel is founded. Strether's renunciation, while a genuine tribute to his experience and a payment for it, is a substitute for the payment that might be made in the life of the emotions and in more complete commitments of behavior. Maria's "defeated protest," when Strether lays claim to his rectitude, bears the pain of her more deeply felt loss and sounds again the wasted feelings which his vision and James's art draw on: " 'It isn't so much your *being* "right"—it's your horrible sharp eye for what makes you so.' " His "advance" and his "retreat," his success and his failure, his commitment and his abdication measure each other, and the folly which is all of these forms the basis for both the comedy and the tragedy of *The Ambassadors*.

Miss Gostrey had once pledged herself to the success of Streth-er's mission by saying " 'And to that end I'm yours. . . . Till death' " but when she now admits that " 'I can't indeed resist you,' " she confesses her failure to win the argument and shat-ter the cruel logic of his decision. Yet in the same phrase she expresses also her irresistible love for him, and with touching resignation she "sighed it at last all comically, all tragically, away." (I, 75; II, 326-327.)

In *The Ambassadors* James discovered that his newly consti-tuted art could sustain, without becoming the obsessive aberra-tion displayed in *The Sacred Fount,* the perilous equilibrium of tragi-comedy. But it attains the fullness of the illusion it pro-jects and its virtually perfect formal symmetry by holding care-fully in abeyance "the point where the death comes in," ac-knowledging it only as Strether acknowledges the memories of his dead wife and son, and revelling, with Strether, in the "postponements" which contain the imminence of death within a musing interplay of wishful fantasies, delicate evasions and controlled indulgences, enchanting hypotheses and entertaining forms. In James's next novel, the imminence of death becomes paramount: subjected to a more intense focus, it presses more violently and intimately against the form which would attest its presence yet survive or triumph. And the dream of marriage presses more firmly against the "game" of courtship which its heroine and her suitor play, against the affairs of her closest friends, and against the craft of the novel devoted to her. The result is a fully tragic drama in *The Wings of the Dove.*

CHAPTER FIVE

"The Sketch of the Affair":
The Wings of the Dove

"Men must endure
Their going hence, even as their coming hither;
Ripeness is all."

Shakespeare, *King Lear.*

This effect of certain of the manifestations of wealth in New York is, so far as I know, unique; nowhere else does pecuniary power so beat its wings in the void, and so look round it for the charity of some hint as to the possible awkwardness or possible grace of its motion. . . . The whole costly up-town demonstration was a record, in the last analysis, of individual loneliness; whence came, precisely, its insistent testimony to waste—waste of the still wider sort than the mere game of rebuilding.

James, *The American Scene.*

[I]

LANGUAGE AS FATE

"It was not till afterwards that, going back to it, I was to read into [Kate's] speech a kind of heroic ring, a note of a character that belittled [Densher's] own incapacity for action. Yet he saw indeed even at the time the greatness of knowing so well what one wanted." The quoted sentences, drawing attention to the heroism of one character (Kate Croy) and comparing it to the passivity of the novel's hero (Kate's fiancé, Merton Densher), occur at the height of the scene which constitutes the drama of *The Wings of the Dove* by bringing the novel's crisis to its culmination and at the same time providing the basis for its resolution. At so crucial a point, James speaks, in the first American edition, for the only time when his voice emerges in the first person to help bring an important matter, Kate's heroism, into definite focus; Densher's ready admiration for her at the time enforces a tribute felt later but openly by James. In the first English edition as in the subsequent New York collection, the "I" is replaced by "he," whether because James detected a typographer's error, corrected his own mistake, or decided on second thought to substitute one form of expression for another.* In any case, the "muffled majesty of authorship" and the entire insight into Kate's heroism are delegated in the revisions to Densher—his "bland Hermes," as James was to call him in the preface, the god of theft and commerce who gave Apollo his lyre.[1] In all versions the tribute to Kate helps to define the novel's form by straining it, in an effort to encompass both a prospective and a retrospective view, so as to define an act of confession of which the quoted sentences are part. (II, 226.)

The act of looking ahead or anticipating the completion of

* *The Wings of the Dove*, 2 vol. (New York, 1902), II, 241; *ibid.*, 2 vol. in one (Westminster, 1902), II, 434. Subsequent references to James's fiction, enclosed in parentheses in the text, are, unless otherwise identified, to the New York Edition, *The Wings of the Dove* being volumes XIX and XX of that collection. Other footnotes appear at the bottom of the page.

1 *The Art of the Novel,* p. 298.

the action and the act of reconsidering it in memory, whether performed ostensibly by James or ostensibly by Densher, are joined in a tribute to Kate's heroism at the moment when she has expressed a willingness to " 'do what I don't like' " in encouraging her own fiancé to marry a dying and wealthy American girl, Milly Theale. James's intervention at this point to pay tribute to Kate, in the unrevised version, would implicate him explicitly in the plot, thus associating him intimately with Kate's and Densher's deed. But the tribute assigned wholly to Densher in the revision is a degree of consciousness and conscience *imputed* to him by James, and it is likewise an effort to confess James's responsibility for the action and to confess as well his form's involvement in the action and his intimate involvement with his medium.

The narrative convention of *The Wings of the Dove* is founded on neither the author's voice alone nor on the center of consciousness alone but on the intimate connection between them, on the shared burden and responsibility which the narrative's gestures confess; it is articulated consistently and frequently, in all versions, when the narrative momentarily reveals James's presence in such carefully unobtrusive phrases as "I say" or "our analysis," "our young lady" and "our subject." Being the very image of the vicarious imagination, the narrative exercises authority by delegating authority and confessing responsibility for it, and the scene which includes the tribute to Kate's heroism twice reveals explicitly, then again veils, James's presence in the phrase "we know." [2] (I, 275, 141, 157; II, 204, 222.)

James's emergence intermittently in the first person is paradoxically both a lapse or flaw in the "guarded objectivity" of his drama and the fulfillment of its logic as a novel which builds, as the preface was to point out, on its own failure. His acknowledgment of the role of narrator, the pretentious "majesty of authorship," is the flaw in his form and a questionable commitment, matching that of Kate and Densher, which must be answered and redeemed. Yet it articulates also James's confession of his commitment. But James's confessed presence is revealed more profoundly, in all versions, in the projected *ac-*

2 Cf. the American version, I, 300, 157, 175; II, 223, 243.

tion of the scene, for what Kate and Densher do on that occasion—what they do for James—is to "suit the action to the word, the word to the action" of James's novel by agreeing to enact its plot, with Kate forcing Densher to put her plan into words and then joining him in the phrasing of it. Moreover James's complicity and the involvement of his form are revealed implicitly also in the rendering of other characters who are James's instruments and who contribute along with Kate and Densher to the plot. Indeed, the very behavior of language itself as an instrument is revealed to be one of the sources of the novel's tragic vision.

If it inheres in the very nature of a language, as Santayana has written, that it gives "perspective" to experience but in that act also "vitiates the experience it expresses," the "kindly infidelities" of language, as Santayana called them, define the verbal action which mediates the tragic vision of *The Wings of the Dove:*[3] the behavior of a medium which at once expresses and betrays its subject or vision and accordingly is inseparable, in *The Wings of the Dove,* from the tragic action it renders. The novel's language is shaped by three principal vocabularies —one commercial, one religious, and one aesthetic—which are defined by characteristic metaphors or phrases: for instance, the phrase "a capital case" which a doctor uses to describe the dying and wealthy heroine; or the description of doves who are "picking up the crumbs of perpetual feasts" in the square before a Christian church in Venice; or the description of the heroine as "embodied poetry." Each of the phrases, and each of the larger vocabularies of which it is part, helps define the novel's relevance to the actual world beyond it—to the institutions, attitudes, formulations of value, and forms that comprise the culture of capitalism, or the Judaeo-Christian tradition, or the fine arts. But the field of relevance they define is a field of behavior in which they act, not a safely remote and independent realm of actualities to which they refer, and the language functions so as to draw the practices and values it suggests *into* the "crucible" of the imagination and into the fictive action, to include them in the world it creates, and, conversely, to bring the "penetrating imagination" into an intimate encounter with

3 George Santayana, *Reason in Art* (New York, 1905), p. 82.

its materials, the actualities in the world of which it is part.

The consequence is that the language, as an instrument, is subject not only to all the pressures which have already endowed it with the conventional implications that it brings into the novel but to the pressures it undergoes as the mediating instrument of James's imagination. Its behavior is far from the "merely referential" function which James was to disparage in the preface to *The Ambassadors,* in being at once more anxious or apprehensive and more powerful. It is closer rather to the explorative maneuvers he attributed to himself, as a "wary adventurer," in the preface to *The Wings of the Dove,* "standing off" from the "situation" of the wealthy dying girl, but then "coming back to it," walking "round and round" the "case" that "invited and mystified" his fascination.[4] The language does not so much stipulate its meanings or describe its action as *suspend* them in a mode which is epitomized by the novel's opening sentences, where Kate Croy's hesitation between departing or remaining, between going away or staying to see and help her father, presents the first version of the novel's central action and its basic rhythm. The paleness, the waiting, and the decision to stay, here touched on for the first time, are crucial motives in the novel, and the opening sentences virtually postpone Kate's decision to remain, suspending it in tension with the temptation to go away so as to evade a confrontation with her father, while literally pausing and lingering over her name, the detail of the mirror above the mantel, and her momentarily pale face: "She waited, Kate Croy, for her father to come in, but he kept her unconscionably, and there were moments when she showed herself, in the glass over the mantel, a face positively pale with the irritation that had brought her to the point of going away without sight of him. It was at this point, however, that she remained. . . ." (I, 3.)

While the language, in this dramatic suspension, both expresses and betrays its subject, rendering it by approaching it but holding off from it, the prose serves the several functions that are paramount for James's art and govern his characters as well as his language. The prose can be as intimate and compressed in its irony for James as it is for Kate, with her de-

4 *The Art of the Novel,* p. 288.

sire when talking of her family's predicament "to work off, for her own relief, her constant perception of the incongruity of things," and to devise, for intimate conversation with her fiancé, a shorthand of "fantastic" phrases and "the happy language of exaggeration," exaggerations which constitute their intimacy and manage to be more true than the less intimate make-believe which they indulge in public. In its analytic probing the prose risks the cruelty of exposure which Kate fears when she learns that she might be written up in a book: " 'Chop me up fine or serve me whole'—it was a way of being got at that Kate professed she dreaded." Yet if it is intimate in its devious exaggerations and painfully close in its exposure of the characters it depicts, the language is, nevertheless, conspicuously restrained even when subservient to James's analytic strategy, as when sheer observation of the ailing heroine becomes a risky adventure for her hired traveling companion, Mrs. Susan Stringham, whose watchful care is dangerous and is inseparable from the reader's and James's own. She knows that she would not (or at least "shouldn't") *lunge* at the girl in her efforts to keep track of her and watch for symptoms of her illness, but she has "almost the sense of tracking her young friend as if at a given moment to pounce" and fears that her aid is "secretive," that her "observation" is "scientific." She fears that she is "hovering like a spy, applying tests, laying traps, concealing signs," and while she continues to do this nevertheless, satisfied because "to watch" is "a way of clinging to the girl" and gives access to her "beauty," she does so with the tact of reticence and with restraint. The same probing analysis which risks exposing or chopping up Kate, and spying on or trapping Milly, is, in its restraint, a measure of solicitude and care. (I, 65-66; II, 46; I, 117.)

So infused is the language itself with the creative aim it serves and the drama it projects that it becomes at once a rich resource and a virtual fate, endangering and enclosing its subject in the very act of focusing loving attention on it, intimating what lies beyond its vocabularies but failing to free itself from them. The novel distinguishes the heroine's doctor's services from exclusively commercial ones, for instance, but does so in terms which remain distinctly pecuniary: "Sir Luke had appeared indeed to speak of purchase and payment, but in reference to a different sort of cash. Those were amounts not to be named or reckoned, and such moreover as [Milly] wasn't sure of having at her command." Whether because it clings perversely to the terminology of cash when it might try to abandon it, or because it dramatizes by that means art's inescapable dependence on its medium and the "kindly infidelities" which are unavoidable necessities inhering in the nature of language, the prose creates the very possibility of the impending tragedy, prepares the very "fallibility" James was to speak of in the preface as the foundation of artistic mastery, the failure of beguiling intentions which is made part of the very creative process and helps stage the destruction and transformation through wastage—in sum, the tragedy—of Milly Theale. (II, 142.)

The "amounts" not "named" or "reckoned" and the failure to name and reckon them are so central to the tragedy that the "kindly infidelities" of words, the verbal drama suspended in the movement of the prose, virtually defines the plot of the novel, when Densher tries to define in his own case the relations among words and action and inaction, telling a lie and "acting it out," telling the truth and keeping it secret. He decides that truth and candor inhere only in naming the names and declaring the reckoning, in openly "speaking the particular word," and that measured by this standard, any behavior short of it— silences, verbal evasions, and inaction as well as overt action—is "acting" in the sense of histrionic illusion or affectation, and that such "acting" in his case makes him responsible for acting out a lie. Accordingly, the very sentences which suspend, postpone, and prolong their import and action, the "kindly infidelities" of the prose which hovers "round and round" its subject in a verbal drama and holds off from naming and reckoning, are, in their style, part of the very drama they help enact. Indeed, the "particular word" that Densher speaks of is a secret that is crucial for the novel's plot—the fact that Kate still is in love with Densher—and Densher goes on to pledge himself to continued silence out of loyalty to Kate and a consequent loyalty to her "design," a design which at that point in the novel has not been fully divulged to Densher, has not been made explicit to the reader, and *may* not even be fully formulated yet by Kate.

But that emerging "design" is crucial in James's novel, for it is his own plot which, along with the prose, helps to project the tragic action. It helps to create the design and the movement which James was to call, in the preface to *The Ambassadors*, the full "process of vision," the firm "march" of his novel's "action." [5] (II, 76-77.)

[5] *Ibid.*, p. 308.

[II]

THE "SACRAMENT OF EXECUTION"

THE PLOT has one origin in the fact that Kate and Densher, the English writer she loves, have not enough money to marry. Nor can they get help from Kate's wealthy Aunt Maud, a philistine social climber who will share her money only if Kate marries the impecunious aristocrat Lord Mark. For obvious reasons, Kate's widowed sister and ruined father want her to please her rich aunt, and Densher's meager salary provides no satisfactory alternative. Accordingly, Kate, whose family "piety" is genuine and whose assessment of her predicament is astute, resorts with Densher to a familiar strategy of deception, a secret engagement. Kate will pretend to oblige Maud, to favor Mark, and to remain indifferent to Densher while she and her fiancé wait out their secret engagement in hope of winning all of Maud's consent and at least some of her cash. (I, 71.)

Much later Kate stumbles on an unexpected opportunity in the novel's heroine Milly Theale, a young American orphan who is fabulously rich and who seems, and later proves, to be dying. Kate alters her scheme so as to do justice not only to the need for deceiving Maud and acquiring money but to the genuine pity and affection she feels for her friend. She will induce Densher to be friendly with Milly, helping with his attentions to give Milly the strength to live. Milly will be encouraged, through Maud and Susan, to think that Kate is not interested in Densher. Then Kate will induce Densher to pay court to her and marry the dying girl. Though there is a risk that Densher might genuinely fall in love with Milly and that Milly might live, Kate makes the gamble: Milly will die; Densher will inherit her cash; he and Kate can marry.

As enterprising schemes have a way of doing, this one works, even though it is threatened twice by contingencies Kate had not anticipated or had hoped to avoid. One is Densher's demand, to which she consents, that she pay for his cooperation by sleeping with him. The second is Mark's shrewd guess that Kate and Densher are engaged, a fact he reveals to Milly in hope of gaining her hand and her purse for himself: in his unthinking crudeness he precipitates her death. But Milly has come to love Densher, she agrees to see him before going away, she forgives him in a letter and bequeathes him a fortune when she dies. In the last chapters, Kate and Densher confront the fortune which has become for them, as it became for Milly, a tragic destiny.

That portentous destiny is established as an immanent possibility in the earliest elaborations of the plot, the early configurations which ominously, however tentatively, sound the note of bargaining, bankruptcy, and sacrifice. All but vulgar and forceful Aunt Maud (she is "Britannia of the market-place," secure as a "lioness" in the "cage" that is her "counting-house") are shown to be rootless and insecure in the social environment James labels "middle-class." Kate's widowed sister, pinching pennies with her four "greasy children" in grubby quarters, has shown that marriage for love can be like being squeezed through a funnel. Though Kate's penniless and shifty father seems "the fortunate settled normal person," he deals out lies like cards from a "greasy old pack"; Kate can virtually taste the sordidness, the " 'something wicked' " which his late wife made a successful secret of, his "failure of fortune and of honor." (I, 30, 174, 65, 7-8, 67, 4.)

His faked pretense of willingness to sacrifice himself for his daughter's advancement introduces one of the novel's earliest motifs of sacrifice, as does indeed his name Croy, which Kate feels to be a "bleeding wound." In the first chapter Kate is genuinely willing to sacrifice herself to help her father, and even when he spurns the offered gift the prospect of sacrifice still threatens. Haunted and menaced by her relatives, in their eyes a commodity or "tangible value" that is "chalk-marked for the auction," Kate likens herself "to a trembling kid" being saved to feed her aunt, and she reflects "that the more you gave yourself the less of you was left. There were always people to snatch at you, and it would never occur to *them* that they were eating you up. They did that without tasting." In one argumentative conversation about whom she should marry, Kate can be reduced to denying "everything and every one," even, as a conversational gambit, to "paying with the sacrifice of Mr. Densher." (I, 6, 32, 9, 6, 30, 33, 44.)

If the language of feasting and auctions suggests the possibilities that threaten in Kate's world, so does the vocabulary of the arts. Maud's furnishings are vulgar "signs and symbols" which "syllabled [Densher's] hostess' story." Lionel Croy's letter to Kate announcing that he is too sick to leave his room and asking help is called "the sketch of a design" lacking even "the moderate finish required for deception." Densher's journalistic mission to America (when he first meets Milly Theale) is called a "parenthesis" in an otherwise ordinary "sentence" on "a great grey page of print." Indeed, Kate lives not only in Chelsea and Kensington but in the space defined by a virtually Faulknerian sentence which is nevertheless the medium of James's own syntax: Kate's family "history . . . had the effect of some fine florid voluminous phrase, say even a musical, that dropped first into words and notes without sense and then, hanging unfinished, into no words nor any notes at all." With her admirable determination, she plans to survive even the test of Jamesian prose: "She hadn't given up yet, and the broken sentence, if she was the last word, *would* end with a sort of meaning." (I, 76, 6; II, 11; I, 4, 6.)

Kate will have the novel's last word, but she can scarcely anticipate that with certainty on page six. The tempest that rumbles in Aunt Maud's world threatens also within the contrivances of a magician-artist. No wonder that Kate hopes, by her strategy of deception, to avoid for herself, her family, and Densher the sacrifice that threatens: " 'I shall sacrifice nobody and nothing, and that's just my situation, that I want and that I shall try for everything.' " No wonder that the rootless engaged couple, each raised as a child on the Continent by transient impecunious families, should have acquired what Kate recognizes as most highly developed in Densher: the "religion of foreign things." One wonders only at the "process of vision," the "march of the action," when the foreigner from America with her ample checkbook, her hunger for cultivation and affection, and her strange beauty descends into the broken sentences of James's novel and onto Aunt Maud's London; there, in search of a doctor, she takes her place in Kate's design. (I, 73, 92.)

It is at this point that the novel extends the range and renders more precise the evocations of its medium, speaking more frequently now of imagined realms, of "imagination" and "fancy" and "legend" associated with Milly. It begins to focus on the realm in which her "New York history" and her "New York legend" coalesce, namely her manner. It is the medium of forms which both reveals and shapes her character, because the manner is created in response to inner pressures of will, moral intent, and aspiration and outer pressures of decorum, social accommodation, and moral strictures. There are four components in Milly's manner, merely acquired at first but then possessed more consciously and used articulately in the course of the novel's development. (I, 104-106.)

One of these (and one of civilization's most problematic creations) is her money, a symbol always of the economic power it represents, in this case power which Milly simply inherited as the " 'survivor of a general wreck,' " pecuniary power which is the speaking record of its sources, "the record" namely "of used-up relatives, parents, clever eager fair slim brothers . . . all engaged . . . in a high extravagance of speculation and dissipation that had left this exquisite being her black dress, her white face and her vivid hair as the mere last broken link. . . ." As all can see who notice her clothes and other visible signs of her affluence, Milly is an " 'angel with a thumping bank-account,' " and as her companion Susan knows, "the girl couldn't get away from her wealth," she "couldn't have lost it if she had tried." On one occasion the costly pearls she could afford to purchase are acknowledged to lend something to her "style." (I, 241, 174; II, 51; I, 121; II, 217.)

To be so clearly the " 'capital case' " is, as her doctor recognizes, to be the American, and Milly is imaged as an explorer and adventurer, at once naïve and empirical. Wanting in culture, odd looking and new, she is the "potential heiress of all the ages" that it took Europe centuries to produce—the American, that is, of history and legend whom Densher calls simply "the American girl" and whom the novel renders in terms of "spontaneity" and simplicity, with her way of doing always "the natural thing." (I, 242, 109; II, 215; I, 295-296.)

Yet this simplicity of temperament and manner is a formed one and comes to be the cultivated and artful one of a civilized showpiece. When on display at Lord Mark's party or in the National Gallery, she displays the "bland stare" of conventional society that she has learned to adopt, and a "glassy lustre of attention" as a social conversationalist. As she looks over the ornamental objects in her doctor's office while waiting for him, she wonders what gift she will give him in gratitude, and imagines that she should be "one of the circle of eminent contemporaries, photographed, engraved, signatured, and in particular framed and glazed, who made up the rest of the decoration." The girl who may one day hang in this office behind glass is later referred to as "embodied poetry." She is imaged as a cloistered princess of Byzantium, an image as stylized, as rigidly two-dimensional as the courtly figures against a gilt background in the Ravenna mosaics that the novel mentions. (I, 219, 301, 237; II, 217; I, 256.)

To have one's place like the Empress Theodora in the Ravenna mosaics, however, is to have a place in a church, and Milly's manner is that of a cloistered princess and an object of worship in a world of ceremonious decorum, in a novel where offices and houses are called temples and Kate's hoped-for marriage with Densher is called "a temple" without a street running up to it. Milly at one time is imaged as a communicant, at another as "a priestess." When she is first introduced, sitting on a ledge overlooking a valley in the Alps, her calm self-possession is likened to Christ's in the face of Satan's demand that he prove his divinity by leaping from the steeple or Satan's tempting offer of the kingdoms of the earth; her companion, Susan, is relieved to find that Milly was not driven by some "horrible hidden obsession" to commit "suicide" in a "flying leap" and that if she was overlooking the "kingdoms of the earth" it was because she felt no intention of "renouncing them" but, already in a state of "unlimited possession," was prepared to accept the "human predicament" and take "full in the face the whole assault of life." Kate declares very early that " 'we all adore you' " and recognizes Milly as a dove, calling her a dove "not with familiarity or as a liberty taken, but almost ceremonially as in the manner of an *accolade*." (I, 241; II, 146; I, 59; II, 135; I, 123-125, 228, 283.)

While these are the patterns of Milly's manner, bestowed by her past and by Kate's naming of them, Milly's way of acting with them is equally part of the manner. The phrase for this is given in connection with the empirical procedure and comforting bedside manner of her doctor, Sir Luke. Milly notices that he gives her no facts about her illness, and that he is perpetrating a "beautiful beneficent dishonesty" in pretending to be her friend; but she senses also that, when he assures her she will not suffer " 'a bit,' " he is probably trying to "let the patient down easily" in his mission to the doomed, that he is " 'acting,' as they said at home, as if she did matter" medically, acting as if she were seriously ill. (I, 252, 240, 246, 253.)

And *acting as if,* or playing a role, characterizes precisely Milly's conduct. With the motifs of wealth so clearly, if tastefully, a part of her, she begins to act the part. She had to begin with "no manner at all" about her money; unlike Maud who sits "in the midst of her money" and had a clever "high manner about it," Milly sits on the frontier of her fortune and one can "get at her nature" without having to cross "any piece of her property." But the anticipation that Milly might eventually acquire a "motive" in using her money and that "then she might very well have, like Aunt Maud, a manner" is fulfilled when Milly begins to think consciously of her money, begins to measure its impact on others, and plans finally to use it to buy her rented palace in Venice as a last "counter-move to fate." Also, she begins to look and act the part of the spontaneous American, sounding at will "her own native wood-note" in making conversation with Densher: "She still had reserves of spontaneity . . . so that all this cash in hand could now find employment. She became as spontaneous as possible and as American as it might conveniently appeal to Mr. Densher . . . to find her." When she sees the conventional "bland" stare of polite society, she adopts it. (I, 196-197; II, 142; I, 295-296.)

When, finally, Kate calls her a dove, Milly adopts it as "the revealed truth. . . . *That* was the matter with her. She was a dove. Oh, *wasn't* she?" And she "studied . . . the dovelike," beginning to act out the role named for her by Kate. She'll be kind, she'll protect her friends' interests and feelings, even by telling lies. Chiefly she does this by the lie that her health is better than she feels it is, though she creates this illusion "with no consciousness of fraud, only as with a sudden flare of the famous 'will-power' . . . which was what her medical adviser had mainly thrown her back on." If she will lie to help others, she will also muster courage and tact so as to help her doctor treat her: "him too she would help to help her, if that could possibly be," virtually becoming a "physician" to help him as "patient." Moreover she will accept the attentions and deferences with which they honor her. If her doctor and companion offer her "devotion" on a platter, she will "consume it as the dressed and served dish. . . ." For "devotion" her "appetite would be of the best. Gross, greedy, ravenous—these were no doubt the proper names for her." (I, 283-284, 258; II, 124-125; I, 261.)

The adoption and gradual perfection of a manner by Milly accompanies her initiation into the complexities of the society she confronts and her growing understanding of it. Indeed, the development of her manner is shown to be inseparable from her initiation, her deepening understanding, and her consequent gain in self-possession. Not only does Milly learn from her immersion in Maud's world: she illuminates and begins to mold *it*, revealing a process of ferment which is altering a stratified society, a process which her presence and manner quicken and eventually govern. It is profoundly significant that in presenting Milly's confrontation of unfamiliar social realities James reveals a British society in which some of the marked contours seem arbitrary and are subject to challenge and alteration while being nonetheless oppressively real. The society, moreover, is one in which the "manner" devised merely to *adjust* to *given* social differences displays the latent capacity for a more creative social function, that of salvaging or reconstituting the very basis of a community which is threatened by intermissions and cleavages within it.

Unfamiliar in America with the differences in social "position" which prevail in England and the "awfully good manner" which functions to "bridge" the distance between them, Milly arrives in Europe stripped by death even of her immediate family and, with an isolation enforced by her huge fortune, she is " 'independent,' " as Kate declares enviously, of the " 'tiers and tiers' " of groups in an "hierarchical, an aristocratic order." One thing her native society lacks is the vast "interval" between classes, which is associated metaphorically by James with blocks of "skipped" pages in a book or "social atlas." Another thing it lacks is a "manner"—accompanied by a "sinking" or repressing of the "consciousness" (but not the ignoring) of social intervals by both the privileged and unprivileged classes but particularly by the privileged—a manner which bridges the intervals, acknowledging the intervals by the fact of bridging them but repressing the awareness of the differences so as to be able to bridge the intervals at all. In the world of Matcham and Lancaster Gate, social distinctions are still to *some* extent founded on settled arrangements but are also founded on the manipulations, powerful and enterprising, of middle-class Aunt Maud. Not only is she devoting her money, talents, and practiced manner to gaining higher status in the traditional "order" for Kate, and an attractive well-financed wife for the aristocratic Lord Mark; she has brought about by willed effort, virtually created, an otherwise nonexistent social distinction between Kate and her widowed sister Marian—a distinction which to Milly seems forced. (I, 191-192, 281.)

Though the position of the Croys was once "settled" in the successful middle class, static *status* is no longer the apt term for Lionel Croy's precarious and shifting position as he moves downward through bankruptcy toward oblivion, and though Marian Croy may have married beneath her station while Kate is being groomed for higher things, James's treatment of the "social atlas" suggests that the "order" is no longer fixed under the impact of Maud's counting-house, that Kate and her sister have not simply fallen or been sorted into different fixed social positions but that a position for Marian has been "established" by Maud's maneuvering, exaggerating whatever interval might otherwise extend between the two sisters, a feat which will be completed if Kate marries the impecunious Lord Mark. The "vast interval" which places Marian on virtually a different "map," in "quite another geography," is defined by skipping, willfully and habitually, "page after page" of the actual social fabric; to locate and acknowledge Marian in the book at all (with a benevolent " 'Here!' " to mark the discovery) is virtually to salvage a community of pages from which she was otherwise willfully excluded. Status and class divisions seem falsely sharp, yet appear more malleable than fixed, in Maud's England as the governing fact of her money produces ferment and the

prospect of change. Milly confronts not the old "hierarchical
. . . order" of settled divisions but its remnants, in a middle-
class world which subjects everything to change in its struggle
for power. and secure position, and where everyone talks (as
Milly notices) of money and threatens to put people and opportunities (as Kate warns Milly) to "use." (I, 191, 281.)

James's rendering of Milly's explorative reaction to the
world of the Croys and Aunt Maud reveals a characteristic American view in speaking of social divisions as gaps or voids rather
than as tangible barriers, as spaces that can be spanned by a
manner which responds to the need for it instead of as walled en-
closures. The suggestion is not that the intervals are unreal or
inconsequential but that they are not impassable. Furthermore,
to bridge them (rather than either to obliterate or fortify them)
is to define a community which will encompass several geogra-
phies without relegating one to another atlas and which will
compensate for the "skipped leaves" or pages in the total community—the network of social distinctions and the continuities
between them—which the larger contours of class division and
Maud's forced exaggerations obscure.

The metaphor of a book—conceived both as an integral
whole and as a series of discrete pages—governs James's analysis of Milly's initiation into English society and enables him to
define the complex and unresolved relation between that social
world and both his heroine's action and his novel's action in it.
The glaring, cruel, operative distinctions are there for Milly to
discover and confront, the manner which bridges gaps by suppressing consciousness of them is there to emulate. The full
sequence of the "atlas" from page to page is there to suggest the
density of the existing community behind its more obvious cleavages, but to suggest also the long chain of intervals between pages
which must be bridged by a "manner" if the society or book
(with its broken sentences and parentheses) is to hold together
at elemental levels and attain beyond that the full coherence it
seeks. Milly's American manner, like James's, is adopted in the
process of coming to understand society and its sharp divisions
and, while moderating her consciousness of them, to bridge the
intervals which separate her from it or from the groups and individuals in it whom she encounters. In the process, her manner

has the effect of enabling Milly to play a role in her world and to share in altering and shaping it. Vulnerable in her illness but powerful with her money, she begins with her manner to take precedence over Aunt Maud and to become the governing center for the schemes and aspirations of the world which begins to form around her under the impact of her power and presence.

Both her impact on that world and her gain in understanding and self-possession are vivid in the scene when Lord Mark unexpectedly proposes marriage to her and Milly discerns an "ugly motive" dimly and briefly showing in his request. But she suppresses the recognition that the combination of her money and "the ravage of her disease" together make her attractive to him, decides that his "motive shouldn't matter" because he was "kindly, . . . humanly, concerned for her" anyway, and with perfect ease and candor tells him openly that she is " 'very badly ill,' " doing so out of kindness to soften the blow of her refusal. Her dove-like concern for his feelings is combined not only with a repressed understanding of his motives but with firm self-possession and with an exercise of her influence; she now can bring herself to talk openly of her illness and impending death and can *use* her influence, enforcing Aunt Maud's desire by suggesting that Mark seek to marry Kate. (II, 149-150, 155, 165.)

Eventually Milly's self-possession, power, and manner survive an even firmer test at a time when Milly so dominates the lives of the others that Densher feels it is Milly who accomplishes everything, governing, even purging, his and Kate's relation to her (if indeed "practically purged it was"): it was Milly herself, "Milly's hospitality, and Milly's manner"—it was "Milly's character, and, perhaps still more than anything else, Milly's imagination" that worked in his and Kate's interest; and "not to profit by it, so far as profit could be reckoned, would have been to go directly against" it and against the "spirit of generosity" which Milly instills in him. In his last conversation with Milly before the exposure of his engagement, Densher faces Milly's second request that she visit his rooms for tea, planning to refuse a second time because he thinks of his rooms as sacred to Kate alone. His own manner falters in awkwardness as he inadvertently alludes to Milly's illness; Milly, by contrast, registers first "for twenty seconds an exquisite pale glare" and then declares that she is " 'splendid' " and " 'capable of life,' " declaring that she " *'can'* " and " 'will' " live in a tone that converts the solemn "weight" of her determination into "mere light and sound." Moments later, when Milly asks again to visit Densher's rooms for tea, the "sense of her own reality" which overwhelms Densher as he consents is not adequately revealed in "his face or his manner," and Milly takes his reaction for bored politeness instead and withdraws her request, speaking not with the "hand-to-mouth" improvisations which characterize Densher's attempt to help *her* but "gently" and with the smile that characterizes the kindness, ease, and assurance of her American and dove-like manner. As Milly questions him finally about his motives for staying on in Italy, his "anxiety" and "vagueness" are countered by her determination to help and by the grace with which she draws back from further questions out of kindness, and phrases an answer for him: " 'You stay because you've got to.' " In her mercy she lets him depart with the simple and genial but forceful declaration that will later become a formidable burden and tax his conscience: she says lightly that he "must judge" whether, as he has suggested, it is " 'enough, whatever may be one's other complications, to stay after all' " for her. (II, 239, 245-250.)

In Milly's *acting as if* and in the patterns of her action are the manner which yields the appearance, at least, if not the very image of Milly herself. Yet it is the very fact of having a manner and using it, however, that the novel develops into ambivalent and disconcerting expectations for the reader. They and the actions which occasion them establish the main rhythm of the novel, one movement of which is revealed fully when Milly, at a party in her honor, confronts a protrait by the Mannerist painter Bronzino which everyone says looks just like her.[6] Moved in her excitement to tears, Milly senses, in a feeling which the novel suggests has nothing to do with the portrait's subject, that the woman is "dead, dead, dead," and says " 'I

[6] Miriam Allott identified the portrait as that of Lucrezia Panciatichi in "The Bronzino Portrait in *The Wings of the Dove*," *Modern Language Notes*, LXVIII (January 1953), 23-25.

shall never be better than this.' " She is reminded, of course, of her own death that she fears is imminent, but the reader is also reminded of a sense in which any work of art, no matter how brilliant, is dead, all art being lifeless in a way which the gestures, postures, and high finish of Mannerist painting display in a particular and extreme version: no blood flows through a painting or novel and no breath breathes there; one can smear greasy oil upon a yielding canvas, but no womb will conceive new life. The association of the realm of art with death is reinforced instantly, for it is immediately afterward that Milly, her illness upon her, sinks fainting into a chair. In this incident, however, Milly willingly takes passive refuge in her sickness—"in a manner plunge[s] into it"—overcome by envious resentment toward Kate who seems so familiarly the friend of Densher. (I, 221, 225.)

This action gives one of the novel's main movements: the anguished withdrawal from life into death, a movement that is confirmed and deepened by one of the evocations of the novel's title, Psalm 55. There, in fear and trembling at "the oppression of the wicked," a voice cries out: "O that I had wings like a dove! / Then would I fly away and be at rest. / Lo, then would I wander far off, / I would lodge in the wilderness. / I would haste me to a shelter / From the stormy wind and tempest." The voice then asks the psalmist's God to "Destroy, O Lord, and divide their tongue . . . For it was not an enemy that reproached me— / Then I could have borne it— / Neither was it he that hated me that did magnify himself against me— / Then I would have hid myself from him— / But it was thou, a man mine equal, / My companion, and my familiar friend. / We took sweet counsel together, / We walked in the house of God with the throng. / Let death come suddenly upon them, let them go down alive into the pit: / For wickedness is in their dwelling, in the midst of them."

Counter to this movement is the other: not to withdraw but to stay, to live on "for a long time" as she declares "with her eyes again on her painted sister's" in Bronzino's portrait, to live by an act of will and, as the doctor urges, to " 'accept any form in which happiness may come,' " to turn her "anxiety" and utter uncertainty into a "great adventure, a big dim experiment" and with whatever resources she can muster to act out her role as "the American girl." This is the dove hailed in Psalm 68 as Jehovah leads his favored nation into the promised land: " 'Kings of armies flee, they flee, / And she that tarrieth at home divideth the spoil'— / 'Will ye lie among the sheepfolds?'— / 'The wings of a dove covered with silver and her pinions with yellow gold'—." (1, 227-228, 242, 250, 248.)

To the extent that a resolution of this tension is prefigured in the first half of the novel, it is in the gesture Milly makes to Kate after feeling so resentful of her. Recognizing that Kate has a right to friends, Milly makes up for her silent injustice by a gesture of devotion to the friend whom, in her momentary withdrawal, she had left behind; in a gesture of devotion, she asks Kate to accompany her to her London doctor's office, pledging her to join in the " 'wicked and false' " deed of keeping the visit secret, and adopting her clearly as a companion and friend. (1, 226.)

It is not in London, however, where the novel approaches its final crisis, but in Venice, the declining city of luxury and intrigue which James had called (in 1882 in an early piece on Venice) a "great bazaar," a "curiosity shop" itself like the many "halls of humbug" which it harbored. In 1907 in *The American Scene,* Venice was to remind James of New York City and Venice's annual ceremony of marriage to the sea was to seem the analogue of New York City's welcome to the immigrants who sought a new life there. It is in Venice that James's New York heroine confronts the ultimate crisis of her adventure and presents to the friends who follow her there the ultimate challenge of their lives. The drama hinges finally on three crucial scenes. Of these, the third is never described, that in which Kate spends the night with Densher in his rented rooms. The first, however, is one of the most brilliantly rendered in the novel; it is the occasion when Densher, frustrated and impatient, makes his request of Kate. He had broached the subject before in London—protesting against the need to improvise furtive meetings with Kate and to see her always in public places or at Aunt Maud's Lancaster Gate or Milly's apartments, and proposing to Kate that instead she " 'come to *me.*' " Then, out of pity he drew back from his request. Now he makes it a demand as part of a desperate bargain.[7] (II, 5, 29.)

Milly is too sick to go on an outing, but Maud and Susan, Kate and Densher, make a trip to the great St. Mark's Square. Gradually the architecture of the scene comes into view. Three sides of the Square are surrounded by shops, and it is shopping that Susan and Maud plan to accomplish and spend the chapter doing. The fourth side is dominated by the huge cathedral, the "biggest booth" in the "bazaar" of Venice (James had written in 1882), filled with Renaissance paintings and Byzantine mosaics and with the bread and wine sacred to the claims of Christian communions. Densher and Kate do not plan to shop; they plan to have a "look-in," as Densher says, at the cathedral. Early in the chapter they do, though the novel scarcely mentions it. Then they come out and walk about the Square, which, since the Venetians are having breakfast is deserted except for the "pigeons picking up the crumbs of perpetual feasts." As Kate and Densher talk, Densher insists on his impatience and threatens to leave Venice. At the chapter's end, with Kate turned so that she twirls her parasol in the direction of the cathedral, Densher makes his proposition. She dodges his question, turns toward the shops, and is rescued when Maud and Susan, their commercial errand over, emerge from the stores and interrupt the private conversation. Though he has not yet received an answer, Densher takes satisfaction in the masculine ascendancy he has now asserted and feels certain that Kate will oblige him.[8] (II, 190.)

In the next chapter comes the dramatic scene for which the entire novel has been preparing. Possibilities which have been latent in the action since the beginning now materialize and are revealed in their full depth and power, their furthest implications embodied in the very simples of a party scene which present by intimating the sacrificial drama which the novel's action has become.

Densher drops around at Milly's palace as usual and is asked to stay to dinner and then for a party afterward in honor of Sir Luke who has just arrived in Venice. Milly is too sick to

---

[7] *Portraits of Places* (Boston, 1884), p. 9; *The American Scene*, pp. 184, 206.
[8] *Portraits of Places*, p. 9.

come down for dinner, but she does come down for the party. There are musicians hired for the occasion, and Milly gives them instructions and spends the rest of the time mingling with her guests. Densher and Kate both serve as delegated centers of consciousness, joined for the occasion to make a "represented community of vision," as James called it in the preface, in a chapter which bears the "double pressure" of "picture" and dramatic "scene." During most of the scene, Densher and Kate stand in the foreground watching Milly and talking to each other.[9]

The foreground in which they stand is one of immense scope as is suggested by remarks Susan makes when asking Densher to stay for the party—remarks about one of James's favorite painters, Paolo Cagliari, the expatriate who was known in the Venice where he flourished by the state where he was born, Veronese. To John Addington Symonds, Veronese was "precisely the painter suited to a nation of merchants," who depicted religious martyrs as "composed, serious, courtly, well-fed personages who like people of the world accidently overtaken by some tragic misfortune, do not stoop to distortion or express more than a grave surprise, a decorous sense of pain." For Berenson, writing in the fourth quarter of the last century, Veronese displayed a "happy combination of ceremony and splendour with almost childlike naturalness of feeling," a "frank and joyous worldliness, the qualities . . . we find in his huge pictures of feasts. . . ." Two of Veronese's huge feasts became for James, in one of the boldest appropriations of his expressionism, the instrumental forms for the making of his own composition.[10]

The two are introduced by Susan's reply to Densher's remark about the festive decorations of Milly's palace. She says: " 'bringing out all the glory of the place—makes [Milly] really happy. It's a Veronese picture, as near as can be, with me as the inevitable dwarf, the small blackamoor, put into a corner of the foreground for effect.' " She should have a " 'hawk or

<hr />

[9] The Art of the Novel, p. 300.

[10] Symonds, The Renaissance in Italy: the Fine Arts (American Edition, New York, 1888), p. 373; Bernard Berenson, Venetian Painters of the Renaissance (New York, 1895), p. 64.

hound' " or borrow a " 'big red cockatoo' " to " 'perch on [her] thumb for the evening.' " Though Densher feels out of place in so grand a "composition," Susan insists: " 'Besides you're in the picture. . . . You'll be the grand young man who surpasses the others and holds up his head and the wine-cup.' " (II, 206-207.)

One of the paintings is evoked by Susan's echo of Veronese's defense when summoned before the Inquisition (Ruskin had printed a transcript of the proceedings in his guide to the Academy at Venice); it was and is known as *The Supper in the House of Levi*. As recounted in the Bible (Luke v, 27-35), Christ was entertained on that occasion by his wealthy tax-collecting disciple Matthew, along with a company of publicans and sinners. When asked why he associated with such persons, Jesus replied: "They that are whole need not a physician; but they that are sick"; Jesus declared that he came "not to call the righteous, but sinners to repentance," and warned against the day "when the bridegroom shall be taken away."

In Veronese's treatment of the tale, a dwarf stands in the left foreground. (The dwarf aroused the Inquisition's suspicion, but it was placed there, Veronese informed the Inquisitors, "For ornament, as is usually done.") A blackamoor reaches for the bird perched on the dwarf's wrist. Above them on the landing of a staircase in a Venetian palace, in a strikingly mannered pose, stands a figure in green who seems about to descend the stairs and depart; he affords an analogy to Densher. At dinner, far in the background but centered, is the doomed and sacred figure of Christ; he, and his wealthy host, afford analogies to Milly.[11]

The second painting is *The Marriage Feast at Cana*. On that occasion, singled out as Christ's first miracle by the Gospel of John (II, 1-11) and regarded as one of the precedents for the Christian sacrament, Jesus and his mother attended a wedding banquet where the host ran out of wine. Asked to help, Christ first refused, then instructed servants privately to fill the jugs with water and serve that; it proved to be a very fine wine indeed. After tasting it, the banquet's steward made a speech,

---

[11] John Ruskin, *Guide to the Principal Pictures in the Academy at Venice* (rev. ed., London, 1891), p. 55.

explaining that most hosts serve their best wine first, then offer cheaper kinds when guests can less easily taste the difference; this host, by contrast, had saved the best wine till the last.

In Veronese's picture (the Louvre version which James knew), a dark-skinned dwarf, with his bird, stands inconspicuously in the left foreground of a sumptuous banquet scene. On the right, holding up a wine cup, stands the steward; he is the figure Susan associates with Densher. Dominating the composition in the center foreground is a small group of musicians, including a portrait of Titian and a self-portrait of Veronese. They draw the eye in the direction of the figures directly behind, but, in their business as performing artists, they distract attention from the others; behind them at dinner, analogous in their position to Milly, are Mary and Christ.

These are the instrumental forms introduced early in the chapter by Susan's remarks. Later Densher speaks of "the Veronese painting . . . as not quite constituted," but by the end of the chapter the import of Veronese's subjects and the compositional patterns of his canvases have been constituted as part of James's medium, and they inform the composition of James's own canvas and the drama they reveal. (II, 213.)

The chapter's central action is enclosed in a frame outside itself (by the proposition which precedes and the assignation which follows) and by one within it. It opens with Susan's urgent request that Densher stay for the party and stay in Venice; it ends with Densher and Kate making urgent requests to each other and consenting. Kate urges Densher to remain in Venice, to pay court to Milly and marry her. Densher agrees to stay. But in return, Densher presses his demand that Kate sleep with him in his rooms, and Kate, reluctantly but without flinching, agrees to do it.

But within this frame of requests and answers, demands and commitments, a proposition and an assignation, lies a vision of Milly which it is the burden of the chapter, and indeed of the entire novel, to make vividly present, a vision which she makes real by enacting it and which sinks so deeply into Densher's consciousness that he can never get away from it, even though at the time he does not fully appreciate it.

It is rendered entirely through Kate's and Densher's perceptions, and while they spend much of the time watching Milly, talking and thinking about her, Milly herself is scarcely even seen. She is far off in the background most of the time, almost obscured in any literal sense by Kate and Densher, the writer, in the foreground. Only once does Milly pass close to the pair and then only to say three words which are not given: it is a "single bright look and the three gay words (all ostensibly of the last lightness) with which her confessed consciousness brushed by him." Densher admires in her the infectious geniality of a civilized hostess and, feeling that she has never before been so much "the American girl," he sees her "as diffusing, in wide warm waves, the spell of a general, a kind of beatific mildness." In the deep waters of that spell, he feels that all of them are swimming around "like fishes in a crystal pool." She is like a " 'new book,' an uncut volume of the highest, the rarest quality," and Densher feels "again and again" the "thrill of turning the page." Later in the chapter, Milly communicates again specifically with Kate and Densher; from across the room she sends a silent message, "all the candour of her smile, the lustre of her pearls, the value of her life, the essence of her wealth." (II, 214, 215, 213, 222, 229.)

The closest view of Milly herself, actually, is a look at her costly pearls. Kate points them out to Densher and they both stare at them; the "long, priceless chain, wound twice around the neck, hung, heavy and pure, down the front of the wearer's breast." Looking at these pearls of great price, Kate remarks: " 'She's a dove . . . and one somehow doesn't think of doves as bejewelled. Yet they suit her to the ground.' " Densher agrees, and, as the novel says, a dove "was the figure for her, though it most applied to her spirit." (II, 217-218.)

What lies revealed in the impress of Kate and Densher's experience is that Milly, though sick, has put on the superlative performance of her career so far, as the sumptuous hostess, the spontaneous American, the dove. It is revealed, too, that she has become one with the role she began earlier to play, for the illusion is so amply complete, so intensely and tangibly real, that one of Densher's phrases for her is perfectly apt: he thinks of her as "embodied poetry." And in becoming one with what she seems, she wears a dress whose color Densher notices, for the first time appearing, like Christ at the moment of his transfiguration, in white. The embodied poem, the wealthy dying dove, has become the perfect host. She has spent more lavishly of her money for the party—Densher noticed more candles burning when he entered her " 'temple to taste' "— and she has been spending more lavishly of her energy, her life. Milly has had to miss dinner to save strength for the party, and Densher could even *taste* the question of her health when he entered the palace; toward the end of the chapter, Kate insists that Milly's health is worse. The entire chapter, in its form or composition, focuses attention on Milly while not showing her directly to reveal and shield the torment of her triumph as host, the agony within a radiantly glad and splendid surface. Milly has been inspired by the occasion (chiefly, Densher notices, when Sir Luke arrives), and it is under the nourishing stimulus of this ceremonious affair that she diffuses her "beatific mildness." And while she is finding sustenance in the occasion, Kate and Densher feast their eyes on her. Although Densher at best only half grasps, and Kate now scarcely appreciates at all, what is before their eyes, Milly has become the sacrament, the sacred thing, prefigured in the temples, histories, and legends which the novel evokes but embodied now in its stricken heroine, the treasure, dove, and muse of James's imagination. (II, 217, 146, 203.)

Milly's sheer presence in this chapter has two important effects on Kate and Densher, even though she speaks to them only once and looks at them only twice. First, her sheer presence makes Densher aware of Kate's limitations; judgment is passed against Kate through Densher's consciousness. By comparison with Milly's strange beauty, he reflects, Kate would be more appropriately dressed in black. Then he feels that Kate, when looking at Milly's pearls, is thinking not of their purity and genuineness and what they reflect in Milly, but of the cash value which they also represent while lending something to Milly's "style." And to this measurable extent, Kate and Densher are momentarily separated and their "community of vision" is threatened. Judgment is passed against Kate without Milly's saying a word or even knowing that it happens. She does not condemn Kate or try to separate the two, but her sheer presence brings it about. Momentarily the close intimacy of Kate and Densher is destroyed, and divided is their tongue.

The other effect of Milly's sheer presence proves to be disastrous for Milly. Part of her triumph has been to bring people together, to make them, as Densher says, "more finely genial." The effect of this is to bring Kate and Densher closer together too. When Milly sends across the room "all the candour of her smile, the lustre of her pearls, the value of her life, the essence of her wealth," the tragic consequence is that it brings Kate and Densher more intimately together than they have ever been before. They have begun to talk over whether Densher should stay in Venice, and it has dawned on Densher what Kate has been scheming for so long. At Kate's insistence, he invests with words, as he does in deeds, the design that unwittingly he has been enabling Kate to realize. And Kate, as listener and participant, knowing that Densher is now "in possession," finds courage to "pronounce the words she hadn't pronounced"; she breaks "the grace of silence" to join him with the echoing responses which seal their union. " 'Since she's to die I'm to marry her?' " Densher asks; Kate replies " 'To marry her.' " " 'So that when her death has taken place I shall in the natural course have money?' " " 'You'll in the natural course have money. We shall in the natural course be free.' " (II, 213, 225.)

It is at the precise moment when Densher is struggling with Kate's proposal that Milly happens, by chance accident and James's careful management, to smile at them: her smile "brought them together again with faces made fairly grave by the reality she brought into their plan." Within a matter of minutes, under the protective "cover" of the music of Milly's orchestra, Densher has agreed to stay, to pay court to Milly under false pretenses, and to propose marriage to her if she lives long enough and seems to give him the opportunity. With her smile as well as with her cash, with the "essence of her wealth" and her benign manner as well as with her money, Milly has tempted her two friends and helped to bring them together in Kate's design. Moreover, by sustaining and making vivid the beauty of her role, she not only tempts Densher but makes it easier, virtually helping him, to betray her. Milly will not cough blood, seize her heart, or show herself to be wracked with pain. For her friends who are feasting on her she will not (as Kate has known she would not) " 'smell . . . of drugs' " or " 'taste . . . of medicine.' " Kate reminds Densher that " 'She isn't for you as if she's dying.' " It is in the full face of the vision Milly now embodies that the reader is forced to witness this betrayal by her own equals, her companions, her familiar friends. (II, 53, 229.)

But if together they so betray Milly in accordance with Kate's evil plan, Densher compounds the outrage by adding another: his betrayal of Kate. For the first time he applies successfully a strong pressure to Kate, asserts his dominance, and forces her consent to surrender her body to him. Impatient and frustrated, he has begun to fear that Kate, succumbing to Aunt Maud's arguments, may abandon him for Mark, and he feels that if he is to bargain his integrity for Milly's money, he prefers a partner to share the responsibilities and risks: Kate too should spend and pay. The assignation is the payment he demands. And this demand is not only an assault on the sexual scruples which the two so far have respected, it is a challenge to Kate's sincerity in their engagement and to the ardor of her love for him. While she is not shocked in the conventional sense, she seizes on pretexts, trying to evade the question at the end of the scene. But Densher, pleased with his new-found mastery and admiring Kate's ability to rise to the occasion, persuades her. He will stay in attendance at Milly's rented palace if Kate will accede, just once, to his demand. " 'You'll come?' " he asks. And the chapter closes with Kate's answer: " 'I'll come.' " (II, 231.)

This double betrayal is the very action that promises at the same time to be a triple guarantee. For by promising to insure the success of Kate and Densher's terrible deception, it promises to gain them the money and entrance into the "temple" of marriage, and it promises also to sustain the beautiful illusion of loving adoration for Milly which they have helped to create and to which they have already given more substance than they know, the illusion founded to begin with, as Milly knew, on sheer pity, but now become the vision of the life to which Milly clings so desperately. In persuading Densher to stay in Venice, Kate insists, with genuinely affectionate concern for Milly and even more point, that to break up their act now would be a heartless cruelty: it would kill Milly. Susan, too, wants Densher to stay for Milly's sake. When Densher agrees to stay in Venice, he agrees to perpetrate the fraud which is Milly's betrayal, fixing himself squarely in the picture at *The Supper in the House of Levi,* there to hear the call to repentance. Yet the same action, staying in the picture at Venice, fixes him squarely as the admiring young man with the wine cup, still sampling the sacred wine in *The Marriage Feast at Cana.*

[III]

ANALOGOUS FORM AND TRAGEDY

IT IS the echo of that call and the aftertaste of that wine which dominate the last two books of the novel. In being the mere echo and aftertaste, however, they call into question the novel's very form. Why does it not give directly the scene which precipitates the final crisis, the scene where Lord Mark (whose thoughtless brutality is the very cruelty which Kate and Densher strove to avoid) tells Milly of the secret engagement? Why does it not show Milly's final visit with Densher, or the agony of her last days alive? Why does it give, instead, the stricken conscience and tortured feelings of Densher, and why is it through these only, in fragments based on hearsay, memory, and imaginings, that it renders the final crisis of Milly's tragedy? The novel takes this form for the reason that its governing perspective is what the Narrator in *The Sacred Fount* called " 'the torch' " of an " 'analogy.' " Instead of the central passion it gives the analogies or embodied likenesses in which the mysterious passion itself is refracted.

To do so becomes the burden of a passage near the novel's end, where, even when it is wrenched from context, one can imagine an unspoken statement of Milly to Densher, as she leaves him to face alone her doom:

"She had throughout never a word for what went on at home. She came out of that and she returned to it, but her nearest reference was the look with which, each time, she bade him good-bye. . . . 'It's what I *have* to see and to know—so don't touch it. That but wakes up the old evil, which I keep still, in my way, by sitting by it. I go now—leave me alone!—to sit by it again. The way to pity me—if that's what you want—is to believe in me. If we could really *do* anything it would be another matter.' "

There is the form of Milly's passion, rendered by a passage which describes not Milly, but Kate, the look Kate gives Densher to say that she must leave him to sit alone by her penniless, sick, and ruined father. And her suffering, so similar to Milly's yet so different, is so precisely analogous to Milly's that the same passage can give the form for both. Yet that form is resilient enough to sustain the immense difference between the two friends, for Kate's suffering is imaged not as the dove's but as the "bleeding wound" she carries in her name, and Croy, in a dialect of the penny-pinching Scots, means the legal penalty paid, whether in goods or cash, for murder. (II, 394-395.)

The refractions of analogy, in phrase after phrase, play about the textures of the prose, which serves to distend, in the taut lucidity of its simplifications and abstractions, the paradoxes which yield its tragic vision. When, for instance, Milly sits in the park in meditation after seeing her doctor, she is surrounded by impoverished people in whom she recognizes the likeness of her own predicament; *she* is "a poor girl—with her rent to pay" and shares with them "their great common anxiety," and the phrase on which the poor have been taught to base their desperate hopes—"they could live if they would"—echoes in diction and syntax the phrase which sounds the imminence of a common doom: "they would live if they could." Terror and compassion become inseparable when the phrase which renders Milly's substance and integrity, her generosity and aspirations—"*That* was the matter with her—she was a dove. Oh, *wasn't* she?"—renders also the other things which matter for the reader as they do for Maud and Kate and Densher, for anxious Susan and Sir Luke: "the matter with Milly" is her money or her mortal illness, the prospect of her dying. (I, 250, 253-254, 117, 209, 253.)

The same task of refracting Milly's passion through analogous enactments becomes the burden of the novel's action. Milly's sacrifice and Kate's sexual surrender to Densher in his rooms are shown, without being identified, to be each the likeness of the other. A garbled sentence in James's preface testifies to the power of the analogy which joins Kate's sacrifice to Milly's and suggests the importance of the analogy to the novel's structure: "heaven forbid we should 'know' anything more of our ravaged sister [Milly] than what Densher darkly pieces together, or than what Kate Croy pays, heroically, it must be owned, at the hour of her visit alone to Densher's lodging. . . ." [12] A profound analogy links Milly's "mercy"—which by the end of the novel has shamed Kate and Densher and split them asunder—to Mark's cruel bluntness when he discloses the fact (which he has guessed) of Kate's and Densher's secret engagement, exposing Milly's naïveté to shame yet *saving* her from being duped and used unwittingly by the other two. These actions are prefigured earlier in Sir Luke's "merciful" concern for Milly which, during her meditation in the park, she finds nonetheless "chilling," his "compassion" which is "divesting, denuding, exposing." And these actions are echoed in the analogous incidents which occur in the closing chapters, when Densher's effort to repay Kate for her act of devotion in Venice and to salvage their love is combined with a cruel test of her affection and moral fiber—which pains her as if she were a sick patient being examined by an "exploring medical hand" probing to locate an illness or injury. Then indeed Kate and Densher's attempt to redeem their efforts echoes at every turn the analogous attempt by Milly. (II, 242; I, 252-253; II, 398.)

One of the formal triumphs of the novel is that, despite the disproportion between the two halves for which James apologized in the preface,[13] the early action in its main dimensions prefigures the later action by establishing the basis for exploratory analogous forms which join the two parts and reveal the actions of Lionel Croy, Kate and Densher, and Maud to be part of the very matrix of Milly's effort to redeem the world in which they live. Lionel Croy, surviving his secret "failure of fortune and of honor" with his pretense of self-sacrifice, his lies, his letter to Kate containing the "sketch of a design," finds not only his moral opposite but his tragic and transforming likeness in the American girl who survives for a while *her* "general wreck," tells lies while studying "the dove-like" to help her friends, and, while she " 'can't make a bargain,' " finally writes a letter and uses her wealth in a last "counter-move to fate." Kate—with her secret engagement, her immense vitality, her brutality which is nonetheless a "strange grace," and with the "bleeding wound" in her name—and Milly—with her mysteri-

12 *The Art of the Novel,* p. 301.
13 *Ibid.,* p. 302.

ous illness and her dove-like radiance—are not so much opposed or divorced from each other as joined, in different measure, in a tragic action; and Kate's efforts to please and beguile
Maud early in the novel are the same efforts which later please
and beguile Milly and help create the crisis which Milly undertakes to redeem. (II, 161; I, 182.)

Even Aunt Maud, though she lacks Susan's depth of tenderness and Sir Luke's professional insight, is joined in a community of interest with Milly finally, despite the opposition
between her effort to separate Kate and Densher and Milly's
attempt to protect them. Though Maud is a " 'vulture' " rather
than a dove, she is also an " 'eagle—with a gilded beak . . .
and with wings for great flights' " who can eventually share
sympathetically in the tragedy of the gilded dove. With Milly's
money "fairly giving poetry to the life Milly clung to," and
with Milly's vision of the " 'might have been,' " the "possibilities" which life might have afforded, so "at one" with Maud's
own view, Maud is moved to tears at the time of Milly's dying
and recognizes in the "cruelty of the event" a "cruelty, of a sort,
to herself." It is with Maud that Densher can bring himself to
speak of Milly's farewell to him and of her "unapproachable
terror" as she "held with passion to her dream of a future" and
then was torn from it "as one might imagine some noble young
victim of the scaffold, in the French Revolution, separated
at the prison-door from some object clutched for resistance."
These conversations with Maud he keeps secret from Kate, as
later he keeps secret his exchange of letters (his "transatlantic
commerce") with Susan, finding in that duplicity the only rock
to cling to in a vast "waste of waters," the "grey expanse" of
stark, drab candor. (I, 73; II, 341-432, 391.)

All these dimensions of the action and all the probing analogies are most revealing and moving when the reader tries
to make out what Milly saw in the dark shadows of her
last days alive, and to imagine what she made out of the life
that consumed her.

She made two things simultaneously which were joined in
the process of her making: the final passionate surrender of devotion, and the image of it, as she acted out, with genuine passion, the complex role she had been playing and now filled

completely. It is this double action which the novel can not allow the reader to see and will not allow him to glimpse (shielding the privacy of Milly's shame and the mystery of her agony), but which, with all the power at its command, it urges him to imagine. First, Milly put into words which the novel does not give the lie Densher has been acting out: she told Mark the lie that Densher's motives were genuine, and Mark returned to London duped by this delusion which he passed on to Maud, for he had paid Milly the tribute of believing her. Then Milly " 'turned her face to the wall' "—her pride injured, her folly denuded and exposed—excluding Densher and shaming him. Since her money and her life proved to be both a blessing and a curse, she told Susan and her Italian doctor to leave her alone and to " 'talk of the price of provisions.' " (II, 270, 276.)

That anguished statement is, in this profoundly economic novel, the turning point in the novel's drama, for while marking the catastrophe, it reveals Milly's recognition of the meaning of her "dim experiment." Knowing finally the "price of provisions," she began in her dying days to pay it and to act it out. She agreed to see Densher again and mercifully "let him off" (to use one of the novel's recurring terms for kindness and mercy) by not asking him to state openly his motives, her mercy enabling him to evade the choice between herself and Kate; in her mercy she held back from creating the occasion when Densher would be forced actually to make that choice— in which case, as he remembered it later and declared to Kate, he would have lied to Milly in affirming his love for her, would have " 'denied' " Kate, and then redeemed his lies, made them true, by sticking to them. In her mercy Milly has saved him from the cruelty of that choice but ironically has created for him the cruelty of a later choice which he faces in the closing pages of the novel. She did the kind and cruel thing, the civilized, dove-like, and naïve thing in mercifully forgiving him. Then, like a civilized person and like the adored princess who feeds on the devotion of others, she acknowledged the devotion in a letter to Densher, sending him a message and arranging that it arrive on Christmas Eve from across the interval of silence which now separates them. (II, 301, 325.)

Finally she did the dove-like thing which is the civilized and naïve and American thing: she spent her money, spent it lavishly, in the act of giving it away to Densher. She took possession of herself and of her money, in her act of spending them to give away, bequeathing to Densher an image of her love for him. She joined in her friends' commerce, completed their transaction, redeemed their enterprise by transforming it into a gift, making her loving surrender to her tragic fortune and joining to "the imagination of expenditure," which Kate had early attributed to her, the "imagination of terror, of thrift, the imagination . . . of a conscious dependence on others," which for Milly is of more recent acquisition. (I, 175.)

In this action Milly gave final form to what had been the rhythm of her life, suspended as she was between moments in which she encountered, recognized, and accepted her impending doom and moments when, mustering the "famous 'will power' . . . which was what her medical adviser had mainly thrown her back on," she struggled to live. While she had succumbed willingly to her illness at Matcham before the Bronzino portrait, she had on other occasions as a "counter-move to fate" turned away from death and had clung to her appointed role as "the American girl"; the end of the first volume had left her feigning an interest in the American West because Densher wanted to talk about the States, prolonging the conversation and clinging to "the Rockies" so as to avoid facing her doom. At her death she clung again to her role as the American girl and dove, clinging as a "counter-move to fate" to the illusion she was making real. When she died, only the three images which embodied the illusion were left: her letter, her money, and the memory of her. But she now made at the same time an anguished withdrawal *into* her doom, her death, accompanying it by a tribute of devotion to the life which brought on her death and which she left behind. It was a tribute to Densher, whom she then knew fully and nonetheless loved. And it was a tribute also the the illusion of love which he, more intimately than anyone else, had helped to sustain. (I, 301-302.)

To speak of this rhythm, however, is to speak of the novel's form, though to speak thus is to "act as if" the form and the

substance of the novel were completely separate, which is the
lie we tell, the murderous violence we must risk, in any act of
historical and critical analysis. In the rhythm of *The Wings
of the Dove* the form is made to be analogous to the action
which the novel is about. Instead of merely describing its subject, the form acts it out. The form enacts the passion which
lies at the novel's center and is revealed, chiefly through Milly's
sacrifice, in the action which she, helped by the others, brings
to pass. The novel tacitly acknowledges that it cannot completely or directly embrace the ultimate reality—neither the
ultimate horror nor the ultimate beauty, neither the pulsing
actuality of life beyond art, nor the completely imagined vision which was the novel's origin or muse before, in the dance
of James's imagination, it was wooed, seduced, and made into
the rhythm of his words. But the novel is not content to acknowledge this by saying it. Instead it acts as if its vision lay
within the presence but beyond the reach of language: as if its
horrors were unspeakable horrors and its beauties too beautiful for words, the novel intimately acknowledges the fact in the
contortions of expressive movement, the rhythm of approach
and withdrawal as a tribute of devotion to what it leaves behind.
As a gesture of love, this rhythmical form falls short of the full
communion it manages nonetheless to intimate and celebrate;
as an act of devotion it reveals by betraying the life and sacred
presence it adores.

Early and again late, it presses close to Lionel Croy, then
draws back from the terrible—and pitiful—truth about him.
Twice it moves toward temples—St. Mark's and later the
Oratory in London—and sends Kate and Densher, then Densher alone, into them, but itself withdraws without entering
them. It presses toward Kate's assignation, but draws back
without entering that scene. It draws close to Milly's illness
but leaves it unnamed, just as it presses closer and closer to her
suffering but even at her party scarcely shows it at all. And the
novel makes an anguished withdrawal from the crisis occasioned by Mark's visit in Venice, and from both the utter horror
and the utter beauty of Milly's final agony—and in this very
withdrawal it pays tribute to what it leaves behind: to what
Milly actually suffered, to the validity of the role she enacted,

and to the created vision which she finally made, in dying, out of the life that consumed her.

But in approaching Milly only to draw back from her, even while paying tribute to her, it becomes what Densher calls the action they all have been engaged in: just before exclaiming " 'the mere aesthetic instinct of mankind!' " he calls their action "a conspiracy of silence" which has suppressed "the great smudge of mortality across the picture," and has surrounded "the truth . . . about Milly" in an "expensive vagueness," an "impenetrable ring fence" made up, with Milly's help, of "smiles and silences and beautiful fictions." The novel enacts the other dimension of its passion: in failing to do justice to Milly, it betrays her. It draws back into a world which has only fragments and images of Milly, and set against her actual suffering and the envisioned glory she embodied, the novel confesses in guilty terror the necessity it accentuates and gives assent to. Like the rich color and gilt background of a Byzantine painting, like the hard stony glasses of a mosaic, like the mannered art of the Bronzino painting, it is in the candor of its own confession "dead, dead, dead." As in the case of the pictures in Sir Luke's office, which were "in particular framed and glazed," so Milly is *framed* as well as glazed by the novel which takes her to use as the subject of its chilled embrace, and arranges, in the eighth book, that "her death" shall have "taken place." She is betrayed by the very fiction that enshrines her. (II, 298-299.)

This is the form—the design and the movement—that gives shape to what otherwise would be a miscellany of irrelevant notations: The fact that Milly is placed in canvases of Veronese whose compositional modes are like James's own. The fact that in the circle of her friends Milly numbers two professional writers, Densher and Susan. The fact that, in the rite which constitutes her worship, she acknowledges two friends who carry the names of devoted writers: Mark, the patron saint of Venice and author of the Second Gospel; and Luke, the physician-evangelist, the patron saint of painters, and author of the Third Gospel. The fact, finally, that a remark of Densher's early in the novel reveals in Kate's scheme or plot, the plot, the design in deed, of art. He had been admiring Kate's plan to deceive Maud, the plan that was broadened to embrace Milly: "It had, [Kate's] sketch of the affair, a high colour and a great style; at all of which he gazed a minute as at a picture by a master." (I, 74.)

For the novel, like all its characters, is caught in the tragic passion it celebrates. In varying degrees they all, even Mark, pay Milly the tribute of devotion which she exacts, but together and at the same time they all, even Susan and Luke, "frame" her and betray her. For novel and characters alike are consumed in the tragic passion which the novel reveals life to be: this world which mercifully gives life, hope, love, and even money to Milly, enabling her to envision the complete life, only to make these things cruelly impossible of full attainment and to waste them. By the end of the novel, life—with the help of Milly's "disconcerting poetry," her "inscrutable" mercy, and what Maud calls " 'the mere *money* of her' "—has done that to Kate and Densher too. It is a world which is enlightened and ennobled by its suffering but which is also ruined and consumed by it. And it is this consuming passion, the tribute of devotion joined with the betrayal, that the novel's form enacts. The consuming passions of life and art were joined in Milly and they are joined by *The Wings of the Dove* in the "sacrament" which "marries" form and content, for the passion is enacted by the form, which is the telling likeness of it. (II, 184, 242, 341.)

It is with the novel's form in view that one is moved by its withdrawal into the agony of Densher, which transpires on the stage of Densher's memory as he recalls his last sight of Milly, seated talking to him in a room that was "all gaiety and gilt," instilling in him the sense that he has been "forgiven, dedicated, blessed" in a "scene" which he relives in memory as if reading it "from the page of a book." Then on the stage of memory he imagines the torment of Milly's death and tries to redeem at once his love for Kate and his devotion to Milly. His effort, along with the reactions of Kate and Maud, the novel can pretend to give with comparative directness. Moreover, it is chiefly through the sensitive medium of Densher's conscience and imagination that the novel can undertake its most difficult task: to make a likeness of the passion it cannot embrace directly, revealing it in the likeness of analogy. Like Milly, Densher feels intense shame. Like Milly, he feels that "while the days melted, something rare went with them." Like Milly he must face as closely as he is allowed, and as a living person can, the horror of her death, "the price of provisions." Like Milly, at the end, he creates a moral crisis for the living person he loves by trying to give Milly's letter and then the money to Kate, trying to surrender them in honor of the memory he adores. It is because Densher's suffering, and to some extent Kate's and Maud's, is so like Milly's that Milly's tragic presence hovers over the closing chapters even though she is never otherwise seen. (II, 342-343, 395.)

And it is because Densher's and Kate's predicament and suffering are so like the central predicament and passion of the novel that the last two chapters not only complete the novel, as they must, but do what words and novels can do only when they achieve in narrative prose the movement and power of the drama: they not only complete the novel but virtually reenact the entire work.

Life before had surrounded Milly and the others with actual opportunities for life and love along with visions of even more glorious possibilities. Now Kate and Densher confront the actual opportunity they have longed for, the opportunity for their marriage. And they try, despite the widening gap between them—the momentary scorn, the disgust, the recriminations, and the "dim terror" of their final confrontation—to prevent the waste of their passion. But they confront also the images of more glorious possibilities which constitute Milly's last "counter-move to fate." They confront her letter, and then they confront her cash. That money is, as Shaw wrote in his preface to *Major Barbara,* "the most important thing in the world"; it affords the enabling condition which will permit them to have the civilized life and married love they want. The money is, at the same time, a sacred symbol, important (again as Shaw knew) for the very reason that it is a symbol of economic power and that, in modern commercial society, it is made a symbol of the "health, strength, honor, generosity and beauty" which it "represents." In a world which needs and worships the almighty dollar, a world where Milly's compassionate devotion and last "counter-move to fate" find in a gift of cash the necessary form that reveals and makes them possible, that money is made a sacrament, a sacred symbol "set apart and sanctified," as Melville wrote of the doubloon, "to one awe-striking end." It is a symbol, sanctioned now by James's art, of the finest possibilities, revealed in Milly, that they want to pay tribute to. And it is intimately bound to the memory of Milly (with "the mass of money so piled on the girl's back" she "couldn't have lost it if she had tried"), bound to the image of her which is embodied in the memories of Kate and Densher and the others. Milly had had to decide what to do about her memories and had paid them the tribute of devotion; now Kate and Densher must decide what to do about theirs.[14] (II, 401; I, 106, 121.)

Even in situation and setting, the last two chapters are a re-enactment of the whole. Maud is still around, touched to the heart, still confident, and still, thanks now to Milly, deceived. Mark is still available, though Kate has turned him down once; he is simply a bit poorer and closer at hand. Lionel Croy is back, a more ominous and pathetic presence than before. And the setting returns in one chapter to the environment where it began—to the dingy quarters of Kate's family. There Kate and Densher confront Milly's letter of forgiveness on Christmas Day.

With the knowledge of himself that he cannot bury, and with his devotion to Milly, Densher feels he would desecrate the letter by opening it, and he refuses to read it: in a tribute of devotion to Milly, he draws back from the "undisclosed work of her hand," just as Milly, in her tribute of devotion to life and to Densher, drew away and bequeathed him an image of something so glorious and shaming that it insures his refusal of it. (II, 388.)

Then Densher makes a gift to Kate of Milly's letter, making it a " 'tribute' " and " 'sacrifice' " and " 'symbol' " of his gratitude for Kate's " 'sacrifice,' " the " 'act of splendid generosity' " she performed when surrendering her body to him in Venice. And Kate proceeds to reenact the crime which she

---

[14] George Bernard Shaw, *John Bull's Other Island and Major Barbara* (New York, 1907), p. 271. Herman Melville, *Moby-Dick*, eds. Luther P. Mansfield and Howard P. Vincent (New York, 1952), p. 427.

and the world have been committing for some time in an incident which has the terrifying power of the scene in Ibsen's *Hedda Gabler* when Hedda ruthlessly destroys the manuscript which had been inspired by Thea's love for Lövborg, whispering "Now I am burning your child, Thea! . . . Your child and Eilert Lövborg's . . . I am burning your child." Kate, accepting what the letter surely promises, "with a quick gesture . . . jerked the thing into the flame," the "thing" being the "sacred script," the still "undisclosed work of [Milly's] hand." In that action Kate betrays life and betrays herself, for at the novel's end she has, finally, paid with "the sacrifice of Mr. Densher." And Densher suffers the letter's loss, keeping the "pang" of memory wrapped in a "sacred corner" of his room and undoing the wrappings, "handling" the memory "as a father, baffled and tender, might handle a maimed child." His imagination "filled out" the distinctive tone and manner of Milly's letter, and the loss of the "revelation" he imagined is like "the sight of a precious pearl cast before his eyes—his pledge given not to save it. . . ." It was "like the sacrifice of something sentient and throbbing" which "might have been audible as a faint far wail." He clings to the memory so that it might "prevail" as long as it can before the "inevitable sounds of life . . . comparatively coarse and harsh," would "smother and deaden it" and "officiously heal the ache in his soul that was somehow one with it." [15] (II, 385-387, 395-396.)

Then a few months later, as the seasons move (without ever getting there) toward the full bloom of spring, the money comes and Kate and Densher confront that, the novel recalling insistently that they are, once again, alone in Densher's rooms. And Kate, who if no one else in the novel can see, sees now the glory of Milly's love and asserts her claim to having helped prepare for it: " 'she died for you then that you might understand her. From that hour you *did*. . . . And I do now. She did it *for* us. . . . That's what I give to you. . . . That's what I've done for you.' " The only proper tribute to Milly's generosity is to take the money; to "refuse to profit by it" would be to deny Milly and the life she clung to so passionately; it would be to spurn the offered gift, as Lionel Croy had done when Kate

15 *Eleven Plays of Henrik Ibsen* (New York: Modern Library, n.d.), p. 287.

offered her help to him. Milly gave Densher the condition of life that he might have it: To take the money. But Densher, who if no one else in the novel now can feel, feels that to take the money would be to complete his betrayal of what the money symbolizes. To take the dim reflection and soil it with his lips would betray the impassioned love it represents: Not to take the money. Then, to prevent the waste of his and Kate's passion, Densher like Milly tries to give away the money to the living person he loves, adding out of his devotion to Milly the stipulation that Kate in turn renounce the cash. (ii, 403-404.)

This action, in which Kate agrees to join, is at once a tribute to their own love and to Milly's memory, but at the same time it is a refusal of the cash which would enable them to marry and a refusal of Milly's generosity: it is a tribute of devotion, but it is also an assignation. Accordingly, as Densher awaits Kate's decision, the novel evokes as a memory the earlier assignation, never described, in Densher's rooms: "Strange it was for him then that she stood in his own rooms doing it, while, with an intensity now beyond any that had ever made his breath come slow, he waited for her act." As before, Kate consents, determined if she can to prevent the waste of their passion, but consenting only on one condition: " 'Your word of honor that you're not in love with her memory.' " She demands that he deny the dead image of a girl now dead, but an image of a passion beyond any he could otherwise imagine. Densher squirms in making an exclamation which tries to hide, without openly denying, the memory that now possesses him: " 'Oh—her memory!' " But within that exclamation Kate sees instantly the truth that separates them: " 'Her memory's your love. You *want* no other.' " When Densher offers again to marry her, and stands, without moving, awaiting her answer, Kate "turned toward the door, and her headshake was now the end." She has withdrawn from a passion which, she knows, is spent. They have made an anguished withdrawal into the sterile isolation of their lives apart while paying a desperate tribute to the passion—their own and Milly's—which they leave behind. (ii, 404-405.)

Densher is left with the memory of what the novel, with Densher, calls in genuine seriousness the " 'act of splendid generosity' " performed by Kate in his rooms in Venice. Both have the memory of the marriage they had hoped for, that institution a temple still and still without a street running up to it. And each has the memory of the money which sits on the table at the novel's end, the check not acknowledged or endorsed, the gift still not possessed, the grace of forgiveness and love still operative but balked of fulfillment: it is "untouchable and immaculate," like Melville's doubloon, and wasted. And each has the memory of the American girl who made on the occasion of her party a "brief sacrifice to society" in a world where "ripeness is all," a world which cannot make the most out of its money.[16] (II, 295.)

Every attempt Kate and Densher have made at the end to salvage their love and pay tribute to Milly's has involved them in the throes of transformation, in the process which Milly's suffering brought to light and which her redemptive imagination created in partial fulfillments for herself and for her friends. But these efforts, finally failing, have inescapably divided and destroyed them at the same time, revealing the possible *might-be* in the form of the *might-have-been* and its betrayal, rendering the world not redeemed but redeemable in the process of its tragic wastage. The double burden of this double recognition is carried by Kate's closing cry, the novel's last sentence before, "hanging unfinished," it drops "into no words nor any notes at all." Kate says simply: " 'We shall never be again as we were!' " The novel's vision yields itself, as the form reveals itself, in its spendthrift waste of passion—their own and Milly's—the tragic waste which is the appalling cost of Milly's tragic triumph. The novel's action spends itself, as the form completes itself, in the consuming passion with all its waste which James found life and art to be.

16 Melville, *Moby-Dick,* p. 427.

CHAPTER SIX

The Marriages:
The Golden Bowl

Can Wisdom be put in a silver rod?
Or Love in a golden bowl?
William Blake, "Thel's Motto"

It is by words and the defeat of words,
Down sudden vistas of the vain attempt,
That for a flying moment one may see
By what cross-purposes the world is dreamt.
Richard Wilbur, "An Event"

It is becoming clear that plastic art never derives
from a special way of seeing the world, but from a
way of making it.
André Malraux, *Museums Without Walls*

[I]

THE VENDING OF THE BOWL

FRAMED in doorways at opposite ends of the long picture gallery of their country estate at Fawns, Maggie Verver and her
father, Adam, stand mute in a confrontation which becomes
an unexpected "communion." With the strained, obsessive reg-
ularity of its geometry, the stunning scene (Chapter IV of Book
Fifth), to which the late F. O. Matthiessen called attention,
can stand as the epitome of James's artistry in *The Golden Bowl*
and as an image at once of the crisis it brings to life and of the
process which resolves it. For along the axis of Maggie's and
Adam's vision lies the terror of what they have helped to make
and the compassion which is created in the willed effort to redeem it. (II, 292.)*

Midway between the father and daughter is a cluster of visitors on a tour through the collection, nominally neighbors but
actually "neighbourly from ten miles off"; the group listens
to their guide's lecture as attentively as if the gallery were "a
church ablaze with tapers" and the speaker were "taking her
part in some hymn of praise," while a friend of the Ververs,
Fanny Assingham, stands on the periphery, "rapt in devotion."
The speaker who holds the group tightly together "by something almost austere in the grace of her authority" and draws
Maggie toward her, is Charlotte Stant, Maggie's friend, the
lover of Maggie's husband, and the wife of Maggie's father whose
infidelity to him has recently become known to Maggie. As Charlotte speaks she displays "her cheerful submission to duty," but
her words are a perilous blend of relevance and inconsequence
on the ostensibly trivial subject of a large vase with garlands
draped around it; the garlands are " 'the finest . . . *vieux
Saxe*,' " Charlotte intones, but they are inferior to the vase itself,
having been " 'put on at a later time' " by a rare " 'process known
through very few examples,' " and they render the whole some-

* Citations enclosed in parentheses in the text refer to The New York Edition,
The Golden Bowl being volumes XXIII and XXIV of that edition. Other footnotes
appear at the bottom of the page.

what " '*baroque*' " though its value is " 'inestimable.' " (II, 290-291.)

Mrs. Assingham masks the feelings stirred in her by Charlotte's performance, but her look conveys a message to Maggie: " 'You understand, don't you, that if she didn't do this there would be no knowing what she might do?' " And as Charlotte strives to "justify the faith with which she was honoured," Maggie turns away on the verge of tears at the sound she has heard within the "quaver" of Charlotte's voice, the tormented "shriek of a soul in pain." Maggie exclaims silently to herself " 'Hasn't she done it *enough*?' " and turns to see her father with "strange tears in his own eyes." Maggie and Adam share his pity and admiration for Charlotte (" 'Poor thing, poor thing . . . *isn't* she, for one's credit, on the swagger' ") and together recognize "the shame, the pity, the better knowledge, the smothered protest, the divined anguish," which applies to all of them. By the end of the chapter, Charlotte's cry has produced for Maggie a shared communion over even vaster distances, not with her father but with her husband, Prince Amerigo, in London. There in an empty house where two servants "were alone in possession" and surrounded by the "pale shrouds" of furniture covers, he paces the floor or sits restlessly smoking "ceaseless cigarettes," trying to escape the sound of Charlotte's "high coerced quaver" but determined to face the consequences of his marriage and waiting, in the confines of his own domicile, for nothing more or less than to be at his wife's side. (II, 291-294.)

Charlotte's remarks about the layers of history contributing to the "baroque" effect of the vase and the spatial composition of the scene hold in a taut suspension the main patterns of movement in *The Golden Bowl* which radiate from the tortured sacrifice sounded by Charlotte's shriek of pain to be revealed in the imagination of Maggie: the commemoration of a past life, its memories accepted as past, and the launching of a new life constituted as new. Personal crises for the principal characters are joined in a social crisis which signals at once the passing of a lost Roman imperium and a prevailing Pax Britannica, both transformed under the ruinous but creative impact of the Ververs' culpable innocence and projected confidence, their nascent responsibility and infused power. As part of this process Charlotte Stant's role as hostess in a crumbling world of the upper middle class and European aristocracy, and Adam Verver's role as entrepreneur, are converted into a public mission for the American City in the new imperium where Adam plans to erect the "temple of taste" that Strether in *The Ambassadors* had hoped to build.

As part of the same crisis, the institution of the family is profoundly altered: the large tribal family of old—the "wealth of kinship" which journeys from Italy for the Prince's wedding or the cluster of children, aunts, and uncles which witnesses the preliminaries of Adam's engagement to Charlotte in Brighton —is reduced to the constricted limits of the immediate family (husband, wife, and child) and sheer domesticity, the veritably appalling intimacy of the immediate family which is the stage for most of the drama of *The Golden Bowl*. And the " 'ghastly' " and "magnificent" form of marriage is made sacred in the process, tested, reduced to the mere shell of conventionality yet stretched to sanction familial perversions and betrayals, until reconstituted as the basis for Adam's project for American City and for Charlotte's role in service to it, and as the basis for the fruitful intimacy and passion of the Prince and Maggie. (I, 145, 18.)

What Maggie calls at one point the " 'funny form' " of her life with her husband, father, and stepmother and their interlocking marriages is matched by the funny form of James's novel, and the scene in the gallery at Fawns, with Charlotte's speech releasing her shriek of pain, illuminates the form of *The Golden Bowl* and the perilous marriage it achieves with its materials. The speech, though brief, is distinctly set off from the narrative, and the haunting relevance of prose which verges on the irrelevant, suggesting an immanence of meaning beyond what is, word for word, quite lucidly clear, recalls the scene in *The Scarlet Letter* on which it seems to draw for resources of formal effect. In the second from the last chapter of Hawthorne's work, Hester Prynne listens to Dimmesdale's sermon, standing "statue-like" at the foot of the scaffold outside because she cannot find room inside the crowded church. Hester's "intentness," the resonant power of Dimmesdale's voice, and the fact that the church walls filter out the "grosser medium" of words and leave only the "murmur and flow" of Dimmesdale's voice, enable Hester to hear only the "undertone" and "solemn grandeur" and to catch in the sermon "a meaning for her, entirely apart from its indistinguishable words." What her ear discerns beyond the words—across the interval of social space and through the walls which separate her, as in Maggie's case, from the rest of the audience and from the speaker himself—is "the shriek, as it might be conceived," the "cry of pain" of a "human heart . . . telling its secret" and asking "sympathy" for sorrow or "forgiveness" for sin.[1] (II, 25.)

James's prose acknowledges a comparable tension between words and their more compressed or intimate meanings and seeks a comparable communion across intervals of social space and the barriers of a verbal medium. But it recasts Hawthorne's ratio between idiom and implication, clinging to, rather than trying to abandon, the solidity of a "grosser" linguistic medium, yet clinging also to the depths or far reaches of implications beyond the medium. And in the light of his own warning against the limitations of allegory in his *Hawthorne* (allegory being apt to "spoil" both a "story and a moral, a meaning and a form"), James avoided the severance between surface and substance, between instrument and import, on which Hawthorne's allegorical mode rests and made the interaction of medium and substance more intimate and more compressed.[2]

The result, culminating in *The Golden Bowl* and epitomized by the scene in the picture gallery, is an art which swells or burgeons with the force of realities which press upon it and the comparable pressures which it creates and projects, yet sustains these acknowledged pressures almost entirely on the surface of its medium. As in the case of a number of distinctly modern modes in painting and the architecture of reinforced concrete which Siegfried Giedion has analyzed so brilliantly, the "surface" itself has challenged "perspective," in the illusionistic or three-dimensional sense, as "the basis of composition," and instead of possessing a merely "decorative" function, the "surface" has been endowed with an "intrinsic capacity for expression." The motives of characters and the ambiguities

---

[1] Hawthorne, *The Complete Novels and Selected Tales*, p. 228.
[2] *The Shock of Recognition*, p. 474.

which are part of James's expressive form, whether they become lucidly known or remain densely mysterious, are luminously and almost nakedly present on the surface of the art. The "confounding extension of surface" which Densher associated with Milly at her party in *The Wings of the Dove* characterizes the mannered form of *The Golden Bowl*. Though there are realities which lie beyond both its grasp and its reticence— sexual intimacies among them, certain social conditions and occupations, and the "great smudge of mortality across the picture" which shadowed without actually entering *The Wings of the Dove*—their felt presence looms pervasively in the very manner of the prose and saturates the symbolic actions which it registers and projects.[3]

The Golden Bowl's strange candor, including the confession of its own responsibility, is derived not only from the fact that it is as " 'accessible to experience' " as James himself hoped to be but from the fact which makes that accessibility possible: the fact that its own medium is confessed in the gestures of dramatic presentation, its own artifice is displayed as transparently in its manner as the feelings of its characters, and the artifice is thereby intimately exposed both to the characters and to its readers. Its encounter with reality and its rhetoric become one.[4]

Both the architectural settings and the images of architectural structures serve this confessional function among others, hovering or obtruding with obsessive power and characterizing not only the world of social and psychic experience which the characters encounter but the universe of the particular House of Fiction which helps shape their environment. The chapter which sounds Charlotte's cry in the picture gallery and culminates in the view of the Prince waiting for Maggie alone in London renders the lives of the characters in a surrealistic image which serves also to characterize the stunning symmetries, the strained eruptions, and the displayed manner of James's novel. Desperately seeking relief from the strain of their private lives, the characters find release in "the possible heroism of perfunctory

---

3 Siegfried Giedion, *Space, Time, and Architecture* (Cambridge, Mass., 1941), pp. 380-381. James, *The Wings of the Dove*, II, 215, 298-299.

4 *Autobiography*, p. 124.

things," the rituals of sociable entertainment when their lives assume "finally the likeness of some spacious central chamber in a haunted house, a great overarched and overglazed rotunda, where gaiety might reign, but the doors of which opened into sinister circular passages. Here they turned up for each other . . . with the blank faces that denied any uneasiness in the approach; here they closed numerous doors carefully behind them—all save the door that connected the place, as by a straight tented corridor, with the outer world" of tourists and closer acquaintances and, "encouraging thus the irruption of society, imitated the aperture through which the bedizened performers of the circus are poured into the ring." Earlier, when rendering the impact on Adam Verver of his future son-in-law, the Prince, the novel presents the image of a Palladian church, geometrically angular "with a grand architectural front," dropping suddenly as in a hallucination into the "pleasant public square" of Adam's life and the reader's vision and so dominating the scene as to press the confines of the square and block any view of "the future." But in the resiliency of Adam's experience and James's medium, the "sky" has soon "lifted, the horizon receded, the very foreground itself expanded," creating room to walk around the building and disclosing access to it through doors, as its façades prove to be not dangerously angular but " 'inexhaustibly round.' " (ii, 288-289; i, 134-138.)

The House of Fiction is more distinctly visible in the novel's most famous exotic image, the "beautiful, but outlandish pagoda" planted in the "garden" of Maggie's life by her marriage, which leaves sometimes "ample," sometimes "narrow," room to walk about. The "tall tower of ivory"—a "structure plated with hard, bright porcelain" and ominously remote—is a figure for the pair of marriages which leave the four principal characters interlocked, publicly joined in what their startled acquaintances call the "highest amiability" and privately joined in what Maggie has just recognized as an unusual intimacy: with Maggie married to the Prince but still as intimate with her father as before, and with Charlotte married to Adam Verver but still frequently associating with the Prince and now, as Maggie has just discovered, renewing her sexual affair with her stepson-in-law.

The pagoda is presented as a figure for the curiously short-circuited relations which prevail among the four, and Maggie is struck by the fact that neither marriage has been "measurably paid for" and that to make bold to enter the pagoda might entail "paying with one's life." (II, 3-6.)

But if the pagoda suggests the complex social, psychological, and sexual situation which Maggie confronts, it presents also an exotic version of Gilbert Osmond's formidable house in *The Portrait of a Lady* with its "jealous apertures" which defied entrance, its "small high window" from which Osmond scrutinized the world and looked upon Isabel Archer to court, to use, and to "mock at her." The pagoda which entices yet repels Maggie displays openings "that must serve from within, and especially far aloft, as . . . outlooks," but Maggie can as yet find no door which gives "access from her convenient garden level." Its "great decorated surface" is fascinating but "consistently impenetrable and inscrutable." It represents, finally, not simply the fact of the interlocking marriages but precisely the fictive process which formed them, and more particularly, the crisis in their development which the novel is constructed to focus on as its very center at the opening of Volume II: "The pagoda in her blooming garden figured the arrangement—how otherwise was it to be named?—by which, so strikingly, she had been able to marry without breaking, as she liked to put it, with her past." (II, 4-6.)

As a consequence of James's aim to make novels that are, as H. G. Wells discerned, "continuously relevant," [5] the formal novelistic "arrangement" which created *The Golden Bowl* is confessed continuously in its style and in the deeds of the characters whose watchful provisions for each other implicate also the author who created and used them as the instruments of his craft, the watcher through the windows of his form, the shopkeeper who came upon them in his commerce with life and with his readers and became their vicarious companion in the arena of his fiction. The novel sustains an unbroken analogy between itself as a fictive creation and the action it projects or the

---

[5] H. G. Wells, *Boon* (London, 1915), reprinted by Leon Edel and Gordon N. Ray in *Henry James and H. G. Wells: A Record of Their Friendship, Their Debate on the Art of Fiction, and Their Quarrel* (Urbana, Ill., 1958), p. 240.

life it images. And while this analogy by no means exhausts its significance, it illuminates the shaping impact of its form at every turn, and the interaction of James with his centers of consciousness is articulated consistently in the textures of the prose and in the "intimate connivances" (to use Gide's term again) of its plot. The relevance of James's form to the suspense and moral import of *The Golden Bowl* is clearly established in the treatment of Fanny Assingham and her husband, Bob, and in the negotiations of the unnamed shopkeeper with the Prince and Charlotte, and later with Maggie, over the purchase of a golden bowl.

The opening sections which define a double "crisis" for Prince Amerigo—his restlessness as the plans for his marriage take shape around him, and the crisis which is created when his former lover, Charlotte Stant, unexpectedly returns from America to attend the wedding—are the very sections which establish the Assinghams' role in terms which reveal the complicity of James's art. Fanny Assingham is the one, the Prince gratefully remembers, who not only is " 'launching' " him on " 'adventures' " but " 'had the conception' " of his marriage—indeed, she has *"made* his marriage, quite as truly as his papal ancestor had made his family," though for what "profit" he cannot imagine. Costumed with the indulgence of a "pampered Jewess" and a "lazy Creole," she is "covered and surrounded" by the " 'things' " or "toys" with which she amuses her friends; the native New Yorker, with her "eyebrows marked like those of an actress," has not only made matches but "invented combinations," and she shares the relish James was to express in the Prefaces for difficulties and complications: " 'I really like them. They're quite my element.' " (I, 19-21, 27, 34-36, 43.)

When she invites Charlotte to move from the hotel and become her guest, and when she sanctions Charlotte's plan to shop for a wedding present with the Prince as escort, she has become implicated in a crisis which her husband acknowledges to be their concern. The situation " 'isn't *your* fault,' " he first insists, wondering what "she was so bent on being responsible for," but he himself engages in a world of playful fantasy, finding in his habitual "extravagant language," his "wealth of expression," an equivalent for the military maneuvers which, as

THE VENDING OF THE BOWL

a retired colonel, he is cut off from. And he is not dissociated from his wife's maneuvers: he has habitually "edited, for their general economy, the play of her mind" just as he edits her "redundant telegrams," and whether by listening attentively and reading between the lines, or by asking probing questions, he serves the reader as well as his wife and James to help establish important matters: the fact that Charlotte and Amerigo had been intimate but, with marriage apparently out of the question, had precipitously separated just before the Ververs' arrival in Europe; Bob's suspicion that Charlotte may have suggested her wealthy friend, Maggie, as a wife for the Prince before separating from him; Fanny's recognition that Charlotte and the Prince had been more intimate than she first knew; Fanny's certainty that the Prince had never heard of Maggie until Fanny herself introduced them. (i, 63-67, 70-75.)

Together the Assinghams establish the tension between a detachment which is guiltless—whether because Fanny played only a mediating role to begin with or because now she can wash her hands of the arrangements which make her so " 'happy' " and " 'quiet' "—and the guilty involvement which leaves Fanny patently *not* " 'quiet,' " the feeling that the situation is as " 'grave' " as the Colonel suspects, despite his claim that the situation is " 'theirs now; they've bought it, over the counter, and paid for it.' " (i, 82-83, 73, 75.)

As they continue their conversation, they deepen their involvement and project it into the future. For Fanny's dubious declarations of confidence are "words" which she seizes on frantically "very much as if they were the blue daylight towards which, through a darksome tunnel, she had been pushing her way" and the effect is a shrill mixture of anxiety and forged confidence which makes her husband even more interested; the Colonel's response is to persist in his questioning, not to abandon it, for "his interest might in fact have been more enlisted than he allowed." He casts aspersions on her morality, but he no more strenuously objects than he had objected to the " 'meddling' " which eventuated in his own marriage to her: it had ceased to be " 'meddling,' " he admits, from " 'the moment I didn't object.' " And he has already pointed to the even deeper and more active involvement of his wife, claiming that she, like Charlotte, had fallen " 'violently in love with the Prince' " and finds vicarious satisfaction in arranging a marriage for him with someone else. However the marriage began, " 'the effect was produced, the charm began to work' " from the moment she introduced Amerigo and Maggie, and Fanny's " 'only course, afterwards, had to be to make the best of it.' " (I, 76-77, 86, 80-81.)

She defines her responsibilities for the affairs and for the novel's plot more precisely when she declares her belief that Charlotte, in leaving for America and " 'the undertaking of a new life,' " has helped the Prince break from her and " 'helped me to help him' " and that " 'it's for us on our side to see *her* through' " by marrying Charlotte to someone so as to " 'make up' " for any possible faults in the arrangement already made. Charlotte and the Prince are " 'my own' " as much as the Colonel himself is, Fanny declares; " 'our relation, all round, exists. . . . We must live *in* it and with it. . . . I shall give, for the next year or two if necessary, my life to it.' " When she rests her claim finally on the assertion that " 'it's all, at the worst, great fun,' " and the Colonel infers that she alludes to sex, she denies meaning " 'the fun you mean' " and (turning out the light) says good-night, but she and her husband have together defined the many dimensions of intimate experience and social forms on which the " 'fun' " or entertainment of James's novel rests. (I, 76, 84-86, 88.)

Late in Volume I, when the Prince and Charlotte show clear signs of becoming intimate once more despite their marriages respectively to Maggie and Adam—when in fact, unknown to Fanny, they have renewed their affair in Gloucester—Fanny is so appalled that she comes close to denying the " 'responsibility' " which the Prince claims she has to continue as " 'my original sponsor' " and to " 'see me through.' " Indeed, she does deny being responsible specifically to *him*. But she cringes in terror at the imminent consequences of her actions, smarts when accidently caught in the glare of a policeman's flashlight, yet continues to play her imagination upon the lives of those around her in the dangerous game where even " 'asking' " questions is to suggest the possibility of the things one asks about, where indeed finally to have so much as "uttered a question" is to have "plunged" into the waters where Fanny has ventured. Her husband, though standing on shore, keeps her "well in sight," relieved finally that she "was making for land," but prepared to "make some sort of plunge" should her boat founder. When he feels "her boat bump" land, she has reached the at best temporary safety of a forged confidence, a projected version of the situation which renders the Prince and Charlotte faithful to their marriages despite their companionship in public, an illusory assurance which collapses suddenly, leaving her with no more than the protest that she has tried to benefit " 'them *all*' " before she breaks into tears and tries to hide in shame from her husband. (I, 274-276, 279, 365-366, 377.)

But the very collapse of her confidence creates for herself the intimacy, the compassion, and the imaginative daring which are to be created in more profound versions later in the novel. The Colonel holds her for a moment in the "small crisis" of an embrace while the knowledge they share closes the door that shields their communion and they look out "through the dim window that opened upon the world of human trouble." The "beauty of what thus passed between them" is sustained because it "passed with her cry of pain" and with the culminating "moments of their silence." He feels that he has sunk with her, "hand in hand," in the waters where she earlier ventured alone. (I, 377-378.)

They emerge in their intimacy with renewed powers of expression and with the vision which prefigures the subsequent action of the novel, projecting it for James in a monstrous but profound pun on the phrase "must be saved" which forges the union of the plot and the moral impulsion of *The Golden Bowl:* "What was the basis . . . but that Charlotte and the Prince must be saved—so far as consistently speaking of them as still safe might save them?" To declare that the pair must be saved in the sense of *saved already* and must be saved in the sense of *rescued in the future* is to define the very viability of their lives, the ratio between their latent capacities or merits and their possibilities for the future. For if, in accordance with some other fiction, James's novel were to speak of them consistently as damned they would not be at all "safe" but irrevocably doomed. If they were damned even by some merely willed fancy, some projected judgment, of Fanny, *The Golden Bowl* would have to be rewritten. As it stands, instead of condemning Charlotte and the Prince, it performs the act of "consistently speaking of them as still safe," and that enactment not only risks the dangerous comfort of a verbal evasion or lie but sustains the purpose which Fanny and later Maggie come to share with *The Golden Bowl*, the redemptive effort that eventually "might save them." (I, 377-378.)

It is that aim which is worked out by and through the Assinghams at the end of the first volume as their anticipations form the sketch for Volume II. Fanny has detected in Maggie's " 'manner' " slight indications that her " 'natural' " behavior is being supplanted by a more calculating performance, the first " 'pale pathetic blinking efforts' " effectively to *appear* " 'natural,' " and she explains this by supposing that Maggie has begun to doubt her husband's fidelity, to suspect the friendship of Amerigo and Charlotte. Fanny imagines that instead of imposing the guilt on Charlotte or Fanny (who admits that " 'I did it all. I recognize that—I accept it' "), Maggie will assume the responsibility and " 'carry the whole weight of us.' " As again Fanny "projected her vision"—pleased with the prospects which "under so much handling" have begun to emerge but knowing that eventually she must " 'pay for . . . my damnable, my unnecessary interest' "—she impresses Bob "with her mastery of her subject" and with "her exposition" that tends "more to create than to extinguish in him the germ of a curiosity." (I, 380-383, 386-389, 399.)

She has seen earlier that Maggie will now have to open her mind " 'to what's called Evil—with a very big E,' " to " 'the crude experience of it' " or at least " 'to the suspicion and the dread' " of it, for evil has emerged in the life she knows. It has emerged despite " 'beautiful intentions all round' "—Charlotte's and the Prince's genuine intention to respect Adam (which has held for two years), the "intensity" of Maggie's conscience that made her want to provide Adam a wife yet remain close to him herself, the irresistible charm of the four characters for each other, leading Charlotte and the Prince " 'guilelessly' " to accept Maggie's intimacy with her father and permitting Maggie to hold the " 'guileless idea of still having her

father, of keeping him fast, in her life.' " Fanny may discount
the Prince's culpable passivity and Charlotte's risky initiative
in inviting the Prince's attentions, yet her views help define
the moral issues of the novel, and her excessively favorable
view of the situation is part of the feat of "consistently speaking
of them as still safe": the creation of a form which projects the
possibility of their redemption. What Fanny's improvisations do
is to suggest that all of the characters need saving, including
Maggie with the " 'unfortunate even if quite heroic little sense
of justice' " which has led her to imperil her marriage by clinging to her father and welcoming the compensatory companionship which Amerigo and Charlotte find with each other. Fanny
imagines that Maggie will find her salvation in sparing her father from the knowledge of their betrayal, and imagines that
Maggie now is taking command and that like " 'an old woman
who has taken to "painting," ' " she will " 'lay it on thicker,' "
learning with new-found audacity to " 'gloss things over' " and
" 'for that sacred purpose' " to do so " 'consummately, diabolically' " lest her performance show for mere " *'rouge.'* " To
help her in her folly, Fanny and the Colonel engage to make
fools of themselves, to be " 'absolute idiots' " in pretending
that " 'nothing *has* happened' " and that " 'nothing *is* happen-
ing' " while imagining surely that it has and is. In so doing
they not only help define but help create the moral drama of
The Golden Bowl. (I, 385, 387, 391-393, 395-397, 401-402.)

That drama is shaped also by an extended action which
concludes Book First but which is completed only at the culmination later of Book Fourth, the act of buying the golden bowl
in the Bloomsbury shop which constitutes the novel's central
symbol. Bluntly obvious but no less significant are three features of the action once it is completed: the bowl is cracked to
begin with, Charlotte wants to buy the bowl but does not, and
Maggie later does. The bowl is resonant already with its echo
of Ecclesiastes ("Remember also thy Creator in the days of thy
youth, before the evil days come . . . before the silver cord is
loosed or the golden bowl is broken") and its equally strong
echo of Blake's haunting question in "Thel's Motto": "Can
Wisdom be put in a silver rod? / Or Love in a golden bowl?"
But the bowl in the novel and the field of form it consti-

tutes are rendered inseparable from the arrangements which
bring them to light; the first of these is the surrender which
Charlotte initiates and risks when she secures the Prince's company on her shopping expedition to find a wedding present for
Maggie.[6]

She explains that her gift cannot be " 'expensive' " and " 'competing,' " that it must perforce be incongruously " 'funny,' "
by which she means " 'absolutely *right,* in its comparative
cheapness,' " because it will be something that " 'no rich person
could ever give' " and that Maggie is " 'herself too rich ever to
buy.' " But deeper than the desire to commemorate Maggie's
marriage is the longing accompanying it which has brought her
from America, the longing, as she confesses to the Prince on the
way to the shops, " 'to have one hour alone with you.' " Her desire to present a gift to Maggie is spliced paradoxically with the
deeper offer of herself to the Prince which supplants it, the offer
which Amerigo had anticipated with a "mixture of pity and
profit" when he met Charlotte at the Assinghams: "the doing
by the woman of the thing that gave her away" and the arranging of "appearances" by which she dresses it up. (I, 92,
89, 49-50.)

He had appreciated her physical attractions and had regarded
them as "a cluster of possessions of his own" which he might
enjoy, like art treasures stored in a cabinet, when he chose;
she seems a silken purse drawn through a ring at her "flexible
waist" whose weight he has measured in his hand and whose
value he has heard in the clink of coins. Now Charlotte's every
gesture betrays her desire and reveals her abjection and the
gift she is willing to make. She wants to instill in him the inescapable memory of her presence: " 'that I was here with you
where we are and *as* we are—I just saying this. Giving myself,
in other words, away—and perfectly willing to do it for nothing.' " She takes full responsibility for it, without even asking
an answer from the Prince, who is morally self-indulgent by
comparison. Even when she adds that he " 'may want to know
what I get by it. But that's my affair,' " the offer stands as an
authentic revelation, on Charlotte's part, of love. The moral

6 Ecclesiastes XII, 1-6. Blake, *Poetry and Prose of William Blake,* ed. Geoffrey
Keynes (London, 1939), p. 162.

viability of Charlotte's action, the problematic nature of her relation with the Prince, and the coupling of her desire to give Maggie a present with her determination to express her love for the Prince, reveal in Charlotte the moral heroism which Louise Bogan and Jean Kimball have rightly discerned in her.[7] (I, 46-47, 97-98.)

The Prince does have the insight to anticipate that one's " 'affection' " for Maggie may make a telling difference in one's relation with her, but it is Charlotte who defines the " 'terrible' " predicament of people who must rely on " 'prayer and fasting' " or take special pains of *some* sort not to take advantage of Maggie since Maggie herself makes no demands, with her " 'disposition to be kind' " and " 'does everything herself.' " In the context provided by Charlotte's and the Prince's conversation as they approach the shops, avoiding the expensive Bond Street stores which Maggie frequents, their negotiations over the bowl relate to both the intended gift for Maggie and Charlotte's intended offer to the Prince. By the time they fail to buy the bowl, because it is flawed and the Prince thinks the price too high, both the offer of the bowl and the failure to purchase it establish perspectives on their affair and on Maggie's marriage, and by analogy, on James's art as well, and thus define further the novel's moral issues. (I, 102.)

In the shop in Bloomsbury, surrounded by the "faint poetry" of "cups, trays, taper-stands, suggestive of pawn-tickets, archaic and brown, that would themselves, if preserved, have been prized curiosities," they encounter the shopman with the careful hands of a "chess-player" considering a move of his players, the "interesting dealer" whose manner, though not "importunate," is "intensely coercive" and who "fixed on his visitors an extraordinary pair of eyes." He is "clearly the master, and devoted to his business," and he strikes Charlotte as more interesting than his stock of curios not only because he " 'cared so for his things' " but because he cared for his customers, and (like the author of the preface to *The Portrait of a Lady*) would

---

[7] Louise Bogan, "The Silver Clue" in *Selected Criticism* (New York, 1955), pp. 264-268, 267. Jean Kimball, "Henry James' Last Portrait of a Lady: Charlotte Stant in *The Golden Bowl*," *American Literature*, XXVIII (January 1957), pp. 449-468, 458, 468.

prefer to keep the "things" if he could or "sell them to the right people." He overhears and understands the Italian spoken by his present customers as they talk not of a present for Maggie but of selecting presents for each other. When the Prince rules out a gift from Charlotte to himself as " 'impossible,' " the dealer tries to interest them in a special item: James's artistry is clearly implicated when "their entertainer" takes out "a drinking-vessel larger than a common cup" and, handling it "with ceremony," exclaims " 'My Golden Bowl' " and places it before them "to produce its certain effect." "Simple, but singularly elegant," it seems to have "justified its title by the charm of its shape as well as by the tone of its surface." (I, 104-107, 110-112.)

The Prince almost instantly leaves the shop, convinced as he tells Charlotte later that the man is a " 'rascal' " and that the bowl has a crack which is an ill omen for his marriage: " 'If it had cost you even but five pence I wouldn't take it from you. . . . I saw the object itself. It told its story.' " He insists that anything *he* ever gives *her* will be " 'perfect' " and that he will someday give her something, namely a present when she marries. He salves his conscience, as Charlotte realizes, by anticipating her marriage and holding to the strictly conventional proprieties. (I, 118-120.)

It is Charlotte, however, who in her dealings with the shopkeeper stands closer to the drama of *The Golden Bowl*. Acknowledging that it is not pure gold as he first claimed but gilded crystal, the shopkeeper gradually concedes its imperfections while underscoring its merits as a beautiful substitute; but he insists that one will never " 'find' " any " 'joint or any piecing' " because the gold is so fused to the surface that it cannot be scraped off. When she persists in asking " 'what's the matter with it,' " he simply returns the question, though she asserts that it is his responsibility " 'honestly to tell.' " He declares that to present a gift with a known flaw is acceptable, if the flaw is confessed to the recipient and if " 'good faith' " accompanies it and assures Charlotte that no recipient would " 'find' " the flaw even if warned. Then, however, he is forced to admit that flawed crystal is peculiarly subject to splitting. When Charlotte wonders if the recipient might not find the flaw " 'if the thing should come to pieces,' " if " 'he should have to say to me "The Golden Bowl is broken," ' " the shopkeeper concedes that it could be broken by a hammer or (foreshadowing the later scene when Fanny breaks the bowl) " 'by dashing it with violence—say upon a marble floor.' " When he taps it, its clear sound fails to disclose a flaw, and Charlotte leaves to consider the purchase further and to rejoin Amerigo outside. (I, 113-117.)

The Prince's reaction to the bowl, accompanied by his departure from Charlotte's side and from the shop, is distinctly correct but crudely simple in view of the moral complexities which Charlotte explores while bargaining with the shopkeeper, and his attitude is perfunctory in comparison with the commitments which Charlotte confronts in wanting to give a present to Maggie and then to buy the bowl for a gift to the Prince. The bowl brings into a strained harmony the many issues and values which surround it in the action, giving a single, tangible shape to the variety of purposes, feelings, and forms which play about it. Held together by its strange symmetry are both the flawed perfection of the impending marriage and the failure of Charlotte and the Prince to pay tribute to it with a suitable gift; the imperfect love of poor Charlotte and the disdainful Prince; a world whose surfaces gild its hidden faults; a beauty whose hardness renders it safe from dissolution but vulnerable to splitting; the careful craft with which the shopkeeper will produce and sell the bowl for the appropriate people; the courage Charlotte would display in buying and offering it despite its flaw; the passion with which Charlotte longs to offer herself to Amerigo; the hard and crystal form of James's novel which presents so tempting and formidable a challenge to Charlotte, so dangerously " 'exquisite' " a golden opportunity to whomever might stay within the shop and buy the bowl. (I, 119.)

When the bowl is bought, later in the novel, it is bought by Maggie, and purchased not as a wedding present but as a birthday present for her father. Her difficulty in selecting a present is comparable to Charlotte's, since Adam is sure to have seen, or bought already anything distinctly " 'good.' " Presents to him must perforce be a "foredoomed aberration," and Maggie's "candour of affection" must find its "tenderest mementoes" in "the infirmity of art," the "ugliest objects" which are "dedicated to the grimacing, not the clear-faced gods." Strolling aimlessly alone in London one day, she recalls Charlotte's speaking of out-of-the-way shops in Bloomsbury, remembers Adam's birthday, and finds the bowl, which is to stand later on her mantel with its "stupid elegance" and "conscious perversity," a " 'document' " which is somehow "ugly, though it might have a decorative grace." (II, 156, 165.)

When Maggie later confronts her husband over the pieces of the broken bowl and tells the circumstances of its purchase, the Prince thinks it " 'the sort of thing that happens mainly in novels and plays,' " and Maggie divulges her interview with the conscience-stricken shopkeeper when he calls to confess for James that the bowl is flawed and that he charged Maggie an unjustifiably high price. Because he has " 'taken an interest' " in her and she has " 'inspired him with sympathy,' " he tells her of Charlotte's and Amerigo's visit. Recognizing the injustice of his price and its unsuitability as a gift, "the vendor of the golden bowl," Maggie's "partner" in "her bargain," has tried to undo his doing, since he "hadn't liked what he had done, and what he had above all made such a 'good thing' of having done." Yet he does not try to retrieve the bowl but to prevent her using it as a gift and to "return her a part of the money." But Maggie finds that, in view of the knowledge that the shopman's information has brought into focus, she does not want her money back, that she is " 'getting its worth' " by virtue of being in " 'possession at last . . . of real knowledge.' " (II, 195-196, 222-224, 198, 201.)

The symbol of the bowl helps govern the novel because the bowl and the act of buying it or possessing it, of breaking and salvaging it later, inform each other, and the bowl itself does not stand as a merely referential or imposed symbol but serves as part of a profoundly creative act to constitute a field of form, a formal nexus. At times the bowl or cup, on its shallow stem, is a tangibly distinct figure, as when Fanny holds it high and dashes it to the floor and Maggie gathers up the three pieces and holds them in her hands; at other times it is not named or shown but echoed almost inaudibly in allusions to cups overflowing, to "gilt and crystal" and the "florid features . . . of Fanny's drawing-room," to things broken or the act of breaking, to the act of gathering up pieces. (I, 378.)

In the resiliency of James's medium, it can suggest both the book which it affords a title, and perspectives and actions contained within that book. It can suggest either the perfect equilibrium of the pair of marriages or merely Maggie's sanguine ideal for them; its breakage can imply either the betrayal of the marriages or "the dire deformity of [Maggie's] attitude" toward the others; its pieces, "the terrors and shames and ruins" with which Maggie's imagination could but refuses to people the stage she looks at when watching the others playing cards. When Maggie awaits Amerigo's return from the weekend at Matcham and his sexual reunion with Charlotte at Gloucester, the bowl is charged with erotic longing, becoming the " 'cup' " of Maggie's " 'need' " for the Prince, too full to carry and spilling over him. It becomes later charged with the passion of the Prince and Charlotte when Charlotte is imagined to say to Maggie: " 'You don't know what it is to have been loved and broken with. You haven't been broken with, because in your relation what can there have been worth speaking of to break? Ours was everything a relation could be, filled to the brim with the wine of consciousness.' " (II, 240, 236, 18, 329.)

In the next to last chapter, when Maggie manages to "wait" and to postpone an embrace and final confrontation with the Prince, the bowl hovers off the edges of the prose, an image of the girlish immaturity, the past that is "lost and gone" which "it was vain, now, wasn't it? to try to appear to clutch or to pick up." Much earlier it serves to illuminate the relation between the Prince and Adam Verver and the complex social configuration which the novel begins to develop in its opening pages: the Prince is rendered as a "pure and perfect crystal" in Adam's admiring eyes, and "nothing . . . could more have confirmed Mr. Verver's account of [the Prince's] surface than the manner in which [the] golden drops [of Adam's praise] evenly flowed over it." The process of gilding the bowl renders the process of appreciation which involves James's artistry and Adam Verver's fortune with the history of the Italian Prince. (II, 351; I, 138.)

[II]

THE CRISIS OF TRANSFORMATION

THE IMAGE of society presented in *The Golden Bowl* is built on the pair of fictive marriages, projected first and then achieved, and the strange family they institute, which are central to both the form and the import of the novel because they are made symbolic not only of marriages in actual life but of other social institutions and processes which are fused with them. Yet the fusion of these other social patterns with the marriages is so complete that the marriages acquire a heightened significance in their own right. They are at once the stage for the drama and part of the drama itself, and *The Golden Bowl* not only acknowledges the importance of the institutions of marriage and the family in the culture it represents by holding so sharp a focus on them but helps create those institutions in their modern form by imposing on them burdensome functions beyond their customary capacity and infusing them with the power to sustain them. James's novel devotes its full power simultaneously to sanctioning the institution of marriage as a convention and to challenging its given conventional status, exposing the flaw in the "ghastly form," demanding of the "magnificent form" and of the partners in it the full redeeming intimacy of intense passion, a willed fidelity within the tightened bond, an authentic commitment to the communion it affords and to the larger community of purpose it can make possible. Terrors and cruelties are revealed within the form, easy convenience and profitable usage, the façade of decorum as well as the sustaining form of passion, the mere mask as well as the speaking form of love or the abysmal passion Maggie comes to know. The perilous mixture of weakness, convenience, utilitarian usage, a flawed harmony, and a community of devotion which the form affords is characteristic of the society in its larger dimensions which *The Golden Bowl* helps to mold, with the result that "the marriages" (as James intended to entitle the novel until recalling that he had already used that title) are at once part of the novel's subject and, like the bowl itself, a containing metaphor for its social vision.[8]

The plans for the Prince's marriage that occupy his thoughts in the opening chapter harbor an historical drama of larger proportions in which Adam Verver, his prospective father-in-law, holds, to begin with, a more important role than the Prince's fiancée. The handsome Prince seems an architectural façade to Adam, and the enigmatic millionaire seems shielded in the "flawless freshness of [his] white waistcoat" by the mysterious "great white curtain" which the Prince associates with the fate of Poe's Gordon Pym, with the American imagination and "the state of mind" of his new American friends. Both are revealed in the contours of the social roles and historic missions which first characterize them. (II, 305; I, 22.)

Restless and unoccupied after the recent exertions which have brought the "capture" of Maggie, the Prince stands looking at a heap of objects in a shop window that seem the "loot" accumulated by the "insolence of the Empire." Latent in his career are combined precisely the predatory "insolence" and, in larger measure, the massive power of an established "empire" which he associates with the modern London that has replaced the older *Imperium* of his native Rome. The older empire seems to be recovered in memory by the sight of modern Bond Street. If he seems strikingly unoccupied and place-less in relation to this imperium, as he does in relation to the wedding arrangements made in his behalf (the "inspired harmony" reached by the Ververs' lawyers and "his own man of business"), he is nevertheless ready to make a place for himself in the new life being prepared for him. His traditional past still receives his respect—indeed, his habit of simply receiving its inherited benefits, including the attentions of some twenty women, links him to traditional aristocratic customs and he looks forward to resurrecting his past with Adam Verver's money, excavating the family estates now buried by a "cloud of mortgages" as "thick" as the ashes from Vesuvius. (I, 3-5, 164.)

Yet he knows that his traditional security has lapsed into the mere momentum of its past vigor and that he has at least a tenuous claim to a place in the imperium of the present: his

8 *The Notebooks*, p. 233.

familiar name, "Amerigo," which associates him, as Fanny Assingham puts it, with the " 'pushing' " adventurer who followed after Columbus and managed to become at least " 'name-
father' " to the new land. If his efforts are less inventive and
aggressive than luckily opportunistic, he is nevertheless aware
of the limitations of his past and regards his marriage as the
quest "for some new history that should, so far as possible,
contradict, and even if need be flatly dishonour, the old." His
family archives include the deeds of some men of good character
and the " 'crimes' " and " 'follies' " of others, but his past has
become singularly ineffective and he cannot simply inherit it:
"If what had come to him wouldn't do he must *make* something
different," and the "material for the making," he recognizes,
"had to be Mr. Verver's millions." The crucial difference between the Prince's history and Adam's is that the Italian's is a
record of money spent and gone while the American's is a current account of cash available for spending, the veritable bath
of fluid wealth in which Adam has soaked his future son-in-law,
with Maggie adding drops of "good faith," "innocence," and
"imagination." The financial arrangements in connection with
his marriage have scarcely invoked "the principle of reciprocity," but the Prince hopes to move closer at least to that enviable equilibrium: having mastered the English language for
its utility in all but the most intimate transactions, he is now
as his marriage approaches "practising his American"; Amerigo practices it so as "to converse properly, on equal terms as it
were, with Mr. Verver." (I, 78-79, 9, 16, 10, 5-6.)

The drama of *The Golden Bowl* rests in large part on the
tensions created by Adam Verver's money and the other values
associated with the American character. Together they constitute a language which the others are induced to speak, and the
drama's irony arises from the fact that the language of the new
imperium does provide an effective medium of communication
but threatens to rule out, by its very power and fluency, the
"reciprocity" the Prince aspires to, the shared relationship he
seeks, the veritable equality which communion in the new language might afford.

The language, the " 'manner,' " the power and the system of
morals which operate alike with the swift efficiency of a ma-

chine, and the enigmatic whiteness which the Prince associates with the American character are in Volume I embodied chiefly in Adam Verver, who dominates the Prince's attention at the start almost as thoroughly as he proves later to dominate his daughter's. The Prince, whose crystal form Adam gilds and appreciates, is to Adam " 'an object of beauty, an object of price,' " in the art collection with which Adam plans to endow the museum he is building in American City, the community which he has adopted as home in his native state. Adam's "apprehensive passion" is appreciative, whether in matters of business or of taste, and James's diction in Book Third places Adam precisely on the threshold of the creative imagination. His " ' "peak in Darien," ' " comparable to that of Cortez in Keats's sonnet, was the transforming discovery of "the affinity of Genius, or at least of Taste, with something in himself," the discovery that he was "equal somehow with the great seers . . . and he didn't after all perhaps dangle so far below the great producers and creators." He is the "financial 'backer' " rather than "stage-manager" or "author of the play," but he is associated intimately with the "grasping imagination" and with the exercise of power to which Professor Edel has drawn attention in James's own ambitions.[9] (I, 12, 145, 141, 170.)

In Adam's case, "acquisition of one sort" has proved "a perfect preliminary to acquisition of another," and he has learned to enjoy the pursuit just as he had learned to like in business the "calculation and imaginative gambling all for themselves," the combination of exploitation and luck, "the creation of 'interests' that were the extinction of other interests, the livid vulgarity . . . of getting in, or getting out, first." The "insolence" of empire which is, at the most, quiescent in the Prince and safely established in Britain's shops has been more powerful in Adam. His ambition to become a "Patron of Art" is presented as involving release from his first marriage, breaches in decorum, a challenge to established authority. His first wife, with her uninformed tastes for the merely decorative, was alien to the ambitions he discovered on a trip to Europe after her death; no decent or "real lady," it occurred to him later, could have

---

[9] Leon Edel, *Henry James: The Untried Years* (Philadelphia, 1953), p. 71. James, *Autobiography*, p. 196.

been a "companion of Cortez," and while the new ambitions of the "plain American citizen" appear to himself as the imperial vision of Cortez, they appear also as the " 'cheek' of the young man who approaches the boss without credentials" or acquires a friend by accosting a stranger on the street. (I, 141-144, 150.)

His particular "real friend, in all the business," is his own self in its new role as Patron, a self which he discovers by intruding without a formal introduction; knocking at the door of its "private house," and admitted only after humiliating delay, he stands "twirling his hat, as an embarrassed stranger," or, "trying his keys, as a thief at night." The freedom to *see* which he asserts is the result of the bold determination figured in the comparisons he makes between himself and two popes, earlier and inferior patrons who neglected Michelangelo. And the museum he plans for American City is not simply the product of earlier ages, the "Golden Isles" which he has been able to "rifle"; it is "positively civilization condensed, . . . a house on a rock . . . from whose open doors and windows, open to grateful, to thirsty millions, the higher, the highest knowledge would shine out to bless the land." (I, 145, 149-150.)

Adam Verver's embarrassment in connection with the memory of his first wife, his temporary rebuff at the house of his aspirations, and the pride he takes later in the possession of a grandson, point ahead to Faulkner's Thomas Sutpen and his design for a community and a dynasty in *Absalom, Absalom!*, but Adam Verver in contrast to Faulkner's protagonist has had exceptionally good luck; he is a strikingly successful, fortunate, and amiable magnate whose "years of darkness had been needed to render possible the years of light" in his marital life as well as in his business affairs, and James's analysis accords to Adam the dignity of a complex, essentially mysterious, integrity. The density of the figure derives from its puzzling mixture of affability, compressed imaginative power, and insolence, his insolence being the assertively proud exertions of an entrepreneur whose enterprise works independently of older customs and decorum. The novel acknowledges that "amiability" is often helpful if not the very "principle of large accumulations," but the novel probes unsuccessfully for the link in Adam's case between so "insolent" a concentration in business matters and so sociable a temperament in all other affairs. That "variety of imagination" on which "amiability" depends is "fatal, in the world of affairs," unless, as in Adam's case, it is "so disciplined as not to be distinguished from monotony"; Adam Verver has for several decades been "inscrutably monotonous" behind the "iridescent cloud" of his native American manner, the "soft looseness" which displays few folds but has nevertheless a "quality unmistakable." (I, 144, 128.)

Both screened and expressed by that manner is the "special genius" of the American businessman, a "spark of fire" shining in Adam Verver's "inward vagueness as a lamp before a shrine twinkles in the dark perspective of a church." Fanned by youthful vigor and the good fortune of being an American—the encouragement given by "example and opportunity" in the New World—his "genius" has converted his mind into "a strange workshop of fortune," a "mysterious" though plain and "almost anonymous" factory which enclosed, at the height of his business activities, "a miraculous white-heat." This power is joined with the "perfection of machinery" it has produced and with the "acquisitive power engendered and applied," but it is enclosed in the virtually "anonymous" and child-like manner which Adam displays at the opening of Book Second, when he indulges in a rare moment of privacy in the billiard room but feels ashamed of his concern for his own "personal advantage" and acknowledges it with "confessing eyes." His manner shows that he is playing at "depravity" for the "amusement" of it, knowing that his moments alone are doomed to be short because of the demands upon him (which he welcomes) and the power which almost despite himself he communicates to others. An "impersonal whiteness" is a screen for which his "vision sometimes ached" in the face of the "many-coloured human appeal" of social intercourse—and the novel's first detailed treatment of Adam shows him seeking that refuge in a retreat through the "tortuous corridors" of Fawns. (I, 125-128.)

But the power of his money is inescapable and is augmented by the awe in which people hold it—by the "attribution of power" beyond what he may otherwise have, which others, reading the symbolism of his cash, infer that he *must* have as a virtually "infinite agent." Together they have an effect and constitute a burden which he cannot pretend to escape, for he has made himself vulnerable to social demands: his manner reveals the amiable *accessibility* of one American archetype, the individual longing for a community. His youthful eyes make it impossible to tell whether "they most carried their possessor's vision out or most opened themselves to your own." In their watchful gaze other persons are drawn toward possible communion, whether with Adam himself or with others, "moving about, for possible community, opportunity, the sight of you scarce knew what," either "before" or "behind" the focus of Adam Verver's attention. It is precisely that kind of attention that *The Golden Bowl* fixes in turn on Adam Verver at the opening of Book Second, following his retreat through the "tortuous corridors" only to infringe on his "achieved isolation," envying his sense of "having the world to one's self" and aiming to "share this world," subjecting him to its possessive scrutiny but rendering that scrutiny "tender indeed almost to compassion." (I, 131, 170-171, 125.)

The novel's intrusion on Adam's privacy simply anticipates the social demands from which he had taken flight, which are the efforts represented by the Mrs. Rance who pursues him into the billiard room at Fawns, the efforts to get him remarried. By the time the routinely determined efforts of womankind have been replaced by Maggie's own, and such available spouses as the Misses Kitty and Dotty Lutch have been replaced by the beautiful Charlotte Stant, *The Golden Bowl* has projected the form which it tries at once to challenge and to redeem: the "arrangement," the "pagoda," the funny form in which marriage as a constituted convention, familial affection of father and daughter, the business transactions entailed in the purchase of a work of art and an expanding imperialism, and an affair of sexual passion are interdependent, each relation contingent on the others for both the opportunity and the sanction to develop. All are or soon become monstrous: the conventional marriages become hollow if convenient shells; the familial affection becomes instituted incest; the business transactions become merely acquisitive instead of productive as Adam's "workshop of fortune" had been when operating at its earlier "miraculous white-heat"; the affair of passion culminates in an adulterous betrayal. But these distortions do not simply express the perversions that each relation has become; they express also the power and validity which each is in some measure acknowledged to have, the heightened pressure of energy and form which each acquires in interaction with the others, and the double pressure which James exerted in the effort to preserve "his form with closeness" while at the same time infusing the novel with an energy which "strains, or tends to burst, with a latent extravagance, its mould."

The first half of the novel—including the chapters which culminate in Adam's marriage and those which culminate in Charlotte's and the Prince's assignation in Gloucester—is informed by all these pressures and by James's willingness (a combination of desire and resignation) to incur in the arena of his fiction the risks of his art and the sacrifice it enacts. Adam's courtship of Charlotte, and the renewal of her affair with the Prince, are part of James's effort to construct a novel that will both accede to the conditions of his world and celebrate them while challenging them in the attempt to redeem them. Adam's marriage and Charlotte's assignation tax the flaw in the golden bowl and prepare for the incident later when it will be broken on the marble floor; but they also prepare for, and thus help to create, the possibility that it may be salvaged and filled with love. Each of the relations, the marriage and the affair, is a flawed bowl which images a sought perfection.

The institution of marriage which the Prince recommends blandly to Charlotte early in the novel (she should " 'marry some capital fellow' ") is the social relation which, in his eyes, most reveals people to each other and is acknowledged by Charlotte to be succinctly " 'the condition' " on which a place in her world depends since she declines the position of a " 'shop-girl' " or " 'old maid.' " Marriage, she declares to Adam, would give her " 'an existence' " and " 'a motive outside of myself.' " But the marriage arranged for her is as much a part of the world of shops as Maggie's marriage, whereby the enterprising Prince captured his bride and Adam Verver bought a precious title for his collection. Compensation for Charlotte's sacrifice of the Prince is what Fanny Assingham wants a " 'good' " marriage to bring her, as well as protection for the previously arranged marriage of Charlotte's lover to Maggie. Moreover, Maggie recommends marriage for Adam specifically as compensation for the loss of his daughter; Maggie's leaving his house, where she had been virtually " 'married' " to him, has thrust him on the " 'market.' " And when Maggie persuades Adam to invite Charlotte for a visit, she does so as an act of beneficence and as an opportunity to put Charlotte's talents to use in the new program of entertaining which Fanny has urged on her diffident American friends; Maggie will both help Charlotte and use her, though she will " 'admire her still more than I used her.' " (I, 58, 121, 311, 219, 85-86, 172, 181-190.)

Convenience, compensation, aesthetic mastery, and the careful negotiations of a tactful bargain characterize Adam's courtship and Charlotte's acceptance, and both the utility and the bargain in the beginning serve chiefly Adam's and Maggie's affection for each other. Having agreed that Charlotte's talents should not be " 'wasted,' " Adam finds himself liking what Maggie and Fanny tell him about her, "almost as if her portrait, by some eminent hand, were going on, so that he watched it grow under the multiplication of touches." He finds her "a domestic resource," meeting her often in his grandchild's nursery when she fills Maggie's place during Maggie's trip to Italy with the Prince. Adam has at least "an inkling" that he is, "as a taster of life, economically constructed" and that he has the odd habit of applying "the same measure of value" to "new human acquisitions" such as Charlotte as he does to "old Persian carpets," Oriental tiles, or Luini paintings. And James presents this "aesthetic principle" in Adam as something dangerously illicit but as yet contained safely within the tidy confines of Adam's domestic self and within the control of his bookkeeping. Though one of the "profane altar-fires," it feeds exclusively on "the idea (followed by appropriation) of plastic beauty," not spreading to consume the rest of the "spiritual furniture" of Adam's mind as it does "in so many cases." It has not "raised the smallest scandal in his economy at large," though Adam's aesthetic power is in the dubious position of lucky "bachelors or other gentlemen of pleasure who so manage their entertainment of compromising company that even the austerest housekeeper . . . never feels obliged to give warning." (I, 185, 193, 200-201, 196-197.)

The telling consideration for Adam, finally, is moral and aesthetic as well as compactly economical: by marrying Charlotte he will serve Maggie, playing along with her fancy that he is younger than his forty-seven years and convincing her that by marrying she has not "forsaken" him. The "whole call of his future to him, as a father" lights the landscape at Fawns (as it does the entire novel) as if by "some strange midnight sun," giving it "a spoken pretension to beauty" and the "inordinate size" of an "hallucination." The aim to serve Maggie falls in "beautifully" with the prospect of his marriage, and for Charlotte to serve likewise will be "the proper direction" for Charlotte's "leisure" to take. (I, 206-208.)

The marriage which Adam proposes to Charlotte, with Maggie's tacit encouragement, is well within the range of Adam's aesthetic and moral economy, as are the terms of Charlotte's acceptance. The occasion which brings Adam to the point of a proposal is his trip with Charlotte to Brighton to inspect the Damascene tiles which he has heard are in the possession of Mr. Gutermann-Seuss. The negotiations constitute a ceremony which precipitates and illuminates his decision to propose marriage. He girds himself for both the marriage proposal and the negotiations for the tiles, and Charlotte's sharing the trip with him not only quickens his affection but opens up new vistas for his future exploits as a buyer and connoisseur. With her enviable appreciation of " 'type' "—even, as the Prince has noticed, when it appears in "cabmen" and "faces at hucksters' stalls" in the vast London democracy—she leads Adam to relish the distinctive Semitic features of the numerous Gutermann-Seusses and to anticipate new delights in his future bargain hunts. She had seemed earlier to the Prince to match his "notion, perhaps not wholly correct, of a muse," and now her "free range of observation," her habit of registering "almost any 'funny impression,' " renders for James as well as for the reader and Adam the postures and accents of the "fat, ear-ringed aunts," the "glossy, cockneyfied . . . uncles," and the eleven "graduated offspring" of Mr. Gutermann-Seuss, the swarming family who surround the purchasers as if gathered "for some anniversary gregariously and religiously kept." Adam reflects that Charlotte's taste for the "funny" would in the future alter his "customary hunt for the possible prize, the inquisitive play of his accepted monomania" and make of it a "somewhat more boisterously refreshing . . . sport." For the transaction proper, Charlotte and Adam are led into a private chamber, but afterward they rejoin the family and Adam is "merged in the elated circle formed by Charlotte's free response to the collective caress of all the shining eyes," and they share "heavy cake and port wine" in a ceremony which gives "their transaction," as Charlotte notices, "the touch of some mystic rite of old Jewry." (I, 106, 47, 212-213, 216.)

So solemnized and celebrated, the transaction is one of the most complex events in the novel since it founds his proposal of marriage on an act which is both a commercial transaction and a ceremony, which the proposal itself consummates but also supersedes. On the way to the Gutermann-Seuss's Adam considers his "majestic scheme" of securing happiness for himself, Maggie, and Charlotte as carefully as if he held "a glazed picture in its right relation to the light." He first associates his intention with the volatile young heroes in fiction who pour out the language of love in enviable soliloquies; in the abstract diction assigned him by James, Adam speaks enviously of the sheer power to " 'speak.' " Yet he distinguishes his "scheme" from theirs, since they pursue the feverishly impetuous "path of passion properly so called"; Adam feels that his plan to marry is "a thing of less joy than a passion" but that it might nevertheless "have the essential property" and "dignity" of "providing for more contingencies." Marriage as he envisions it is a substitute for the difficulties and deviousness encountered on "the path of passion properly so called," and it gains its more lasting utility at the cost of passion. (I, 210-211.)

Correspondingly, when with Charlotte and Mr. Gutermann-Seuss during the transaction, Adam finds that his experience is different, though different not from transactions in fiction but from those in comparable "bourgeois back parlours" when he has "pried and prowled," risking "the very bloom of honour." On those typical occasions he lingered over inspecting the purchase, enjoyed the "criticism" of the treasure, the bargaining ("what was called discussion") and thought predominantly of "his acquisition and the figure of his cheque." Now, by contrast, he finds that the transaction proceeds swiftly in silence because his attention is engrossed by Charlotte's presence; the "predominance of Charlotte's very person" makes the deferment of talk about the purchased tiles as pleasant "as some joy promised a lover by his mistress, or as a big bridal bouquet held patiently behind her." The tiles are perfect—"scarcely more meant to be breathed upon . . . than the cheek of royalty"— but the monied American Patron with the simple insolence of empire buys them in a transaction which for the first time in his career is as "fine as the perfection perceived" in the regal treasure he buys; and the swift perfection of his decision is owing to Charlotte's presence and his accelerating intention to propose to her. It is in view of "the relation of intimacy with him . . . which she had accepted" by virtue of being present with him and, particularly, hearing the stipulated "sum"—as a consequence, that is, of Adam's "having exposed her" to the "hard business-light" of the chamber where they negotiate "with the treasure and its master"—that Adam carries through his proposal. James declares that, "fabulous as this truth may sound," Adam finds in the experience they have shared the grounds for proposing to Charlotte, either as an obligation incurred by affection or as a penalty for transgression: it is "a sentimental link, an obligation of delicacy" or it is "perhaps one of the penalties of its opposite," that is, a penalty for compromising her. (I, 214-216.)

The espisode is crucial for James's fable because it reveals in a fantastic light indeed the faults of the marriage arranged for Adam and Charlotte while also providing the basis for according their marriage any stature at all as a moral and intimate form. Their intimacy during the transaction is exaggerated if not created in Adam's anticipations, for the implications of Charlotte's silent presence remained undefined except insofar as they are anticipated hopefully by Adam. But the occasion brings into new focus both the earlier affair of Charlotte and the Prince and the episode in the Bloomsbury shop.

The earlier affair had been an affair of passion without contractual or commercial considerations, though the Prince's ap-

preciation of Charlotte's charms is possessive and his willingness to take them or leave them is condescending. Their affair
was an emotional and sexual involvement which was stronger
on Charlotte's part but one which could be abruptly terminated on grounds which the Assinghams and the reader must
hypothesize. The transaction at Brighton, by contrast, is a stunning and appalling amalgam of intimacy and commerce, with
Adam breathing more intimately on the cheek of the tiles he
buys than on Charlotte and sacrificing appreciative pleasures
to the efficiency of his purchase, and with Charlotte indifferently
taking part, then responding freely to the "collective caress of
all the shining eyes" of the Gutermann-Seusses. The incident
is made to seem decidedly more illicit than the affairs of the
fictional gallants which Adam contrasts to his own because it
is distinctly void of the "passion properly so called" which
theirs, like Amerigo's and Charlotte's, may claim.

Yet the scene presents paradoxically at the same time the
image of a relation intimately engaged in and publicly sanctioned by a ceremony, and if it lacks the "joy" presumably
known to the Prince and Charlotte, this ceremony nevertheless, like familiar engagement and wedding ceremonies in western culture, sanctions a marriage which is not yet consummated
as a marriage or fully achieved: it does not celebrate a marriage
already accomplished but one which it provides for and helps
create. Though Adam's and Charlotte's relation during the negotiations lacks the passion of love, it has the sanction of ceremony and it is closer to a shared communion than the business
deals which Adam has known to the peril of his honor in other
parlors.

Moreover, it is closer to intimacy than were the Prince and
Charlotte on the telling occasion when they found the bowl in
Bloomsbury. Then they talked in their familiar Italian, but
the Prince left the shop, leaving Charlotte to negotiate alone
with "their entertainer." Now Charlotte remains with Adam
in the parlor where they are together closeted with the tiles
and their "master." Her silent presence inspires Adam not only
to his suspiciously speedy efficiency but to the "perfection"
of his purchase and then removes his mind from the tiles to
talk with Charlotte about them, the lover's gift or "bridal

bouquet" he anticipates enjoying. In other words, she inspires the transformation of an ordinary business negotiation into a more intimate transaction than Adam has ever known, stimulating Adam to imagine the incident, at least, as an affair, with Charlotte as his intimate partner. At the same time, she leads him to give precedence, over the business deal and the beautiful tiles, to her. In the context of the novel the two are compromised by the incident yet bound closer by a certain measure of affection and interest, and the incident moreover joins them by anticipation in the imagined or prospective form of union in marriage. And Adam, unlike the Prince in his affair in Rome, finds in the event at Brighton the grounds of an obligation to propose marriage, as he proceeds instantly to do.

The fantastic scene is powerful because of the many pressures it exerts which contribute to the *funny form* of James's novel. It makes of the fictive courtship and marriage of Adam and Charlotte inside the novel a contorted image of numerous actualities which either do or might exist outside it, all the more contorted an image for the range of its relevance and the variety within the conjunction it forges: conventional marriage as a domestic, sexual, and commerical convenience, deliberately chosen by the partners but subordinating marital to familial and occupational concerns; the traffic of prostitution; the transformation of an ordinary acquisitive enterprise in the realms of business and of taste into a more discriminating, intimate, and viable experience.

Within the novel, the fictive marriage is a promising though perilously flawed form which virtually demands that it be either violated or reconstituted in the name of passion, a terrifyingly brittle vessel to sustain the burden of advantages, kindnesses, and other expectations intended for it and the pressure of needs and impulses which may threaten it from without. The fictive marriage subjects the actualities of the institution to an appallingly intense light while embodying also the promise or ideal communion of the form: yet the promise itself is flawed and must be recast in the crucible of experience. When the action of Book Second culminates in Charlotte's agreement to marry and the messages of approval which Maggie and the Prince (with what amounts to their "caressing eyes") send on to Paris, the dialogue and the telegrams simply complete the odd arrangement already provided for in the exotic "back parlour" at Brighton.

In discussing the proposal, Adam and Charlotte display a mixture of candor and of intentions unexplored or undisclosed, contingencies anticipated, dismissed, or veiled. They bargain tactfully, and Charlotte warns that he may learn later or perhaps never know the unpleasant things about her; she asks him to consider that she might " 'get what I want for less' " than marriage to him would entail and that he might express his kindness in some other way, and warns that his wife might be his daughter's rival for his affection. Adam encourages her to " 'make something' " or get some advantage from his affection for her, and, to reassure her concern for Maggie, admits that he is marrying in part to relieve Maggie of the fear that she has "forsaken" him. Though Charlotte questions whether this idea is " 'quite enough to marry me for,' " she concedes that the plan is " 'beautiful' " and that Adam has " 'certainly worked it out!' " She must suppress a sudden "small cry" when Adam suggests that they join Maggie and the Prince in Paris to seek their approval, so keen is her excitement and anxiety at the prospect of being often near the Prince, but she agrees to await Maggie's approval. (I, 220-225.)

Adam's "majestic scheme" hinges on Charlotte's accession to his insistence that his " 'luck' " is nothing without Charlotte to complete his good fortune and " 'make me right,' " and it hinges too on the approval of his daughter and son-in-law. Maggie's telegram of congratulations lacks her usual " 'grace' " as Charlotte sees it in being addressed to Adam alone, and Adam mistakenly thinks that the second telegram, to Charlotte, is also from Maggie and thanks his daughter for in effect giving him his wife. But under the odd circumstances James has contrived, Charlotte tells Adam succinctly " 'I'll give you what you ask,' " and the novel's "majestic scheme" is given the sanction of this crucial incident. The second telegram, drawn from the "cartridge-box" of a uniformed messenger as he approaches the "stronghold of the concierge," is addressed to Charlotte alone and is not from the daughter but from the son-in-law. And the **telegram**, which Adam in his confidence feels no need to read when Charlotte offers it to him, is one which might prevent the marriage if Adam knew its contents but which secures Charlotte's consent. When the message is later divulged, it completes the fascinating though terrifyingly grotesque design on which the novel is founded. James puts the opening phrase in the Prince's original French (the language he had once intimated was the "most apt" for "discriminations . . . of the invidious kind"), then translates the rest into the Jamesian English which Amerigo speaks perfectly: " '*À la guerre comme à la guerre then. . . . We must lead our lives as we see them; but I am charmed with your courage and almost surprised at my own.*' " (I, 235-240, 6, 290.)

Even two years later Charlotte cannot resolve with certainty the ambiguities of the treasured telegram. She wonders whether the Prince, in giving his more than perfunctory consent, was indicating that he felt "secure" in resisting the temptation which her proximity would present or "seasoned" in welcoming it, or whether he had the courage simply to face the increased strain on his conduct which her marriage would entail. But the telegram defines the "moral energy," as James had called it in "The Art of Fiction," which is required of his art, and of Charlotte and Amerigo, by the fantastic arrangement which James's "scheme" (the "sacrament of execution" which "marries" form and substance), along with the motives of characters and the habits, conditions, and goals of their society, together have produced. (I, 291.)

Within two years, the arrangements have produced the "crisis" which Charlotte is prepared to enjoy at the opening of Book Third, a crisis which challenges not only the marital and familial lives of the chief participants but the exceedingly fortunate society which their interlocked marriages represent. The marriages not only facilitate but institutionalize the dangerously close though authentically tender affection of Adam and his daughter and grandchild, while institutionalizing also, in an accepted and even familial form, the charged companionship of Charlotte and the Prince, renewing the passion they have known. The marriages singly and together become in fact a mockery of the form; they are a mere convenience, serving the almost indolent domesticity of the wealthy father and daughter (whose disappearance from society at large into the limbo of their affluence and familial intimacy is dramatized by the novel's focus on the experience of Charlotte and Amerigo and the Assinghams), and sustaining the fruitless public rituals when the Prince and Charlotte appear together on formal occasions. When Charlotte is first seen by the reader after her marriage, at the Ambassador's reception, the flaws in the original arrangement have already come more vividly to light, but Charlotte and the Prince are not the only ones who have threatened the marriages and the possible communion which, along with the possible debasements, they might afford. (1, 246.)

In his use of Charlotte and the Prince as centers of attention James presents the deterioration of the marriages through the eyes of characters whose opportunism and passivity have contributed to the crisis but who also suffer from it and are in part its victims. Adam's career as a Patron has (for all we hear about it) virtually ceased, and since the birth of the Principino, he and Maggie have retired within the debilitating ease of the marriages. Adam has thought proudly of Maggie and the Prince as an image of "marriage demonstrated" beyond the experience of his own first marriage, particularly since the birth of their male child, and his affections have become monopolized by his daughter in her familial role as wife and mother and by his grandson. The novel presents this affection as an out-and-out usurpation of the Prince's position as father and husband.

Both the attitudes which *distinguish* Adam's feeling for his grandson from his feeling toward art and those which *connect* the two, contribute to his displacement of the Prince. Adam insists that a painting resemble the master who is thought to have produced it, but he does not judge other matters by their "looks," and "so far as he was not taking life as a collector, he was taking it . . . as a grandfather." Yet if the Principino's features display any claim of Amerigo's to his paternity, Adam ignores them, and while he thinks the boy more "precious" than other "small pieces he had handled," he can "manipulate and dandle," "toss and catch again" the infant with what prove to be possessive hands. In what the novel wryly brands an odd twist to the "old story," Maggie and Adam have "converted the precious creature into a link" not between parents but between "a mamma and a grandpapa," and readers are asked to see the boy as "a hapless half-orphan, with the place of immediate male parent swept bare and open to the next nearest sympathy." The child is cloistered at Fawns in chambers as guarded as the nursery in "a royal palace," yet even in the case of the royal Prince his "absence" is preferred; he must enjoy the child when Adam's priority allows a merely "auxiliary admiration" and must accept wonderingly the American's characteristic surrender to the young and Adam's "impunity of appropriation." (I, 146-147, 156-157.)

Adam's companionship with Maggie likewise has relegated the Prince to the periphery of their family circle, leaving it to Fanny Assingham to amuse him (as she is left to amuse callers) while Maggie and Adam converse apart in a tête-à-tête of their own, a situation that has become more outlandish after Adam's and Charlotte's marriage. And while Charlotte's disdainful irony in explaining the situation to an appalled Fanny Assingham at the Ambassador's reception is a clear sign that Charlotte and the Prince are contemplating doing something about their plight, the irony does not discredit Charlotte's assertions but highlights glaringly the abnormalities of the situation and the crisis in which she determines to act.

A slight indisposition has kept Adam from the reception, Charlotte explains, and he had insisted that both Maggie and Charlotte go to the party with the Prince; Maggie has suddenly left before even entering the reception rooms to return to her father, and consequently Charlotte and the Prince are there alone; the father and daughter doubtless are enjoying a "little frugal picnic," a "little party at home." Their separation after Adam's marriage has simply increased their desire to be together, and since they now no longer literally live together Maggie arranges for visits; they virtually pay calls on each other and engage in "make-believe renewals of their old life." Though the two couples live in separate households, Adam and Maggie now have "more contact and more intimacy" than before. The affectionate and wealthy father and daughter have in effect " 'placed' " both Charlotte and Amerigo on the edges of their routines, if not of their affections, and one should, " 'as they say . . . know one's place.' " In sum, Charlotte's husband treats her as being " 'of less importance to him than some other woman,' " despite her efforts to " 'make him capable of a greater' " affection than what Fanny calls his " 'natural interest in his daughter.' " (I, 162, 252, 256-262.)

The Prince, on the same occasion, brings out the effect on all of them of Maggie's and Adam's wealth and good nature, which is namely to bring to bear, as the Prince had noticed early, astonishing amounts of "American good faith" and to afford, for themselves at least, "innocent pleasures, pleasures without penalties"; the "absence of prejudice backed by the presence of money" suggests the open high confidence, and the power which implements and protects it, that the Ververs display. At the Ambassador's reception, the Prince points out that he as well as Charlotte is " 'in Mr. Verver's boat,' " which floats at all, as Fanny understands, only because his "father-in-law's great fortune" has provided "the element" in which he "could pecuniarily float." Whatever the motives of the characters to begin with, and whatever their motives become, the Verver money, affluence, and trusting kindness toward others have a tangible impact, both corrosive and creative, on the action. (I, 10-11, 17, 268.)

With their solicitude for each other, Adam and Maggie are able to spend hours and evenings together (there are quarters at the Ververs' house for Maggie and the baby when they stay over), while encouraging Charlotte and Amerigo to find companionship with each other and indeed using them to represent the two families in social affairs. Charlotte cannot escape the responsibility she shares by claiming that the " ' "doing" ' " has *all* been the Ververs' and that " 'it's all a matter of what they've done *to* us,' " nor is the Prince exonerated by simply noting that they themselves have been more than passive in accepting the Ververs' beneficence and the marriages. But James's "language of exaggeration" (like Kate's in *The Wings of the Dove*) does define a real pressure which bears down on Charlotte and the Prince in declaring that "no more extraordinary decree had ever been launched against such victims than this of forcing them against their will into a relation of mutual close contact that they had done everything to avoid." (I, 374, 289.)

And the Prince reveals more than his own negligent and

shrewd deference to Adam's power ("treating him" as he and Charlotte do with the deference due "a Pope, a King, a President . . . or just a beautiful Author") when he wonders at the connection between Adam's familial affections and his banking affairs: Adam governs the Prince's relation to Maggie as he does "everything else," relieving him of "all anxiety about his married life in the same manner in which he relieved him on the score of his bank-account." The Prince is amused rather than irritated by the situation which leaves him still on the circumference of his new family, but he perceives that Adam's strangely close relation with his daughter has "the same deep intimacy as the commercial, the financial association founded, far down, on a community of interest." Like "capitalists and bankers," "illustrious collectors," "American fathers," and Americans generally, the Ververs do each other favors and do him the favor of the " 'treat' " he is enjoying "at his father-in-law's expense." (I, 205, 292-293.)

The " 'treat' " is the fluent "ease" which is "guaranteed" him in his marriage, but it brings with it the situation which leaves him literally jobless (as Bob Assingham emphasizes) and with no office other than those of father and husband, and with nothing in *these* roles to do. The Ververs in their marriages stifle the imagination; the "dagger" and poisoned cup imply admittedly old-fashioned plots, but the Americans rule out any comparable service "worthy" of a truly "personal relation"; they rule out any intriguing responsibility, any "charming charge," any genuinely interesting burden to assume in tribute to "confidence deeply reposed." The Prince's situation is the "dreary little crisis" which he considers, just after ruminating on the Ververs' money, in the empty drawing room of his own house and begins to pace "again and again the stretch of polished floor," to discover in a moment that Charlotte, having found Maggie in charge and safely occupied in Adam's household, has come in private to visit her stepson-in-law and former lover. (I, 292, 294, 314-315.)

It is the " 'bore of comfort,' " as Lord Warburton called it in *The Portrait of a Lady*, as well as good fortune's protecting ease, which helps produce the crisis for the marriages, but Charlotte seeks excitement in the life that with their help and consent has

been arranged for all of them. She relishes the opportunity at
the Ambassador's reception to be seen, "in truth crowned," in
the Prince's company, "exposed" and "a bit brazen" but stunning, and convinced, like Gilbert Osmond, that "materials to
work with had been all she required and that there were none
too precious for her to understand and use." And there is mounting evidence that she and Amerigo may begin, as Fanny thinks,
"*really* treating their subject" in intimacy and "finding it much
more interesting." Yet Charlotte finds it boring to spend hours
sight-seeing alone, and equally dull to perform, as " 'part of one's
contract,' " the "duties of a remunerated office" as formal hostess
for both households, putting up with the "arid social sands"
which seem to her astute eye the forged coins in the "debased
currency" which their lives have become. (I, 246-247, 271, 303,
317-318.)

A "debased currency" is an apt metaphor for the adulterations
which characterize the domestic lives of Adam and Maggie, innocent and benign but relaxed and withdrawn in the perfunctory routines of their familial lives, and it is apt also for
those adulterations that permeate the society surrounding them
which is epitomized by the party around Easter at Matcham, a
reincarnation of Newmarch in *The Sacred Fount* where Charlotte and the Prince plan their assignation. Maggie and Adam
decline the invitation to Lord and Lady Castledean's house
party, but Amerigo and Charlotte attend. And the Prince reveals for James, within the tawdry though glittering textures of
the life around him, the rudiments of social intercourse which
become the matrix for both the imminent betrayal and the
imminent redemption in James's drama. At Matcham, as at
Newmarch, people are brought into an arranged though shifting scene which stirs with change, creating the prospect of
"possible new combinations" and "the quickened play" of sheer
"propinquity," even if it produces no more than the assignation
which Lady Castledean will arrange, once her titled husband returns to town, with the "sleek," "civil," white-collared Mr.
Blint. (I, 330, 352.)

The Matcham world is more practiced in sociability on the
grand scale than the Ververs', and it displays no trace of familial
concerns; but in crucial ways, which the abstract diction and

extravagant oddity of James's form bring to light, it fosters the notably relaxed tolerance and risks the specifically comfortable freedom which Adam and Maggie encourage in their spouses and which, in an utterly different but equally risky version, they display in their own strange intimacy. The "happy boldness" with which the Prince and Charlotte, and others at Matcham, mingle together and accept it as simply "funny" is precisely that "eccentricity of associated freedom" which in a different version characterizes Maggie and Adam also. Matcham has simply done *to* the conscience in a cruel way what Maggie and Adam unintentionally have done *with* it in their benign manner: they have isolated it and rendered it safely ineffectual in its subservience to bland good faith in their own proprieties and the services others perform for them. Matcham keeps the conscience at hand as a harmless and useful seamstress, a "snubbed" but docile "poor relation . . . for whose tacit and abstemious presence, never betrayed by the rattle of her rusty machine, a room in the attic and a place at the side-table were decently usual." (I, 330-331.)

In the world of Matcham, Amerigo's innermost self stands half outside or half hidden by its rites, while the "good people who had, in the night of time, unanimously invented them . . . still, in the prolonged afternoon of their good faith, unanimously, even if a trifle automatically, practised them." The "complacency" and "seated solidity" leave the Prince "puzzled as to the element of staleness in all the freshness and of the freshness in all the staleness, of innocence in the guilt and of guilt in the innocence," the mixture by which the "enquiring mind" is so "sharply challenged." The Prince's actions themselves remain rather "automatic," but the more courageous Charlotte finds a way within those drab rituals to renew her love with the Prince, and the re-emergence of their passion is at once the final debasement of the form their lives have taken and a challenge to it which provides the half-furtive, half-bold basis for its redemption. (I, 327-328, 354.)

The "congruity" of Charlotte's visiting Amerigo in private at Portland Place which strikes him as almost an act of "violence," the "harmony" of her "breaking into" his vision, is incorrect but nonetheless consonant not only with his increasing desire but with the negligent good faith of the Ververs and the design of the novel whose marriages have sanctioned and even plotted the deepening association of the two, and the developing affair is presented with all the taut ambivalence of its strange morality and its dubious beauty. For the marriages have produced an almost "ideal perfection" of "freedom," a measure of license which is not only shielded but actually created by the interlocking marriages which facilitate their relation, and the Prince feels "the sense of the past" so intensely "revived" when Charlotte suddenly appears that "the future" is joined with their past passion "in a long embrace of arms and lips." As he and Charlotte try again " 'the old feelings' " and compare the pathos of Charlotte's childless marriage to the strange intensity with which Maggie and Adam " 'adore together' " Amerigo's son, Charlotte insists that they must, like Adam and Maggie, " 'act in concert' " —have faith indeed, the Prince adds, " 'as we trust the saints in glory' " and as " 'fortunately . . . we can.' " They can oblige Maggie and Adam while converting their companionship into intimacy, shielding it from observation and shielding Adam and Maggie from knowing it; they can, as the Prince sees later, so guard their "intimacy" with the "vigilance of 'care' " as never to expose it and never "consciously to wound" the feelings of husband or wife. Then they join, "grasping and grasped," in an embrace which converts the delight of "response" into the "pressure" of more intense desire and "with a violence that had sighed itself the next moment to the longest and deepest of stillnesses they passionately sealed their pledge." (I, 295-298, 300, 307-312, 325.)

This intensely sensuous passion is illicit when judged by the moral codes of their society, though that society's affluence encourages it and its behavior sanctions it, but their renewal of their past love has a dignity which the perfunctory professions and habits of their world (notably Lady Castledean and Mr. Blint) do not display. And their love brings to a crisis the passion which the novel must control but which it must also with envy and terror bring into play to infuse in turn the forms which threaten passion. Charlotte provides the initiative and the train schedule for their afternoon at the inn in Gloucester, but the

Prince recognizes the strange opportunity that is presented him, the occasion which calls for the combination of abandon and responsible decision which Charlotte and he finally display. The sun-lit day before him seems "a great picture, from the hand of a genius, presented to him as a prime ornament for his collection"—as if he, like Adam, were enjoying "his absolutely appointed and enhanced possession of it." He expects as usual in his "commerce" with women that his books will show a "balance in his favor," and the "sense of beauty" which he shares with James is stirred by the opportunity prepared for him by the vague permissiveness of Maggie and the calculations of Charlotte —by what, in sum, the novel has provided for and calls his "remarkable fortune." (I, 350-351.)

As he watches the other men (excepting Mr. Blint) leave to return to their occupations, each a "lubricated item of the great social political administrative *engrenage*," he recognizes that for Maggie's "convenience" he has lost the respect of these people (and probably the reader) by relinquishing any role as provider, prince, father, or husband: he has relinquished "his real situation in the world," and welcomes the chance to do something "quite beautiful and . . . harmonious, something wholly his own." The opportunity looms before him like a "precious pearl" in Charlotte, with her traveling jacket and her time-table, in the beckoning cathedral towers of lustrous " 'Glo'ster, Glo'ster, Glo'ster' " and the " 'tomb of some old king' " that Charlotte vaguely recalls, the tomb of Edward II, the deposed king who was betrayed by his wife and then wrongly murdered, whose grave became a shrine for visitors bringing rich gifts to the cathedral. The opportunity shines forth too in the radiant day at Easter time which is " 'a great gold cup that we must somehow drain.' " Amerigo is, to his calculated advantage, simply "taking . . . what had been given him," and Charlotte reminds him of her earlier offer of " 'the gilded crystal bowl in the little Bloomsbury shop,' " the " 'beautiful one, the real one, that I offered you so long ago and that you wouldn't have.' " The Prince does recall the " 'treacherous cracked thing' " that she had wanted to " 'palm off on me' " and the " 'little swindling Jew . . . who backed you up,' " scorning any imperfections in its harmony for himself and leaving it to Charlotte to "risk" them while he takes a more complacent view of their good fortune.[10] (I, 352-354, 357-359.)

Their afternoon in Gloucester is never rendered in the novel, but Charlotte's consciously arranged offer, and the Prince's eager exploitation of it, project in anticipation a more fully achieved relation, a more intensely intimate passion, and a greater strength of commitment than anything yet rendered in the novel, including Adam's and Maggie's tender and terrifyingly close regard for each other and for Maggie's son, though these are vividly enough suggested through the minds of Maggie and Adam and through Charlotte's and the Prince's wonder at them. And the scene at Matcham which prepares for the lovers' reunion exceeds in impact the other scenes which come closest to matching it in power, the scenes in the Bloomsbury shop and in Brighton and Paris which bring the action of the earlier sections to tentative, preparatory resolutions. These scenes, each given prominence in the novel's structure, establish the context and rhythm which define Charlotte's and Amerigo's reunion at once as a tentative or partial consummation of the novel's design and a betrayal of its aims. Charlotte's and the Prince's affair of passion, and Maggie and Adam's relation, are given the same status in the novel: that of a strained and contorted fusion of what is authentic, normative, and good with what is false, perverted, and evil. And both relations give the measure of the other and in their antagonism create the pressure for the remaking of the marriages and the reforming of the love contained within them. Charlotte now finally offers the Prince the flawed bowl she had not bought, and it may now be possessed and filled with the conscious enjoyment of the passion they will drain from the cup.

But if the metaphor of the cracked and gilded bowl which Charlotte invokes defines the prospect of a more intimate communion in passion, it defines with equal clarity another perspective: the golden bowl remains in Bloomsbury still unpurchased, and what Charlotte offers and the Prince delightedly

10 Henry D. M. Spence-Jones, *The White Robe of Churches . . . Pages from the Story of Gloucester Cathedral* (New York, 1900), pp. 147-149.

takes is a treacherous substitute for the wedding gift she did not buy for Maggie and the gift she could not offer to a lover who will not deign to consider receiving it from her. Their reunion, while it is not at all what Adam would knowingly sanction, is in strange keeping with Charlotte's agreement " 'to give what you ask' " and with Adam's behavior since, asking for very little and relegating Charlotte to her serviceable " 'place' " while closeting his affections principally with Maggie and her son. Yet the furtive affair with the Prince is a betrayal of the confidence Charlotte had encouraged at Brighton, and it exploits the trust which she and Amerigo have encouraged in Adam since, as well as being a betrayal of the partnership he had imagined sharing with her in buying the tiles and sharing the cake and wine afterward with the admiring family of Mr. Gutermann-Seuss. The effect of Charlotte's and the Prince's strange daring is an action which creates the evil of the betrayal they perpetrate yet creates also the promise of redeeming passion, and James's art is implicated in both the evil and the promise of redemption by the crisis to which his fictive marriages have given form.

The challenge of that crisis to the marriages and to the form of James's novel is dramatized in the last chapters of the first volume when the Assinghams confront it, with terror and compassion, from within the communion of their own intimate embrace. They confront it in the way the reader must—namely, by imagining it—and they begin already for James, within the achieved form of the first volume, to salvage the situation and redeem the promise of *The Golden Bowl*. James's narrative strategy in these chapters is the epitome of the form of the entire novel, for instead of rendering the reunion in Gloucester he gives the imaginings of the Assinghams which anticipate it and then project beyond it the prospect of a denouement. Without the grounds for picturing the towers of Gloucester at Easter time or the " 'tomb of some old king' " which James has given the reader's imagination, they sketch in and prepare for the sacrificial drama which Maggie and the others enact in the second volume, imagining in their desperation that "Charlotte and the Prince must be saved—so far as consistently speaking of them as still safe might save them," and beginning, with the absolute idiocy which is imaged in their name and which Maggie will bring to perfection, to project the faith and sustain the illusion which gild the bowl so as to join in the process of transforming it.

[III]

THE REDEMPTIVE PROCESS

THE PROCESS is redeemed, and its risks and the cost in suffering are measured, through Maggie's assumption of responsibility for it as she becomes James's mediating center of consciousness and the heroine of the drama being built around her.

The drama is at once "more abstract and more living" (as James had written of Ibsen) for the bare " 'middle-class' " austerity of its materials, and it takes place in a world which is both discovered and constructed, a world which is a combination of pressures and forms that James earlier could define, in the famous passage in his study of Hawthorne, only in terms of their absence. But these "absent things" are articulated in the novel in the glaring abstraction of its materials and forms: they are present in *The Golden Bowl* but present only as ghosts of their former embodiments or projected versions of their future forms, and the ostensible England of its setting is a world in decay which is still continuous with a world in the making, a world which James's imagination had recognized in the America of Hawthorne.

In James's novel as in Hawthorne's America there is "no State, in the European sense," and "no sovereign" and "no aristocracy"; only their dim remnants appear at times in the mere office and costume of an unnamed Ambassador, the glimpse of Lady Castledean absorbed in Mr. Blint, a disembodied "Personage" at a reception, the title "Prince" with no family name given to fill in the lineage of Amerigo. Servants are reduced to mere names or shrink into a single appendage which defines their utility: "the hand employed at Fawns for mayonnaise of salmon." [11] (I, 264; II, 301.)

There is "no church, no clergy," only their remnants and effigies in the pendant Maggie wears or the "good holy hungry" Father Mitchell who conducts for two weeks the "local rites flourishing under Maggie's munificence" and who attends a "ceremonious semblance of luncheon" at Fawns, prattling and

[11] *Hawthorne*, in *The Shock of Recognition*, p. 460.

twiddling his thumbs over a "satisfied stomach," with no more than a perfunctory guess as to the moral crisis around him. His is the Catholicism of the Prince's Rome that the principal characters are dispensing with. Adam prefers to peruse his mail on Sunday mornings, though he is "loosely willing, always, to let [the Roman Church] be taken for *his*" and is pleased that his and his first wife's affiliation with it made "the stage firm," provided "the solid ease," for the "drama" of Maggie's marriage to the Prince. Charlotte's "apparent detachment . . . from any practices of devotion" is conspicuous to Maggie, and Charlotte may have lied about her obligations to Father Mitchell, but Maggie admires Charlotte's strength and ingenuity in having to do without the solace afforded by exposure and confession. Maggie is aware how she herself "has dispensed with him," intending someday "to confess that she hadn't confessed" but fearing now the "breath of a better wisdom . . . , of heavenly help itself" lest it upset her undertaking: she keeps the burden "on her own conscience" and carries in her own "weak, stiffened hand a glass filled to the brim." [12] (ii, 297-298, 300-301; i, 152.)

There is indeed "no Epsom nor Ascot" in the accessible environs of Matcham and Fawns, or Eaton Square and Portland Place, but what looms large instead is not a void but the forms (the "joke," as James called them) which remained for the provincial American of Hawthorne's and later generations: the strained institutions of the family, commerce, marriage, and the arts which James challenges but also celebrates, the funny form of his own novel, the great "over-glazed rotunda" which shelters an affluent society undergoing a crisis of transformation and mustering the "possible heroism of perfunctory things." The ritual forms and actions which James's novel joins with Maggie in making, rather than any comparable given resources which comprised the mere stage for the drama itself, confront the crisis of transformation and sustain the process of redemption.[13]

Late in the novel James remarks that Maggie's "place" is not charted on any "map of the social relations," but James provides the new geography: the atlas of the "fundamental pas-

12 *Ibid.*
13 *Ibid.*

sions." Maggie's location on the chart of elemental passion and the vocabulary for expressing it James renders in a bizarre contrast between the Prince and Maggie at the time when they have abandoned the grandeur of Fawns and have settled in the more constricted comfort of their London house—an act which is the " ' "reduction to its simplest expression," ' " as the Prince puts it for James, " ' "of what we *are* doing." ' " The Prince's "place" is that of an ancestral statue fixed on its pedestal, the position "made for him beforehand" by history, by "ancestors, examples, traditions, habits." But if Maggie resembles a statue (as she does to Adam), her nymph-like, nun-like form has been cut loose from her pedestal, "set in motion by the remarkable infusion of a modern impulse," and her position moves. Her "place" is the "improvised" outpost of a "settler or a trader in a new country": it is even that of "some Indian squaw with a papoose on her back and barbarous bead-work to sell." Maggie begins to demand the "privilege of passion," possession of her claim as settler, and her right of access to the trading post as squaw at the opening of the second volume when her place on-stage is converted by her imagination and James's fiat into a generically dramatic and moral role and, trying to find access to the forbidding Pagoda which looms in her garden, she begins consciously and deviously to play her part. And the innocence which heretofore it has been her good fortune simply to exemplify, in a version made dubious by her easy diffusion of confidence and good intentions, becomes the culpable innocence—what Professor R.W.B. Lewis has called the "aggressive innocence"— which her performance at once tempers and makes effectual.[14] (II, 323-325; I, 187-188.)

Maggie looks back on her welcome to the Prince after his return from Matcham (and the afternoon in Gloucester) as if the scene were a "great picture hung on the wall of her daily life, for her to make what she would of," and the novel forges in her remembered scene the inseparable fusion of her passion, her sense of possession, and her drama. Seminal though discomforting doubts have begun to interact with her good faith, and she can recognize that for the first time she was "acting up to the

[14] R.W.B. Lewis, *The American Adam: Innocence Tragedy and Tradition in the Nineteenth Century* (Chicago: Phoenix Books, 1955), p. 154.

full privilege of passion" and can see the need for "the proper playing of one's part." In arranging by "calculation" that Amerigo should not find her, as usual, at her father's house but find "his wife" waiting for him "in her own drawing-room at the hour when she would most properly be there," she has staged herself in a carefully chosen dress and has staged a succession of "moments" which seem effective in retrospect "almost in the manner of the different things done during a scene on the stage." The "violence" of his "surprise" is marked, and, without her saying aloud that the "cup" of her need for him is "too full," he sees that she is *"testifying"* in deed and gesture "that she adored and missed and desired him." For Maggie, both the need for "self-control" and the need for "large expression" are met by her action, and it leaves her with an "excitement" so intense that she feels she must conceal it as if it were a "thing born" of an illicit "misadventure." The excitement of "acting up to the full privilege of passion" is something which she, like the "clinging young mother of an unlawful child," must keep hidden. She does not go up with the Prince while he bathes for dinner (Maggie recalls offering to help him dress, but he had thought he could best go "straighter and faster alone"), but when he returns she is thrilled with her newly felt "sense of possession." (II, 7-11, 16-20.)

The grace of Maggie's histrionic performance and the actions she helps others perform become the foundation for the entire novel, with the following consequences: her marriage is prepared for passion, Adam can live vicariously in Maggie's experience while separate from her and can return to America and his cultural center there, and Charlotte is led to make herself "interested" in her husband and his career as Patron in the new American imperium. In achieving this resolution, James does not hide his commitment to the action any more than he conceals the willed deceit—the make-believe—which Maggie's performance entails. Nor does he hide the arbitrariness or luck which favors the "good fortune," as Maggie calls it, of her marriage, and arms her with knowledge by bringing her to the shop in Bloomsbury and the flawed beauty of the bowl she buys. Instead, he acknowledges them and brings into the drama the torment of their recognition and the recognition of the limitations of Maggie's and the Prince's sheer domesticity, the limitations of Charlotte's and Adam's childless, passionless marriage, and the shortcomings of the civilization to which they devote their efforts. The second volume is tense with terror while measuring the cost in beauty, integrity, and suffering which is exacted in the process of breaking with the past and redeeming it, while discovering that the bowl must not only be gilded to salvage the past but that it must be broken, it must be sacrificed in order to create even the promise that the reality it symbolizes may be transformed. (II, 21, 304.)

It is not only the playing, but the creating, of her role that joins Maggie to James in the arena of *The Golden Bowl* and brings about her acknowledgment of complicity in the action and prepares for the full assumption of responsibility for it that Fanny has imagined Maggie will adopt. Moreover, it is finally her performance that renders her a sacred symbol in the sacrifice which the novel enacts. Only when she begins to perform, does Maggie begin to recognize that she has been too passive in her marriage, that she has " 'accepted too passively the funny form of our life,' " and as she begins more actively sharing in their lives, she reminds "herself of an actress who had been studying a part and rehearsing it, but who suddenly, . . . before the footlights, had begun to improvise, to speak lines not in the text." By "heroically improvising," Maggie "invented from moment to moment what to say and to do." Later she is pleased to find herself "possessing the constructive, the creative hand." (II, 25-26, 33, 145.)

Her performance involves "humbugging" Adam so as to deceive him into thinking nothing wrong and to prepare herself to leave him to "go his own way and take his risk and lead his life," redeeming in this way his intention to marry Charlotte for Maggie's sake, so as to free Maggie for a life of her own. Maggie recognizes that she desires "to possess and use" the others, that she is indeed "exploiting" and "enjoying, under cover of an evil duplicity," her onlookers' startled attention to her performance while she "plied her art upon the Matcham band." Later, one of her "dissimulated arts" is to "interweave Mrs. Assingham in as plausibly as possible with the undulations of their surface." When at last Fanny is summoned by Maggie to confront the golden bowl and the information provided by the penitent shopman, Fanny is startled to see Maggie dressed to the point of "extravagance" and "incoherence," costumed "like some holy image in a procession, and left . . . to show what wonder she could work under pressure." Fanny is in the position of a "pious priest" "when confronted, behind the altar, before the festa, with his miraculous Madonna." (II, 79-81, 49, 54, 144, 152-153.)

The power which makes Maggie sacred as its incarnation is a function of the drama she enacts as wife and helps to create, and her playing her role is the basis for the attempt to recreate her married life which she has started undertaking before she accidently comes upon the bowl. It is after she begins to act dramatically with a conscious view of her own effect and with duplicity that she can recognize that Charlotte and the Prince are themselves acting in concert and "*treating* her," "treating" her moreover with "a plan that was the exact counterpart of her own," namely with a "bath of benevolence artfully prepared for her," and "baths of benevolence," fit only for a sick "patient," a "nervous eccentric or a lost child," become suspect in her eyes. Simultaneously she begins deviously to test Charlotte and the Prince and to recognize her own complicity in the imperfections of her marriage. She recognizes that it was the second marriage which she inspired that toppled the "house of cards" and that if she lives " 'in the midst of miracles of arrangements' " a substantial " 'half' " of them are her own. When she persuades her father not to leave for a trip abroad, disguising her anxiety but acting on her suspicions, she agrees with Adam that their comfort has brought irresponsibility, that, as Adam says, " 'a wicked selfish prosperity' " has settled in after they have " 'grabbed everything,' " that they " 'haven't . . . enough, the sense of difficulty' " and " 'are lying like gods together, all careless of mankind.' " Serene though they remain, they begin to see that their happiness is a virtual " 'opium den' " and, lolling in " 'pigtails' " on their " 'divans,' " they sense only vaguely " 'whose . . . personal expense' " their happiness depends on. Moreover, Maggie recognizes the "hypocrisy" of her performance—scrutinizing the Prince yet concealing any signs of her newly informed and deviously assertive role by keeping up the illusion of her familiar simplicity. And this "hypocrisy" prepares for a strange intimacy between Maggie and her husband, the "steel hoop of an intimacy compared with which artless passion," mere uninformed, aimless passion, "would have been but a beating of the air." (II, 41, 44, 113, 81, 110, 90-92, 141-142.)

It is in the context of Maggie's tormenting suspicions and her attempts to forestall an outbreak while yet testing Charlotte and the Prince, that she broaches her suspicions to Fanny and Fanny lies to sustain Maggie's good faith and to bolster her courage (as she had hoped Fanny would) in determining to hide her mistrust and not force the Prince to make a declaration. Fanny is all but speechless in the face of Maggie's declaration that she " 'can bear anything' " for love itself, and she finds, in Maggie's ability to make the Prince and Charlotte " 'do what I like,' " the same terror that the Prince had found in Charlotte's capacity for arranging their assignation in Gloucester. Fanny sees finally the logic of Maggie's desire to avoid risking an outbreak by refusing to make an accusation. Maggie wants not " 'proof' " but " '*dis*proof,' " Fanny explains to the Colonel; she " 'irresistibly *knows*' " but " 'insurmountable feeling' " makes her prefer being at sea to utter certainty and she avoids an outbreak so as to forestall disaster. Accordingly, when Fanny lies in swearing that she had never even " 'entertained' " the possibility that Charlotte and the Prince are lovers, she not only covers her own errors but gives Maggie the help she wants in maintaining her faith while testing her suspicions. Fanny tells the lie, then induces Maggie to declare that she believes it, knowing however that Maggie's declaration is half a lie—that it is, as she tells Bob, at best the " 'pretence that she believes me.' " (II, 115-116, 119-120; I, 362; II, 131.)

The courage behind their lies, and the good faith that each hopes to secure by perpetrating it, are challenged by the crisis which occurs when Maggie accidentally buys the bowl in Bloomsbury and learns the circumstances of its purchase from the "vendor of the golden bowl" who has "made such a 'good thing' " out of its availability and is now moved to confess the "embarrassed truth" (as James spoke of his own responsibility in the preface) about the condition of the bowl, the price he charged, the terms of its sale. The reader first learns about the incident through the drama Maggie stages and takes part in at the culmination of Book Fourth when she deliberates confronting the Prince but postpones that scene and first calls in Fanny.

What Maggie has done is simply to dress herself in finery, clear her mantelpiece, and place the golden bowl, her "odd acquisition," at its center " 'for my husband to see, . . . where it would meet him almost immediately if he should come into the room.' " On that day he has stopped paying her even casual attentions—he has " 'given up even his forms' "—and with touching resignation she has placed the bowl in its central position, without knowing what she will say about it, on the mere chance that Amerigo will enter but fearing that he " 'may never again come into this room.' " She counts on the bowl to work its effect itself, uncertain whether she will " 'speak' " to the Prince at all about how she acquired it or what she thinks it " 'represents.' " But she summons Fanny first to tell her of finding the bowl and Fanny, after sounding out the situation, performs the deed which precipitates Maggie's commitment to her role. (II, 164-166, 178, 200-201.)

Fanny smarts with guilt and half anticipates that Maggie will openly denounce her but then feels instead the sharpness of Maggie's method; Maggie does not administer the "stab" of explicit "denunciation" but, like Milly in *The Wings of the Dove,* exerts her pressure, exercises her power in the grace of abstention and Fanny feels her responsibility "drilled into her" by "this intensity of intimation." In view of what Fanny proceeds to do, her excuses or her explanations for her past conduct are less important than the future objectives she hopes to secure. She protests that she has " 'tried . . . to act for the best,' " that she had thought the past " 'solidly buried.' " She claims that not evil intention but good faith has produced the situation and the evil in it, that the good faith which all had in Charlotte, and the confidence in herself that Charlotte accordingly was encouraged to have, heightened an otherwise manageable temptation and invited the betrayal. With even more telling insight, she insists on crucial possibilities which are not ruled out by the uncertainties of their knowledge. Adam may or may

not have discovered or divined the facts, and with his " 'extraordinary' " way he will not want to hurt Maggie but " 'do for himself whatever there may be to do' "; it may be that he and Charlotte are " 'intimately together' " still. Also it may be that the
Prince and Maggie are, as Fanny hopefully asks, intimate still
" 'in spite of everything' ": Maggie's reply is that " 'it remains
to be seen,' " and she concedes that even his staying away from
her that day may be an indication that he is interested enough
in her to be apprehensive about her feelings. (II, 162-163, 168-
172, 175-178.)

In view of the possibilities, Fanny insists that Charlotte and
Adam should be left to each other and that Maggie should
" 'take' " from Adam whatever mode of conduct his own behavior sanctions. Then she picks up the gilded cup and, "possessed of the bowl, and possessed too of [the] indication of a
flaw," she declares that, like the bowl, Maggie's conception of
the situation " 'has a crack.' " And she hazards her claim (at
best a determined hope which she wishes to bring about rather
than a well-founded certainty) that Amerigo has " 'never been
so interested in you as now' " and raises high above her head
what she regards as the only evidence of the infidelity, the only
visible threat to the continuance of the marriages, the only barrier to the reconciliation of Amerigo and Maggie. She holds
high the flawed and gilded bowl, and with "due note taken of
the margin of the polished floor," she "dashed it boldly to the
ground, where she had the thrill of seeing it with the violence
of the crash lie shattered." Precisely at the moment when it
breaks upon the floor, the Prince, returning to his attentive
forms, opens the door just enough to see the ruined fragments.
And when Fanny exclaims to Maggie " 'whatever you meant by
it—and I don't want to know *now*—has ceased to exist,' "
Amerigo's voice shatters the silence between the two women
"with a sharpness almost equal to the smash of the crystal." He
does not seek ignorance of Maggie's meaning but asks her
" 'what in the world, my dear, *did* you mean by it?' " and his
question has all the piercing impact of Fanny's destruction of
the bowl. (II, 176-179.)

For a moment his eyes meet Fanny's in search of the guidance
she has provided in the past and the two "communicants" re-

new "something that took up that tale and that might have been a redemption of pledges then exchanged" to see each other through. James's authority and Maggie's role hang in the balance, challenged by the Prince's turning to Fanny for help yet constituted in its main design and movement by Fanny's next act: the tale *is* taken up, the pledges *are* redeemed, when she leaves the room, abdicating so as to redeem the marriages, abandoning the Prince with the injunction that he seek an answer not from her but from his own wife. Maggie's answer is given first in deeds rather than in words: it is the "prompt" though only partly successful "tribute to order," the "positive pomp" with which, in her "rustling finery," she stoops to gather up and reassemble the pieces of the golden bowl. (II, 179-180, 182, 185.)

Fanny's breaking of the bowl has no consequences for the action other than the rudimentary but crucial one of presenting an express form which enables author and reader, along with Fanny, Maggie, and Amerigo themselves, to explore the situation and talk about it, symbolizing as it does the central crisis of the novel and the energies and forms of movement which impel the action toward its resolution. Her act exceeds not only what Maggie has intended but Fanny's own intention of removing the evidence and encouraging Maggie to think her marriage more safely intact than her anxiety over its flaws will permit her to count on. Fanny's deed is in keeping with the characters' pervasive strategy of concealing the imperfections of the arrangements but goes beyond it in all but destroying the evidence. Moreover, Fanny's act destroys also the wholeness of the imperfect bowl and accordingly expresses in excess the betrayals that have been perpetrated earlier, the imperfections that have been gilded over. Yet the same act which destroys the integrity of the bowl images the break with the past that Maggie has begun to seek and that Fanny thinks necessary, and it also rends the gilded surface which has obscured the faults; it reveals by annihilating the hidden " 'weak place' " in the crystal which the Bloomsbury shopman had confessed to Charlotte but neglected until quite late to point out to Maggie. Fanny destroys the novel's governing symbol in an expression of James's effort to re-create the novel which contains it—the novel being the marriage of form and substance, the larger community of experience and form, which the bowl symbolizes—and the bowl becomes accordingly the "wasted symbol" (as the Narrator had called May Server in *The Sacred Fount*) that is spent in the exacting service of James's art. In Fanny's undoubted deed is compressed the creative act which would enact and redeem James's novel as well as form and redeem the marriages, the commerce, the life it represents. And Maggie's burden, as she stoops to gather up the pieces, is to make each of the marriages a " 'true' one" so that "the scandal of a breach" (to use again James's phrasing in the Prefaces) will not "show."

That process is the tortured sacrifice enacted in the closing sections of the novel to secure Maggie's break with the past, her possession of the Prince, the resumption of Adam's project for American City and Charlotte's subservience to it as his helpmate and wife, and the remaking of Maggie's marriage in the name of passion. And the almost explosive power of the action derives from the dilemma (for James's language as well as for the imaginations of his characters) that the redemptive efforts cannot—and must not, to be effective—escape from their dependence on the very materials and instruments they seek to transform. To acknowledge that dependence is the crux of the redemptive act for Maggie as for James. The process of forging a marriage in which no breach shows because none exists virtually requires the lie which James's mannered style creates: the pretense that any " 'weak spot,' " any division in the past or any impending breach, does not exist by making certain that it does not show. The marriages can *become* true only by pretending that they are so *already*. Only by gilding the bowl—by consistently speaking as if the characters and marriages were still safe, by giving form to ignorance, blindness, projected faith as well as to knowledge and insight—can the novel appreciate what is given even in the flawed or fragmented remnants, and restore their promise by transforming and making good on it.

Maggie's role is to forge the lies, illusions, and devious pretenses which redeem the promise of their lives and to suffer vicariously the cruelties which the process entails for those who have less nascent virtue and less " 'good fortune' " than her age and inheritance provide. Charlotte becomes a scapegoat

whose suffering Maggie imagines undergoing herself. And the
novel's vision is polarized along the double axis of the two
marriages, with Charlotte's willed marriage to Adam being
made the constituent or conventional form which makes accessible for Maggie and the Prince the possibility of marriage
as an achieved form of passion.

When Maggie confronts the Prince over the pieces of the
bowl and tells him of her interview with the Bloomsbury shopkeeper, she works out the basis for their accord, offering Amerigo a measure of help "that wasn't to have been imagined in
advance" and requires "some close looking at before it could
be believed in and pronounced void of treachery." He persists
in avoiding details about his earlier affair and lies about the
circumstances of their shopping for the bowl. His one forceful
declaration is that Maggie has never been " 'more sacred to
me than you were at that hour—unless perhaps you've become
so at this one,' " and that assertion, like something "unimagi-
nable" arising from "his strange consistency," chills Maggie for
it defines so precisely her gamble; her being "sacred" to him
may count for no more than it did before, but his devotion, if
genuine and now stronger, is the ground on which she must
build. She has brought him to this declaration by the control
with which she has presented the fact that she is now in " 'possession . . . of real knowledge.' " (II, 187, 199, 201.)

The "positive pomp" of her performance with the fragments
keeps the urgency of the crisis before him while permitting her
to turn away, as if with "bandaged eyes," from the sight of his
wound "flaming there in his beauty." She dreads saying what
she might have to say and "taking from him what he would
say," then she finds that the very "taste of [the] wrong" he has
done her is softening under the strong "desire to spare him"
that is born in the mere experience of "being *with* him there in
silence." What is created is his "need" for her "which she was
rapidly taking on." Heretofore he has simply "used her" and
"enjoyed her" but now she can give him an unexpected kind
of support: she has "got into his labyrinth," is "in the very act
of placing herself there, for him, at its center" and, like Ariadne
with Theseus in the Cretan labyrinth, she "might securely

guide him out of it" not only by "helping him to help himself"
but by helping him "to help *her*." And this effort will make
their relation a more nearly reciprocal union (of the order
Fleda Vetch had dreamed of in *The Spoils of Poynton*) than
his contempt for her simplicity earlier, or her utter condemnation of his infidelity now, would permit. She relies on an intimacy, in the strict sense, between them which exists at best
only latently but which she creates by projecting it in this
scene. She intimates her charge without making it explicit so
as to bring the Prince to his choice, to lead him to make a
commitment to her and his marriage. (II, 182, 185-188, 193.)

Maggie accomplishes this by a double effort: by impressing
on him, without stating outright, a sharp sense of his wrong,
the burden of his responsibility, the " 'advantage' " he may gain
by choosing her, and correspondingly the stiff " 'price' " he
must pay and the person (Charlotte) " 'whom [he] may have to
pay *with*' "—and by sparing him the severe penalty in outrage
and scorn and rejection which he might fear from her and which
might permanently scar their relation. Accordingly she speaks
almost exclusively about the Bloomsbury incident, the Prince's
earlier affair, and her own negotiations with the shopman—
the crucial difference, as she tells the Prince, between " 'my
having made the purchase where you failed of it' "—and she
scarcely alludes to the more recent renewal of the liaison. When
she does refer to her suspicions (now her certainty) about his
conduct since the visit to Gloucester, she refers abstractly to
the two " 'kinds of relation' " with Charlotte, the one being the
public companionship with his stepmother-in-law which Maggie does not even sketchily describe or name, the other being
the " 'something else' " which was hidden. When Maggie speaks
of knowing now about the earlier affair and knowing by inference " 'the other things [more recent] that were before me,' "
and Amerigo asks whether her knowing " 'would have made a
difference, in the matter of our marriage,' " she replies that it
would have made none " 'in the matter of *ours*,' " suggesting
without saying that the second marriage is the one they have
most betrayed. But she insists in carefully chosen words, which
heighten the urgency of the question by virtue of not filling in

specifications, that the issue is " 'bigger than that. You see how much what I know makes of it for me.' " (II, 188, 195, 190-191, 200.)

The result is that both Maggie and the Prince can sustain, even in private, the illusion of an undisturbed marriage, while undergoing the tortured process which Maggie launches to transform their love. She wants to tell him to take his time so that he will " 'suffer least' " or be least " 'distorted and disfigured' " but does not say so. She feels that he is "straightened and tied" in his uncertainty as to whether Adam, too, knows, but she does not relieve his anxiety, saying nothing but what will achieve the combination of rigor and mercy for which she works. Later, consequently, he can present to her as to others the astonishingly reserved, "undisturbed manner" displayed by members of his "class and type" who after a political revolution seek to "re-establish a violated order." There is no apparent " 'intimate' result of the crisis she had invited her husband to recognize," but his "possibly almost too polished surface" harbors a "working arrangement" whereby his allegiance to her may be brought about. (II, 184, 192, 219-221, 228.)

What complicates Maggie's redemptive effort and sharpens the terrifying impact of the ensuing drama is that the proof of their intimacy will be the intimate communion itself, in its privacy, and that their transformed relation will necessarily be their *own*, shielded even from those whose lives are closely connected with theirs. The institution of marriage which Maggie sanctions is by its nature possessive, the propriety which Maggie would charge with faith and passion belongs exclusively to the contracted partners in it. Their talking together, their circling about the question of their marriage, and the terms of their accord will be *theirs* alone to know from within the form of their marriage; others will be excluded from the property they claim on the frontier of the "fundamental passions" by the propriety of intimacy, by the veil of the unspoken on which intimacy depends, by the walled chamber, citadel, or fortified outpost which the imagination, alone and vicariously, can penetrate.

Maggie notices that the Prince will not bring himself to name Adam, holding back from the "particular ugliness" of drawing attention to Adam's shame and betrayal, and that he will not mention Charlotte, since to do so would call into question embarrassingly their betrayal and would further expose Charlotte's complicity, would at once reveal and betray his partner or "give Charlotte away." When Amerigo asks cautiously whether anyone but Fanny and Maggie knows the facts, she learns that Charlotte does not know whether Adam suspects her infidelity, for Charlotte otherwise would have told the Prince. It is then that Maggie conceives clearly the design of concealing her knowledge from Adam and Charlotte as a condition of creating the full intimacy she wants. Uncertain though she will remain about Adam's motives, she imagines that Charlotte is keeping up the appearance of a tranquil marriage while tortured within by the unanswered question of whether Adam suspects her, and Maggie imagines that Adam *does* know the facts but that he is keeping quiet so as to sustain the illusion of a happy marriage out of consideration for Maggie. She imagines "the possible identity of her father's motive . . . with her own," and supposes that he is protecting her from the shock of disappointment just as she makes his "serenity" her obligation, protecting at least the "marvellous enamel" or "firm outer shell of his dignity." When she answers the Prince by telling him to " 'find out for yourself,' " she is gambling that he will not be able to find out and that he will not tell Charlotte whether Maggie knows, that even if he is asked by Charlotte he will lie. (II, 192, 202-203, 218.)

For either his silence or his lie will be proof that their marriage is a community of interest and commitment which now excludes Charlotte. And if neither he nor Maggie can find out whether Adam knows, then the form at least of Adam's and Charlotte's marriage has become inviolate and their relation is accordingly salvageable. By playing her role as wife and sustaining the illusion of the unbroken marriages, Maggie helps to create realms of intimacy within a larger community of knowledge and possession, but she can do so within the limits of her world and vision only by staking out claims and insisting on the forms which mark the frontiers of those dominions. And at the opening of Book Fifth she is stunned by her own "sense of possession" and the burden of "humbugging" which she has assumed, like a young actress "engaged for some minor part in the play" who now finds herself "promoted to leading lady and expected to appear in every act." But the drama built around her projects not only the beauty and heroism of her triumph but the horror of its cost and the peril of unfulfilled promise which it faces at the end. (II, 207-208.)

The new relation with her father that Maggie works out with his help is founded on the probability that he knows the facts, on the illusion he sustains (whether true or not) that he does *not* know, and on Maggie's corresponding pretense to undisturbed happiness. That either might have to sacrifice something for the other is a prospect they both deny, but the sacrifice by Abraham of Isaac (an imagined sacrifice, never otherwise enacted) plays about Maggie's imagination when she hopes that Adam will lift the burden of sacrifice from her, or when conversely she feels that Adam is preparing to be sacrificed as if he were "her child." Finally Maggie recognizes that it is Adam who is "practically *offering* himself . . . as a sacrifice," that she is committed to accept it, and that he is strengthening her to perform the deed. In this reversal of roles she takes the responsibility for accepting his offer and performing the sacrifice, branding him the " 'victim' " to her happiness and suggesting subtly that he return with Charlotte to the safely distant American City. His eager acceptance of the proposal is accompanied by his declaration that he will not feel the sacrifice unless he discovers that Maggie has " 'ceased to believe in me,' " and Maggie, grateful but determined now to separate from him, is filled with admiration for the figure of the "perfect little father" he presents. (II, 82, 269, 267, 271-273.)

Only when Maggie is in clear view of the need to separate from him does the novel, in full accord with her affection, render Maggie's tender praise of her father: the " 'successful' beneficent person," both "beautiful" and "bountiful," the "dauntlessly wilful great citizen, the consummate collector and infallible high authority" that Adam is for her. She will always think of him with both "pity" and "envy," and, holding him "in her eyes as no work of art probably had ever been placed in his own," like "the typical charmed gazer, in the still museum," her love acknowledges the "pride of the catalogue, that time has polished and consecrated," and she declares that she believes in him " 'more than in any one at all.' " Believing in her likewise, Adam has discerned in her the "fine pulse of passion" of a "creature cradled upon depths, buoyant among dangers" and feels "hushed," even "admonished," in view of a life so far now beyond his own. In one of James's most moving passages, the "plash and play" of her experience "become for [Adam] too a sensation," but a vicarious one as this "infallible high authority" now recognizes. Though he is not "personally floating" or "even sitting in the sand," it could "pass very well for breathing the bliss, in a communicated irresistible way— for tasting the balm." And the greatest satisfaction for Maggie's father becomes the knowledge that "without him nothing might have been." When they embrace at the end of the scene, the embrace is "august and almost stern" and any trace of the perverted or of the sentimental is gone, since it "produced for all its intimacy no revulsion and broke in no inconsequence of tears." (II, 273-275, 263.)

When contemplating Adam's departure for American City and the public which might simply take his reputation and " 'tear it to pieces,' " proving again that his efforts are all at his " 'expense,' " Maggie imagines Charlotte's departure as that of a convict or indentured servant dispatched to colonial America, "transported, doomed." And the prospect for Charlotte is revealed in the deepening insights of Maggie's imagination to be an increasingly tortured one. The novel's aim, like Maggie's, is not to indulge in righteous condemnation of Charlotte's errors but to muster compassion for the gorgeous woman who has been otherwise excluded from the community of passion she has sought (by the disdainful Prince in Rome, by the "stiffer proprieties" of marriage that are now enforced upon her by James as well as by Fanny, Maggie, Adam, and the Prince) and to create in her a new commitment to her marriage, the redemption of her bargain with Adam. The horror of the closing sections of the novel derives in large part from the fact that everything they do to make this possible heightens the torture of the sacrifice they enact. The bland affluence and beauty of Fawns becomes the nightmarish "overglazed rotunda" and "haunted house" where the "heroism of perfunctory things" accomplishes the transformation and exacts the payment for it. (II, 267, 271.)

It is in the card-playing scene at Fawns that Maggie assumes the full burden of her role in the drama she helps to create. Amerigo and Charlotte, Adam and Fanny, form partners at bridge, while the Colonel writes letters at a desk to one side, and Maggie wanders in and out of the room or watches from the terrace like "a tired actress who has the good fortune to be 'off,' while her mates are on" the stage. But she finds that she is virtually in their midst, so intense is their consciousness of her, and Maggie feels that she is virtually "holding them in her hand" because they observe so perfectly the "stiff standard of the house," and because, suppressing any friction among them, they have achieved a taut "security," a complete "conquest of appearances." Her sense of power tempts her toward an action that is "monstrous" and "horribly possible"—to "sound out their doom in a single sentence"—but she rises instead to move about their table, bending "a vague mild face upon them, as if to signify that . . . she wished them well." She senses in them the hope that she might spare each one "the actual present strain," the "complexity of their peril," and, "adopting it from them," she assumes this burden, reminding herself of "the scapegoat of old, of whom she had once seen a terrible picture," which was "charged with the sins of the people and had gone forth into the desert to sink under his burden and die." (James remembered seeing Holman Hunt's *Scapegoat* in 1858 and felt that it was "so charged with the awful that I was glad I saw it in company. . . ." [15] (II, 231-235.)

This scapegoat Maggie becomes, after once again feeling the temptation of "the straight vindictive view." Finding that her friends resemble "figures rehearsing some play of which she herself was the author," she recognizes that on that "stage" was a "scene she might people . . . either with serenities and dignities and decencies, or with terrors and shames and ruins, things as ugly as those formless fragments of her golden bowl she was trying so hard to pick up." She decides with James to hold to the illusion of "serenities and dignities and decencies." To find "evil seated, all at its ease, where she had only dreamed

[15] *Autobiography*, p. 178.

of good," to meet it like a thief or "some bad-faced stranger surprised in one of the thick-carpeted corridors of a house," is terrifying, but the figures seated at cards bring home to her during the "crisis" that to act in outrage would be "to give them up." Instead, Maggie determines to save them. (II, 235-237.)

The "breakage" of the bowl, she concludes, stands now not for any "wrought discomposure among the triumphant" partners to the marriages but merely for the "dire deformity" of Maggie's vision of them. If Charlotte gains any indication that Maggie knows the truth, Charlotte might create a chasm of distrust between the father and his daughter. As things stand, there may be "still firm ground between the elder pair," some bond of will on Charlotte's part and confidence on Adam's, along with "the beauty of appearances" which has been "so consistently preserved." When Charlotte seeks Maggie out on the terrace, approaching with all the "portentous intelligent stillness" of a "creature who had escaped by force from her cage," Charlotte simply impels Maggie to see the advantage of keeping up benign appearances whose mercy Maggie has already decided to sanction while watching the card game. (II, 240-241.)

The cage of half-knowing uncertainty to which Charlotte has been doomed by Maggie's refusal to bring charges and by the Prince's "false explanations" has become unbearable, destroying, whether or not she at first realizes it, the intimacy which Charlotte and the Prince once shared. Charlotte's explanation for what has happened is never revealed, but whether she thinks the Prince is simply growing indifferent to her or that he is responding to pressure from Maggie or from his own conscience, what she bargains for with Maggie is her own safety within her marriage and her husband's trust. It is clear to Maggie that "her old possession" of her father is now "divided," that Charlotte is asserting her claim to him, trying to gain her own "security at any price," and expecting Maggie to pay by leaving undisturbed Adam's good faith. Maggie's decision is to place her shawl over her head "for humility" and under this "improvised hood" to become "the poor woman at somebody's proud door." When Charlotte asks whether there is " 'any wrong you consider I've done you,' " whether she is responsible for committing " 'unconsciously' " some " 'fault,' " Maggie replies with the lie that Charlotte is " 'mistaken' " in thinking her suspicious and with the half-truth that " 'I accuse you of nothing.' " (ii, 229, 244, 247-250.)

It is impossible to ascertain whether Charlotte actually hopes to relieve her uncertainty and to rest content if Maggie seems not to know of the infidelity, or whether Charlotte has seen a way to establish an accord with Maggie whether or not Maggie surely knows of Amerigo's liaison, an agreement which will simply insure Charlotte that Maggie will not divulge any suspicions or information she may have to Adam. There are no indications that Maggie, performing under her "improvised hood," thinks naïvely that Charlotte will simply believe what she is told. The suspense and phrasing of Maggie's answer— " 'I accuse—I accuse you of nothing' "—establishes the basis for a working agreement even if Charlotte should remain suspicious of Maggie's assurances. Maggie counts on Charlotte's being guided by what she does and refrains from doing, not on her being utterly convinced by what Maggie says, for the tormenting " 'ignorance' " which Maggie later posits for Charlotte is not the tranquillity of oblivion but a compound of uncertainties. Maggie, like Charlotte, performs during the scene with an increasingly sharp awareness of the many contingencies they face. (ii, 250, 336.)

Maggie's willingness to carry through with her lie is strengthened by her supposition that Amerigo, too, has had to lie in some comparable way to "this admirable creature" and it enables her to carry her lie further, to deny that she ever so much as " 'fancied I could suffer by you' "—a statement which not only sounds deceitfully the note of utter good faith in the past but rings with present triumph and the assurance that Charlotte is no longer a threat. For Maggie feels that by this lie she and Amerigo are joined "close, close together" leaving Charlotte "in some darkness of space that would steep her in solitude and harass her with care." In this way the scene dramatizes the painful separation of Amerigo and Charlotte, along with his commitment to Maggie and Charlotte's resigned commitment to Adam. The willed deceit which Charlotte and Maggie together enact, "their conscious perjury," the lying fiction which enacts their accord, is completed when Charlotte asks " 'Will you kiss me on it then' " and Maggie turns her cheek "in her passivity" to receive the "prodigious kiss," just as the others rise from the bridge table to witness the embrace. When Maggie discovers the onlookers, she breaks away as from "some absurdity" and they, not knowing whether to display "sympathy" or "hilarity," and not daring to disclose how much they understand, greet the scene with the "consecration conferred by unanimities of silence." (II, 248-251, 276-277.)

The abject surrender which Maggie is willing to perform makes her the scapegoat she has imagined being, for she takes on herself the burden of the wrongs done her and removes from Charlotte (as she will later from the Prince) any enforced demand or pressure to confess. Yet "their conscious perjury," and the accord it sanctions, enable Maggie to secure the love of the Prince, while abandoning Charlotte to the dark solitude of severance from him and yoking her more firmly to her comparatively passionless marriage with Adam. The same accord which keeps Charlotte within the community of the marriages expels her from communion with her lover. And the scapegoat who pays most in deprivation, who suffers the doom of separation, is Charlotte. Maggie so concerns herself for the fate of her partner in "their conscious perjury" that in her imagination she follows Charlotte about the corridors of Fawns, wondering what she made out of her lover's "rebuke," imagining the dissolution of their affair and the "forms that had lost, all so pitifully, their precious confidence." Joined vicariously with Charlotte in her plight, Maggie faces with her the "cold air" of Amerigo's indifference, with her turns away in pain from him, turns "in growing compassion, this way and that" as she lives with Charlotte through the nightmare of her anxiety. (II, 280, 282, 284.)

What Maggie also sees, as she follows Charlotte's search for "her issue and her fate," is the figure of the "little quiet gentleman" with the white vest who "measured the perspectives of the park" and keeps "weaving his spell" and measuring "the impression he produced": Adam Verver walks about alone or with Charlotte near at hand paying the attention due his "rarities" as she had always "most freely paid him" since her marriage. She displays "her appreciation of his taste," taking "possession of the ground throughout its extent" as "the most breathable medium common to them," while he holds (so Maggie imagines) "in one of his pocketed hands the end of a long silken halter looped round [Charlotte's] beautiful neck." He need not "twitch it" or "drag her," but in the now tightened bond of their marriage Charlotte is at hand. (ii, 283-287.)

As she justifies "the faith with which she was honoured," lending "the grace of her authority" to the "heroism of perfunctory things," she takes visitors through the echoing galleries beneath the "overglazed rotunda," where doors open and close onto "sinister circular passages," and she pays the tribute to art, her husband's possessions, and her marriage in which Maggie hears the repressed "shriek of a soul in pain." Charlotte's cry is the source of the communion Adam and Maggie share when watching her from the doorways of the picture gallery; her pain releases the "shame" and "pity," the "better knowledge, the smothered protest, the divined anguish" which they all feel and know. Her torment is the cost of the Prince's marriage which he shrinks from recognizing when he takes refuge in his empty London house, leaving Maggie to divine how he still hears the "strange wail of the gallery" and to imagine his lesser torment as he waits to be alone with Maggie by his side.

Maggie's final effort to help Charlotte in her struggle to make her decision takes place when Maggie, leaving the Assinghams, Father Mitchell, and her father behind, follows Charlotte through "exposed and shining spaces" beneath the "high glare of noon" to an "ancient rotunda" which has been, like everything at Fawns, "conscious hitherto of no violence from the present and no menace from the future." There Charlotte, like stricken Io in her "frenzy," has sought refuge, just as Maggie sought refuge earlier on the terrace during the bridge game. Instead of bringing the charges that Charlotte fears, Maggie comes simply to make Charlotte's effort "as easy for her as the case permitted," to "produce in her" the felt experience "of highly choosing." Maggie knows her to be "doomed to a separation that was like a knife in the heart," and if Maggie has felt like Ariadne leading the Prince out of the labyrinth, she now sees Ariadne in Charlotte too, the abandoned **Ariadne** later, "roaming the lone sea-strand." Maggie's only pretext for intruding is to bring the first volume of a novel to replace the second volume which Charlotte has brought by mistake, but it permits Maggie to draw attention to Charlotte's new opportunity by saying: " '*This* is the beginning; you've got the wrong volume, and I've brought you out the right.' " She sees in Charlotte's "blinded physical quest for a peace not to be grasped" the starkly "tragic" ravages of her abjection. When Charlotte's pride moves her to forego confessing, conceal her "horror" at her "doom," and find some way to assert her free consent, Maggie once again helps Charlotte by feigning the abject simplicity which Charlotte expects of her. Charlotte announces that she has determined on a " 'definite break,' " that she intends to " 'take [Adam] home to his real position' " and to " '*keep* the man I've married.' " Maggie's folly is to provoke Charlotte to even firmer effort by pretending to object. Mustering a "sharp successful almost primitive wail" she protests: " 'You want to take my father from *me?*' " and Charlotte is impelled to declare: " 'I want really to possess him. . . . I happen also to feel that he's worth it.' " Maggie allows Charlotte to assert her claim and to charge Maggie with having " 'loathed our marriage' " and " 'worked against me.' " She sanctions Charlotte's new determination with the confession that she has worked against her but " 'failed.' " (ii, 307-312, 315-317.)

Maggie's compassion for Charlotte deepens during the closing scenes of the novel though it must yield precedence finally to the pressure of her marital obligations and the mounting intensity of Maggie's passion for Amerigo. So strong is Maggie's desire to soften Charlotte's "humiliation," release Charlotte from the solitude of her separation, and know "the *whole* history" of the passion which Charlotte has been cut off from, that she imagines Charlotte's speaking proudly of the " 'relation' " which has been " 'broken' " and the " 'wine of consciousness' " that filled it to the brim, virtually hears Charlotte question Maggie's right to " 'breath upon it . . . for blight' " and protest the fate that deals her out deceptions and turns to " 'black ashes' " the " 'golden flame.' " The "ingenuities" of Maggie's pity tempt her, with the assumed burden of guilt, to remind

Amerigo of Charlotte's plight and to beg him to give his love to Charlotte one time more—to give her "some benefit" to carry off "into exile like the last saved object of price of the *émigré,* the jewel . . . negotiable some day in the market of misery." But strong though her compassion is, Maggie is saved from that folly—and Charlotte is denied the solace of that negotiable security—by the sight, sharp to the point of "concussion," of her father veiled in his manner and "white waistcoat," wrapt at once in "detachment" and "attention," holding the "silken noose" of Charlotte's "tether" under whatever "tension" was required, or coiling the "gathered lasso" with whatever "magic" he knew how to practice. (II, 329-331.)

In view of her own desire and the power and principle Adam's claim represents, Maggie cannot act in such a way on her compassion, but later she invokes it to protect Charlotte from the callous scorn of the Prince. He has so cut loose from his usual "touchstone" of "taste," and has so completely surrendered to the interest which Maggie now arouses in him and from which she is so clearly "profiting," that he can speak without apparent regret of Charlotte's and Adam's departing to " 'live into' their queer future." Maggie must suggest that he should at least " 'miss her a little,' " that Charlotte is in effect " 'dying for us—for you and me,' " that it is " 'as if her unhappiness had been necessary to us—as if we had needed her, at her own cost, to build us up and start us.' " And it is in the clear recognition of Charlotte's payment as one source of their good fortune that Maggie protests against the Prince's cruelly untrue statement that Charlotte is " 'stupid.' " Charlotte understands Maggie better than he allows, she insists, and if Charlotte does not wholly understand her it is partly because Maggie's deceptions have deceived her. To protect her from the Prince's scorn, Maggie protests that Charlotte knows the torture of unhappiness and even credits her, despite the inescapable uncertainties, with having seen through Maggie's deception and known the shame of exposure along with the pain of bafflement: " 'She knows, she knows!' " Though the Prince can see profoundly that " 'everything's terrible, *cara,* in the heart of man,' " and that Charlotte is undertaking to forge a

new life and that she will " 'make it,' " Maggie must bring out
that also " 'she's making ours.' " (II, 345-346, 348-349.)

Maggie's compassion for Charlotte is more than matched by
her passion for the Prince, and while Maggie's determination to
possess her husband forces Charlotte into the "cage" of torment
and the "silken halter" of marriage, it brings Amerigo from
Fawns into the caged confines of his domicile at Portland
Place. There Maggie can anticipate the departure of the Ververs and feel with new intensity the pressure of her passion for
the Prince that is rendered in the mounting rhythm, the charged
and expressive manner, of James's prose: "He was with her as
if he were hers, hers in a degree and on a scale, with an intensity
and an intimacy, that were a new and a strange quantity, that
were like the irruption of a tide loosening them where they
had stuck and making them feel they floated." She can virtually
feel him displacing her father in her longing to embrace him:
"What was it that, with the rush of this, just kept her from putting out her hands to him, from catching at him as in the other
time, with the superficial impetus he and Charlotte had privately inspired to impart, she had so often, her breath failing
her, known the impulse to catch at her father?" Though she
knows that the next days promise the consummation of her new
passion, since she holds the telegram announcing Charlotte's
and Adam's last visit to say farewell, she reveals the full depths
of the transforming crisis they confront when she imagines that
Amerigo is about to be executed and that she is "losing her
head" in some break with the past comparable to the French
Revolution, and she imagines that she is sharing with Amerigo,
in his prison cell, his "last day of captivity" and celebrating it
like "noble captives" with a "feast" made from their "last poor
resources." The "sudden freedom of her words" is the "diverted
intensity" of her passion to "seize him." Maggie is virtually in
Charlotte's position and her own at the same time: she imagines
the somber ecstasy of grasping at the last chance to commemorate their passion before sentence is executed against them,
yet she thrills in anticipating the next days when Amerigo and
then herself with him will be released from the constraints
which now imprison them. (II, 339-341.)

Sustained by this passion and in "present possession of her ground," Maggie can safely expand on the joys of her earlier companionship with Adam, can consider spending the last evening alone with him, and can suggest that the Prince for a final farewell to Charlotte might want to " 'carry *her* off somewhere' " alone and " 'do as you like.' " For these fancies are part of her effort to provide for their separation from Adam and Charlotte "with a due amount of form," to commemorate their past affections as memories, rather than to escape back into their enchantment. She recalls staying with Adam " 'ever so late, in foreign restaurants . . . with our elbows on the table and most of the lights put out,' " talking about the " 'things he had secured or refused or lost.' " The main force of her desire, however, is to "seize" the Prince, and her extravagant fancies are simply "the diverted intensity" of her desire to do so. Even the need to separate from him for a few hours has the intensity of an embrace which she virtually enjoys while being obliged to postpone it. She is persuaded to postpone it, despite a pressure of longing which almost terrifies her, because the Prince asks her precipitously to " 'wait,' " anticipating that he will be obliged to make a confession and wanting to wait until they have said farewell to Charlotte and Adam—until, that is, he and Maggie have made their break and are truly alone in their marriage, having observed the "due amount of form" which Maggie insists on in her strange way and which matches nevertheless his own "touchstone" of "taste." (II, 342-343, 345, 351-352.)

Formerly it was Maggie who had felt that the gesture of an embrace, and the sexual or affectionate power which was offered and appealed to, were ways which the Prince used to escape responsibility and evade the pressures Maggie might exert to enforce it; three times she had consented, on the evening of his return from Gloucester, happy that she had held him to his offer of affection but fearful that this was for him a substitute for "the words he hadn't uttered" and that her "weakness" in consenting so readily might encourage his laxity. Later during a ride in a cab the Prince had resorted to comparable gestures, and Maggie, though responding to "his genius for charm, for intercourse, for expression, for life," resists his intent in her effort to strengthen her claims to his affection. Now, while they await Adam's and Charlotte's last call, Maggie is consumed with desire and the Prince must beg her to " 'wait.' " She has received Amerigo's declaration of good faith and, standing in his study, she feels that they are so "shut in together" that they have "gone too far" to permit her leaving, that to leave him would be a futile attempt to "recover the lost and gone," to retrieve the "something" that had "slipped away from her" during the last few minutes and that "it was vain, now wasn't it? to try to appear to clutch or to pick up." The very movement of the novel has become their courtship of the passion that awaits them, and both the concern for form and the consuming passion which Maggie now can sustain prepare for the embrace that closes the novel; the suspense creates a charged intensity beyond any suggested for Charlotte and Amerigo at Matcham or beckoning to them from the ancient inn, radiant towers, or somber tombs of Gloucester. The Prince, so close that she could "touch him, taste him, smell him, kiss him, hold him," and all but "pressed upon her," bends over her "with the largeness with which objects loom in dreams," and Maggie, responding with his own words to the pressure of his request, agrees to " 'wait.' " (II, 28-29, 56-57, 351-352.)

The "form of their reunion" is rendered by their anxious suspense as they await the Ververs at the opening of the last chapter, and by their embrace at the novel's end. And within the tense symmetry of his novel, the strange and unnerving intimacy of its tenderness and terror, James's art strains still in the last chapter to quicken and give form to the vision it projects. As if "comparing notes or nerves" before some official visit, Maggie surveys the room and the Prince paces the floor whose "perfect polish" reflects the flower arrangements and the tea table. His nervous pacing and the inviolate arrangement of the surroundings qualify each other, and both are sounded in Maggie's charged remark: " 'We're distinctly bourgeois!' " James comments instantly that this was rendered "grimly" as an "echo" of their "old community," then projects an hypothesis, creates a perspective, which does not contradict Maggie's view but lends to it an increment of grandeur and power which accrues to it from older social perspectives: for "a spectator sufficiently detached," the couple might have been "quite the privileged pair they were reputed" if one assumed that in preparing to greet Adam and Charlotte they were "awaiting the visit of Royalty." (II, 354.)

Maggie forbids the Prince to confess his lie or divulge Maggie's to Charlotte when he threatens to do so, willing to remain a " 'fool' " in Charlotte's eyes or if Charlotte thinks otherwise to let Charlotte " 'think . . . what she likes,' " and suggesting with a "majesty" new to her that for the Prince to think he might " 'correct' " her is to forget who and whose wife Charlotte is. When Adam and Charlotte arrive, any question of correction dissolves before the impact of her "beauty" and the clear note of the "official" with which she accepts her "mission." The " 'burial,' " as Maggie had once disliked calling it, of going to American City, the "doom" which Maggie and Adam have known Charlotte feared there, has become instead the "mission" as Charlotte sees it of "representing the arts and the graces to a people languishing afar off and in ignorance," when the "final rites" of Adam's ambitions will become the " 'opening exercises' " he has hoped for, the ceremony of dedication of his new museum. The broken golden bowl in all its ugly fragile beauty is restored momentarily as an echoed memory once the scene has "crystallized . . . to the right quiet lustre" when Charlotte takes her seat, "throned, as who should say, between her hostess and her host." The "only approach to a break" in the "harmony" occurs when the Prince awaits Adam's permission before offering Charlotte some refreshment, then offers it when Adam fails to notice or understand. But Charlotte's "consummate" manner of accepting it removes any danger to the perilous equilibrium and they continue the ceremony of farewell which they can stand only by avoiding reference to its "finality," sustaining the harmony only by "the firmest abstention from pressure." (II, 355-358; I, 14, 145; II, 361.)

The Prince and Charlotte are alone for a few moments before the couple departs, and Maggie and her father have a longer interview, parting in an accord which binds in a new tightness the connections among their various acquisitions. Adam looks at a Florentine religious painting he is parting with as a "sacrifice" for Maggie, and she thinks of it from then on as framing "a part of his palpable self" for her to hold in her arms. He asks if it is " 'all right,' " meaning the picture, and she agrees, but they feel that the rightness has "symbolized another truth," and they look about at the other things which it encompasses, taking in piece by piece the poetry of things, the "other pictures, the sofas, the chairs . . . , the 'important' pieces" which stand there "for recognition and applause," along with the figures of Charlotte and the Prince which are fused with them, the "high expressions of the kind of human furniture required aesthetically by such a scene." Taking the inventory of his accumulations, Adam concludes that " '*Le compte y est*. You've got some good things.' " James comments, in terms which encompass the economic and aesthetic dimensions of the drama as well as the moral and emotional, that Charlotte's and Amerigo's "contribution to the triumph of selection, was complete and admirable," then adds that, to "a view more penetrating than the occasion really demanded," their "contribution" was no more striking than the "rare power of purchase" displayed by the fortunate Ververs in acquiring them. (II, 359-360.)

The pain for Maggie of separating from her father is intensified because she has always anticipated such a separation "only on the basis of the sharpest of reasons" and has colored the crisis with fears of his death and the haunting imagery of the River Styx. She is apprehensive that if the two couples separate "sombre ghosts of the smothered past" might "show across the widening strait pale unappeased faces, or raise in the very passage deprecating denouncing hands." Now the "finality" of the separation produces a torment which they both suppress. Maggie avoids the pain which "would have torn them to pieces, if they had so much as suffered its suppressed relations to peep out of their eyes," by referring instead, as "a bold but substantial substitute," to the gap in her life that Charlotte's absence will mean. They face the crisis of their parting by joining in praise of her, acknowledging the " 'risk' " and rightness of Adam's marriage; Adam agrees with Maggie that " 'Charlotte's great,' " and adds the tribute that crowns his appreciation: " 'She's beautiful, beautiful.' " Maggie hears the "speaking

competence" of Adam's declaration, the "note of possession
and control," and she can "speak her joy," though parting
from her father, in praising Charlotte's *"value,"* the assurance
that "her gifts, her variety, her power" will not be "wasted in
the application of [Adam's] plan." Their marriage has become
an instrument of his vision. When the young Principino appears to say farewell, the novel turns sharply away from the
final break, the last ten minutes of the family scene, but returns
to witness the embrace it had postponed, to sound the "stillness" which is "not so much restored as created" when the
Ververs leave and Maggie awaits her reunion with the Prince.
(II, 74, 362-366.)

Secure though she now is in their newly constituted marriage, Maggie is seized with terror at facing the consequences
of the gamble which has brought the Prince from Italy, from
Fawns, into the straitened confines of their marriage. She does
not know the size of her "reward" because the Prince's hand
still covers the "dice" she has thrown in the hazard of her "wild
speculation." She is in her good fortune "the creature to be
paid," but she does not yet know the amount. When Amerigo
reappears, the sheer presence of the reserved but alert adventurer, "everything that was deep in his being and everything
that was fair in his face," is enough to make her think she is
"being paid in full," and her anxiety is replaced by concern
for his when she realizes that he is prepared to pay with a confession, that he is "holding out the money-bag for her to come
and take it." Maggie refuses to elicit that confession: "if *that*
was her proper payment she would go without money." She
"should be ashamed to listen to the uttered word" since to
make or hear the confession would be to benefit "too mon-
strously, at the expense of Charlotte," and "Charlotte's mastery
of the greater style," her splendor is what they all do profit
from. " 'She's splendid,' " Maggie reminds the Prince as she had
reminded Adam, and adds: " 'That's our help, you see.' " The
only tribute the Prince can pay to match it is to declare that " 'I
see nothing but *you*' " and, setting the past behind him and
with "his whole act enclosing her," simply to embrace his wife.
Possessed and in possession, Maggie welcomes and returns the
embrace, but "for pity and dread" of the devotion she has

sought and he now tenders, she shields her eyes from the impact of his faith and vision. The burden of confession which she has lifted from him is assumed by Henry James, acknowledging the responsibility risked and sanctioned in the "sacrament of execution" which in *The Golden Bowl* he made his own. (II, 367-369.)

Appendix

When a Japanese says "Japanese," he is trapped on a little definite racial fact, whereas when we say "American" it is not a fact, it is an act, of faith, a matter of lines on a map and words on paper, an outline it will take generations and centuries more to fill in.

John Updike, "How to Love America
and Leave It at the Same Time"

REPRESENTATION AND RENEWAL
IN HENRY JAMES'S
THE AMERICAN SCENE

READERS have long been puzzled, if not disturbed, by the ratio of form to substance in James's fiction, the relation between his representational techniques and his subjects or themes. To H. G. Wells, James's fiction, "magnificent but painful" in its elaboration, was like a "hippopotamus resolved at any cost, even at the cost of its dignity, upon picking up a pea." [1] The ingenuities of James's late style have seemed even more disconcerting in *The American Scene*, where his subject was not a pea but the entire United States.[2] The reservoir of memories and the sheaf of notes that he gathered during his ten month visit to the land he had not seen in twenty years defined subjects as palpable as the Waldorf Astoria Hotel, as complicated as the "melting pot," the vulgarity of middle-class tastes, or society's quest for national identity, "trying to build itself, with every elaboration, into some coherent sense *of* itself . . ." (159.)[3] The sheer size of the country, its vast scale, seemed as challenging to James as it had,

This essay was published in *The American Identity: Fusion and Fragmentation,* ed. Robert Kroes. Amerika Instituut, Universiteit van Amsterdam (Amsterdam: 1980).

[1] *Boon* (1915), quoted by Leon Edel in *Henry James, A Biography,* 5 vols. (New York, 1953-1972), V, p. 235.

[2] Commentary on *The American Scene,* in addition to material cited later in the footnotes, includes W. H. Auden's "Introduction" to his edition (New York, 1946), pp. v-xxiii, and Leon Edel's "Introduction" to his edition (Bloomington, Ind., 1968), pp. vii-xxiv. Edel's includes bibliographical notes, notes to the text, and a chronology and itinerary of James's visit. Edel discusses the trip and the text in *Henry James,* V, pp. 224-320. Peter Buitenhuis's two chapters are useful and informed: *The Grasping Imagination* (Toronto, Ont., 1970), pp. 182-208. A probing essay, relating *The American Scene* to James's novelistic techniques and to his personal autobiography, is Gordon O. Taylor's "Chapters from Experience: *The American Scene,*" *Genre,* 12 (Spring, 1979), pp. 93-116. Other perceptive essays include: William F. Hall, "The Continuing Relevance of Henry James's *The American Scene,*" *Criticism,* 13 (1971), pp. 151-165; B. C. Lee, "A Felicity Forever Gone: Henry James's Last Visit to America," *British Association for American Studies Bulletin,* N.S. 5 (December, 1962), pp. 31-42; and Alan Trachtenberg, "*The American Scene*: Versions of the City," *Massachusetts Review,* 8 (1967), pp. 281-295.

[3] Page references in parentheses are to *The American Scene,* ed. Leon Edel (Bloomington, Ind., 1968). The pagination is identical in W. H. Auden's edition (New York, 1946).

in political terms, to the authors of *The Federalist Papers*. To James himself, the "huge" and "compressed" reality of New York City reduced the Paris of Emile Zola to the scale of a miniature and called for talent and techniques, an "energy of evocation," equal to "wonder-working" Zola's own. (82.)[4]

Different though it is from Zola's, James's power of representation is unmistakable and his techniques for implementing that power are conspicuous in *The American Scene*. When he speaks of "equality of condition" and the "common denominator" his vocabulary is in tune with that of social commentators since Tocqueville, yet his utilization of type characters is derived as much from literary conventions as from categories of social analysis. Indeed, his personifications, and the assignment of speaking voices to buildings and whole cities, are in the mode of hallucination and fairy tale. The functions that govern these techniques of representation must be taken into account and properly measured by readers, whether sociologists, historians, or literary critics, because they prove to interpenetrate with his American subject in ways that define its significance. They reveal for *The American Scene* an importance comparable to Whitman's *Democratic Vistas* in redefining the myth of America and channeling it into the twentieth century. *The American Scene* speaks finally with the apocalyptic fervor that moved Whitman to warn Americans of a fate in hell comparable to that of the "fabled damned" if America did not fulfill its promised mission. And it speaks, as Whitman declared he did, to an audience both disturbed and fascinated by America's prospects, persons "within whose thought rages the battle . . . between democracy's convictions, aspirations, and the people's crudeness, vice, caprices. . . ."[5] My object in this essay is to interpret James's America in the light of James's act of representing it in *The American Scene*. (125, 203.)

A striking instance of what readers are in for is James's treatment of a site familiar from repeated visits: Washington, D.C. Writing after his return to England, from memory and from

[4] James's admiration for Zola is recorded in *Notes on Novelists* (New York, 1914), pp. 54, 56.
[5] *Democratic Vistas* (1871) in Malcolm Cowley, ed., *The Complete Poetry and Prose of Walt Whitman*, 2 vols. (New York, 1948), pp. 258, 209.

notes, James begins Chapter 11 with the notation that he "was twice in Washington" during his visit to the States, but the chronology of his trip proves to be the least important plane of representation in a shifting configuration of planes which, like sheets of translucent plastic, come into or recede from focus, emerging out of and dissolving into each other in moving sequences. The chronology of the visits (the first in the winter of 1905, the second in late spring) is turned swiftly into a chronology of seasonal change across a natural landscape, and the winter scene of his earlier stay there is displaced instantly by the charms of spring and the onset of summer when he revisited the scene. The landscape and the "light of nature" in May continue on through James's description of the place, but the plane of the natural landscape recedes behind a psychological screen. James's sentences acknowledge, as prior to the place itself, his *"sense* of the place" as prior to the landscape, the *"impression"* of May which is representing the seasons to us; this impression, infused with the memories of the city dating from much earlier in James's life, is "washing" the entire landscape, as if a cleaning agent or a watercolorist were at work, washing it not with the silver tones of winter but the "half green, half golden" light of spring. Then James indicates that the impression sustained in memory, or the "veil" of representation—the representation in the mind that can wash the changing seasons in green and golden light—"operates, for memory," in collaboration with the burgeoning vitality of spring to serve a function on yet another plane of activity, namely, the strictly *social* milieu of the "American scene at large." The *natural* landscape is becoming a representation of or figure for a *social* enterprise that it implements, matching the operative and projective force of representations or impressions in the observing mind. They— the advent of spring and the images operative in memory—are "dressing up" the landscape at large, "preparing it for social, for human intercourse," and doing so, moreover, "with an energy of renewal and an effect of redemption not often to be noted . . . on other continents." (332, 333.)

By the time the chapter's opening paragraph is finished, the images recollecting in James's memory are collaborating with the natural landscape, and with figures of the arts, to figure forth or represent "an energy of renewal" and "an effect of redemption" that are operative in the dynamics of American society. "Nature, the great artist of the season," will not paint on the American canvas until she has swept it clean of, or toned down, the unwanted relics of the past, the "old material [already] at hand." Nature is a portrait painter who does not like the costumes, household objects and "paraphernalia," the surroundings and "signs of [already] existing life" that are the habitat and favorite possessions of his subject; the painter excludes them from the emerging portrait or tries to hide them, "dissimulating with the . . . freest brush their impertinence and their ugliness." (333.)

I want now to refine more precisely than I have the uses of the term "representation" in which I have been indulging so far, and add later one more. Let me point out that the representation of Washington, D.C., given at the opening of this chapter is quite different from the measurably full, measurably accurate rendition of the appearance of the site that we can confirm by direct observation, the notion of representation suggested by the popular myth of the photograph and so-called representational realism in art. Notably "representation" does not consist of the sheer act of repetition, re-peating and substituting a re-presentation for an original pre-sentation that preceded it. "Representation" is a process of "redemption" and reinvigoration or "renewal." Representation is an activity or kind of work, an "energy of evocation" as James called it in Zola's case. It is a presentation with reverberations, a process including projections ahead and generating its duration in time by echoing itself in the progeny of its repercussions. That process James finds to be actually operative in American society and figured in the generative power of nature that sponsors it and in the operations of the enabling imagination that engages in it or commits itself to it.

James's imagination, challenged by the scale and urgency of his undertaking, is operating in the ways we usually associate with the so-called "romance" in fiction, magnifying or enlarging the scale of his setting, accenting the *possibilities* immanent in the material rather than giving priority to the more plausible actualities already given, welcoming the liberation of more extravagant maneuvers and speculation than is usually permitted in more novelistic modes or in historical narration and social commentary.[6] When, in the Prefaces to his novels, James speaks of fiction as an "appreciation" of life he means not only that the writer's treatment entails relish for the material but that it entails an enlargement or augmentation of the given material, as with an investment that appreciates in value.[7] In the Preface to *The American Scene* he declared that "the appreciation of life" is related to the "question of literary representation" and acknowledged that his habits would produce "an enrichment of my subject." The increment of "appreciation" in James's representation of the American scene is the projection of "redemption" or "renewal" that he discovers on the site and articulates in his impression of Washington, D.C. The act of representation in *The American Scene*, James's representation *of* the American scene, has become a commitment to the quest for redemption or renewal that, ever since Cotton Mather called for "REVOLUTION" and "REFORMATION" in his *Magnalia Christi Americana*, has been one main thrust, one deep impulsion, of the American dream.[8] (xxvi.)

This is to say that James's book is not simply an astute examination of and protest against traditions and conditions in American culture but an engagement with the American myth that is central to those traditions, an engagement that James's techniques of representation are designed to bring about. It is not to say, as I hope is obvious, that James was complacently confident of America's prospect of fulfilling that dream or realizing the renewal inaugurated in its traditions. To speak as he does of Nature's costuming American society for an eventual public appearance, as if disguising the detritus of the past or

[6] See James's Preface to *The American*, collected in *The Art of the Novel*, ed. R. P. Blackmur (New York, 1934), pp. 25-34, and "The Art of Fiction," in *Partial Portraits* (London, 1888), pp. 315-316, for James's discussion of the "romance" and the novel, and for his insistence that the powers usually attributed to the "romance" may be found in the best achievements of either genre.

[7] See *The Art of the Novel*, pp. 65-67, and my discussion of the subject on pp. 166-167.

[8] *Magnalia Christi Americana*, 2 vols. (Hartford, Conn., 1856), II, p. 653. James Kraft has been alone in measuring the strength of the American dream in its appeal to James in *The American Scene*. See his "On Reading *The American Scene*," *Prose*, 6 (1973), pp. 118-119, 127.

dissimulating the ugly "signs of existing life," draws attention to discrepancies between the myth and the actual stages of its realization. Commitment to the myth enables James to take part in the American experiment while also measuring the degree of its success and failure in the undertaking.

How he took part in it is amply illustrated as his account of the capital city proceeds. He shifts the focus to Washington's parks and urban design, then later enlarges the landscape view to include the nearby site of George Washington's home at Mount Vernon. Simultaneously he interlaces "refinements of response" to the "impressions" he brought back from the States, refinements of his memories that his account "translates." He does this in a way that reveals another plane of representation that is important throughout the book: a histrionic mode of representation that is as important in *The American Scene* as in James's fiction, whereby Nature becomes a figure preparing America for a public performance onstage, a painter performing in dissimulating ways with free brush strokes, and whereby James becomes a *performer* with his own impressions, defining and taking on roles that he shares with figures who people his drama, who enter and exit from his scene. The result in Washington and environs is astonishing. (338-339.)

James approaches Mount Vernon eventually with a "sacred terror" that registers finally his absorption in the lush natural setting, "masking, dissimulating" the "hard facts" of the building's small scale, its unimportance architectually, but he postpones his account of that visit so as to define first more precisely his situation and his role. Dominating the account first are his recollections that the excursion was rendered glamourous by the fact that he was escorted under exceptionally official circumstances (Navy personnel and a launch got him there), and an impression that he gathered only after his return to the city but presents first. After his return to the city he found it "transfigured" by virtue of its being abandoned by its everyday inhabitants and peopled only by stray foreigners from the embassies: diplomats trained to "smile" and exercise discretion while seeking to understand a capital city so unlike their own. James's interest in Washington becomes more intense as it is adjusted to take account of these alien residents in it. Curious about what their view might contribute to his, he engages, he says, in the "tortuous" task of observing Washington through their alien eyes, "judging . . . , fearing, reporting with the alien sense." Within that perspective, the place is charming because they simply do not see Washington's "as yet unsurmounted bourgeois character"; that character is "screened and disguised," and what emerged to dominate the landscape instead is the park-like aspect created by L'Enfant's design for the city. Their view, heightened by the golden green of spring, enables James to imagine converting the existing statues of American generals into "garden-gods" on pedestals of "mythological marble" such as one knows in European capitals. He could, he says, at some proper time, "diplomatically, patriotically pretend" that such a Washington was the " 'real' " one, but his "assent" now to this view is suspended with the recognition that it is a dissimulating enlargement of the facts, the projection of a mythologizing imagination. (334-335.)

These foreign diplomats (who appear only this once in the narration) obviously serve an implementing function closely related to James's own. Together—the figures of the diplomats he enlists in his service, and the figures James presents of himself as narrator—they define the double role that James speaks of in the Preface as *his* role: the role of "inquiring stranger" (the expatriate, the diplomat) and the role of the "initiated native" (the American-born). The figures defined by such roles operate together in the way James perfected in his fiction and discussed in the prefaces to his novels. Each important figure is a "confessed agent," a "deputy" or "delegate," as James called them, of the writer himself, and they function in close relation to him.[9] He is identified *with* them as he adopts their perspectives and plays out their fantasies to people the parks with statues of gods, though he is distinct from these agents, not identical *to* them. But their voices are so intimately related to his that not only what the narrator says in his own right but the figures who are his agents are engaged in the act of representing the American scene, and the narrative voice is implicated as a

---

[9] Preface to *The Golden Bowl,* in *The Art of the Novel,* pp. 327-328. See also pp. 175-177, for a discussion of this technique in James's fiction.

representative of America, voicing its aspirations and its more somber recognitions. James indeed becomes so implicated in the task of representation that he becomes part of the very American scene he is describing.[10] Not only is he a performing actor working in *ensemble* with other figures in his text, but he becomes a representative American in Emerson's sense: a characteristic product and spokesman of it, and a representative of America in the political sense, one of its delegates guiding his society and shaping the conduct of its affairs, responsible to his constituency. (xxv.)

With roles and functions so defined, James proceeds finally to Mount Vernon and finds the natural setting and the building both yielding priority to the sheer fact of their symbolic "association" with the figure of George Washington. The first President is the very "image" of "public service consummately rendered," and the symbolic association or legend defining that service becomes "the great white, decent page on which the whole sense of the place is written." The actualities of the building are absorbed in the symbolic association they sustain, and James registers an encounter there with the American past that leaves him feeling that he is wrapped in the "star-spangled banner" itself. The incident culminates in an "exaltation," yet, for all the radiance of spring and the comfort of the star-spangled banner, it presents one of the deepest soundings of the American scene. It is a touching but tawdry monetary exchange in which one figure, a pathetic "bleeding Past," dressed in the homespun of 1776, returns a lost wallet that he has "rescued from thieves" to a second figure, the "bloated Present" who owns it. His reward for his trouble is a mere "sixpence." The unfairness of the exchange, James says, "breaks our hearts, if we be cursed with the historic imagination." Inscribed on the "white, decent page"—along with the representation of "public service consummately rendered," the "exaltation" of the sum-

[10] James's entanglement in his subject is suggested sporadically by the eruption of titles of his fiction in *The American Scene*: the features of a rustic New Hampshire clearing are "like figures in the carpet"; in Richmond, Virginia, the Negro question "rose like some beast that has sprung from the jungle"; the burden of marginal, incomplete selfhood is about to be stamped or printed on "the readable page" by "the turn of the screw"; America's yearning for excellent taste is the desire for "the real thing." See pp. 16, 375, 408, 446.

mer day, and the promise of the American past—James stands in the bloated present reconciled, though anguished and ashamed, to the culture of capitalism. (336-339.)

James labels these remarks "fantastications," ex post facto "refinements of response" to the original "impressions," though the "ground had been cleared for them" by the legend of George Washington and what it represented, and the result was the "exaltation" of patriotic feeling that he hopes his account "sufficiently translates." In any case these acts of representation have become virtual acrobatics, and the feat has brought him to a celebration of the American past figured in George Washington and homespun, while implicating him in a monetary exchange that is patently exploitive. Renewal, for the returning expatriate, has come to this commitment and to this confession. (338, 339.)

In these ways James has become a figure in his own account, and if he figures more prominently here than in his later fiction, his relation to other figures on the scene is basically the same: he plays his role as observer with and through those other figures in the cast, who define telling points of view in their alignment with James himself or with the voices in the narration through which James is directly represented.

The voices who represent him as narrating his account, the character or characters he himself plays, display a range of feeling, a strained effort to understand, and a degree of self-consciousness that are conspicuous. He speaks unabashedly as "I" but speaks also of "the observer whose impressions I note," the "observer on whose behalf I more particularly write"—"if I may indeed speak my whole thought for him." He dubs himself on occasion a "pilgrim," a "filial mind," a "fond observer," a "restored absentee." Most often he is the "restless analyst," and twice an "incurable eccentric," a "perverted person" and "perverse person" whose impressions cannot be absolute or certain under the hazards of his adventure. (107, 125, 285, 366, 101, 321, 118, 82, 98, 273.)

He must generate impressions and " 'put in' a certain quantity of emotion and reflection" so as to "read out" what he finds there, because American society's types have too little force of representation themselves to leave a durable imprint on the "etcher's plate." His resort to simple, bold-face symbols (as in George Washington, Mount Vernon, and the American flag), amplifies the semiotics of American society where "symbol and figure" must stand for vast ranges of significance, where "representation" and indeed all social institutions are plastic or "elastic," required, even enabled to stretch like rubber and accommodate desires even for things not yet identified. Such representations prefigure the possibility of their identification and realization. The hazards of observation, so often challenged by realities and incoherences that baffle it, threaten the "restless analyst" with madness when he tries to reconcile "what might have been" with "what so hopelessly is." James's "appreciation" of his subject had to hold against a pressure of anxiety and disdain that at times challenged his hopes, confirmed his fears, and taxed his powers of persuasion and diplomacy. Yet what a nameless voice from New York City declares proves to be true: " 'You *care* for the terrible town . . . as I have overheard you call it,' " New York City proclaims, and since you imagine that it intends to be charming, you are " 'tangled . . . in some underhand imagination of its possibly . . . becoming so.' " The problem is to decide what is worth saving " 'for . . . the better life' " and what should be discarded. Defined in these ways is the complex role that engages James throughout the book: that of suffering and voicing the anxieties generated by American society—voicing the challenge to humane values and the imagination that American society presents—while endorsing, under pressure reinscribing, the myth that envisions redemption and renewal. (321, 291, 101, 108.)

He must invest interest in the subject, "like a fond investor," to make it yield *its* interest, to "make it pay." In his role as participant-observer, "so interested and so detached as to be moved to a report of the matter," James's stance varies between a point that is "distantly-respectful" and only "provisionally-imaginative," and that of a "victim, up to his neck in what I have called his 'subject.' " His aim is to "get into the picture," or to "cross the threshold . . . of the frame," to become indeed a "participant" and to "talk himself back" into the American scene like the American males, adept conversationalists, who have reentered the Washington social scene long dominated by women. To penetrate deeper into his subject, his procedure is to invite or expose himself to a shock that calls for "mental adjustment to phenomena absolutely fresh," then move toward a deeper penetration, a closer affiliation with it. It is that performance—moving toward a deeper affiliation with American society, voicing its challenge to civilized values and registering his protest, while reinscribing the myth—that I shall trace in the remainder of the essay. (272, 273, 122, 5, 351, 118.)

James's "underhand imagination" is also the "historic imagination," that we have already seen at work at Mount Vernon, and that imagination is strongly active earlier in the sections that explore, on foot, by train and carriage, and by automobile, the in some ways charming, in some ways blank and tame, New England landscape. His is an exploration that leads increasingly into James's personal past and the more remote past of the country, so that he can define America's failure to fulfill its promise but also reaffirm the potential, the promise itself, that can be renewed by the investing imagination.

The natural landscape in New England is at first so dominant that it is "unreasoned" in its "appeal," beautifully Arcadian in the imminence of autumn, but the Presidential mountain range is smudged by "a great vulgar thumb," and the Theocritan idyll begins to show as blandly monotonous, though disclosing an underside of incest and debilitation in villages whose population has shrunk as people moved westward, leaving abandoned farms (as in Frost's "The Black Cottage") in a "perpetual repudiation of the past." The blankness of the scene displays a "monotony of acquiescence" to the modern railway that disfigures its valleys and hills. Though it looks beguilingly like the Tuscan hills of Italy, the landscape everywhere speaks of the absence of masculine energy that dominates European societies. On the blank landscape there are signs that the *"will to grow was everywhere written large."* Yet it threatens to produce nothing but mere size and standardized repetition. The "monstrous form of Democracy," like a "huge broom," has swept everything clean under an "empty sky." Through the charming veil of the natural setting, the social scene appears vacant, as James earlier, like Hawthorne and Cooper, had complained, void of the intriguing complications of institutions and manners that characterized older civilizations. (36, 31, 53, 44, 19, 24, 54-55.)

The shock for the "restored absentee" is to receive this challenge to his earlier expectations that the drama of the scene was the society's "general effort" to "gouge an interest out" of the ominously cleared "vacancy." Now the scene suggested that *nothing* might happen, as if a "sleeping child" were about to be abandoned by some "slightly melodramatic mother." The effect of this challenge, however, is to trigger an adjustment in James's apprehension, to quicken in him an appreciation of the "elegance" and "mystery" of the "commonest objects," and to induce him to imagine rescuing the feminine landscape, a woman and her family, from such a fate. Her abject appeal, rendered beguiling by the natural setting, is the stereotype of female submission: the "mild submission to your doing what you would" with her. But the prospect of "summer people," tourists or outsiders, becomes the "author" as James calls it of "another boon," the prospect of a reciprocal effort at renewal. The appeal of the native landscape to " 'Live upon me and thrive by me,' " becomes the plea, to him as to the summer transients, to " 'Live *with* me, somehow, and let us make out together what we may do for each other,' " something that is not measurable in mere greenbacks. James continues his tour, sustained by the expectation that a conjunction of native inhabitants and outsiders insures the "possible evolution of manners," the "aesthetic enrichment of the summer people," and, both groups "conjoined," the "production and the imposition of [the] forms" that would revitalize the culture. (21, 16, 20, 21, 26.)

The foundation of his assurance, however, proves increasingly to be the emergence, within the horizon of the present, of traditions sanctioned in the past, and James's entrance into the New England picture leads time and again to the older institutions and predecessors that define those traditions. The new buildings at Harvard, of little interest in their own right, add something to the quality of the old as the wall around the Yard lends a reassuring sense of enclosure to the entire campus. Literary prospects there are dim, but the houses and careers of earlier Cambridge literary figures, overshadowed now by the football stadium and crowds of tourists, mark the traces of

James's personal and literary lineage. Later in Boston the Italianate Public Library, sacrificing private rooms and quiet to the public display of its paintings and collections to a larger public and to children, is half exciting, half unnerving. But in the Museum of Fine Arts the very paucity of the surroundings throws into stunning relief the ancient Greek sculpture of Aphrodite and accords to that ancient work a new "empire." The Gardiner collection of imported masterpieces testifies to the "fine old disinterested tradition of Boston," though the "perpetual repudiation of the past" may otherwise continue and the Democratic Broom still sweep. (60-63, 253, 255.)

The greatest shock for James is to discover that, during the month intervening between two visits to the family home where he had lived for two years and launched his literary career, the house had been razed to the ground: "It was as if the bottom had fallen out of one's biography, and one plunged backward into space without meeting anything." With his personal connection to the past so threatened, he nevertheless found at the battle monument in Concord, Massachusetts, the tradition receding behind Emerson, Thoreau, and Hawthorne, that sanctioned for him the American dream. The graves of English soldiers, the meager surroundings and bare relic of Hawthorne's Old Manse, and Daniel Chester French's statue commemorating the farmers who fired the shot heard round the world, define the "luxurious heritage" which repays the interest invested by Henry James. Theirs, the "embattled farmers," was the "huge bargain" larger than they knew, that "they made for us, in a word, made by the gift of the little all they had." Theirs was the interest and the devotion to the cause. We accept, James says, the inheritance that it was their fate to bequeath, and we acknowledge our interest in it like "a Jew in a dusky back-shop," who might "providentially bait the trap." (229, 262.)

The figure of the Jew, so closely associated with though not identical to James and the first-person plural of his narrator's "we," is introduced suddenly but deliberately on the rustic Concord scene in one of the most garbled sentences James ever wrote: I have had to read into it a syntax so as to read out the tribute to 1776, and the recognition of complicity in its exploitation by the present, that is figured there. The figure of the Jew has been introduced much earlier, however, immediately after James's arrival in the States. On the New Jersey shore, comfortably affluent "German Jewry," already superceded by a new generation and nostalgic for urban neighborhoods they have left behind, parade before their "huge" white villas in "the chariots of Israel," the houses displaying the "familiar prominence in their profiles" and speaking in an "accent, loud, assertive, yet benevolent withal, with which they confessed to their extreme expensiveness." As a figure the Jew brings into focus the complex of commercial and monetary transactions that pervade the culture of capitalism: he is an alien in the surrounding society who nevertheless serves that society by conducting certain of its affairs that promise profit, and suffering the blame for whatever culpabilities those affairs entail. The figure is singularly appropriate to the commercialism and the vulgarity, as James termed it, of the culture that shows glaringly in New York City and the urban landscape that supplants the village and rural landscape for long stretches of *The American Scene*. James's distaste for what he found to be vulgar—common, standardized and pervasive, and demeaning—and his refusal to settle for it did not blind him to its importance or suppress its fascination for him. In 1897, indeed, he had noted that the "triumph of vulgarity," as manifest in the commercialization of Victoria's Jubilee, was "the muscular triumph of the inevitable," and that "history" would have eventually to "accept vulgarity or perish." Vulgarity is "the show itself" now "pushed aloft by deep forces."[11] In view of its importance he could risk a closer look and probe the realities it expressed. (7-8.)

The "bristling" and "extravagant" energy of New York City, the "vehemence" and "power" of a metropolis whose network of bridges seemed the "horizontal sheaths of pistons" in a theatening machine, suggested a "frenzied dance, half merry, half desperate" on the bottom of some ocean, and defined a "menaced state" for all concerned, those rising in it but particularly those lower classes whose freedom consisted of the freedom merely to "grow up to be blighted." The new skyscrapers defy the order of any urban plan. Their wide expanses of windows

[11] "London Notes" (1897), reprinted in *Notes on Novelists*, p. 432.

APPENDIX

express the brash competitiveness of commercial society, their height expresses the cult of novelty and the perpetual replacement of even the more recent by the yet more new. The "vast money-making structure" had all but obliterated the Castle Garden concert hall and old Trinity Church. New buildings have scarred Washington Square and "amputated . . . half my history," James said, by effacing his birthplace without leaving so much as a commemorative plaque to mark the spot. (74-77, 137, 95-96, 83, 91.)

Yet James's text charts the path of his accommodation of the scene. Delighted to find that the old City Hall has survived the threat to replace it, and that its handsome façade forces the nearby vulgar buildings to "stand off," he boldly enters it—an "audacious" act for ordinary citizens in Europe, he says, but the custom of the country here—with something like the illicit excitement of secretly entering a harem: he is surprised to be invited for a chat with the mayor in his office. Crossing that threshold he confronts the gilt-framed portraits of the city fathers of the past. The encounter is a mute tribute to, and a stark exposure of, the "unsophisticated provincialism" in their faces that explains what was coming to pass in the "terrible town." (97-99.)

A comparably critical but appreciative encounter is his entrance into the Waldorf Astoria Hotel. He found it a welcome refuge from the "inconceivably bourgeois" constrictions of the city's grid plan, the "assault of the street" and the "violence" generated by its intersections, unrelieved by squares or other variations, the violence compacted in the tram cars, so congested and hemmed in as to suggest the "projectile in the bore of a gun." The "violence" extended even to the threshold of the hotel, but once projected inside James finds an oasis of socialized activity that characterizes the entire society. It is the triumph of American gregariousness. Within the limits set by the high rates, and by the demand for unmitigated respectability, a wide variety of social groups and ages, even scarcely supervised children, are at home, finding their social aspirations satisfied not in private and exclusive domains but in the full light of "publicity." It is a "labyrinth" James chose never to enter again, but the "hotel world" it represented impressed him everywhere in

425

America. "Consummate management" of a characteristically American degree accounts for the mélange of historical decorative styles, the efficiency with which countless groups and purposes are served simultaneously, and the virtually drugged satisfaction of the guests who are so completely at home there. Inside it James sees "the American spirit most seeking and most finding itself," a " 'mixed' social manifestation" without trace of discord, yielding one of James's "few glimpses of perfect human felicity" in a society devoted "to the greatest happiness of the greatest number." For all his irony he could record his "ache of envy" of a community that had found "so exactly what it wanted," envy of a society's recognition of a "realized ideal" and its "childlike rush of surrender to it and clutch at it," the note in America of the "supremely gregarious state." (100-107.)

New York City calls forth hope as it asks simply "to lead the life it has begun . . . [and] to enfold generations and gather in traditions, to show itself capable of growing up to character and authority." The promise seems alive at the Metropolitan Museum, where, though it does not encourage the creation of new art, "Acquisition" on a grand scale promises to educate the public's taste, and even de-acquisition or de-accessioning, as we have learned to call it, may purge the collection of inferior works and provide the "warrant for a clean slate" and the certainty of greatness in the future. In Central Park the " 'common man' " and the "common woman," plus "the very common child," display the "ruthlessly pushed-up and promoted look" of those who have risen into public space without the encouragements or acknowledgements known to privileged classes in the old world, and James applauds the children who so thrive on these conditions. (113, 193, 178-179.)

New York's greatest challenge was the concentration there of the immigrants, whose presence James found remarkable and disconcerting in all sections of the country. Their foreignness, in matters of taste, language, and manners, impressed him forcibly, of course, but they had a deeper fascination because their experience of emigration—like himself they had left one land to take up life in another, and they were rising to exposed and public levels on an expanding social scene—typified for James the very basis of the American experience. What American "is *not* the alien" James asks when he first approaches the subject and discovers the need for "mental adjustment" to the challenge of "phenomena absolutely fresh." Later, when analyzing the rise to prominence of the middle class, exemplified by country clubs with relatively open membership that dominate the social scene and give free play to the institution of the democratic family,[12] James uses the metaphor of emigration to define this form of socialization. Families one or more generations removed from their immigrant progenitors and now relatively acculturated, and Anglo Saxon whites rising in affluence and status, are joining and founding such clubs, and the process is likened to the process of emigration itself. James's representation of these clubs fuses the two processes: the rise to ascendency of, and the engrossment of society by, the middle class and emigration from abroad into the new nation. In Europe such classes, rising in status, have admittedly begun to "arrive," he writes, but in Europe we see these *arrivistes* still on the ship: in America they have not only "arrived" but disembarked and left the docks. The families and guests in the clubs on the Hudson River are " 'what the People *are* when they've disembarked.' " (124, 327-328.)

To see them on Ellis Island or in the ghetto and the Bowery as James did was to see the very process. The shock of sharing "the sanctity of his American consciousness, the intimacy of his American patriotism, with the inconceivable alien" was, James recalls, to "eat of the tree of knowledge" and become a different person, "shake[n] to the depths of his being" by the "indignity of change" he witnessed. In the face of their "settled possession" and the corresponding "*un*settled possession" or threatened "dispossession" of the native-born, James declares that, while clinging to America's national identity, we must recall the multinational identity of the Swiss. Indeed "We must go . . . *more* than half-way to meet them." That becomes his task in the sections devoted to them, though the situation is so new for

---

[12] As Maxwell Geismar and others have insisted, James overstated the case for the "universal eligibility" as he called it, or open membership of American country clubs. Yet James's claim is pertinent, for such clubs were open to groups which were seldom considered for membership in comparable European institutions, and the extension of privileges and membership to entire families, including women and children, was unusual.

them and for him that the language necessary for discussing it seems an *"abracadabrant"* that he has not mastered and he must settle for only tentative conclusions. He is struck that they seem distinctly *"at home,* really more at home . . . than they had ever in their lives been before," and he feels more at home himself and is somewhat startled by "this very equality of condition." Their look, whether "promising" or "portentous," bespeaks at least a minimum of confidence in their new "security and portability," a "growing sense of many unprecedented things," and a total repression or repudiation of the manners of their ethnic past that gave them color and interest in Europe. The "whitewashing brush" that is accomplishing this acculturation provokes in James neither disdain nor repudiation of the process but the hope that once their " 'American' identity" has been established the ethnic values will reemerge, "affirming their vitality and value and playing their part" in the American scene. (85-86, 122, 125-129.)

The "ache of envy" that drew James to the Waldorf Astoria world, and the "equality of condition" that he found "strange" but compelling when observing Armenian and Italian immigrants, are at play in James's representation of the Jewish ghetto, the "Yiddish Quarter" centering at Rutgers Street on the East Side (and later his description of the Yiddish theatre). James heard there the pain-racked cries of the English language being tortured by accents and idioms that presaged its demise, even if he could imagine the possible later emergence of a language "destined to become the most beautiful on the globe," and he saw a blighted populace fattened to feed the "Ogres" of financial trusts. But under the guidance of a Jewish host and a fellow writer (the playwright Jacob Gordin), James was led to deeper recognitions.[13] Torn from context, many of James's metaphors for the Jewish immigrants seem maledictions: they are "fish, of overdeveloped proboscis," "snakes or worms" cut in half and therefore living on in doubled numbers, an "ant-like" population; they are "squirrels and monkeys" lining the miles

---

[13] Maxwell Geismar's diatribe against what he regards as James's "most vicious book" finds James's "barbarous mythology" to be antisemitic in the extreme, comparable to that by which Hitler undertook to "quell the same alien presence." *Henry James and the Jacobites* (New York, 1965), pp. 345, 351.

of fire escapes that render the tenements a zoo. The pressure of antipathy, prejudice, and apprehension is registered by these images, but the counter pressure of the myth of renewal moderates, reorients, and eventually governs them. The fire escapes permit a healthier, safer, and "merrier life" in the congested ghetto, and the animal metaphors insistently project an enviable proliferation and vitality in this "swarming" Israel; the sounds that rise above the housetops are not a "barbaric yawp" but the murmuring waters of fecundity, the force and vitality of the "appealing, surrounding life." He sees in the Jew a "more . . . concentrated person, savingly possessed of everything that is in him," and finds in the neighborhood park and the neighborhood school a "Jerusalem disinfected," indeed the "New Jerusalem on earth" of legend and prophecy. Although James admits he may not have seen the worst, the district's poverty, as manifest in the well-stocked stores that cater to it, is a "new style of poverty" that displays a "*general* lift" and a "general appreciation of the living unit's paying property in himself," prefiguring a case for outright "jubilation." Compared to the "dark, foul, stifling Ghettos of other remembered cities" in Europe, New York's becomes "the city of redemption." (139, 137, 130-136.)

James's representation of the immigrant districts is completed by his visits to the beer halls and restaurants in the German and Slavic quarters. There, in the welcome extended by a German restaurateur who knew only ten words of English, and in the puzzlingly "equivocal" faces of his customers, exposed in their "lowness" and "baseness," James looked in intimate proximity at the famous "common denominator" to which democracy reputedly reduces its citizens, and he found that "certain finer shades" of interest do in America, "by means known to themselves, recover their rights." The restaurateur was not only "a citizen and tax-payer" but a "spokesman, an administrator, an employer of labor and converser on subjects" who knew "delicacies" of tact and hospitality. His simple furnishings and domino boards were a successful "barrier against vulgarity." He had an authentic "conception of decency and dignity" and he had found the "means to make it good even to the exact true shade." In the Slavic restaurant, already catering to an uptown clientele as well as its neighborhood habitués, James detected the usual oblivion to its historic heritage, either American or continental, and wondered whether the "historic consciousness" [was] "too extinct . . . for any possibility of renewal." The political boss of the ward, however, reassured James with a vision of the future based on "*his* inward assimilation of our heritage" which "matched" America's concession to him and his foreignness. The melting pot's fusion of the two, immigrant and native, James figures as an "intermarriage" comparable to the annual ceremony in Venice when the Doge espouses the Adriatic Sea: it is "quite as if" the American Republic, "incarnate in its greatest port, were forever throwing the nuptial ring to the still more richly-dowered Atlantic" and the emigrating thousands disembarking there. (200-203, 206-207.)

The James who had been engaged by the "conjunction" of natives and summer people in New England, holding forth the promise of revitalization of the culture, the James who found, in the "melting pot," in the "intermarriage" of New York City and the alien immigrants, the promise reaffirmed of the "New Jerusalem on earth," was under greater strain as he moved beyond Washington into a South still numb from the ravages of the Civil War. It is a South whose "Confederate dream" was "artlessly perverse"; it is virtually without intellectual traditions, and its sole claim to literary "distinction" recently is *The Souls of Black Folk* by the "accomplished" black writer, W.E.B. Du Bois. The portentous figures of lowerclass Negroes, more "ragged and rudimentary" than those in the North, were a challenge to the "sweet reasonableness about him" that the nation should cling to, and James had to use the irony of quotation marks, indicating the failure of fulfillment yet, when speaking of the black " 'in possession of his rights as a man.' " An impression in Richmond of the "negro really at home" blurs ironically with the ghostly site of the notorious Libby Prison, and the unhomelike prison "home" has no substantial credibility other than "the projected light" of James's own guiltridden "conscience." The statue of Robert E. Lee touches James's "sympathy" by its plea for companionship, but it recedes into isolation, staring off toward a "heaven of futility." The defeated South's one claim to interest is its posture of tragedy, with the loyalty to the lost cause and the vindictiveness that come with it; James concedes the interest but brands it monstrous because it is so clearly founded on a diseased devotion to the slavery system. Even in the pathos of its tragedy it is a South without commitments to a myth that might redeem it. (374, 418, 375, 378, 394, 420.)

As a representation of the American scene, the South constitutes the strongest challenge to the myth of redemption, celebrated in the middle of the book but transposed, now at the end, into the pathos of yearning and an outraged cry of betrayal in the effort to inscribe it in *The American Scene*. The Hotel World alone awakens the hope for a regeneration of taste, the "possibilities [of which] glimmer before one at times," but they are almost overwhelmed by the signs of failure to realize those possibilities and the premonition that "zeal" for more comfort or "convenience" cannot bring them about. The Hotel World is the habitat of two figures, featured prominently earlier in the book, with whom James aligns himself in the pathos of their exposure. One is a Willy Loman, the traveling salesman or bagman, "extraordinarily base and vulgar," who completely dominates the hotel breakfast room in Charleston and later the Pullman lounge car heading for Florida. Shocked at first, then riding with "My friends the drummers [who] bore me company," the "victim up to his neck in [his] subject" comes to the realization that they too are "something like victims or martyrs," exposed to the merciless pressure of a public society, burdened as "the only figures in the social landscape" with responsibilities they had not asked for and without the social resources to support their efforts. They are not the "monstrosity" James had first taken them for but simply yet "unformed," appealing with at least a dim sense of their predicament. Once the social experiment might be completed, "they would then help, quite subordinately assist, the long sentence to read—relieved of their ridiculous charge of supplying all its clauses." (444-445, 424, 426-429.)

The second figure is that of the American Girl, joined in James's recollection with the Drummer in the pathos of their effort to sustain the burden of creating a civilization, but voicing the fear that it may be too late. The Hotel World, representing the triumph of American gregariousness, becomes a metaphor or symbol for the nation's general attempt to redeem its dream of possibilities by realizing it. The easy affluence that produces tasteless extravagance also reveals an "inordinate *desire*" for good taste, a Dreiserian "pathos of desire" which may remain no more than that, but which constitutes all the more urgently the "blessings" of a "sovereign rarity." Given America's power to clear the way of difficulties, the myth or dream—the "creative freshness, the real thing in a word, *shall* have to . . . be represented, indefinitely," by this "gilded yearning." (446-447.)

That yearning is displaced, though not supplanted, by two figures who dominate the concluding chapter of *The American Scene* which recapitulates the entire book against a panorama of prehistory stretching farther back than Egypt's Nile River.[14] Like a primitive, prehistoric Italy, the scene is a "prepared" etcher's plate with "the impression of History" on it "yet to be made." One figure is a ghostly presence, introduced fleetingly much earlier in autumnal scenes, then appearing suddenly at the conclusion of the chapter on Washington, in the wings of the Capitol building: namely the American Indian, incarnate in a "trio of Indian braves." In their "neat pot-hats," with "shoddy suits" and "pockets, I am sure, full of photographs and cigarettes," they are vulgar. Yet they are like alien diplomats, or now, as James conflates the image, "Japanese celebrities." They represent "the brazen face of history" and "the bloody footsteps of time"; they are "dispossessed of forest and prairie." But they are "specimens . . . of what the Government can do with people with whom it is supposed able to do nothing," and they are represented by James's "underhand imagination" as being "free of the builded" edifice on Capitol Hill as once they were free of the forests they made their home. At the end of the book the figure of the Indian has receded, though James, with his "historic imagination," can imagine preferring the South's unpaved roads to modern thoroughfares, were he a "painted savage" or "even some tough reactionary trying to emulate him." Moreover he incorporates the Indian's voice in his own to cry out in outrage against the encroachment on his "solitude,"

[14] This chapter was not included in the original American edition, whether at James's or his publisher's insistence.

against "every disfigurement and every violence," "every wound" which has "caused the face of the land to bleed." But James acknowledges that he is not that Indian, that he in fact accepts the "ravage" that modern civilization has brought to the American scene.[15] (462, 363-364, 463-465.)

The second figure through which he speaks is an image of the Pullman train[16] that has snaked and polluted its way up and down the land, and across the span of James's chapters, scarring the landscape but making it accessible to any traveller who wants to read or write about it. If the "authority of railways" is conspicuous in the United States, the figure of the Pullman train in the book is intimately associated with James himself and it absorbs at telling points, by echoing or amplifying its sounds, the "train of association" as James calls it, the linked sequence of impressions that figure forth *The American Scene*. Time and again James represents himself as seated *in* that train, whose speed and distance from the localities it joins threaten to keep him from understanding, by taking part in, the drama unfolding alongside its tracks. It is, to his acknowledged pride and shame, a seat of power comparable to that of "satraps and proconsuls," a "bought convenience" marking the "superiority" of the classes who, riding on it, dominate the scene. Seated at its window as it speeds through the Carolinas, he enjoys his "awful modern privilege of this detached yet concentrated stare at the misery of subject populations," the inhabitants of the American South. The symbol of the train represents in the book a combination of privileged or exclusive status and, its smoking lounges filled with salesmen, the power and bourgeois vulgarity of the industrial civilization that lies alongside, indeed constitutes, its right of way. It is an alternative image of the American hotel, and like the hotel, which boasted of its "advantages" and challenged the restless analyst to " 'make what you can of it,' " the Pullman train is itself "eloquent." In the final chapter the train speaks in a hypnotic rumble that boasts of its "conquest" as a creative achievement: " 'See what I'm making of all this . . .

[15] The novelist Wright Morris has drawn attention to James's commitment in this passage to modern society. See *The Territory Ahead* (New York, 1958), pp. 112, 210-211.

[16] Leo Marx's comments on the railway in *The American Scene* are in *The Machine in the Garden* (New York, 1964), pp. 239-240, 350-353.

what I'm making!' " Seated at the window inside that train, an alienated native committed still to the promise of the promised land, James voices that boast and triumph but also counters that boast by denouncing the world the railroad represents for failing to redeem its promise, for its irresponsibility as measured by that dream.[17] (27, 148, 142, 1, 433, 406-407, 463.)

Castigating the monstrous "ugliness" and abortive "crudities" that modern America engenders, the callousness of its institutions and its irresponsibility—and asking will it ever stand for anything but "the triumph of the superficial and the apotheosis of the raw"—the vehemence of James's rhetoric has the force not of disassociation and repudiation but of a shared commitment betrayed, the power of a challenge generated by that commitment and augmented under the pressure of the threats to its fulfillment. The civilization is behind in its payments on the debt it owes to its own highest aspirations. James's *American Scene* brings that charge against its subject, but in another sense it charges its subject with the "energy of renewal" and "redemption" that are the basis of its claim to interest, representing the promissory note, inscribed still and reindorsed, in *The American Scene*. (463-465.)

---

[17] David L. Furth speaks for many readers in finding James to be "unreconciled towards America," a modern America that has repudiated the models against which James measures its achievements, models generated in its own past and in European civilization. See *The Visionary Betrayed: The LeBaron Russell Briggs Prize Honors Essay in English* (Cambridge, Mass., 1979), pp. 56, 58.

INDEX

435

Chase, Richard, *The American Novel and Its Tradition*, 60f, 67-68
Cheney, Sheldon, *Expressionism in Art*, 77n
Chopin, Frédéric, 132
Clairmont, Jane, 132, 135
comedy, 131-32; in *The Papers*, 149-50; in The Prefaces, 159, 161; in *The Fount*, 184, 193-94, 223; in *The Ambassadors*, 237, 241, 264, 266, 271, 282. *See also* caricature, entertainment, parody, tragi-comedy
confession, x; in The Prefaces, 3-4, 9, 11f, 159f, 170f, 176f; in *The Portrait*, 33, 35-36; in *The Spoils*, 95-96; in *The Papers*, 148-50; in *The Wings*, 286-87; in *The Bowl*, 335ff, 383-84, 402, 404, 406-07. *See also* art and moral commitment, authority, entertainment, intimacy, victimization
constructive imagination, 118f; in The Prefaces, 4, 164-66, 170-71; in *The Portrait*, 38; in *Partial Portraits*, 120ff, 129-30; in *The Papers*, 152; in *The Fount*, 184, 193-94, 196, 198-99, 200-01, 208ff, 213ff, 221-22; in *The Ambassadors*, 230, 232, 234, 246, 278, 280; in *The Bowl*, 357, 375, 377-79, 381. *See also* analytic imagination, vicarious imagination
convention, 33-34, 39, 161, 190, 388
Cooper, James Fenimore, *The American Democrat*, 61, 63-64, 64n
crisis and art, 76ff, 83-84, 88-89, 117-18, 134f; and society, 18-19, 78-79, 83-84; in *The Portrait*, 25, 51-52; in *The Spoils*, 97, 100ff, 111-13; in *The Papers*, 134-35; in The Prefaces, 158ff, 168-69; in *The Fount*, 186-87, 193, 222-24; in *The Ambassadors*, 231-32, 270, 272f, 279; in *The Bowl*, 322-23, 338, 341, 365, 369, 371-72, 375, 378, 398, 401, 406. *See also* revolution

Dante (Alighieri), 72-73, 76
Daudet, Alphonse, 71, 124; *Le Nabob*, 125; *Les Rois en Exile*, 125
Daumier, Honoré, 129
Defoe, Daniel, *Robinson Crusoe*, 68
democracy, 65, 86
Dickens, Charles, 71
drama, 8, 58-60, 80-81, 83-84, 85ff, 225; in Hawthorne, 70-71; in Franklin, 74-75; in Melville, 75; in painting, 80; in Maupassant, 127-28; in *The Spoils*,

101ff; in *Partial Portraits*, 121-22, 126-128, 130, 137-38; in *The Papers*, 139, 141, 150f; in The Prefaces, 159, 162ff, 172-73, 177-78, 180-81; in *The Fount*, 189, 192-93, 196-98, 210; in *The Ambassadors*, 230, 241 248-49, 257-58, 269f, 278; in *The Wings*, 285, 290-91, 296-98, 305-06, 308f, 311-13, 317f, 320ff; in *The Bowl*, 338, 343, 350, 379ff, 392, 394-97, 399. *See also* comedy, tragedy, tragi-comedy
Dreiser, Theodore, 67
Dumas, Alexandre, fils, *La Dame Aux Camélias*, 85, 102-04
Du Maurier, George, 129-30
Dupee, Frederick W., *The Question of Henry James*, 15n; *James*, 156

Edel, Leon, 35n, 45n, 183, 183n, 238n, 252, 252n, 267n; *Henry James: The Untried Years*, 353
Edward II, 373
Eliot, George (Marian Evans), 14, 122
Eliot, T(homas) S., 66; *Selected Essays*, 19-20
Emerson, Ralph Waldo, 19, 90, 122, 176
entertainment (and amusement), ix, 126ff, 225; in The Prefaces, 5, 7, 14, 178f; in *The Portrait*, 18, 29, 33, 53; in *Partial Portraits*, 126, 130, 137; in *The Papers*, 140-41; in *The Fount*, 180-84, 188, 195-96, 207f; in *The Ambassadors*, 238-39, 270, 282; in *The Bowl*, 340
expressionism, 58, 76ff, 77n, 87-88, 118, 225; in *The Spoils*, 111-12; in The Prefaces, 155, 162, 168-69, 172-74, 180-181; in *The Fount*, 220-21; in *The Wings*, 288-89, 306, 320-21; in *The Bowl*, 334f, 356-57, 363, 386f, 401. *See also* caricature, Gothicism, mannerism

family (and parenthood), ix; in *The Scarlet Letter* and *Adam Blair*, 21-25; in *The Portrait*, 17, 33-34, 37, 52; in *The Spoils*, 91-94, 100; in The Prefaces, 157, 169-70; in *The Ambassadors*, 234ff, 243, 246f, 259f; in *The Wings*, 325; in *The Bowl*, 356ff, 359, 363, 366ff, 374-75, 378, 392-93, 401f, 405-06. *See also* marriage
Faulkner, William, 294; *Absalom, Absalom!*, 354

INDEX

Fitzgerald, F. Scott, *The Beautiful and Damned*, 66
Flaubert, Gustave, 72; *Madame Bovary*, 130
Follett, Wilson, 181, 183
form, vii-viii, 117-18, 124, 222, 225; in *The Portrait*, 26, 41f; in *The Spoils*, 103f; in *The Fount*, 210, 214, 217. See also allegory, analogy, analytic imagination, caricature, constructive imagination, drama, expressionism, imitation, intimacy, manner, manners, mannerism, narrative form, painting, parody, symbolism, vicarious imagination
Franklin, Benjamin, 66; *Autobiography*, 74
Fry, Roger, 77

Gibbon, Edward, 63
Gide, André, 15, 338
Giedion, Siegfried, *Space, Time and Architecture*, 334
Gombrich, Ernst H. J., *Art and Illusion*, 43, 130
Goncourt, Edmond de and Jules de, 81
Gordon, Caroline, 275n
Gothicism, 72, 117, 136-37, 143, 147, 155-156, 185. See also caricature, expressionism
Grunewald, Matthias, 77n

Halliwell-Phillipps, James O., *Outlines of the Life of Shakespeare*, 180
Hauser, Arnold, *The Social History of Art*, 77n, 78-79
Hawthorne, Nathaniel, 59, 61, 70-71, 73, 75; James on, 10, 20-27, 44, 72; *The Dolliver Romance*, 20; *The Scarlet Letter*, 21-27, 70-71, 333-34; *The Blithedale Romance*, 70, 176; *The Marble Faun*, 81
Homer, 73
Howells, William Dean, 44-45, 62, 72, 252
Hugo, Victor, 233
Hunt, Holman, *The Scapegoat*, 394

Ibsen, Henrik, 85ff, 377; *John Gabriel Borkman*, 87; *Hedda Gabler*, 325
imitation, 118f, 124, 126, 130, 159, 179. See also representation
Impressionists, 77

intimacy, x-xi, 225; in The Prefaces, 163-66; in *The Fount*, 188, 200-01, 207-08, 210, 214, 218; *The Ambassadors*, 259-60, 269, 271f; in *The Wings*, 286-90; in *The Bowl*, 340-41, 360f, 370, 384, 389f, 393, 401f
irony, 68f; in *The Spoils*, 104-05; in *The Papers*, 141, 143, 147, 150; in *The Fount*, 183-84, 192; in *The Ambassadors*, 240, 252, 263-66, 273, 275-77, 280; in *The Wings*, 288

James, Henry, on American culture, vii-viii, 61f, 64-66, 377-78; on the British Empire, 90-92, 112-13; on Europe, vii, 62
  on Balzac, 71, 95, 120, 179; on Browning, 163-64; on Daudet, 71, 124f; on Flaubert, 72, 130; on the Goncourt brothers, 81; Halliwell-Phillipps, 269; on Hawthorne, 20-27, 72, 81, 334; on Howells, 44-45; on Ibsen, 85ff; on Janin, 81; on mannerism, 81-82; on Brander Matthews, 180-81; on Maupassant, 71, 123, 127f; on George Sand, 131f; on Shakespeare's *Tempest*, 179-81; on Stevenson, 124; on Zola, 179
  The American, 249; *The Ambassadors*, 229ff, 223, 225-26, 333; *The American Essays*, 45; *The American Scene*, 64-65, 77, 304; *The Aspern Papers*, 139ff, 117-18, 132, 137-38, 155-156; *Autobiography*, 232, 335; *The Bostonians*, 117; English Hours, 257; *French Poets and Novelists*, 11n, 72, 72n, 95, 96n, 125, 125n, 131, 131n, 132; *The Golden Bowl*, 331ff, 12, 223, 225; *Hawthorne*, 20-22, 44, 61, 334, 377-78; *Italian Hours*, 82; *The Ivory Tower*, 62; *The Lesson of Balzac and The Question of Our Speech*, 69-70, 70n, 179; Letters, 35, 72, 73n, 137; *Literary Reviews and Essays by Henry James*, 44, 44n, 62; *The Notebooks*, 84-85, 90, 106, 252, 350, 351n; *Notes of a Son and Brother*, 232, 238; *Notes on Novelists*, 62, 85n, 95, 112-13, 119, 130-35, 163-64, 179; *The Painter's Eye*, 78n, 90; *Parisian Sketches*, 85, 131, 145; *Partial Portraits*, 120ff, 5, 16, 118, 137, 148, 159, 238, 365; *Portraits of Places*, 305; The Prefaces, 155ff, 3-16, 72, 90, 97-98, 119, 135-37, 217, 220-21, 238, 279, 338, 387; *The Portrait of a Lady*,

INDEX